the Modern Movement in Architecture

Selections from the DOCOMOMO Registers | Dennis Sharp & Catherine Cooke editors

With an introduction by Hubert-Jan Henket Chairman DOCOMOMO International

010 Publishers Rotterdam 2000

Apart from any fair dealing for the purposes of research or private study, or criticism or review, this publication may not be reproduced, stored or transmitted, in any form or by any means, without the prior permission in writing of the publishers or in the case of reprographic reproduction only in accordance with the terms of the licences issued by the appropriate Reproduction Rights Organisation.

executive editors	Dennis Sharp
	Catherine Cooke
advisory board	Maristella Casciato
	Hubert-Jan Henket
	DOCOMOMO International Specialist Committees on Registers and on Publications
design	Malcolm Frost
pre-press	Igma Presentation Imaging London
printed by	Snoeck-Ducaju & Zoon Ghent

©2000 DOCOMOMO International
www.docomomo.com
and 010 Publishers, Rotterdam
Watertorenweg 180,
3063 HA Rotterdam,
The Netherlands
www.010publishers.nl

Bibliographies ©Cooke/Sharp

ISBN 90-6450-405-9

This book was initiated by DOCOMOMO International and has been made possible by the generous support of the Netherlands Architecture Fund and the Faculty of Architecture at Delft University of Technology, the Netherlands.

Acknowledgements

This book shows a selection of a much larger, more extensive and standardized documentation of buildings and sites of the Modern Movement, compiled by hundreds of active DOCOMOMO members worldwide, over a period of eight years. Out of the 40 national or regional working parties participating in the DOCOMOMO network at this moment, 32 of these were in time to present their contribution to this book.

It was only after months into this book's collation and assembly – an innocent period of naiveté perhaps – that we discovered why such a survey had not been done before. It needed the continuous efforts of those involved not only to produce the rare material but also to help refine and edit it. Although this has taken up an inordinate amount of time and energy it is now in a fit state to present to the reader and to connoisseurs of modern architecture.

While acknowledging the enormous debt we all owe to the efforts made by those members of the individual DOCOMOMO national and regional groups who have provided the raw material for publication, I wish to specifically acknowledge the enormous effort put in by the editorial, design and production team working out of London.

Hubert-Jan Henket
Delft, The Netherlands June 2000

Editor's Acknowledgements

From the outset, the graphic designer Malcolm Frost has set out the concept of the book, adapting it from an original idea for a series of fiches into a full-blown publication. He has worked closely with Graeme Martin, the proprietor of Igma Presentation Imaging, who have set the book to disc. His patience and willingness to work as a member of the team has been of paramount importance to the book's production.

However, without the patient and painstaking effort on the editorial side by Dr Catherine Cooke, I doubt if we would have completed the task at all. She has graciously and precisely dealt with the inevitable conflicts of producing a book assembled from a multitude of sources and we have worked together agreeably and I hope effectively in providing the reader with a sustained and accurate narrative. The meticulous checking and double-checking of thousands of details is reflected in almost every section of this book. On behalf of the International Registers Committee and DOCOMOMO International I extend to my colleagues my grateful thanks for all their effort and skill.

The production team is also indebted to Maristella Casciato, Marieke Kuipers, Wessel de Jonge, Eleonoor Jap Sam and Professor Hubert-Jan Henket for help and guidance on this book and contributions to it. For help of a more general nature in various stages of the production of the book I also wish to thank Yasmin Shariff of Dennis Sharp Architects for basic research work and mutual support, as well as our firm's secretary Susan Finn, who sorted out many a disc problem besides patiently typing out copy after copy of drafts and amendments.

Dennis Sharp
Hertford, England June 2000

contents

6	**The Idea of DOCOMOMO** Hubert-Jan Henket Chairman, DOCOMOMO International		**Register selections :**	97	France	185	New Zealand
		17	Argentina	105	Germany	193	Norway
		25	Australia	113	Greece	201	Quebec
8	**Documenting Modern Architecture** Maristella Casciato	33	Belgium	121	Hungary	209	Russia West
		41	Brazil	129	Iberia	217	Russia East
10	**Registering the diaspora of Modern Architecture** Dennis Sharp	49	British Columbia	137	Iceland	225	Scotland
		57	Bulgaria	145	Israel	233	Slovakia
273	**Bibliography** compiled by Catherine Cooke	65	Czech Republic	153	Italy	241	Sweden
		73	Denmark	161	Japan	249	Switzerland
		81	Estonia	169	Latvia	257	United Kingdom
		89	Finland	177	Netherlands	265	USA

The Idea of DOCOMOMO

Hubert-Jan Henket
Founding Chairman
DOCOMOMO International

This book presents a survey of buildings of a style and type that are not always popularly admired, largely because their unique origins are ill understood. Today, many of them are under serious threat of being lost to us through factors intimately related to those origins. But a growing international movement is working to reduce the misunderstandings and reverse this neglect. Why are these buildings so special and how has all this come about? Having stepped into the beginning of a new century let us step back to the early years of the last one.

In 1926 the young Dutch architect Jan Duiker was asked to design a sanatorium near Hilversum for the diamond workers of Amsterdam suffering from tuberculosis. He believed strongly in the rapidly developing areas of science and technology. His client, the Diamond Workers' Trade Union, shared with him the belief that effective medicines would be developed within twenty years thereby rendering the sanatorium redundant. What purpose, therefore, would be served making a building having a longer technically viable existence than functionally required? True to the Modern Movement ideals of applying rational procedures for social ends, he designed a complex of buildings in which every space precisely fitted specific functions, employing a minimum use of materials and effort while exploiting technical innovation to the maximum. This approach he called 'spiritual economy' the result being both practically efficient and poetically beautiful. The quality of these buildings was such that many architects considered them among the most outstanding buildings of the twentieth century.

Following his death in 1934 Duiker's prescience was vindicated – by the early 1950s effective cures for tuberculosis had been evolved and the need for a sanatorium evaporated. This so-called Zonnestraal complex was converted into a general hospital. For as long as the functional requirements remained unchanged Duiker's principle of 'spiritual economy' proved its worth, but when new uses were introduced the principle of tight fit between form and function became a liability. As a consequence, some elements of the complex were abandoned and fell into ruins while others were changed beyond recognition. Only the memories of a social and cultural monument survived. Gone were the poetry and beauty.

Even in the Netherlands Zonnestraal was not an isolated case. In that country alone there were many Modern Movement buildings of significant cultural value displaying similar social, technical and aesthetic characteristics whose fate and future usefulness were uncertain. Among these were such world-famous buildings as the van Nelle Factory by Van der Vlugt and the Kiefhoek housing estate by Oud, both in Rotterdam, and the Schröder House in Utrecht by Rietveld.

Faced with this new cultural phenomenon the Dutch Government Heritage Department approached me in 1982 to develop a methodology enabling them to make accountable decisions concerning culturally important Modern Movement buildings. Since Zonnestraal was notorious and technically the most complex, as well as being in dire need of intervention, it was used as the main research project for investigation. I invited a student of

architecture who had special knowledge of Duiker's work, Wessel de Jonge, to assist in the project. One of the main recommendations in our final report was to contact architects and researchers faced with similar problems outside the Netherlands. To our great surprise colleagues in other countries were operating just like us in a similar ad hoc, isolated fashion notwithstanding the shared view that the Modern Movement has exerted the most significant influence on twentieth century architecture and urbanism.

Many questions emerged. Since it is not feasible to keep them all, which buildings and building groups should be conserved, and why? Each case is specific; not all buildings need the same type of protection. But what does protection imply? How is it possible to extend the economic and functional life of particular buildings in environmentally acceptable ways without sacrificing the authenticity of the original idea, including visual and tactile qualities? Can the paradox of preserving 'throw away' buildings be justified? In what way can experiences drawn from many countries be shared for mutual benefit? How can the public at large be informed of the cultural significance of the Modern Movement and those in power reminded of their responsibilities to celebrate and conserve our recent heritage?

These questions, and many more, convinced us of the need to get ourselves organised. In 1988 DOCOMOMO was founded at the School of Architecture in the Eindhoven University of Technology where I held a Chair in Building Technology. The memorable and rhythmic acronym DOCOMOMO was selected not only for its intrinsic appeal but, by placing

DOcumentation ahead of COnservation an inherent, realistic priority is established for posterity. In 1990 we organized the first international DOCOMOMO conference in Eindhoven. To our astonishment representatives from 13 countries arrived, all keen to join and launch Working Parties on their home territory. The question then arose, how to structure a voluntary organisation to unify disparate cultural, legal and hierarchical traditions. Wessel and I although interested in organizing DOCOMOMO for a few years were also busy as teachers and in practice and had no inclination to embed ourselves in bureaucracy. With the invaluable help of Christopher Dean, John Allan and James Dunnett from the United Kingdom we designed the DOCOMOMO constitution leaving each country to organise its own affairs within a unifying framework having minimum constraints. The rules would be formalised by a meeting of Council which consisted of representatives appointed by each National Working Party. One country, one vote. And so it happened! The constitution was accepted and DOCOMOMO was on its way.

Now, after twelve years, the network consists of active working parties in 40 countries and some 1400 participating architects, historians, students and technicians world wide. The International Secretariat once established in Eindhoven, was suddenly inundated by an avalanche of local initiatives from a diversity of locations such as La Plata in Argentina, Quebec in Canada and Belgrade in the former Yugoslavia, seeking help in the fight to protect their modern built heritage. Very often we had no idea of the importance of particular buildings or the urgency of the local situation. We were in danger of getting our priorities wrong which would result in undermining the authority of the organization. It was decided to establish a register of the most important buildings in each participating country to be composed by the national DOCOMOMO working parties which, by definition, operated from first-hand knowledge. In order to keep numbers manageable and oblige each working party to make choices, a maximum of fifty buildings per country was allocated. The choice also had to be justified and each contribution informed and enriched our Modern Movement archive. These cultural donations helped to establish the Modern Movement as heterogeneous, full of regional variations and thereby to dispel its erroneous representation as a unified, universal movement dubbed in 1932 the 'International Style'. This publication demonstrates the diverse richness.

After a few years of experimentation Council decided that registers should be more clearly structured, and standardized in accordance with universally accepted methods of documentation. An International Specialist Committee for Registers was established and a standard format was developed together with a comprehensive approach to selection. The latter was necessary because DOCOMOMO was invited by the International Council on Monuments and Sites (ICOMOS) to make a proposal for Modern Movement oeuvres (buildings and sites) to be included in the World Heritage List of UNESCO, together with a set of criteria for the selection of 20th century buildings. In addition to assembling the national registers, the national working parties were also asked to present buildings which might prove sufficiently important for inclusion in the International DOCOMOMO selection. This has resulted so far in some six hundred buildings world wide being equally and thoroughly documented, probably one of the most extensive sources of documentation in the history of architecture. Over three hundred DOCOMOMO members from across the world participated in this vast operation under the guidance of successive chairs of the International Specialist Committee: Gérard Monnier from Paris, France; France Vanlaethem from Quebec, Canada; Maristella Casciato from Rome, Italy. Other major contributions have come from Marieke Kuipers (The Netherlands), Allen Cunningham (UK) and David Whitham (Scotland). This book can only illustrate a small number of buildings from the total international DOCOMOMO selection on which detailed information fiches have been compiled. The complete archive is held at the Nederlands Architectuurinstituut (NAI) in Rotterdam and is available for study. Currently, the DOCOMOMO working parties are preparing the documentation of significant Modern Movement urban sites and landscapes which will be ready in 2004.

In the meantime, what happened to Zonnestraal? A lot, and yet nothing. Many serious initiatives emerged. These included a conference resort for trade union members, an Aids centre, a meditation resort, and a preventive and curative centre for heart patients, all of which were investigated. The general hospital has departed, the buildings are empty but no restoration or conversion work has started due to lack of money, bureaucracy, conflicting interests, demanding requirements and inflated expectations. Zonnestraal provides clear proof of the necessity for such buildings to be registered with, and kept under the continuous vigilance of an organization like DOCOMOMO. We receive many complaints from all over the world about the general lack of interest in preservation of twentieth century architecture and urbanism. I even experience this incredible lack of understanding and care in the highest echelons of international heritage circles. Not only buildings like Duiker's Zonnestraal, Aalto's Viipuri library, Ginzburg's Narkomfin housing in Moscow but also, many lesser known masterpieces around the world were designed to fit the demands of our dynamic era. Precisely because of that they are easy prey to rapid change or demolition – often before it is recognized they are under threat.

And yet their social, technical and aesthetic innovations are representative of the best architecture of our time, and for many of us these are objects which, quite simply, we love. This book shows clearly the rich variety and exceptional architectural quality of Modern Movement buildings. They belong to the continuity of our civilisation and varied cultures and must be retained in one form or another for the enjoyment of future generations. This is a responsibility for us all.

Postscript
Literally on the day this book is being sent to the printers, good news for Zonnestraal has finally emerged after some 18 years of continuous struggle. All parties concerned have signed a covenant agreeing the future use of the complex, the restoration work to be done, the degrees of intervention to be allowed, the time-table and above all the financing. This optimistic future for Zonnestraal is in line with the optimistic ideas and endeavours characterizing the Modern Movement: hard to realize but very much worthwhile.

Documenting Modern Architecture

Maristella Casciato
Chair, DOCOMOMO International Specialist Committee on Registers

The rhythmic effectiveness of the acronym DO-CO-MO-MO has become enjoyed in its own right by aficionados world-wide. My colleague Hubert-Jan Henket has explained its meaning and origins in his Introduction. He has also stressed the clear methodological priority which lies behind the ordering of its first two phonemes.

When our international working party started, this confident identification with MoMo – with that part of the acronym which represents 'the Modern Movement' – was itself an attempt to overcome what by then, in the late 1980s, were deeply rooted historiographical prejudices. But the very act of linking Documentation with Conservation was itself far more radical than it seems now. They had not previously appeared to be areas where common strategies were readily agreed.

This book demonstrates how documentation is necessarily the prerequisite for any effective action to safeguard. It also shows how conservation receives its authority and acquires its successes from detailed knowledge of the historical, economic, aesthetic, social and constructive motivations which guide the architectural process. This is no small matter when the objective is to create a methodology for safeguarding the heritage of modern architecture.

Back in 1980, when one of the first international meetings was held to discuss the sources of modern architecture, Manfredo Tafuri made the following observation in his introduction: 'History can in some way contest and indeed destroy not only a work of architecture in itself, but also the context in which it was made, by concentrating on production methods, writing the history not of works or personalities but of methods and relationships. . . . To be truly sophisticated, a historiographical tool must not, therefore, serve simply to eliminate critical impressionism.' It must, as he insisted, 'act on the perspective of the disciplinary statutes of history itself.'

This move from object to process is one of the fundamentals on which the DOCOMOMO Register is based. It is a tool which primarily aims to advance modern architectural historiography, freeing it from worn-out art-historical itineraries and creating a methodology of knowledge and procedures for working on the modern heritage.

As Italo Calvino has written, 'Memory has true value only if the traces of the past and the project for the future are held together, if it makes it possible to do what one wanted to do without forgetting, becoming while never ceasing to become.' The Register fiches fit this dimension exactly, for they document not only the status quo of the object concerned, but also its conception, the stages in its design, the final results, the processes of its transformation, its sedimentation in collective memory. To sum up, recalling Calvino once more, the Register fiche forms part of an on-going process of construction so that, as the inhabitants of Tecla replied to the traveller, destruction can never start.

This is the only means we have of bringing our past (especially our most recent past) into our present space and of letting it penetrate our lives. In this way the Register fiche becomes an instrument of that complex phenomenon we call modernity. This is no longer something regarded either as the 'heroic' period of modern architecture, or as the idea of a style. It is rather a cultural mode, a form of civilization which permeated the world in opposition to all earlier traditions, and is dedicated to fundamental economic and social transformation.

Twentieth century architecture stands before us as a living heritage which is to be defended from oblivion and destructive aggression. This is a great responsibility which needs urgent action. With the help of the Register we need to select those works which represent its most significant heritage.

In 1992 the second international conference of DOCOMOMO was held in the extensively restored buildings of the Bauhaus in Dessau. With the east-west divisions of Europe newly removed, it was an extraordinarily evocative and challenging event. Assembled delegates from across the world concluded that there was an urgent need to start up strategic research projects. These would be entrusted to small committees who would be nominated by working parties in the various countries and elected by the movement's unifying Council. Thus it was that an International Specialist Committee on the issue of Registers was created, along with parallel ones for Technology and Education.

The foremost task of the International Register Committee was to devise a register system appropriate to twentieth century architecture with which working parties across the world could create national or regional registers of their own key buildings.

The first draft of a register form or 'fiche' was drawn up soon after that conference. This task in itself prompted debate about the content of the register itself and about the need for it to act as a driving force enabling each national or regional working party to plan their own work. Plainly all this had to be linked, where necessary, to other public institutions involved in aspects of this process.

There was always heated debate about the selection criteria and about the extent to which the final aim of such registers was preservation of the object itself. This debate was partly fuelled by the various currents which had pervaded modernity throughout the twentieth century in geographical areas which were profoundly different from each other. Thus the aim of the national or regional register for each territory has been the selection of a limited number of modern buildings and sites which are representative of the manifold and complex courses that modernity has taken in each geo-political area. Within the common cultural project launched by DOCOMOMO International, the guidelines for register fiches specified that 'the selected buildings and sites should be shown to be innovative technically, socially and aesthetically, and that 'their historical significance should be evaluated.' From these National Selections it became possible to create an International Selection of over 500 works which was presented for debate to our fourth international conference at Bratislava in 1996. This provided the scientific and methodological basis for discussions with ICOMOS about criteria for inclusion of twentieth century buildings in general, and Modern Movement ones in particular, within UNESCO's World Heritage List.

The issues to be addressed in nominating modern works for inclusion alongside more ancient cultural products on such a list are to some extent the universal ones of supreme creative quality. The vexed issue of 'authenticity' is equally central and involves scrutiny of what remains in relation to four dimensions of the original object: its key idea; its form, spaces and appearance; its construction and details; its materials. It was agreed that the life work of four great masters, Le Corbusier, Frank Lloyd Wright, Ludwig Mies van der Rohe and Alvar Aalto, were of such importance to twentieth century culture that their oeuvres should be recognized as a universal heritage.

As this work has expanded and progressed, the debates it has provoked have been intellectually and professionally challenging far beyond the boundaries of the immediate task, which is represented in this first selective book. The logic and content of the record fiches has evolved in parallel as they have become increasingly authoritative and public documents. One consistent feature of the work, which this book inevitably reflects, has been its international perspective. The International Specialist Committee on Registers which has guided this work has profited from different people's time and perspectives at different stages. Thus its chairmanship has shifted across the Atlantic from Gérard Monnier in Paris to France Vanlaethem in Quebec and to myself in Rome. Its members at various stages have been the following: Marieke Kuipers and Dirk Baalman (Netherlands), Jorge Gazaneo (Argentina), Xavier Costa (Iberia), Dennis Sharp and Alan Powers (United Kingdom), András Ferkai (Hungary), David Whitham (Scotland), Panayotis Tournikiotis (Greece), Luca Veresani (Italy), David Fixler and Anthony Merchell (United States of America) and Luc Verpoest (Belgium).

As that list indicates, DOCOMOMO is a polyglot network which spans the globe. In assembling a first summary of the Modern Movement heritage identified by our fiches, purely practical reasons have prevented us even including material from every one of the forty countries where we now have working parties. We hope another volume may follow to complete the global picture. Meanwhile we are particularly grateful to Dennis Sharp and Catherine Cooke of DOCOMOMO-UK for editing this volume and coordinating its production. As English is DOCOMOMO's common language their participation has been vital.

Alvar Aalto
TB Sanatorium Paimio Finland
1929 | 1933

Registering the diaspora of Modern Architecture
Dennis Sharp

With the turn of the millennium it is time to take stock. The 'modern' spirit has absorbed the minds and the creative talents of many generations of architects for well over a century and a half. The search for that which is described as 'modern' has been an absorbing intellectual crusade. Viewed as the inevitable result of a long evolutionary process, 'modernization' has slowly adjusted itself socially and politically to the perceived needs of society.

Modernism took art and culture by the scruff of the neck and revolutionized the built environment. Central to its progress were ideas for the reshaping of the city. New ideas were manifest from Chicago and Letchworth Garden City to Canberra and Tel Aviv, through Le Corbusier's ideas for a 'radiant city' to the achievements of European new towns after the Second World War. More recently whole new capitals have been created like Brasilia and Chandigarh. All these examples were planned modern cities.

During the nineteenth century many overcrowded cities were dreadful places. Their inhuman conditions, coupled with a growing need for social equality, expressive freedoms and universal education, conspired to force architects and urban designers to reconsider the formation of city spaces and buildings. Musicians and artists were also engaged in a fundamental reassessment of their arts and the service of their arts to society. Adopting in many cases what have been called avant-garde positions, it was architects, artists, designers and musicians (Picasso and Gris, Marinetti and Boccioni, Le Corbusier and Ozenfant, Berg and Schönberg, Craig and Appia, Hoffmann and Loos to name a few) who were to lead an assault on previously defined aesthetic values. They revolutionized the visual and aural world through the invention of not one but many languages of 'modern' art. We can sit back and collectively call it a Modern Movement. Through its universal appeal which has seeped through the surface of even the most tradition-bound societies, its diaspora has spread everywhere from Berlin to Buenos Aires.

The Register
This book is an attempt to collect data on this phenomenon through the local and national Registers compiled by DOCOMOMO's international member groups. It is the first publication of its kind devoted to recording and documenting the international spread of modern architecture. Its scope is wide and its purpose precise. Drawing on examples from over thirty national groups the book shows nearly six hundred works of modern architecture. It covers much of the classifiable world of Modern Movement architecture monitored by the member groups of DOCOMOMO.

This is therefore a very different type of survey from the selective anthologies of modern architecture compiled during the movement's propagandist and ideological period. It was during this period that formative and propagandist texts began to appear, somewhat different from the Utopia projects and correspondence of the previous era. The definitions of modernism supplied by earlier versions of the modernist language were considerably altered. It had all become rationalized – even homogenized perhaps – and books like Le Corbusier's Vers une architecture (1923) and Gropius's Internationale Architektur (1925) were the manifestos that accompanied the movement's diaspora. Besides the early Bauhausbücher and the internationally orientated articles of the mid-20s in De Stijl and L'Esprit Nouveau, in Wasmuth's Monatshefte für Baukunst, The Studio and The Architectural Review, the first full scale survey of German 'new architecture' (the so-called 'neue Bauwegung in der Baukunst') was Gustav Platz's Die Baukunst in der neuesten Zeit (Berlin 1927), part of the Propylean series. Platz was followed by a much more ambitious and personal survey compiled by the Italian architect and CIAM member Alberto Sartoris: Gli elementi dell' architettura funzionale (Milan 1932). This was followed by a number of textual, critical and visual surveys in various European languages. Few of these however provide such a wide-ranging coverage of built examples as this new DOCOMOMO anthology.

Despite this breadth it is by no means comprehensive, nor, as yet, definitive. It covers regions which have an active DOCOMOMO membership. Furthermore, it includes selected material only from those DOCOMOMO groups which have responded positively to the invitation to submit examples from their national lists. Consequently there are obvious gaps and, inevitably, some regrettable omissions. These include the whole of Africa, China, India as well as some countries in Central and South America. Subsequent editions will make up this short fall. But none of this should obscure the value of this remarkable collection of material, compiled with varying degrees of expertise and enthusiasm by the national group members. It will prove a valuable asset for architects, students and conservationists as well as for Modern Movement historians seeking international comparisons for their judgements and work. Many texts have been especially translated into readable English from a variety of sources.

As a list it is therefore unique. It indicates the widespread nature of modern architecture, its ideological – and sometimes pedagogic – bases, as well as the many interpretations and metamorphoses it has undergone since the early 1920s. The survey also supports the often-stated argument that modernism has a coat of many colours and derives from many sources, although in demonstrating that argument visually this is not to be seen as a history book. Rather, it sheds light on the variations and versions of modern architecture through individual examples and indicates the many interpretative aspects of the diaspora that the Modern Movement produced.

The Modern Movement
So what are the main characteristics of this modern architecture that DOCOMOMO seeks to document and save?

Firstly, it is a product of the twentieth century that derives from the stylistic and creative remnants of the Art Nouveau, Cubist and Art Deco attitudes of the period up to and including the mid-1920s. It incorporates the Zweckkunst of the German Neues Bauen; French ferro-concrete experiments; American health programmes; machine age art, and the social and political bases of Russian

Walter Gropius
Bauhaus, Dessau
Germany
1925 | 1926

Moisei Ginzburg
Narkomfin, Moscow
USSR
1928 | 1930

Constructivism, that lead to the 'functionalist' buildings of the International Style and its seminal regional variations. The special character of these buildings, often related to Le Corbusier's 'Five Points of a New Architecture' of 1926, can be crudely summarized as: spatial exploration, unadorned surfaces, flat roofs and 'white' (or coloured) surfaces of plain concrete or rendered walls.

The widespread dissemination of modern architecture was not monolithic, as I have said, but a series of 'Modern Movements' occurring in various parts of the world. Those who argue that modern architecture was merely a 'cloning' operation have got it wrong, even with the persistent influence of Le Corbusier and the CIAM. We have here over six hundred examples to support this view, that there were a variety of approaches to modernism, some regional and some technical. Some of the national groups in this book see this architectural diaspora as a continuous process, and have indicated the way in which the original tenets of modern architecture were absorbed into post-war architectural developments. In other cases these tenets were modified or extended to meet the extraordinary challenges of post-war reconstruction and the establishment of new towns and new housing programmes. This post-war 'second phase' of modern architecture has been likened to the analytical phase of Cubism although it must be said that modernism in the arts was to change direction far more rapidly than in architecture. Tachism, Action painting and the way in which Abstract Expressionism replaced the figurative abstractions of the inter-war periods, were developments that could not be so easily paralleled in architecture.

However, modern architecture has consistently kept to its aim of revolutionizing modern life. It did this through an architecture that derived its form language from concepts based on the virtues of sun, light and air, and construction systems based on flexibility, repetition and ease of erection. New materials too, many originally developed (lightweight steel, aluminium and plastics) as part of the war effort, played an important part in the post-war modernist experiments.

This publication also has another purpose: to define some of the reasons for the general interest and understanding that has grown up over the past two decades, in the pioneer achievements of inter-war modern architecture.

This enthusiasm has more recently been aided by the events of 1989 and the thawing out and the eventual demise of Communism in Russia and Central and Eastern Europe – an area which is now seen as a crucible of early modern architecture. It was with immense relief that a large number of previously forgotten and certainly undocumented modern buildings – and indeed whole estates – were found to be intact in the Czech Republic, Slovakia, Bulgaria, Poland, Hungary, East Germany and in the former Soviet Union itself. This was at a time when the western nations were seeing their Modern Movement masterpieces threatened, some rapidly disappearing and others altered beyond recognition. Here DOCOMOMO was instrumental in filling the gap that opened up in building conservation and

Postwar optimism and building innovation went hand-in-hand in 1951

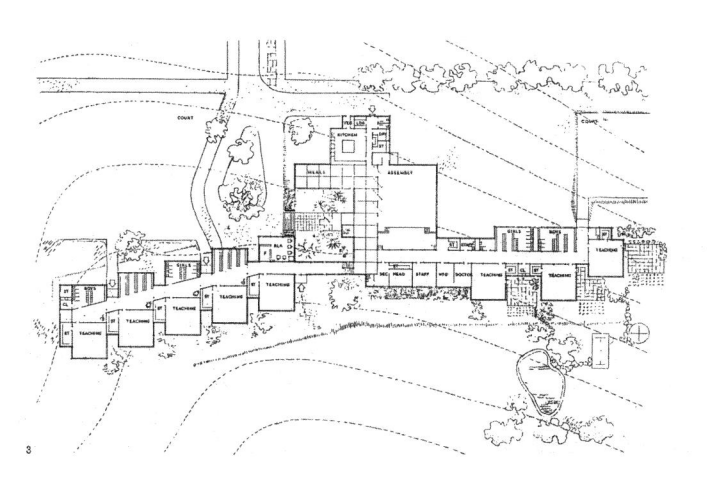

The postwar British Schools programme brought open plans and technological change to an old building type.

documentation by taking on campaigns for various threatened structures in many parts of the world. In Holland for example the neglect of Duiker's Zonnestraal Sanatorium at Hilversum was an incentive to create DOCOMOMO. It has been well documented. The Schröder House in Utrecht by Rietveld, which was also poorly looked after, has now been fully restored. One early campaign led to saving 'Torilla', the first reinforced concrete thin-wall house in England near Hatfield.

However there have been losses too. Another campaign generated worldwide interest for preservation of the Narkomfin building in Moscow, but this has fallen into worsening, maybe terminal decay. In Wales the commercial and economic failure surrounding the famous rubber factory at Brynmawr designed by the Architects' Co-partnership, which was one of the most important innovative post-war modern buildings and the first in that country to be listed, has meant the structure is now almost beyond repair. The iconic Bauhaus complex in Dessau went through a series of changes resulting eventually in its re-use and most welcome restoration.

All these examples justify the need for an organization like DOCOMOMO to prevent the further loss of Modern Movement buildings, whether through deliberate destruction or by careless neglect. The fact that this rescue action occurred during a period dominated by anti-rational and so-called Post Modernist, historicist, tendencies in general architectural taste worldwide has made its energy all the more remarkable and surprising.

13

After years of neglect, the first listed modern building in Wales still awaits a new user :
At completion 1950
Current condition

World Heritage

I must now turn to this publication's raison d'être. The DOCOMOMO International Committee on Registers has been meeting now for nearly ten years. It made a decision to compile an international register of Modern Movement buildings in addition to making all the archive material assembled from individual national groups publicly available in the NAi archive in Rotterdam. To produce a comprehensive list proved impossible. Thus a compromise was reached, based on the experience of selecting Modern Movement examples to be nominated for the World Heritage List. That selection was submitted to ICOMOS in 1998.

At the DOCOMOMO Conference in Stockholm in 1998, a publishing programme for a selection from the national registers of each member group was announced. National groups were invited to select up to twenty examples from their own country. Some have done that. Some have done otherwise! There was no restriction on an end-date for the chosen examples but the buildings and sites were to be extant and visually accessible. The descriptions and supporting information were placed in the hands of the national groups and therefore the responsibility for selection and accuracy rested with their members. Furthermore, the variations – and sometimes infelicities – to be found in the use of English in the text pages have sometimes been retained, although every attempt has been made to achieve a stylistic evenness in the publication. This policy was adopted to obviate the introduction of a bland editorial style and also because many

'Isokon' Flats, London
'Minimum existence' living
inspired by German and
Russian models:
present condition.

national groups will be ordering copies of the separate sections that make up the publication, for their own use. In many cases the full-page illustration chosen to introduce individual countries is a modern building or site previously nominated for the World Heritage List.

This book was originally envisaged as a loose-leaf series. In the manner of various classic Modern Movement publications of the 1920s and 30s, it was to consist of a number of separate fiches produced as a cahier in a slip-case cover. However this proved unsound from the publishing point of view today. Instead, an agreement was reached to issue a book divided into national sections which could later be off-printed in individual booklets for the use of the national groups.

Additionally, it was felt that the book should be reinforced as a reference publication on Modern Movement architecture. To this end its shape has changed considerably from the sizes originally proposed, in order to give much more space for textual material. Some of the national sections – originally restricted to 750 words only – now have longer introductions than was anticipated and a greater emphasis is now given to bibliographical source material. A general bibliography is included covering books and journals related to the Modern Movement in addition to the more specialist bibliographies contained in the national sections.

Finally, despite all the pictorial and linguistic problems, editing this book has been a pleasure and an education in itself. It would not have been possible even to contemplate such a broad selection without the encouragement, help and co-operation of the thirty-two working parties involved. The editorial and design team acknowledges a huge debt of gratitude to each of them.

Argentina

In the mid-twenties, a group of writers, artists and architects interested in the development of European avant-garde tendencies, together with the presence of qualified enterprises and technicians, were the basis for the adoption of the Modern Movement in Argentina. Even when the predominant conservative cultural trends acted as an obstacle to the frank entry of the new waves, European books and magazines allowed Argentine professionals to get in touch with the thought and work of Modern Movement masters while in local magazines some texts were published presenting the fresh ethic and aesthetic ideals and praising their introduction in the country.

In early 1929 the Sociedad Amigos del Arte (Friends of the Arts Society) invited Le Corbusier, to Buenos Aires where he delivered nine lectures. His visit did not leave an immediate result, and his influence would only become evident some ten years after. The same year one of the early examples of Argentine modern architecture was finished: the house of writer Victoria Ocampo. Close friend of some of the most important writers and artists of her time, Miss Ocampo commissioned the project to Alejandro Bustillo, an academic architect, who yielded to the stubborn position of the client, who firmly decided to play a pioneering role concerning the renovation of taste.

In the thirties, a group of outstanding buildings was built in Buenos Aires and other cities, introducing and spreading the Modern Movement in Argentina. Architectural programmes focused in the housing field, including upper middle-class flat buildings and social housing, though the lack of defined policies and the practically total absence of the State meant that the ideas and projects concerned did not find the appreciation for which they hoped. The team Sánchez, Lagos and de la Torre produced some of the most outstanding architectural examples of the decade, as the Kavanagh Building in Buenos Aires, remarkable for the conditions of the site and the way they are taken advantage of. It is no less important for its concrete structure, for many years the highest in South America.

In 1928 the Russian architect Wladimiro Acosta arrived in Argentina. After graduating in his country, a period in Germany allowed him to contact modern architecture. Acosta was concerned about the proper answer to the climatic conditions, proposing the 'Helios' system, based on the consideration of the sun incidence giving adequate solar exposure. He also made important contributions to the relation between architecture and the town, through the proposal of prototypes of high buildings close by related to the urban situation. His built works are perhaps scarce compared to his theoretical contribution.

Antonio Vilar designed several apartment buildings in Buenos Aires, including prototypes for narrow plots. But his most significant contribution is his work for the Automóvil Club Argentino, a vast programme including buildings in the main Argentine towns and gas stations along the whole road system. Vilar employed a rigorous functionalist approach, related to German rationalism, where the composition of different masses showed the diversity of functions. Other important contributions during the thirties are the apartment buildings by Leon Dourge and Jorge Kalnay; some office buildings such as the Comega or Safico in Buenos Aires and the Gran Rex Cinema by Alberto Prebisch.

At the end of the thirties a stylistic regression is noticeable, which would continue up to the fifties. The principles of the Modern Movement were practically excluded from official architecture, and Classicism became the style used in official architecture. One significant exception to this situation is the building for research laboratories in Florencio Varela (1943), belonging to the State petrol enterprise YPF and designed by a team led by Jorge de la María Prins.

The avant-garde attitude during the forties was mainly found among architects with more projects than constructed works. The Austral Group, headed by Juan Kurchan, Jorge Ferrari Hardoy and Antonio Bonet denounced the setting of a new Academy which had produced 'the modern style', while architecture had no power to deal with the problems of the town and was detached from urbanism. The group took the subject of the urbanism and the rural housing, including considerations related to the climate, the habits of people, the architectural traditions and the local materials. Among the buildings erected by members of the group, it is worth recalling the one located on the corner of Paraguay and Suipacha Streets by Bonet and the one in Virrey del Pino Street by Kurchan and Ferrari Hardoy, both in Buenos Aires.

The work of Amancio Williams must also be mentioned. His career began in 1942 with the project for his father's house in Mar del Plata. With just a few buildings materialised, Williams is one of the most original Argentine architects, whose influence would be evident not only in his country but also in the international context. In 1949 Le Corbusier projected the house for Dr Pedro Curutchet in La Plata, the only residential building that the master erected in the Americas.

Argentine architecture post 1950 was influenced by Brutalism and International Style. The headquarters of Teléfonos del Estado (1951) in Buenos Aires, the Town Hall of Córdoba city (1953), both by the team SEPRA (Sánchez, Elía, Peralta, Ramos, Agostini) and the Government House of the province of La Pampa in Santa Rosa city, by Clorindo Testa, are significant examples of the Brutalism and aesthetics influenced by Le Corbusier. These four architects together are the authors of the London and South America Bank in Buenos Aires, one of the landmarks of Argentine architecture.

In 1953 Mario Roberto Alvarez designed the San Martín Theatre in Buenos Aires, another outstanding example of modern architecture in the country. Alvarez, who began his career in the late thirties and is still an active practitioner, incorporated in this building layout many technological advances, including the construction of a whole glass curtain-wall. In his later works Alvarez showed a great coherence, based on a rigorous position concerning constructive and formal aspects.

Stella Maris Casal

1
Victoria Ocampo's House
Rufino de Elizalde Street
Buenos Aires
1929
Alejandro Bustillo

The original owner, Ms Ocampo, was a prominent member of Buenos Aires high society and cultural circles. She wanted a modern house to be erected in the most elegant district of the city, a site surrounded by historicist buildings. Although Le Corbusier was asked to make a preliminary design for a nearby plot, the work was finally commissioned from Alejandro Bustillo, leader of Argentine academics. The house is the best built testimony of the particular local appropriation of early Modern Movement aesthetic ideals, an outstanding 'manifesto' of the international images of built modernism.

2
Comega Building
222 Corrientes Avenue
Buenos Aires
1932
Alfredo Joselevich & Enrique Douillet

The Comega Building was the first skyscraper to be built in reinforced concrete in Latin America. Since it was the result of a real estate investment, the aim was to offer a new image of efficiency and modernity to attract possible occupants, as it did, indeed. It is considered the very first 'monument' of modern architecture in the city, its height and spatial arrangement challenging local standards of its time. The usual combination of different Modern Movement sources, a typical attitude in Argentinian designers, is shown in this unexpected recreation of an idealised German rationalism adapted to a skyscraper.

3
Apartment building
Libertador Avenue 2894
Buenos Aires
1928 | 1934
Leon Dourge

The programme included flats, parking facilities and two shops in the ground-floor. The plan responds to the exiguous dimensions of the plot by means of a compact layout; a little open space allows the ventilation of service rooms, while living-rooms and bedrooms open towards the street. The balconies enjoy the views to the nearby park and river, giving protection to prevailing winds. The formal result is a plain, white mass including a special solution of the corner, defined as a semi-independent prismatic mass. The solution of the ground-floor with big glass surfaces and practically no walls on the façade plane emphasises the purity of volumes, which are seen as independent from the ground.

4
Kavanagh Building
Florida Street & San Martin Street
Buenos Aires
1935 | 1937
Sánchez, Lagos & de la Torre

The Kavanagh Building was for many years the tallest building in South America, the highest reinforced concrete structure and the first apartment building in the world using a central air conditioned system. Its conception links two sides of the modernist world: it is an American skyscraper type using technical resources adopted from German DIN regulations. The programme established that it would contain apartments for middle class individual owners and no initial cost limitations were set up in order to assure the quality of the results. Its aesthetic conception, an outstanding synthesis of Art Deco, expressionism and purism, was innovative for the city of Buenos Aires in 1935. Still today its scale and silhouette adds to the Buenos Aires skyline.

5
Gran Rex Cinema Theatre
956 Corrientes Avenue
Buenos Aires
1936 | 1937
Alberto Prebisch

The cinema, a modern architectural programme, is housed in a simple, stunning building settled on a crowded broad street: a shiny dream-box representing modern urban ideals. The audacious reinforced concrete structure not only allowed a large spectators capacity but gave support to an impressive spatial design. This feature also helped to establish a fluid connection between interior and exterior, emphasised by the front curtain wall, one of the largest, most suitable and technically efficient fenestration of the period. Air conditioning systems, modern electrical and acoustical appliances complete the innovative services of the building.

6
Ateliers Building
Corner of Suipacha & Paraguay Streets
Buenos Aires
1938
Antonio Bonet

After working with Josep Lluis Sert and Le Corbusier, the Catalan architect Antonio Bonet established himself in Argentina in 1938. His first work in the country is the Suipacha & Paraguay Street building, developing a programme that had no precedents in Argentina. Located in a corner plot in Buenos Aires downtown, the building has commercial facilities in the ground-floor and ateliers for artists above. The architect introduced some new solutions, like the double height spaces, vaulted roofs and the unusual definition of the corner. The building was seen as an experiment in the use of new synthetic materials, light construction methods and innovative mechanical systems. It is a turning point in the development of Argentine modernism.

7
Automovil Club Argentino Headquarters
1850 del Libertador Gral, San Martin Avenue
Buenos Aires
1940 | 1943
Jabobs Gimenez & Falomir
Antonio Vilar (engineer)
Sanchez, Lagos & de la Torre
Jorge Bunge, Hector Morixe

The unusual and complex functional programme, very much conditioned by vehicular circulation, required particular structural solutions that were an outstanding testimony of the high construction standards reached by the time by influence of the application of German DIN regulations. The ACA headquarters must be seen as the main component of an extended network of buildings well identified with the institution's purpose to develop vehicular communications and tourism all along the country. In this case Modern Movement technical and aesthetic resources served both as useful means of efficient construction and the successful transmission of the ACA image.

8
Apartment Building
Figueroa Alcorta Avenue 3020
Buenos Aires
1941
Wladimiro Acosta

The Russian architect Wladimiro Acosta was particularly concerned by the relation between architecture and climate, looking for proper solutions related to the local conditions of insolation. The building occupies a narrow urban plot facing a park. The plan is conceived in order to profit from the views to the park and the proper orientation, and, at the same time, providing protection against the summer sunlight. This work can be considered as an example of Acosta's concern about the relationship between architecture and climate. It reflects more than a decade of white Modern Architecture, plus an outstanding constructive quality and the ability to insert new buildings in the existing context.

9
The House on the Stream
Williams House
Mar del Plata, Province of Buenos Aires
1942
Amancio Williams

With only a few buildings erected, Amancio Williams is one of the masters of modern Argentine architecture. The house built for his father in the sea-side town of Mar del Plata was his first work, and the main project Williams would ever build. The house is supported by a bridge-like concrete structure over the stream that crosses the vast plot. The house itself, located in the first floor, is based on an open plan. A continuous 'fenêtre en longueur' allows inhabitants to enjoy the view to the surrounding park. In this work Williams introduced some fresh aesthetic ideas, like the exposed concrete.

10
Apartment Building
Virrey del Pino Street
Buenos Aires
1942
Juan Kurchan & Jorge Ferrari Hardoy

After a period of practice in Le Corbusier's Atelier, Kurchan and Ferrari Hardoy founded, along with Antonio Bonet, the AUSTRAL group in 1939, introducing fresh ideas in the local milieu, though with just a few buildings actually erected. The building of Virrey del Pino Street shows new concepts concerning location on the plot, plan layout and aesthetics. Located in a tiny urban plot with boundary walls on three sides, the building itself is placed at the bottom, allowing a generous free space towards the street. Part of the front space is occupied by a restaurant, with entrance both from the street and from the building hall. The building includes three types of flats in an original plan, with all main rooms opening to the front garden. The solution of the light façade is completely original for the time and shows the influence of Le Corbusier on the young architects.

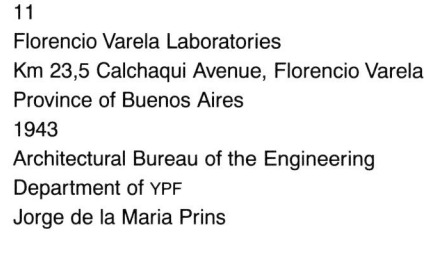

11
Florencio Varela Laboratories
Km 23,5 Calchaqui Avenue, Florencio Varela
Province of Buenos Aires
1943
Architectural Bureau of the Engineering Department of YPF
Jorge de la Maria Prins

The building (originally the research centre for the national petroleum company, YPF, and currently used by La Plata National University with the same aim), was conceived as three independent blocks (laboratories, social and administration facilities and a workshop and experimental area). The spirit of the aesthetic solution adds up to 'form follows function' and thus each particular area of the programme is expressed according to its particular need of space, scale, form and use of modern materials. The rationalized design and high quality materialization were conceived according to standards adopted, once more, from German DIN regulations. It is interesting to point out that the solution for the auditorium was inspired by the Gran Rex Cinema.

12
Curutchet House
La Plata, Province of Buenos Aires
1948 | 1954
Le Corbusier

The Argentine surgeon Pedro Curutchet commissioned Le Corbusier to design his house in 1948; it is the only Le Corbusier residential building erected in the Americas, though the architect never visited the site or met the client. The programme included the family house and the working area; according to Curutchet's requirements and although the exiguous dimensions of the plot, all rooms should open to the street, in order to enjoy proper sunlighting and the views to the nearby park. Le Corbusier organised the layout locating the medical practice area on the front in the first floor, and the house at the bottom and over the working area level.

A ramp connects the entrance, working and the house areas, introducing a pleasant 'promenade architecturale' linking the different parts of the building. It is also remarkable the fitting of the building with the neighbouring ones, which belong to different periods and styles.

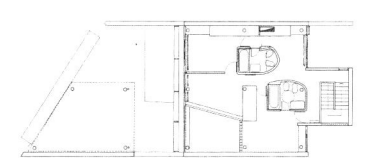

Third Floor: bedrooms

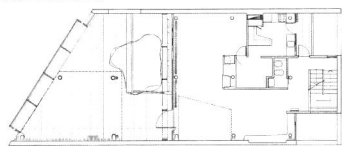

Second Floor: Living areas of the house, and terrace

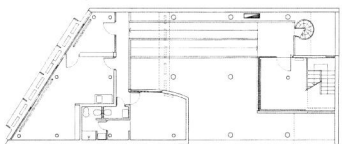

First Floor: Entrance to house and doctor's surgery

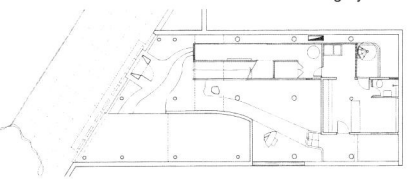

Ground Floor

13
San Martín Theatre
1530 Corrientes Avenue
Buenos Aires
1953 | 1960
Mario R Alvarez

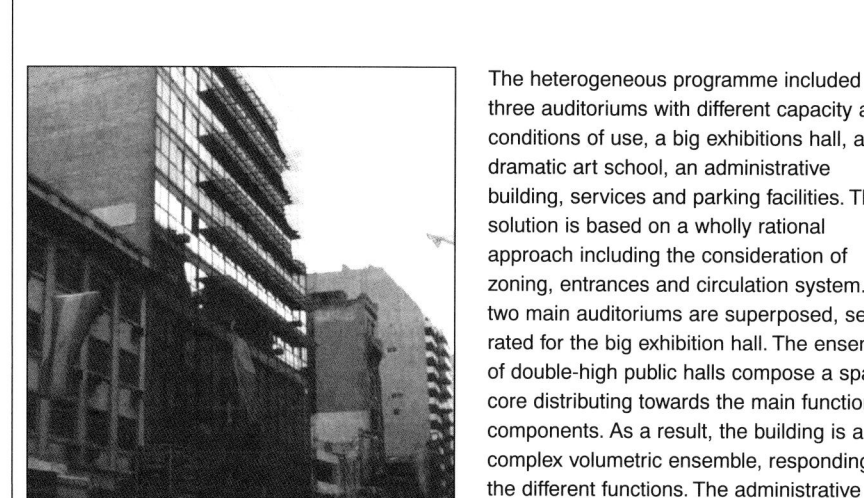

The heterogeneous programme included three auditoriums with different capacity and conditions of use, a big exhibitions hall, a dramatic art school, an administrative building, services and parking facilities. The solution is based on a wholly rational approach including the consideration of zoning, entrances and circulation system. The two main auditoriums are superposed, separated for the big exhibition hall. The ensemble of double-high public halls compose a spatial core distributing towards the main functional components. As a result, the building is a complex volumetric ensemble, responding to the different functions. The administrative building is on the front, forming a continuous glazed façade on Corrientes Avenue.

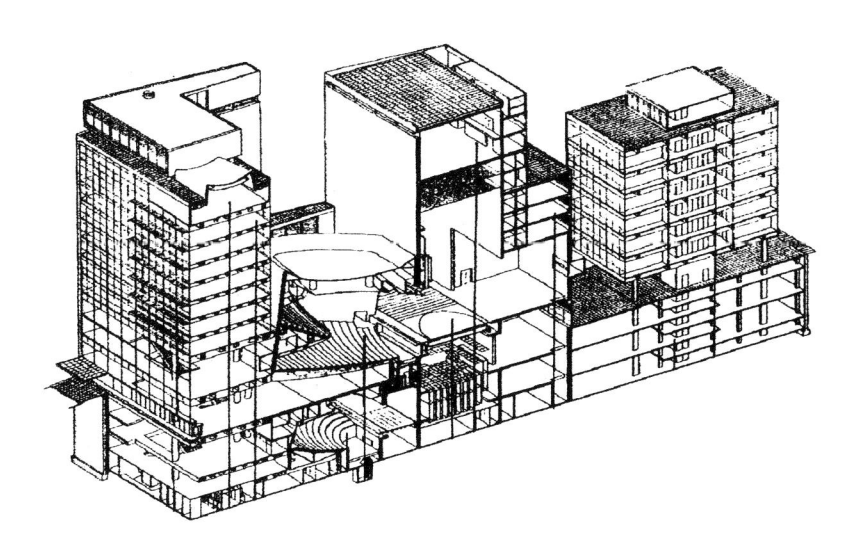

14
Hipotecario Nacional Bank
Formerly London and South America Bank
Reconquista & Bartolomé Mitre Streets
Buenos Aires
1959 | 1966
Clorindo Testa & SEPRA

The building is one of the most important examples of Argentine modern architecture of recent decades. Located on a corner plot, the intention of the architects was to separate clearly the public and private spaces while developing the building in an unique multi-storey high space. The first and second floors containing public areas have a cantilevered concrete structure, while the three-storied offices area is suspended from the concrete roof. Big concrete columns support the roof on an independent plane of that of the glazed curtain-wall, defining the exterior image. The building resulted in a sort of experimental laboratory for architectural solutions. It is an exceptional synthesis of brutalist, metabolist and organic influences.

Selected Bibliography :
'Treinta años de arquitectura en el Rio de la Plata'
Revista de Arquitectura
Buenos Aires no 378 Decembre 1960

Méndez MC
Arquitectura y Urbanismo en Argentina 1930-1960
Buenos Aires 1961

AA VV
Documentos para una historia de la Arquitectura Argentina
Buenos Aires 1984

Glusberg J
Breve Historia de la Arquitectura Argentina
Buenos Aires 1991

Photographic Credits :
A Conti
1, 5, 6, 12, 13
SM Casal
2, 3, 4, 9, 11
Antonio Vilar and others
7
Summa Magazine
8, 10, 14

Australia

The following selection of twenty buildings represents a cross section of Australian modern work ranging across most states and territories, a variety of building types and the various strands of modernism which developed in Australia in response to location, climate and building programmes. The selection does not necessarily represent the 'best' twenty modern buildings but each of the buildings has achieved the status of icon in the Australian architectural community.

Architectural modernism in Australia, as elsewhere, encompasses a broad spectrum of attitudes and techniques which probe the possibilities of cultural and economic modernity. Whilst modernist trends existed from the beginning of the century recognizably 'modernist' buildings emerged in the middle of the 1930s. These early examples inhabited a landscape of eclectic styles, where a minority of architects such as Walter and Marion Griffin were noteworthy for their integrity in welding architecture to belief. A small percentage of practices with a deep interest in the 'new architecture' left a legacy of fine schools and hospitals from the same decade, which for many years were held up as representative of Australian modernism generally.

As the full extent of economic depression unfolded across the country in the early 1930s, large numbers of Australian architects travelled abroad, with many working in England on the eve of the Second World War. Others gained experience in circumstances as diverse as Frank Lloyd Wright's office and the housing programme in Soviet Russia. This experience exposed architects to European modernism and large-scale planned and rationalized production. Impressed by its possibilities, and radicalized by the effects of the Depression, a generation of architects emerged from the war committed to remaking Australia along equitable, progressive lines. Modernism was promoted for this work, with its capacity for rationalized solutions to problems abstractly formulated. The Georgian buildings of New South Wales and Tasmania, with their minimal ornament and dignified proportions, were pressed into service as modernist precursors to lend historical legitimacy to the movement.

The impetus for post-war reconstruction, aided by a widespread Fabianism, propelled modernism to the heart of the political agenda. A lack of resources, though, hindered building until the early 1950s, when a dramatic turn in fortune thrust Australia back into the rank of affluent nations. The austerity of the post-war programme soon gave way to the demands of suburban consumption and the making, along 'modernist' lines, of a progressive corporate world now hand in hand with an expanding welfare state. Through the 1950s and 60s modernism proved its malleability across a range of office towers, shopping centres, sports stadia and highly wrought individual houses. It also showed its hectoring tendencies in schemes which rehoused inner-city inhabitants in mid- and high-rise blocks on the sites of their demolished late-Victorian neighbourhoods. From 1955 onwards city cores began their modern transformations, as the prevailing Melbourne and Sydney building height limits were exceeded by curtain-walled office towers.

The earliest challenges to post-war modernism came in the mid-l950s, at roughly the time it coalesced into an orthodoxy. The link between a new architecture and a spiritual yearning in the face of modernity had been exploited by the Griffins many years earlier, and they had garnered a loyal following. In the 1950s the recent work of their teacher Wright became widely known in Australia, and the charm and responsiveness of his houses from the interwar and post war periods struck a chord with those architects looking for ways to revive the craft-centred tradition of an architecture which was pointedly not commodity housing. Japan, too, was discovered and visited by a generation eagerly searching for poetic alternatives to functionalism. Numerous Californian examples of distinctive houses built at modest cost, such as those by Neutra, Schindler and the Case Study houses, added momentum to this counter-modernism, and the 1960s saw a blossoming of individual houses throughout Australia which were modernist in conception and regional in execution. Queensland and the Northern Territory provided opportunity for tropical and sub-tropical variants, while Perth worked with Mediterranean antecedents. Melbourne's more politicized and urbane culture produced contrasting results to Sydney, where scenic but difficult sites in the city's expanding north and south bushland suburbs gave rise to the distinctive textured houses of the Sydney School.

In the spirit of this divergence, DOCOMOMO Australia is committed to documenting and conserving a wide range of buildings, representative of many modernisms. The divide separating modernism from non-modernism in Australia has not traditionally run between a cosmopolitan internationalism and an introspective nationalism. It runs, rather, between a colonial identity forged in Victorian times, represented by the dark axial interiors of the turn-of-the-century house so vilified by early modernists, and one concerned with adapting architecture to the vicissitudes of modern history and the demands of ancient place. Despite the eager embrace of post-modernism in the 1980s, the legacy of modernism remains strong throughout Australian architecture. Climatic and cultural differences across the country continue to drive architectural experimentation formulated on modernist thinking: it could scarcely be otherwise in a country ill at ease with irony, and with an enduring sense that architecture should strive to be widely accessible.

Jennifer Hill
Noni Boyd
Scott Robertson
Harry Margalit

1
Houses
Castlecrag
1920 | 1935
Walter Burley Griffin &
Marion Mahoney Griffin

Twelve houses within a spectacular setting, designed by American architects Walter Burley Griffin and Marian Mahoney Griffin and their Australian partner Eric Nicholls, survive in the Sydney suburb of Castlecrag. The planning, architectural design and the vision for the community of Castlecrag incorporated the philosophy and political ideas of the Griffins and their experience of theosophy. They formed the Greater Sydney Development Association which purchased 650 acres (236 hectares) in 1920 on a peninsula, jutting out into Sydney Harbour. The Griffin's design for Castlecrag reflected a conscious desire to preserve its topographical features, primarily the rocky sandstone outcrops after which the area was named.

2
Royal Prince Alfred Hospital
Gloucester House
Missendon Road, Camperdown, Sydney NSW
1936
Stephenson, Meldrum & Turner

Royal Prince Alfred Hospital
King George V Hospital for mothers & babies
Missendon Road, Camperdown, Sydney NSW
1938 | 1941
Stephenson & Turner

It is the garden front with its curved glazing to the south-east and the cantilevered balconies that are the distinctive features of Gloucester House. Although the building is discretely tucked away in the hospital grounds the curved glazing was much photographed and published in the international press. The ward block was to be modern in all respects, with internal steelwork and timberwork also influenced by contemporary European buildings visited by Arthur Stephenson. Associated with the new hospital were landscaped grounds and a circular entrance drive, with a central sculpture. King George V Hospital was the second modern building at RPAH. An important modern movement building in Sydney, not only due to its prominent location but also in its dedication solely for mothers and babies. The architects were awarded the '41 Sulman Award for their design. The exterior of King George V also features the distinctive cantilevered horizontal balconies. The two side wings form a front court with a porte cochère, with smaller courtyards to the north and south. Each courtyard contains a sculpture. Due to the strong Australian sun, the building is oriented north-south, with the main courtyard to the west. Royal Prince Alfred Hospital, the teaching hospital associated with the University of Sydney, was the first hospital in Sydney to build a 'modern' hospital block based on European prototypes including Aalto's Paimio Sanitorium.

3
Stanhill
34 Queens Road, Melbourne Victoria
1945 | 1950
Frederick Romberg

Stanhill is the largest of the distinguished series of apartment buildings designed by the Swiss-educated immigrant Romberg before he entered into partnership with Roy Grounds and Robin Boyd in 1953. Regarded as Romberg's finest work, Stanhill is a highly modelled work of reinforced concrete incorporating a complex formal pedigree. Designed in the early 1940s, its construction dragged over five years due to postwar shortages of labour, materials and finance. On completion critical reception was mixed, its busy, sculptural appearance at odds with the rationalist tenor of the times. It has subsequently been reassessed as a striking amalgam of influences.

4
Adelaide High School
Corner West Terrace & Glover Avenue
Adelaide SA
1940 | 1951
EB Fitzgerald & John Brogan

The design of the Adelaide High School was the result of national architectural competition and the building is composed of a series of curves which respond to the curved driveway and contrast with the curved wall of the entry, giving a sweeping horizontality to the building. Each section of the building is composed of an upper large volume, with strip glazing, which is framed and set forward of the brickwork. The upper volume, the first floor, cantilevers over the vertical glazing of the ground floor. The diminishing perspective of the curve is accentuated by the vertical brick piers separating the ground floor glazing and garden bed which follow the curve of the building. The line of the parapet is emphasised, creating a shadow line to each separate volume.

5
Wylde Street Apartments
17 Wylde Street, Potts Point, Sydney NSW
1948 | 1951
Aaron Bolot

This apartment building, containing 38 apartments, was developed as an urban co-operative housing project, which is unusual in Australia. Bolot's Wylde Street apartments was one of the most innovative apartment buildings of its day, with the planning and methods of construction clearly showing the influence of European modernism on Australian architects. Prominently located on a corner, it is one of the first Sydney buildings to employ a segmental radial plan. The sweeping curve of glazing and the spandrels is articulated by the use of breakfronts. The pivot and fixed steel window frames are contained within projecting sills and heads which create shadow lines. The parapet is also accentuated by a shadow-creating capping.

6
Rose Seidler House Group
69-71 Clissold Road, Sydney NSW
1948 | 1956
Harry Seidler

The Rose Seidler House was the first Australian domestic commission of Vienna-born, USA-trained architect Harry Seidler. By 1956, he had designed and built three houses for Seidler family members on a 16 acre (6.5h) bushland estate on Sydney's northern fringe, linking the sloping site with a curving driveway among tall eucalyptus. Rising from natural bush rock foundations, the Rose Seidler House is a flat-roofed, floating cube built of reinforced concrete and timber, featuring extensive use of glass. All twelve rooms have wide views of surrounding bushland with direct or close contact to related outdoor areas. Moveable dividers maximise the flexibility of internal living spaces. The Rose Seidler House was awarded the Sulman Award in 1951.

7
ICI House
1 Nicholson Street, East Melbourne, Victoria
1955 | 1958
Bates, Smart & McCutcheon

ICI House was one of the first free-standing fully glazed curtain wall skyscrapers in Australia. As one of the nation's most stylish commercial buildings, it represented the most refined example of Bates, Smart & McCutcheon's efforts to perfect high-rise office design. Raised on pilotis, the blue-glazed linear stab of open-plan offices, with its clearly differentiated lift core, pierced the city's 132ft (40m) height limit and changed Melbourne's skyline forever. It was the provision of the garden at ground level – designed collaboratively by the architects, sculptor Gerald Lewers and landscape architect John Stevens – which enabled the height limit to be exceeded.

8
Dalton House
Fig Tree Pocket Road, Fig Tree Pocket
Brisbane Queensland
1960
John Dalton

The Dalton Residence is a low-set, flat-roofed building with a direct relationship with its bushland setting. The living areas are orientated to the north, with the adjacent terrace shaded by adjustable louvres for sun control. The language of the building is modified by climatic design elements which directly relate the house to its sub-tropical environment. These elements include floor to ceiling cross-ventilation via full height openings, a parasol roof which incorporates water sprays for cooling, a ventilated clerestory for the venting of hot air, and louvred shades to the northern face of the house. Dalton, while acknowledging the influence of modernist Sydney Ancher and Arne Jacobsen closely tailored the design of this house to the Queensland climate.

9
Summerhayes House
3 The Coombe, Mosman Park, Perth WA
1960
Geoffrey Summerhayes
Graham Glick (engineer)

This locally renowned house is situated on a steeply sloping, limestone cliff site overlooking the Swan River in Perth, the cliff-face forming a natural wall to the undercroft space below the house. A slender steel frame supports and elevates the concrete slab and calcium silicate brick clad structure. The thin, flat roof plane is timber framed. Local dark Jarrah hardwood framing composes a mono-chromatic contrast to the white planar walls. Extensive glazed panels form a transparent end elevation and balcony, orientated towards the river. Interior planning enables open-plan, flexible living, with functional spaces separated by sliding screens.

10
Liner House
13-15 Bridge Street, Sydney NSW
1960
Bunning & Madden

Liner House was erected in 1959 to house the Australian headquarters of Wilh Wilhelmsen Agency Pty Ltd, Norway's largest shipping organisation. The company decided to restrict the building to the company's own use and the building height to that of the neighbouring properties and immediate streetscape. The external walls and ground floor shipping chamber were faced with stone to harmonise with the major part of the street. The RAIA awarded the building the Sulman Award in 1961. The building is dominated by the horizontal louvre framed façade which aligns with the adjacent façades. The façade is set back one metre and comprises aluminium curtain waft patterning and an aluminium panelled cantilevered awning.

11
Woolley House
34 Bullecourt Avenue, Mosman, Sydney NSW
1962
Ken Woolley

The architect's own house stepped down a steep, treed site in a harbourside suburb of Sydney showing the influence of nature and the site on this example of Sydney School architecture. The School was epitomised by modern, rationally planned buildings which were unpretentious, responded to climate and site and used simple, logical structural systems. Architect and writer Robin Boyd described such houses as 'a tamed Australian romantic kind of brutalism' and the Woolley House's use of clinker brick, timber, glass and tile shows this influence as well as the influence of Alvar Aalto. The Woolley House is structured around a 3.6x3.6m grid which is offset 1.2m vertically and horizontally to create a building which steps down the site.

12
Council House
St George's Terrace, Perth WA
1962
Howlett & Bailey Architects
Fraser Consultants (engineer)

Council House – the outcome of a national architectural competition – was designed to contain the new city administration, town hall and council chambers of the city of Perth. Set back from principal city streets and corners, Council House composes a discrete modernist object within a civic square of gardens and reflective water-ponds. Via the granite podium, the building is entered through a Miesian-like open and transparent foyer, elevated by a series of white marble T-shaped pilotis. The façades are clothed in a unique T-section, tiled brise-soleil which appears to float proud of the sheer glazed surface.

Council House is considered an exemplary, yet inflected translation of the International Style to Australia. The building survives (after much campaigning) as an important modernist landmark building within the civic street-scape of the city of Perth. It has been recognized and awarded nationally and internationally as reflecting the vision, prosperity and progress of Australia, post World War II.

13
CB Alexander College
Tocal, Paterson NSW
1965
Philip Cox & Ian McKay

Designed for the Presbyterian Church of Australia in 1963 as a post-secondary level agricultural college it was the first major commission for Cox & McKay, establishing their design reputation for environmental sensitivity. They adapted the principles of vernacular architecture to a large-scale complex, reflecting the grander vernacular of the silos and barns in the region, which was alien to the prevailing modernist institutional architecture of its time. They also incorporated the aesthetics of Japanese architecture in the composition of external spaces and timber detailing throughout the complex. The college epitomises the Sydney School whose principles include loose extendable planning, integration with the landscape.

14
Sidney Myer Music Bowl
Kings Domain, Melbourne Victoria
1956 | 1959
Yuncken Freeman Brothers
Griffiths & Simpson

Named for its retailing benefactor, whose family took a keen interest in the project, the Sidney Myer Music Bowl was the first major purpose-built outdoor venue in Melbourne. The design, with its tent-like roof supported by two tapering cigar-shaped masts, resulted from project architect Barry Patten and his assistant Angel Dimitroff experimenting with various structurally expressive ideas. A model of 6" nails, cotton thread and rice paper was used to develop the idea. The draped structure covers a stage, orchestra pit and fixed seating. An extensive uncovered lawn rises to the south, increasing the capacity of the Bowl to approximately 20,000. The structure reflects the limited means of engineering analysis then available.

15
Ancher House III
Sydney Ancher
Bogota Avenue, Neutral Bay, Sydney NSW
1957
Sydney Ancher

Sydney Ancher was the winner of the 1975 Gold Medal for Architecture as one of the Australian pioneers of the Modern Movement, His houses in the landscape evoke the essence of Australian buildings by the use of horizontality, uncomplicated flat roofs and pergolas in the contemporary mode resembling the traditional verandah function. Robin Boyd stated, 'Sydney Ancher's houses ... are in the best Australian tradition of horizon bleached colours and decorative shadows ... an undeviating search for simplicity.' The first house he built in Villara won the Sulman Medal in 1945. This house, his third for his family, was built as a sophisticated post and beam, flat roofed pavilion-in-the-landscape with a Japanese influence.

16
Robin Boyd House II
290 Walsh Street, South Yarra, Melbourne
Victoria
1957
Grounds, Romberg & Boyd

This house, the second designed by one of Melbourne's best-loved architects and architectural polemicists for his own family, was planned as a narrow rectangle with a catenary roof of planking on wire cables. The draped roof is the guiding idea of the house, with much of its accommodation placed as floating timber platforms under the shelter of this single sweeping gesture. The catenary spans the length of the house, describing a volume which contains a central court, a living and parent's zone at one end and children's accommodation at the other. The horizontal break-up of the window mullions, the refined built-in furniture and the obscured glass side walls of the court are evidence of an interest in Japanese design.

17
Sydney Opera House
Dennelong Point, Sydney NSW
1957 | 1963 (stage 1)
Jørn Utzon
1963 | 1973 (stage 2)
Hall, Todd & Littlemore

'In the Sydney Opera House Jørn Utzon realised the great synthesis of earth and sky, landscape and city, vista and intimacy, thought and feeling, in terms of a unity of technological and organic form.' wrote Christian Norberg-Schutz in 1995. In 1957, the Danish architect Jørn Utzon won the international competition to design an opera house on a peninsula in Sydney's inner harbour, overlooked from the Sydney Harbour Bridge. The design was elaborated over subsequent years resulting, in 1961, in the solution of shells derived from the surface of a sphere of common radius, each vault of precast rib segments radiating from a pedestal. Stress between architect and client forced Utzon to leave the project in 1966 at which stage the monumental podium and soaring shells were in place; the remainder was completed by architects Hall, Todd and Littlemore with newly designed interiors and glass walls. Since its opening in 1973, the Opera House has, nonetheless, been a spectacular success as a venue for the performing arts. Its significance relates to its embodiment of the integration of sophisticated geometry, technology and art and the seminal nature of its sophisticated design and construction techniques. It is important as the expressive culmination of the philosophy of modern architecture and within its ancient harbour setting, as a cultural icon of the twentieth century.

18
Academy of Science
Australian National University, Canberra ACT
1958
Grounds, Romberg & Boyd

The Academy was Roy Grounds' first large building. Grounds, with his first partner, Mewton, was recognized at an early age in 1928 when a recent graduate. Grounds eventually joined Frederic Romberg and Robyn Boyd in partnership in 1953. The client, a learned scientific body, required a large conference hall with raked seating and a second larger space, the Fellows Room, as well as council rooms and offices. The Academy of Science was the recipient of the RAIA's '59 Sulman Award. Grounds deftly moulded these functions into a simple circular plan with circumferential circulation inside and out and housed it all in a concrete copper-clad dome. The dome functions today as designed and the interior details have been retained.

19
Centenary Swimming Pools
Gregory Terrace, Spring Hill, Brisbane
Queensland
1959
James Birrell

The free-form layout of the complex – pools punctuating the concourse and tower restaurant floating above – was influenced by the sculptor Hans Arp and the Constructivist Moholy-Nagy's posthumous publication, 'Vision in Motion' (l947). Birrell intended to generate a 'festive air' and in so doing, he echoed the work of Oscar Niemeyer; the tropical climates of Queensland and Brazil provide the perfect backdrop. The restaurant and pools are of steel and concrete; the pool surfaces are covered in mosaic tiles, patterned in both geometric (main pool) and biomorphic (circular wading pool) designs. In form and function the Pools are one of the most direct adaptations of the Modern Movement to a singularly 'Australian' environment.

20
Australia Square
264-278 George Street, Sydney NSW
1967
Harry Seidler & Associates

The site of Australia Square was the product of a progressive and most extensive protracted site consolidation process which brought under one ownership an entire city block, involving over 30 different properties and more than 80 land titles. The project aimed at bringing a new openness into the congested centre of Sydney with a high rise tower on an open plaza area. The 13-storey, rectangular Plaza Building, was completed in May 1964 and the 50-storey, 171 metre circular high tower in 1967. The project was the recipient of a RAINs Sulman Award in 1967. The precast units serve as both formwork and finish for the surrounding concrete frame. This results in the tapering fin column creating a dominant visual statement.

Selected Bibliography :

Boyd R
Australia's Home, its Origins, Builders and Occupiers
Melbourne 1952

Seidler H
Houses, Interiors and Projects
Sydney 1954

Sowden H (ed)
Towards an Australian Architecture
Sydney & London 1968

Johnson DL
The Architecture of Walter Burley Griffin
Melbourne 1977

Johnson DL
Australian Architecture 1901-51: Sources of Modernism
Sydney 1980

Illustrations courtesy DOCOMOMO Australia

Belgium

This selection of twenty examples of Belgian Modern Movement architecture covers buildings, neighbourhoods and sites designed and built between 1919, Victor Horta's Palais des Beaux Arts in Brussels (1919-1928) and 1960, the Franeau House from Albert Bontridder and Jacques Dupuis (1960). One can identify three phases in the history of modern architecture in Belgium, representative buildings for each of these phases have been selected.

1918-1928 :
Belgium had a very active early 1920s avant-garde movement in the fine arts and architecture, very much in connection with the international scene, more particularly through a series of architectural magazines like La Cité, Opbouwen, 7 Arts, L' Equerre, Het Overzicht, and through very frequent personal contacts during international meetings. Individual housing has been since the late 19th century the main field of architectural practice in Belgium and almost inevitably became so for the Modern Movement. Huib Hoste's Dr De Beir House in Knokke (1924) is very much representative of this, being at the same time, on the international level, one of the first Modern Movement houses, exact contemporary of Gerrit Rietveld's Schröder House in Utrecht. Huib Hoste was an early De Stijl member, while living in Holland during and immediately after the First World War. Hoste also has been one of the most important architects in Belgium in the field of social housing in the early 1920s. He did Klein Rusland in Zelzate, near Ghent (1921-1923) and part of Kapelleveld in Sint-Lambrechts-Woluwe, Brussels (1923-1926), in both cases adopting a straightforward modernist vocabulary, using new building technologies like different in situ concrete systems, industrialization of the building sites and prefabrication. Of great importance is the fact that these modern housing projects have been built during the reconstruction campaign after World War I, a reconstruction (finished in 1928) which is predominantly if not exclusively traditionalist. Another very representative example of Modern Movement collective housing is La Cité Moderne, an early work of another architect of the younger generation, Victor Bourgeois, built between 1922 and 1925. Through this early modernist work in collective housing by Hoste and Bourgeois, Belgium clearly made its mark in the international context of social housing in the 1920s, together with Holland and Germany. The Modern Movement in Belgium was in a certain sense institutionalized through the foundation in Brussels by Henry van de Velde, in 1926, of the Institut Supérieur des Arts Décoratifs (ISAD), better known as La Cambre or Ter Kameren. The 'Belgian Bauhaus' – according to Jacques Aron – had Victor Bourgeois as one of the main teachers, teaching 'practical aesthetics'. Victor Bourgeois was the only Belgian architect to be invited to build at the Weissenhofsiedlung in Stuttgart (1927).

One can interpret as an another international recognition of the importance of the Belgian Modern Movement, the construction by Le Corbusier of the house for the painter René Guiette in Antwerp in 1926-1927. Bourgeois was further appointed secretary of the Brussels CIAM meeting in 1930. Huib Hoste was a collaborator of Le Corbusier for the Antwerp Left Bank competition of 1931.

1928-1940 :
The 1930s show a very intensive production of Modern Movement architecture in Belgium, mainly by architects connected to the La Cambre school of Henry van de Velde. Léon Stijnen became the third director of La Cambre, after Henry van de Velde and the Flemish writer Herman Teirlinck, who had been teaching modern, Bauhaus-like theatre in the school. Brussels was a major centre for the Belgian Modern Movement in the 1930s, with a great variety of different types of buidings, in many cases large complexes of an urban scale. These included hospitals (the Lemaire Sanatorium by Maxime and Fernand Brunfaut, 1933-1937, in Tombeek, near Brussels), multi-functional complexes (the INR-NIR by Joseph Diongre, a radio-building with offices, studio's and concert halls, 1933-1939), collective housing (the Leopold and Albert Residences by Jean-Jules Eggericx and Raphael Verwilghen, 1934-1937), and also individual residences. Eggericx's and Verwilghen's Albert Residence was the first high rise apartment building – 'vertical flats', as they were called by contemporary critics – in Belgium. The Brunfaut sanatorium can stand any comparison with very well known examples of modern sanatoria (almost paradigmata of Modern Movement architecture) by Duiker or Aalto. Of international quality is the work of LH de Koninck, more particularly in the private housing sector: his Dr Ley House in Uccle (near Brussels) (1934), a very interesting Corbusian exercise, is an excellent representative of it and has been recently restored. The international selection of Diongre's radio building is very much relevant because it represents a particular interpretation of the modernist idiom, more particularly because of the use of both modern building technologies and forms and more traditional materials and techniques, eg brickwork masonry as in the work of Dudok in Holland and Mendelsohn in Germany, leading towards a kind of 'moderate modernism'. This is also the case for Henry van de Velde's fourth house – after Bloemenwerf in Uccle, Hohe Pappeln in Weimar and the now demolished De Tent in Wassenaar – called La Nouvelle Maison in Tervuren (near Brussels), built in 1927-1928. The three surviving Van de Velde houses should be collectively listed as historical evidence of his outstanding international career, which has been of great importance for the development of modern architecture in Europe since the late 19th century. Outside Brussels other work of more than national importance has been realized. A recent rediscovery is the very 'constructivist' Albert Residence in Charleroi by Marcel Leborgne (1930). Henry van de Velde's University Library and Art History Institute in Ghent (1932-1936) is undeniably a Modern Movement work of great urban and architectural quality, added to the important historical pattern of this city: an outstanding example of building modern in a historical context. Particularly interesting is the 'moderate modernism' produced by a series of architects in Antwerp, the so called 'Antwerp School' of which the group of six 'Houses for Intellectuals' by Edward van Steenbergen (1932) and the Elsdonck Flats by Léon Stynen (1931-1934) are very much representative.

Research on Modern Movement architecture in Europe should also consider its more 'traditional' aspects, including forms of 'moderate modernism' as mentioned before and the re-emergence of monumentality in modern architecture. This has been the reason for including in this selection, as Belgian representatives of an international development, three exceptional buildings: the Palais des Beaux Arts in Brussels by the former Art Nouveau master Victor Horta (1919-1928), a reinforced concrete structure with a very well designed exterior cladding; an Art Deco kind of classicism in the Perret-like, concrete Saint-Augustine church in Vorst (near Brussels) by Léon Guianotte and André Watteyne (1932-1935), and the Post Office of Ostend by Gaston Eysselinck (1946-1953), the last one being a hinge between pre-war Belgian modernism and post-war late-modernism, a period (1945-1970) which should be focused on very much in the near future.

After 1945 :
Late modernism in Belgium between 1945 and 1970 has been very productive, due to the economic revival after the Second World War. Cities are modernized, high rise office buildings and housing blocks definitely change the traditional urban patterns. At first sight, good quality seems to be rare but still a lot has to be rediscovered. Hugo Van Kuyck's PS Building (1956) in Brussels is an almost unique example of high quality International Style office buildings in Belgium. Two years later, the Expo '58 World Exhibition in Brussels marks the actual success of International Late Modernism. The postwar scene in Belgium is very much dominated by Renaat Braem, once working in Le Corbusier's Paris office in the mid 1930s and now spreading the Corbusian belief in writings, projects and buildings. He designed some of the rare examples in Belgium of large scale social housing ensembles as La Cité Modèle (1958) in Brussels and the outstanding Kiel Housing project (1951-1958) in Antwerp, with a characteristic mix of high and low rise buildings in an open green area, duplex apartments and open galleries. At the same time, in 1957 Braem was building for himself in suburban Antwerp, a very fine private house and office: its evident geometry, clear spatiality and simple technicality already announce the Team X spirit. This is even more the case in Albert Bontridder and Jacques Dupuis' Franeau House in Erbisoeul.

One final consideration as to this selection. For some of the selected buildings an additional important reason for asking for international attention is their actual critical state of preservation: Diongre's radio building, Hoste's house in Knokke and Brunfaut's sanatorium are not in use and even if they are officially listed as historical monuments, their future is uncertain. Bourgeois' La Cité Moderne needs an overall revalorization, for which international support is necessary. There are at present models of conservation namely George Baine's restoration of Le Corbusier's Guiette House.

**Luc Verpoest
Els Claessens
Jean-Marc Basyn**

1
Palais des Beaux Arts
Brussels
1919 | 1928
Victor Horta

Victor Horta was asked by the Municipal Development Company to reorganize the Ravenstein neighbourhood in Brussels (between the Place Royale and the Grand Place) in connection with the construction of the underground north-south railway junction (1911-1952). He first conceived the Palais des Beaux-Arts (1919-1928) and later the Central Railway Station (1937-1952). Horta left his famous Art Nouveau language for a moderate Art Deco, close to monumental classicism. He achieved a feat of strength in this project: the natural slope of the building-site, the ambitious programme of concert halls, exhibition rooms, offices and shops and the strict urban constraints, obliging Horta to design a low building.

The structure of the Palais des Beaux-Arts is a skeleton of reinforced concrete filled with brickwork. The use of concrete and the ability of Horta produce an unsuspected modern free plan and audacious shapes (eg the oval concert hall). The façades are covered with blue stone. The modulated rhythm and the strong relief of the façades, underlining the loadbearing structure, are the main characteristics of the Palais des Beaux-Arts. They strengthen the urban dimension of the building and increase the legibility of its architecture.

2
La Cité Moderne
Sint-Agatha-Berchem, Brussels
1922 | 1925
Victor Bourgeois & Louis Van der Swaelmen

The garden city La Cité Moderne was built in 1922-25. The architect, Victor Bourgeois also designed the urban plan in collaboration with Louis Van der Swaelmen. Together with Kapelleveld (Brussels, 1922-26) and Klein Rusland (Zelzate, 1921-23), both designed by Huib Hoste, La Cité Moderne stands out between other more traditionally built neighbourhoods of that post-war reconstruction period. In style as well as in construction method, Victor Bourgeois joins the experiments of international modern architecture. La Cité Moderne was built to face the urgent need for low cost houses in the early 1920s. The initial project aimed at 500 dwellings together with collective facilities such as a school, a public bathhouse and meeting hall.

3
Dr De Beir House
Knokke
1924
Huib Hoste

After a short participation in the Dutch De Stijl movement, the traditionalist Huib Hoste turned definitely to modernism with garden-city projects in Brussels and Zelzate and this corner house in Knokke. The base of the street façades was originally covered with terracotta tiles while the upper part was plastered and painted black. This composition of planes of façades and roof, form an interesting corner composition that De Stijl principles. Kozijn window frames prove a Dutch influence. There is a clear relationship between the interior organisation and the façades: the ground floor with low windows contained the doctor's practice while the two upper floors with wide and high windows have private dwelling functions.

4
Guiette House
Antwerp
1926 | 1927
Le Corbusier

This house for the painter René Guiette is the only built project of Le Corbusier in Belgium. It refers to the Maison Citrohan of 1920. A long staircase connects the four floors. The third floor contains a duplex studio and a terrace on the mezzanine level. There is a strong relationship between the plan and the façades. The narrow vertical window on the front and back façades lights the staircase and circulation spaces. Large floor to ceiling windows are used on the front façade for the studio, facing north, and for the living room on the garden side. Strip windows are used for the kitchen and for bedrooms. The slightly recessed vertical window, the canopy above the front door and the large balcony of the studio window give some relief to the flat front façade.

5
House in the Weissenhofsiedlung
Stuttgart, Germany
1927
Victor Bourgeois

Victor Bourgeois was only 30 years old when he was asked to design this house for the 1927 Werkbund exhibition. The house was built for a private owner, Dr Boll, who got the plot in lease. Although Dr Boll was very much enthused about Loos' ideas for a Raumplan house on the site, the exhibition direction refused the participation of Adolf Loos and appointed Victor Bourgeois as the architect. In a preliminary design one can see attempts of Bourgeois to create a spatial link between the two storeys, but actually the plan as built is rather traditional. The interior was also designed by Bourgeois and furnished for the time of the exhibition with furniture and works of art by Belgian artists (ao Oscar Jespers).

6
La Nouvelle Maison
Tervuren
1927 | 1928
Henry van de Velde

After a long stay abroad in Germany (Weimar, 1900-1917), Switzerland (1917-1920) and the Netherlands (1920-1926), Henry van de Velde came back to his homeland to found the Institut Supérieur des Arts Décoratifs (La Cambre) in Brussels, to teach at the University of Ghent and to continue his architectural career. The Nouvelle Maison, the fourth house he built for himself, is located in Tervuren, at a short distance outside Brussels. The house is the outcome of a long search by Van de Velde to achieve the modern 'forme pure' through rationality and formal simplification. The plan is strictly functional. The simple, prismatic volume has rounded corners, connecting the different façades to enhance the volumetric aspect.

7
Albert Residence
Marcinelle
1930
Marcel Leborgne

Coming from an architect's family, Leborgne was known as a 'lyrical builder'. He built a famous hospital (destroyed), several luxurious villas but further (mainly apartment) buildings in the industrial region of Charleroi. His most famous work is a pompous, mannerist modern villa in Brussels, the villa Dirickx (1933). The 'Résidence Albert' is located on a street angle, with 10 storeys on the corner and on one side, and 8 and then 5 on the other side. The building has a commercial ground floor. The horizontality is emphasized by the elongated windows and by the alternated use of teak wood for the window frames and the infill in between and concrete for the parapets. The corner is stressed by a cylindrical volume.

8
Elsdonck Flats
Antwerp
1931 | 1934
Léon Stijnen

The 'Elsdonck' is a residential building with apartments as well as shops and a restaurant. Following Le Corbusier's principles, this building was for Stijnen the fulfilment of the ideal way of living: high-rise flats in a green environment. The residence can be considered as a luxurious precursor of the Unité d'Habitation. Preliminary designs for the staircases show affinity with Le Corbusier's Pavillon Suisse (1930-32). The structure of the building is a steel skeleton with infill masonry. By the use of bricks and ceramic elements for the façades, the building shows a rather moderate modernism. The window frames of the apartments are made of Moulmein-teak, those of the ground-floor shops of copper. Rich materials were used for the interior finishing.

9
Six Houses for Intellectuals
Antwerp
1932
Eduard van Steenbergen

On the grounds of the Antwerp World Fair of 1930, architects like Léon Stynen and Eduard Van Steenbergen hoped to participate in the construction of a green residential area, to be built in the spirit of Het Nieuwe Bouwen. This modernist dream has not been realized but a series of interesting modernist houses were built in the neighbourhood, among which these 'Six Houses for Intellectuals', being teachers, librarians etc. Two separate three-façades houses terminate the rows of houses in the two adjoining streets. Four terraced houses form a symmetrical free-standing unit. The lay-out of the rooms is very interesting: a low entrance hall leading to a three storey high staircase with stained glass windows at the back or garden side.

10
Saint Augustine Church
Vorst, Brussels
1932 | 1935
Léon Guianotte & André Watteyne

11
University Library and Art History Institute
Ghent
1932 | 1936
Henry van de Velde

12
Sanatorium Lemaire
Tombeek
1933 | 1937
Maxime Brunfaut & Fernand Brunfaut

13
INR-NIR Radio Building
Brussels
1933 | 1939
Joseph Diongre

The Saint Augustine Church is one of the three churches in Brussels built in concrete, along with the Saint Suzanna church (1925) in Schaarbeek by Combaz and the Saint-John-the-Baptist church (1932) by Diongre in Molenbeek. The church is located on the highest point of Brussels (Altitude 100), on a circular square with 8 radial streets. The central plan of the church is based on a Greek cross. Between the four wings, there are four curved spaces. A central, 50m-high tower gives a strong visual imprint to the church and its neighbourhood. The construction materials are mainly reinforced concrete (skeleton structure, foundations, balconies, staircases, tower walls) and brickwork masonry (elevations of the church up to the flat roof).

Henry van de Velde was asked to build an extension for the University of Ghent in the very centre of the historic city. The programme consisted of a library for some 2,000,000 books and the Arts Faculty building. The library is a high cast-in-place concrete tower of 26 floors, 3 floors are underground, with a square base. This concept of silo-shape libraries was an innovative formula at that time, expected to produce space and time economies. The tower ends with a well-illuminated reception hall. The base of the building is covered with stone while the façades, originally to be in fair-face concrete, have finally been plastered. Each side of the tower has 3 vertical lines of high strip windows.

This sanatorium built for 150 male patients is located on an 85m high table-land, dominating the surroundings. The whole complex consists of the sanatorium and separate buildings (porter's house, house of the director, mortuary, residence of the nursing staff, laundry and technical buildings), all in the same architectural style. The sanatorium is composed of two main volumes, perpendicular one to the other. One wing (115m, four levels) is for the patients while the other wing (80m, two levels) includes the medical and administrative department and the main entrance. At the crossing of the two wings, the main circulation system is situated. The patients' wing has open galleries on the ground floor and three floors of patient rooms with large terraces.

After two architectural competitions for a new National Radio Institute, the project of Diongre was chosen because of its technical and acoustical qualities. The five-storey building is divided into an L-shaped wing for the staff's offices with an entrance on the Flagey square and a separate public entrance to the main concert hall, and a technical wing on the backside. Diongre put the twelve recording studios in the middle of the U-shaped building, being the 'envelope' of a high performance machine. The façades have a horizontal composition thanks to the long strips of windows. Circular corners stress the continuity between the façades. Shops are on the ground level, with large shop windows between dark coloured pilasters.

14
Dr Ley House
Ukkel
1934
Louis-Herman de Koninck

This house for a doctor, built on a steep slope, in the residential commune of Uccle near Brussels, is one of the most evident examples in Belgium of modern architecture and more particularly of Le Corbusier's '5 points d'une architecture nouvelle'. The construction technique of the house was experimental: external walls in cast-in-place concrete, covered with Celotex insulation panels in the interior and a 'grenaille de verre' (glass granules) cement plastering on the exterior. The choice of colour for the façades was very precise and aimed, as in the case of the window frames, at optical or visual corrections. The kitchen was equipped with De Konincks Cubex modulated cupboard units, very much inspired by the Frankfurt-kitchen research.

15
Leopold and Albert Residences
Brussels
1934 | 1937
Jean-Jules Eggericx & Raphaël Verwilghen

These twin blocks on each side of Luxembourg Street on Meeus Square in Brussels have 7 levels on the angle and 14 levels on the square. They share technical and service facilities. The apartments were adapted to the specific needs of individual inhabitants, and some could be combined into a large duplex. The ground floor façade is covered with black marble and has large glazed metal doors. Above the ground floor, the façades are covered with grey-pink concrete tiles, used for the first time in Belgium. The metalwork balconies and window frames are enamelled. Regular alternation of horizontal bands of masonry and fenêtres en longueur all along the façades on top of a dark base produces a refined design despite its volumes.

16
Post Office
Ostend
1946 | 1953
Gaston Eysselinck

In 1945, Eysselinck was engaged to build a new post office in Ostend. His project was considered too modernist for a public building and had to endure many criticisms from the authorities and from Jean-Jules Eggericx, one of the architects of the pre-war Leopold and Albert Residences in Brussels and town-planner of the city of Ostend. Eysselinck did not take into account this criticism and was finally able to achieve his concept. The building is 1.55m above street level. It consists of two volumes: a low public entrance building with the post office counter 1.55m above street level, and a 27m high volume, 10m behind the building line, with offices above and a canteen with roof terrace on the top floor. The main façade of the higher volume is glazed.

17
Social housing Kiel
Antwerp
1951 | 1958
Renaat Braem
collaborators: R Maes and V Maeremans

The 'Kiel' is the most expressive CIAM achievement in Belgium. The main architect of the project, Renaat Braem, worked at the Le Corbusier office in Paris between 1935 and 1937. The complex consists of three high-rise buildings of twelve floors, a crescent of houses for elderly people and the monumental heating building, around a large open green area and six blocks of eight floors in zigzag to allow an optimal view and orientation. Braem is introducing the cluster concept developed by the Smithsons in London as an alternative for the CIAM principles of free-standing high-rise blocks. All buildings rest on 'pilotis' to allow the cluster to breathe and to symbolize the collectivity of the public space.

18
Office building
'Sociale Voorzorg - Prévoyance Sociale'
Brussels
1956
Hugo Van Kuyck

Hugo Van Kuyck studied both architecture and civil engineering. During the World War II, Van Kuyck served in the US Army Corps of Engineers. He practised in Belgium and the United States. The 'Prévoyance Sociale' is an International Style office building with an important urban and visual imprint on the rue Royale, between the royal palaces of Brussels and Laken, and in the perspective of the Avenue Leopold II towards the Koekelberg basilica. After practising in the United States in the 1940s, he brought the latest high-rise building concepts to Belgium. This building shows the influence of the American International Style and the use of specific construction techniques, eg a steel skeleton and an aluminium curtain-wall, the first built in Belgium.

19
Braem house
Deurne
1957
Renaat Braem

'Un jeu brillant de proportions parfaites' (a brilliant play of perfect proportions) wrote Albert Bontridder about the house with studio that Braem designed for himself. As the urban planner of the municipality where he was going to build his house, Braem had to deal with his own prescriptions. The house is an austere three-façade building with a three dimensional framework composition at the backside. One material, red brick, was used for the façades, the slope to the garage, the paths and the low garden walls. The pine window frames, were placed while building the brick façades, an uncommon way of building in Belgium. Between the concrete skeleton filled in with 'Ytong' light concrete blocks, and the brick façades, is a 3cm void.

20
Franeau House
Erbisoeul, route de Ath
1960
Albert Bontridder & Jacques Dupuis

Jacques Dupuis was trained in La Cambre and much influenced by his tutors Victor Bourgeois and Jean-Jules Eggericx. But he clearly opposed the dogmatic side of interbellum modernism, and was more attracted by the Swedish architects Ragnar Ostberg and Gunnar Asplund. He was one of the most important architects of the fifties who defended a 'stylised rustic simplicity'. His oeuvre consists mainly of single-family dwellings, which he designed as isolated units to 'offer full scope to the privileged individual to develop his life'. They combine irregular plans and volumes in painted bricks under sloping roofs shaped to integrate them into their natural surroundings, to assure intimacy to the inhabitants and creating real spatial compositions.

Selected Bibliography :
Meyer H
Junge Kunst in Belgien
Zürich 1925

Kerckhove A de
Tendences de l'Architecture Contemporaine
Louvain 1927

Scmitz M
L'Architecture Moderne en Belgique
Brussels 1936

Kuyck H van
Modern Belgian Architecture
1955

Bontridder A
Le dialogue entre la lumière et le silence
Antwerp 1963

Puttemans P & Hervè L
L'architecture moderne en Belgique
Brussels 1974

Aron J
La Cambre et l'architecture
Brussels & Liège 1982

Smets M (ed)
Resurgam: la reconstruction après 1914
Brussels 1985

Vandenbreeden J & Vanlaethem F
Art Déco et Modernisme en Belgique
Brussels 1996

Photographic Credits :
Jean-Marc Basyn
1, 7, 13, 15
Archives d'Architecture Moderne Brussels
2, 5, 6, 20
Monumenten en Landschappen
Ministerie van de Vlaamse Gemeenschap
3, 8, 6, 10, 12, 14
Luc Verpoest
4
Els Claessens
11, 19

Brazil

The Modern Movement expressed itself in Brazilian architecture through a broad range of interpretations. All these were rooted in a common understanding that a belief in the future and the transformation of society should be main principles guiding the 'new architecture'.

The essence of the Modern Movement in Europe and the United States was quickly absorbed in Brazil. The formal ideas were brought in by the week of modern art in São Paulo in 1922. Practical models were created by the three residences which the Russian-born and Italian-educated Gregori Warchavchik built in São Paulo between 1927 and 1930: the Casa da Rua Santa Cruz, Casa da Rua Bahia and the Casa da Rua Itápolis. These first results were heroic but imperfectly realised due to difficulties in actually applying the new principles and resolving them technologically. But the houses made a fundamental contribution by introducing the appearance of the modern in the Brazilian urban milieu. The architect Rino Levi, also an Italian immigrant, was likewise deeply influenced by functionalism and the use of industrialized materials. Warchavchik and Levi represent the starting point of a Brazilian branch of modern architecture.

São Paulo remained an active centre of modernism until the late sixties due to the presence of architects like Oswaldo Bratke, Lina Bo Bardi and Vilanova Artigas.

In Rio de Janeiro another group of architects enthusiastically developed the possibilities of a new architecture. The driving force here was Lúcio Costa, who abandoned neo-colonialist architecture to embrace the modern. After Le Corbusier's visit to Rio (and São Paulo) in 1929, Costa's work reflected his influence very strongly. Costa became head of the School of Fine Arts in Rio in 1930. Although only 28 years old he made extensive reforms and invited Warchavchik and Alexander Buddeus (an architect from Belgium who arrived in 1925 from Munich, where he designed the airport) to teach there as professors. Costa was dismissed only a year later but he had already made changes that were irreversible.

In 1936, a team of architects composed of Costa, Niemeyer, Leão, Moreira, Reidy and Vasconcelos, with the renowned Le Corbusier as consultant, began to work on what would be a landmark: the construction of Rio's Ministry of Education (MEC). With this building, now the Palácio Gustavo Capanema, Brazilian modern architecture came alive in the world-wide context.

In the 30s other talented architects in Rio de Janeiro had their work recognized. Attílio Correa Lima, who won the competition for the Hydroplane Station, also did city plans, notably for the new city of Goiânia (in the state of Goiás) in 1934.

It is interesting to see that there were several competitions held for hydroplane stations in the rest of the country. The Goiânia plan itself was intended to integrate the coast of the territory by air transport. Communication was also the motivation behind the national agency of Post Offices, a set of similar projects which were spread all over the country. In 1936 the brothers Marcelo and Milton Roberto won the project for the Rio headquarters of ABI, the Brazilian Association of Press Agencies, and they later built the airport Santos Dummont, the Edificio Marquês de Herval and many other schemes.

These works gained special visibility in international terms when the Museum of Modern Art in New York decided to organize the exhibition 'Brazil Builds' in 1943, together with the publication of the book with the same name. This event and the Niemeyer's Brazilian Pavilion at the New York Expo of 1939 were decisive in the crystallization of the so-called 'school of Rio de Janeiro'.

Already in the 1930s Recife, capital of the state of Pernambuco, saw a brief but decisive intervention by a young architect named Luis Nunes, who formed a team to work for the Municipality. This group had certain characteristics which were unique in that period, notably that it was interdisciplinary and it included workers in the design decisions. This offered a first experience of modern architecture to the Pernambuco engineer Joaquim Cardozo, who later became well known for his work with Niemeyer. Another collaborator was the young fine arts student Roberto Burle Marx, who designed his early gardens for this team. This group addressed buildings and their urban context with equal seriousness, in both design and construction. Lacking adequate budgets they researched new materials and building techniques optimizing their use especially in work for the low-income groups. Nunes's work broadened the school of Rio's horizons beyond their established models of Le Corbusier and the German experience opened up by Gropius. Nunes was able to produce superb results with practical interpretations and improvements on these sources.

Salvador, in the north eastern state of Bahia, was a former colonial town and first capital of a unified Brazil. Here too new public institutions were built as part of the renewal of the city and society as a whole. The works executed here make less reference to the French school than to the German. Buddeus designed the Institute of Cocoa in 1933, a building based on notions of the machine and the form of the factory. It was connected directly to the port by subterranean conveyor belts. Another engineering-based work was the tower of the Lacerda Elevator, which links the high and low parts of the city divided by a geological fault. Designed and built by Danes, this intervention offered the experience of verticality and velocity with materials strained to their highest, recalling the discourses of the futurists. Later Salvador saw other approaches such as the brutalism of Diogenes Rebouças in works like the Escola Parque and Escola Classe (with Helio Duarte) and the Hotel da Bahia (with Paulo Antunes) and of Bina Fonyat's work for the Theatre Castro Alves.

In the 1940s Niemeyer began to work for the Mayor of Belo Horizonte, Juscelino Kubitschek, who later became president of Brazil and oversaw the construction of Brasilia as its new capital. While here in Belo Horizonte Niemeyer built one of his main works, the leisure complex of Pampulha. Aided by Cardozo as engineer he achieved a high reputation for his use of reinforced concrete and for commissioning the artist Roberto Burle Marx to do landscape projects. Meanwhile elsewhere in Minas Gerais, in Cataguazes, another avant-garde group emerged that conceived the arts, industrialized objects and architecture, especially housing, as an expression of a new society.

Kubitschek was elected President in 1956 and launched the design competition for Brasilia in the next year. The Pilot Plan was won by Lúcio Costa and those main buildings that were not included in the competition were commissioned from Niemeyer. This established the beginning of a new era.

The architecture of the other regions of this huge country is diverse but in general its products are either considered not strong enough to assert themselves against the big centres, or are seen as late expressions of already existing models. That dismissal is a mistake, however, as architects throughout the country were in close communication with the rest of the world, and in this sense their work contributed to a rich understanding of this movement. There is still a large task ahead in mapping and understanding the range of work that occurred.

DOCOMOMO **Brazil**

1
Pedregulho housing complex
Pedregulho, Rio de Janeiro
1946 | 1958
Affonso Reidy
(engineer Carmen Portinho)

This housing district is composed of housing blocks (with various different floor plans), schools, a nursery, gymnasium, sports pitches, laundry, small-scale commerce and other community facilities. It was a project reflecting serious social concern and aimed at low-income families. The architect believed that such design could help create a better society. Buildings differ in size and form but all display high aesthetic quality and close integration with landscape of the extensive public open spaces. Brises-soleil and shading are extensive. Concrete is the main structural material producing regular and rectilinear volumes. They are enriched by curves in the housing units to take full advantage of the slope and views to the sea.

2
Residência Olivo Gomes
São José dos Campos, State of São Paulo
1953
Rino Levi & R Cerqueira Cesar

This residence is conceived as two main blocks, one for social use and the other containing the private spaces. The planning follows the smooth slope of the site, raised on pilotis and allowing the landscape to invade the interior of the building. The work is very austere but sophisticated. Gardens are composed around curved paths and arranged in groups of local vegetation types which develop outwards into the untamed nature around. The walls incorporate artistic panels by Roberto Burle Marx in a work that creates a transitional space between outside and inside and a typical confrontation between art and nature.

3
Palácio Gustavo Capanema
(formerly Ministry of Education building)
Rio de Janeiro
1937 | 1943
Lúcio Costa et al

This milestone in world architecture was designed by Lúcio Costa, Oscar Niemeyer, Carlos Leão, Affonso Reidy, Jorge Moreira and Ernani Vasconcelos with Le Corbusier as consultant. Burle Marx did the gardens and various artistic interventions are by Portinari, Bruno Giorgi, Celso Antonio and Leipzig. Centred in the city block and raised on pilotis, the building transformed the street corridor into a plaza, reinforcing this by creating gardens that add great quality to the urban space. The T-shaped composition comprises two parts: a 16-storey vertical block and a one-storey block raised on pilotis. The south-east façade is glazed and the north-east has brises-soleil. Brazilian granite and murals are used extensively.

4
Escola Rural Alberto Torres
Recife, Pernambuco
1935
Luis Nunes

Though Nunes had a brief life, the period when he was working for the municipality of Recife was extremely significant. His team developed a multi-disciplinary approach to programmes and plans and they were responsible for creating constructive alternatives matched to very limited budgets. The Rural School represents both a specific social concern and an unusual solution. An audacious ramp is supported by a parabolic structure which links the two floors of the building. This aspect was an early work of the Pernambuco engineer Joaquim Cardozo.

5
Pampulha
Belo Horizonte, Minas Gerais
1940 | 1943
Oscar Niemeyer & Roberto Burle Marx

This architectonic and landscape complex of Pampulha with buildings by Niemeyer and gardens by Burle Marx was further enriched by significant contributions from the artists Portinari, Ceschiatti and Werneck. Disposed around an artificial lagoon are the Church of San Francisco, a casino (now the Museum of Modern Art), a dance hall and a yachting and tennis club. It was the nucleus of a district intended for medium to high-income families. Buildings explore the uses and aesthetic results of reinforced concrete notably in their curved vertical and horizontal surfaces. This successful work was commissioned by the governor Kubitschek who shortly after this became President of Brazil and was the visionary behind Brasilia.

6
Plano Piloto de Brasília
(City Plan of Brasilia)
1957
Lúcio Costa

Costa won the 1957 competition for Brazil's new capital city with a scheme of great simplicity. The brief for a city of 500,000 inhabitants was very general. It did not specify the site. Nor did it specify or request any projections of sociological, environmental or geographical parameters. Costa's scheme comprised two orthogonal axes: the first (Eixo Monumental) contained the public buildings and the second led into the human-scale and open planning of the housing blocks (superquadras). In the spirit of modernity as then understood the plan accorded great importance to rapid free movement of the motor car.

7
Catedral de Brasília (Cathedral of Brasilia)
Eixo Monumental, Brasilia
1959
Oscar Niemeyer
(engineer Joaquim Cardozo)

The expressiveness of this project derives from its simplicity: the great cylinder tapers to enclose the main space then opens again towards the sky. The reinforced structure stretched the skills of Cardozo to the limits. The form is essentially produced by rotation of parabolic columns around a central axis. Surfaces are infilled with polygonal glass panels in a thin wire web. Internally the space created is free and ample with a soft light giving it the necessary introspective mood.

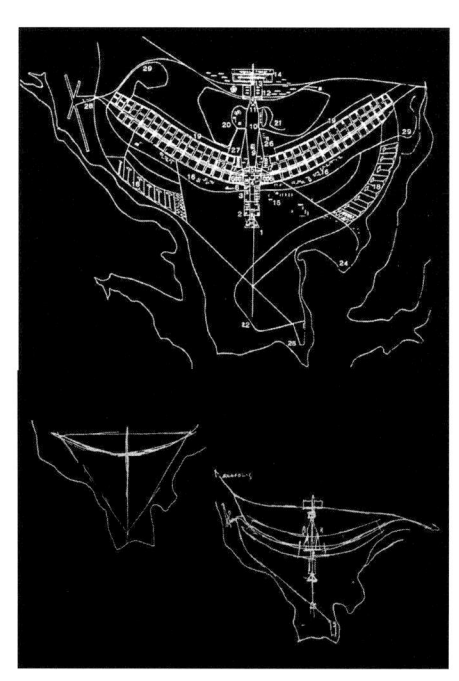

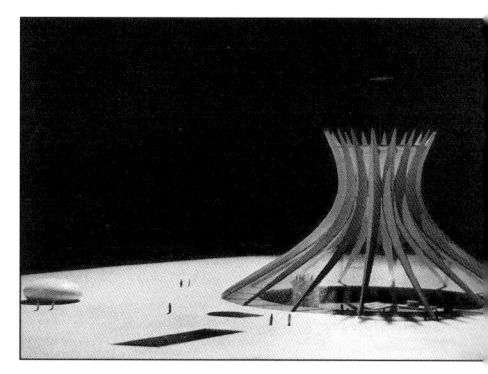

8
Palácio do Itamaraty (Itamaraty Palace)
Brasilia
1967
Oscar Niemeyer

Originally called the Palácio dos Arcos, this Foreign Ministry building is Niemeyer's masterpiece. The magnificence derives from combining the monumental conception with use of simple elements such as reinforced concrete. This is enriched by an extremely well conceived relationship between the inside and outside realm and the use of wide open spaces and large rooms. Formally the building consists of a glass box enclosed by a surrounding structure of high arcs that do not touch each other, rising from a limpid water mirror that reflects and doubles the impression given by the work. The glass box is completed with a garden by Burle Marx with a pergola that produces a rich effect of sun and shade.

9
Elevador Lacerda (Lacerda Elevator)
Praça Municipal, Salvador
1927
Fleming Thiesen for Christiani-Nielsen

The first urban elevators were built in the 19th century but this construction by a Danish architect and contractor marked a second stage. At the time it was the world's highest urban elevator rising to a height of 73.5m, 59m of it used by passengers. It was designed to be built in reinforced concrete but the American consultants did not accept this. It was erected however before they arrived as was a bridge of 28.7m span incorporating a steel structure. The elevator was finished in pre-fabricated concrete plates with iron and glass for the windows. This was an urban intervention through which high and low areas of the city were integrated for the first time. The elevator is still in use with the original machinery.

10
Palácio da Alvorada (Alvorada Palace)
Brasilia
1958
Oscar Niemeyer

This presidential residence was conceived as a monumental noble palace. Formally it is a translucent glass box held between two thin overhanging slabs which appears to float lightly. It is held in an apparently fragile structure of reinforced concrete composed of interconnected columns that are not actually responsible for supporting the building. Thus the underlying rationalist approach was transformed by a lyrical inspiration, expressing the concept rather than the ultimate truth of the structure. In the end of the right-hand wing is a small chapel linked to the main residence though separate from it. Internally the sense of the free plan is maintained by sight of the full ceiling height and an intermediate level.

11
ABI – Association of Brazilian Press
Rio de Janeiro
1936 | 1938
Marcelo & Milton Roberto

The Roberto brothers won the competition for ABI's administrative headquarters in 1936. The twelve storey building stands on the corner of a busy central street. Its plastic solution is strongly conditioned by the intense sunlight it receives, producing a surface entirely covered by brises-soleil. It has an independent structure in reinforced concrete as well as other rationalist elements from Le Corbusier such as pilotis, a roof garden and a free plan. The Roberto brothers became one of the most important architectural offices in the country. Their reputation rested on their serious, exact and laconic approach to design. They won third place in the competition the the city plan of Brasilia.

Not illustrated

12
Clube de Aeronáutica
Bay of Guanabara embankment, Rio de Janeiro
1938
Attílio Correa Lima

The Club was originally conceived as a hydroplane station, to be part of the airport complex in a new embankment area alongside the Bay, but the scale of the final scheme was more modest. The independent structure in reinforced concrete permits a free plan and at second floor a terrace opens up into the floor area. Linking the two floors is a large helical staircase supported on a single central column to great plastic effect. Transparency and visibility was sought linking street to the boarding quay so two façades were entirely covered by glass panels. External gardens of tropical vegetation were designed by Burle Marx.

13
Casa da Rua Bahia
São Paulo
1931
Gregori Warchavchik

This house is designed on a sloping terrain between two streets and was thus divided into three levels. The house stands on the high part and the garden is on the other levels. Construction is reinforced concrete and brick. The structure is orthogonal, resulting in a unit composed as intersecting cubes. Glass bricks are used in the entrance which serve at night for illumination. The outside of the house was originally painted in a mineral green whereas today it is white. This design is considered a better interpretation of the modern house than the architect's pioneering venture in Santa Cruz, where the modernity resides more in the appearance than in the design solution.

Not illustrated

14
Museo de Arte de São Paulo (MASP)
Avenida Paulista 1578 São Paulo
1968
Lina Bo Bardi
(engineer Figueredo Ferraz)

This Art Museum stands on the city's main business street on a site with a 13m slope. The architect thus treated a building as a huge void offering a link and belvedere view to the landscape beneath it. The project consists of a main two-floor high block supported by two prestressed beams which create a clear span of 74m at ground floor level. All functional installations are clearly in evidence and main finishes are glass or concrete. The MASP is particularly distinguished for Ferraz's spectacular structure in prestressed concrete – a unique design that defied traditional concepts of safety and stability.

15
Parque do Ibirapuera
São Paulo
1954
Roberto Burle Marx (landscape)
Oscar Niemeyer et al (buildings)

This park of 1.5 million square meters is the city's main space for leisure and culture. Buildings are scattered across the landscape and include the palace of Nations, the State Palace, the Palace of Industry, the Agricultural Palace, the Arts and Exhibitions Palaces. This last has the form of a flat dome with large round holes at floor level. The others are generally orthogonal in configuration and rationalist in their expression. Beside Niemeyer, architects include Zenon Lotufo, Hélio Uchôa and Eduardo Kneese de Mello. Joachim Cardoso was structural advisor. Other open areas of the park contain children's play equipment and various sports facilities.

16
Casa das Canoas
Rio de Janiero
1935
Oscar Niemeyer

This house was built by Niemeyer for himself. It is a remarkable statement of simplicity, freedom and beauty achieved through curved lines that juxtapose the tropical surroundings of the Tijuca Forest to strict formal solutions mainly of reinforced concrete and glass. The building is enhanced by the view from the cliff to which it is attached towards Guanabara Bay. It is in two main parts. Underneath and out of sight from the approach are the private rooms while the upper part is covered by a sinuous reinforced concrete slab covering the collective spaces and linking them to the garden and the terrace with its pool.

17
Museu de Arte Moderna (MAM)
Avenida Beira Mar
Rio de Janiero
1954 | 1967
Affonso Reidy

The Museum stands at the northern end of the Parque do Flamengo which was laid out by Roberto Burle Marx on Brazil's largest area of land reclamation, along the Bay of Guanabana, and completed in 1962. The Museum building has a powerfully expressive rationalist structure in reinforced concrete, creating the extensive undivided areas needed for the museum. It is rectangular in form, with its wider section developed into tilted pillars that work as pilotis raising the building above ground. Inside reached at intermediary level by a series of ramps, are an internal patio and raised gardens also designed by Burle Marx.

Not illustrated

18
Serra do Navio
200km north west of Macapá, State of Amapá
1955 | 1960
Oswaldo Bratke

The Serra do Navio with the Vila Amazonas constituted an urban nucleus for the State of Amapá which was intended to serve as a base for the ICOMI manganese mining company. The design approach was not strictly functionalist though it observed many rationalist principles. In the housing units in particular, Bratke was very concerned to adapt his use of the available technology and materials to the environmental conditions of heat and humidity and to the cultural aspects of the region, as many workers were native. Serra do Navio enriches our understanding of this period of planning and architecture in Brazil by offering a counterpoint to the ideas being developed in Brasilia.

Not illustrated

47

19
Teatro Castro Alves
Campo Grande, Salvador
1958
José Bina Fonyat

This is the biggest music theatre in a city renowned for its music. It consists of two main blocks linked by an external ramp. The first volume is the main public entrance and foyer, an irregular freestanding prism finished all over in glass wall panels, slab-roofed. It has a reinforced concrete structure and free plan. The second volume contains the 1700-seat auditorium which has very good acoustics and sight-lines, with the stage and its equipment. Internal functions like the raked auditorium floor are powerfully expressed externally. However its brutalist urban-scaled construction of reinforced concrete is not well scaled to the gardens of the Campo Grande with which it was originally intended to be integrated.

20
Instituto do Cacau (Cocoa Institute)
Salvador
1933 | 1936
Floderer & Alexander Buddeus

One of the country's most distinguished examples of the influence of German architecture from the Bauhaus School. It stands alongside the port of Salvador to store the cocoa crop. It has an ingenious internal mechanism, a subterranean conveyor belt which linked it directly to the harbourside and an internal mechanism for regulating humidity through a process using silica gel. The building has a structure of reinforced concrete with columns of mushroom profile. Internally the rigid square division of the floor plan is expectedly all treated in ornamental work typical of the southern area of Bahia State – a product of integration with local Indian art.

Selected Bibliography :
Goodwin PL & Kidder Smith GE
Brazil Builds
New York 1943

'Brazil'
Architectural Review special issue
London March 1944

Papadaki S (Foreword by Lucio Costa)
The work of Oscar Niemeyer
New York 1950

Persitz A
Brésil. Architecture Contemporaine
Boulogne 1952

Mindlin H
Modern Architecture in Brazil
Rio de Janiero & Amsterdam 1956

Giedion S
The work of Affonso Reidy
New York 1960

Papadaki S
Oscar Niemeyer
New York 1960

Amaral A
Arte y arquitectura del modernismo brasileno 1917-1930
Caracas 1978

Bruand Y
Arquitetura Contemporânea no Brasil
São Paulo 1981 & 1997

Harris ED
Le Corbusier: riscos brasileiros
São Paulo 1987

Underwood DK
Oscar Niemeyer and the Architecture of Brazil
New York 1994

Photographic Credits :
IPHAN archive
1, 12, 16
Angela Pedrão
2, 10, 20
Geraldo Gomes
4
Mirthes Baffi
14, 15
Adenor Gondim
19

British Columbia

In the late 1930s, Vancouver, British Columbia, was a relatively small and remote city, physically separated by the Rocky Mountains from the rest of Canada and nestled against the Pacific Ocean. However, a unique confluence of natural factors – temperate climate, a spectacular setting, a rugged and varied topography – combined with rapid growth; a booming economy; a progressive and liberal cultural environment; an influx of young, talented and energetic artists and designers; and a relative lack of an existing design establishment, resulted in the development of a distinctly regional approach to modernism in British Columbia. Although the first modernist homes and public buildings were not constructed until the late 1930s, and construction in general was virtually halted during the war years, the style very quickly gained a popular acceptance in the 1940s, particularly for single family homes. The Vancouver-based magazine 'Western Homes and Living' tapped into this widespread local interest in design and prominently featured contemporary homes, while the Community Arts Council 1949 Design for Living exhibitions at the Vancouver Art Gallery featured house plans and interiors, as well as furniture and tableware prototypes.

The progressive style of design became widely known as the 'West Coast Style', a name which obscures the many sources of architectural ideas which contributed to its development. It is clear that Vancouver Modernists synthesized but simplified diverse European expressions, and blended in more pragmatic and organic interpretations current in the United States in the 1930's. The social objectives of transatlantic modernism – the manipulation of science, technology, industry, and the arts for the betterment of society as a whole – suited a city in urgent need of post-war housing and infrastructure.

Today, despite increasing pressures for redevelopment and alteration, the legacy of this period is still strongly evident in BC, especially in and around the City of Vancouver. Since the late 1980s, many of the buildings from this period have been researched and inventoried, and have been rehabilitated or granted protection through local designation.

In 1995, following a presentation in Vancouver by the Secretary of DOCOMOMO International, Wessel de Jonge, a group of people from the design, civic, academic and heritage communities came together to focus their interest and enthusiasm for the buildings and landscapes of the modern period. Within short order, this group had organized a BC Working Party of DOCOMOMO. A regional list of resources for International Selection was developed, and a series of initiatives was undertaken to increase public awareness and appreciation of the modern period, including hosting a workshop on curtain wall restoration and walking tours of the downtown core, where many of the most significant modern buildings can be found.

This initial work by DOCOMOMO coincided with a major exhibition at the Vancouver Art Gallery in November, 1997 – The New Spirit: Modernism in Vancouver, 1938-1963. The show was organized by the Canadian Centre for Architecture (Montreal), and curated by Rhodri Windsor Liscombe. As noted by Phyllis Lambert, Director of the Canadian Centre for Architecture, in the Foreword to the accompanying guide, 'The New Spirit: Modernism in Vancouver, 1938-1963' charts the emergence of post-war Vancouver as a self-conscious centre for progressive architecture, and shows how the current of international ideas about architecture animated a local culture, allowing the emergence of a distinctive West Coast architecture with a national and international impact of its own.'

In preparing the regional list of resources for submission to DOCOMOMO International, the Working Party selected representative buildings spanning the period during which modernism flourished in British Columbia. The list encompasses various building typologies – residential, religious, institutional, and commercial, as well as the entire planned resource community of Kitimat. The list includes examples of work by many of the key architects and design firms of the period – Peter Thornton; JCH Porter; CBK van Norman; Ron Thom; Arthur Erickson; Semmens and Simpson; and Sharp & Thompson Berwick and Pratt. Almost half of these buildings have been accepted for International Selection by DOCOMOMO International, and are included among the images below.

Many other important designers, educators, builders, artists and architects – Bert and Jessie Binning; Frederic Lasserre; Fred Amess; Cornelia and Peter Oberlander; Underwood McKinley and Cameron; Bill Birmingham; Duncan Mac Nab; Bob Lewis; Wolfgang Gerson; Peter Kaffka; McCarter & Nairne; Donald Manning; Catherine Chard Wisnicki; Fred Hollingsworth and a host of others – are not yet represented in this list, but were equally instrumental in the development of the languid West Coast modernist style.

From the early International Style Thornton House (1939) to the Simon Fraser University (1963), and on to the later Museum of Anthropology at the University of British Columbia (1973-1976), each of the buildings on the regional list exemplify the synthesis of building, landscape, arts and architecture to which the West Coast design aspired. The attention to context and the particular climate and terrain of the Pacific North West, combined with the extensive use of regionally appropriate materials such as wood, concrete and glass, led to the development of a distinctive style of modernism which established British Columbia's reputation as a centre of progressive design and culture.

Mary Shaughnessy
Rhodri Windsor Liscombe
Joel Lawson

1
Dal Grauer Substation
950 and 970 Burrard Street, Vancouver
1954
Sharp & Thompson Berwick Pratt

2
BC Hydro Building
950 and 970 Burrard Street, Vancouver
1957
Thompson Berwick & Pratt Partners

This pair of adjoining landmark modernist buildings, built by the former BC Electric company, front Vancouver's Burrard Street. The Dal Grauer substation (1954) is the earlier of the two buildings. It is distinguished by the grid of its transparent façade, which allows the building's power and mechanical equipment to be viewed by the public. The original colour palette was directed by artist BC Binning who later consulted on the BC Electric Building's mosaic tile murals. The 22 storey BC Electric Building (later the BC Hydro Building) is located on the highest point of land in downtown Vancouver and has been a visual landmark since its completion in 1957.

The lozenge shaped plan, similar to the Pirelli building in Milan, with its shallow floor plate allowed all workers' desks to be near a window. These slender floor plates are due to a hybrid structural system with floors cantilevered from a massive central core, but also supported by slender external columns. The curtain wall cladding is in two shades of anodized aluminum. The distinctive blue, green, gray, mauve and black mosaic tiles, designed by BC Binning, are evocative of the west coast palette of water, forests and mountains. In 1995, the building was converted to residential condominiums and renamed The Electra.

3
Revelstoke City Hall
216 MacKenzie Avenue, Revelstoke
1939
CBK van Norman

The Revelstoke City Hall was commissioned in July 1938 by the Corporation of the City of Revelstoke to provide a new municipal government chamber with ancillary offices, and a new fire hall, on a 50'x100' corner lot (site of former city hall). The building is a surprising early application of modernist principles in British Columbia, predating by a decade the general introduction of modernism on the west coast of Canada (it was constructed in the same year as Van Norman's private residence, since demolished, which shared with the Thornton house the distinction of being one of the first two modern houses in British Columbia). The design is all the more remarkable for its execution and acceptance in a small, relatively remote town.

The design is striking in its simple rectilinear massing and lack of applied ornamentation, and is an early instance of unclad reinforced concrete in a public building. The separate functions of general city administration and fire hall are clearly legible in plan and elevation as two low, perpendicular rectangular volumes pierced dramatically by the vertical shaft of the fire hose tower. The poured-in-place concrete exterior walls are punctuated by strip windows and large glass-block or mullioned glass surfaces straddling the full 2-storey height. The most dramatic use of glazing is on the front elevation, which is essentially a concrete frame defining a recessed wall of glass block providing diffused natural light into the public reception areas.

4
Porter Residence
1560 Ottawa Avenue, West Vancouver
1948
JCH Porter

This significant modern building represents an early use of the modern post and beam structural method, adapted to the particular conditions on the west coast of Canada. The design and the siting permit the house and extensive patios to be fully integrated into the hillside terrain, providing privacy from the street and access to views and sunlight at the back of the house. A butterfly roof covers the carport at the front entry, while the dramatic monopitch roof of the house is raised to allow extra height. Six inch thick fir beams are used for the roof structure, with 4 by 10 inch cedar planking over. The entire south elevation is glass, with sliding panels allowing access to extensive outdoor decks, terraces and the naturally landscaped private yard.

The interior spaces were based on a split level open plan that allowed free movement between rooms. The house received a Massey medal (national recognition) for residential design in 1952. Both John Porter, the architect and the dwelling were very influential in the development of the 'West Coast' regional style of architecture, which adapted the International aesthetic to wood post and beam structures.

5
War Memorial Gym
6081 University Boulevard
University of British Columbia, Vancouver
1950
CE Pratt, Fred S Brodie & Frederic Lasserre

The War Memorial Gymnasium building was commissioned by the Alumni Society of the University of British Columbia to provide a fully equipped modern gymnasium and to commemorate those university graduates killed in the Second World War. It is located on the main access to the University, and is a visually prominent and intensely utilized building, still in essentially its original condition. The overall form successfully relates utilitarianism and monumentalism in a powerfully functionalist solution and a highly effective interplay of vertical and horizontal planes. The rectangular form of the large, multi-use gymnasium is directly stated in elevation.

The large, floating roof structure on slender reinforced concrete columns permits unobstructed sightlines from the bleachers on either side of the gymnasium space. Smaller athletic facilities, offices and changing rooms are located below, defined by four projected corner stairwells. The Pratt-type metal and wood roof trusses extend out into a deep cornice eave, capping the geometric massing and clerestory windows of the walls. This building is the first large-scale unfaced reinforced concrete structure in western Canada, and the first overtly modernist building on the campus of the University of British Columbia. It was awarded a Massey Medal for Architecture in 1952.

6
St Anselm's Anglican Church
5200 University Boulevard, Vancouver
1953
Semmens & Simpson

7
DH Copp Residence
4755 Belmont Avenue, Vancouver
1950 | 1951
Ron Thom

This building was commissioned by the Anglican congregation of University Hill building committee, which consisted mainly of University of British Columbia faculty members. It is located in a clearing off the curving main access to the University. The geometric form of the building is in contrast to the heavily treed site. The Church is especially notable for its sophisticated functional simplicity, providing imaginatively contemporary space for worship and well organized and flexible space for parish activities. A wide variety of local materials, such as a wood shingle roof and masonry walls, contrast with standardized building materials, such as steel framing and large sheets of factrolyte glass.

The steeply pitched nave roof is supported by laminated wood rafters placed on 12 foot centres. The masonry altar wall provides a sense of solidity, and a strong contrast to the glazed entrance wall, in which the structural members create a symbolic cross. Offices and meeting rooms are housed in a subsidiary block, with post-and-beam construction and extensively glazed facades. St Anselm's Anglican Church was the first example of a host of later 'A' frame churches constructed in and around Vancouver. A recent addition was designed by Hugh Ker, architect.

The Copp residence is located on a steeply sloping bluff overlooking English Bay. The house is exceptionally well suited to its site, taking full advantage of its natural characteristics and impressive views. The long, horizontal spreading wings of the house are nestled into the site, rather than being suspended above it. In plan, the upper floor is turned perpendicular to the main floor, the two parts anchored by a massive brick chimney. The open plan allows a free flow of space between the main living areas and to the outside terraces. The house uses a mixed system of wood stud framing and post and beam construction, infilled with unpainted cedar siding and large sheets of single glazed windows.

The colour palette is of nature, soft browns highlighted only with an autumn-red ochre and 'resembles that of native Indian artifacts, baskets and Salish houses then reverently discussed by Thom and local artists.' (McKay, Sherry, 'Western Living, Western Homes', SSAC Journal, Volume 14, September 1989, number 3, page 72). The house continues to be lived in by the Copps who commissioned the building.

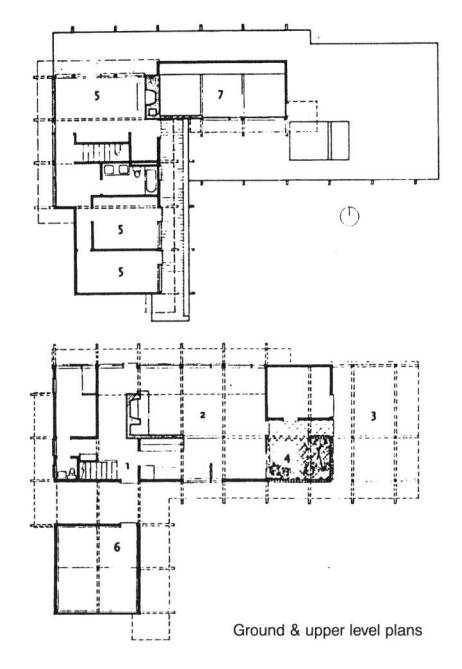

Ground & upper level plans

8
Simon Fraser University
Burnaby
1965
Arthur Erickson
Zoltan Kiss (Academic Quadrangle)
Robert Harrison (WAC Bennett Library)
Duncan MacNab (SFU Theatre)

Perched atop Burnaby Mountain, overlooking the City of Vancouver, Simon Fraser University has evolved into a major Canadian academic institution. The commission was the subject of a well publicized design competition, and saw the emergence of Arthur Erickson as a prominent modernist architect. The university complex reinvents the social structure of the traditional university, organizing buildings by use (residential, academic, recreational) rather than by discipline or college. Traditional university elements and materials are combined in an entirely new way, creating a balance between modernist invention and historical allusion. The campus is organized on a central spine running along the ridge of the mountain with two main public spaces.

The central Mall, connecting the main elements of the campus, is roofed with a structure that combines Douglas Fir beams, steel tie-rods and glass in response to the rainy west coast climate. The academic quadrangle is quiet and contemplative, with landscape features and reflecting pools. Both spaces combine striking monumentality without sacrificing human scale.

9
Smith House II
5030 The Byway, West Vancouver
1966
Arthur Erickson

This striking modern residence, the second designed by Arthur Erickson for noted artist Gordon Smith, has been called the most famous and widely studied modern residence in Canada. The house is beautifully integrated with the terrain, providing privacy from the street and access to views and sunlight at the back of the house. It bridges a natural cleft in a rock outcrop, and was designed in a spiral form on seven levels encompassing a central courtyard. The rough fir beams and posts were cut the same size to add to the desired sense of repose to the building. Each vertical element is capped by extended horizontal beams. Glass sheets form the exterior walls, and allow the interior to open up to extensive exterior patios and natural landscaping.

Interior wall finishes include wood and burlap. In 1967, the dwelling received a Massey Medal for Architecture (national recognition) and a Canadian Housing Design Council Award. Small additions, including a detached artist studio (Russell Hollingsworth, designer) are very much in character with the original design. The Smiths continue to reside in the house.

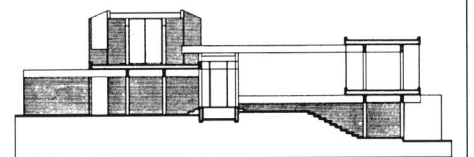

Selected Bibliography :
Ede CM
Canadian Architecture 1960/70
Toronto 1971

Vancouver Art Gallery
Vancouver Art and Artists 1931-83
Vancouver 1983

Erickson A
The Architecture of Arthur Erickson
Vancouver 1988

Kalman H, Philips R & Ward R
Exploring Vancouver: The Essential Architectural Guide
Vancouver 1993

Liscombe RW
The New Spirit: Modern Architecture in Vancouver 1938-1963
Vancouver 1993

Kalman H
A History of Canadian Architecture
Toronto 1994

Photographic Credits :
Vancouver Public Library
1
Robert Lemon
2, 5, 6, 7
Joel Lawson
9
Richard Klopp
3
Gordon Montgomery
4
Simon Scott and
Simon Fraser University
Instructional Media Centre
8

Acknowledgements :
Marco D'Agostini
Bernard Flaman
Susanna Houwen
Joel Lawson
Robert Lemon
Rhodri Windsor Liscombe
Mary Shaughnessy
Peter Vaisbord

Bulgaria

The Balkan Wars (1912-13) followed by World War I delayed the professional development of many Bulgarians. The 1920s were a highly intensive period in Bulgarian culture – a hectic artistic life full of exhibitions, competitions, publications, etc, as if the country was in a hurry to make up for missed opportunities during the wars. This was the time when the first modern ideas made their way into architecture via Bulgarians educated in Western Europe. (There was no academic architectural school in the country until 1943.) The pragmatic views of the Bulgarian public, as well as the comparatively low scientific and technological level at the time, hindered the spread of technical innovation and delayed the introduction of the Modern Movement in the country.

The intensive construction programmes demanded by the post-war housing crises in large Bulgarian cities created optimum conditions for implementing avant-garde ideas about collective living in cooperative apartments. From the mid-1920s on, multistoried residential buildings were constructed by architects committed to the New Objectivity ('Neue Sachlichkeit'). The great variety of typologies and forms responded to the needs of the apartments' owners and future inhabitants. After the 1928 Rules of Construction demanded the use of reinforced concrete skeleton structures, the rational free plan and the flowing spatial composition developed to a mature state.

The Modern Movement gained strength during the 1930s as evidenced by the work in the work of the next generation of professionals educated in western Europe. It was not a fashion but a product of their social commitment and personal convictions. It spread into the public realm after long discussions with the defenders of a traditional vernacular architecture. The architects followed the artistic credo of the epoch most closely thanks to their educated clients from the middle class. For them the modern forms were signs of personal prosperity and integration into the European civilization. Their two-storey residences situated on small downtown plots are typical examples. The functional organization and the furniture served well for the needs of flexibility. Rooms full of daylight, connected by sliding doors, flow one into another. Facing the best orientation with spacious windows and terraces, overlooking a garden or a yard, the private house provided for the continuity between the inside and the outside. The reinforced concrete frame constructions made the free plan possible. Following the Bauhaus, Le Corbusier and Erich Mendelsohn, the functional logic was expressed by clearly defined volumes, sparing use of materials, colours, harmonious proportions and rhythm. The façades were usually asymmetrical and well balanced with horizontal bands of windows, and powerful contrasts of solid/openings, light/dark, vertical/horizontal elements. By the mid-1930s some other typical attributes of Modernism – big windows, horizontal glass bands without columns at the wall-corners, flat roof terraces were more frequently found in housing and public buildings such as hotels, schools, hospitals, and vacation houses.

A dramatic split between national and modern trends was passionately debated in Bulgarian artistic circles, thus compensating for the failure of the nationalist aspirations during the wars (1912-18). Some artists and architects aimed at creating an identifiably national culture and a relevant national style. They founded the alliance 'Native art' in 1919 to promote the traditional folk art and architecture as preferred sources of inspiration.

Architectural manifestations of this 'native' trend spread in residential and religious buildings. Private residences all over the country included rough-stone masonry for the ground floor walls and plinths, projecting wooden parapets and eaves, sloping red tiled roofs, deep recessed terraces, double or triple arched windows often with round columns in between. Until the end of the 1920s Bulgarian medieval fortified houses were paraphrased as expressionist 'brick monumentality' with walls of visible masonry, mystical interiors and pointed-arched openings. This approach was used for public buildings, multi-family and private residences. Designs for public buildings also included vernacular elements from the 19th century, as evident in the modernized clock towers of many city halls. Major opponents to modernism and cooperative housing were the leading investigators of the 19th century Bulgarian architectural heritage, such as Anton Torniov (1868-1942) and Todor Zlatev (1885-1977), who considered the folk house to be the core of the Bulgarian architectural style. Against this conservatism Chavdar Mutafov (1889-1954) proclaimed the self-defined modern architecture as decisive in recreating the spirit of the past through contemporary means. In his essay 'Native architecture' (1927) he stressed the fact that the modern urban life and diverse new building types, materials and structures generate a new architecture. Only exceptional masters could succeed 'to build in the everlasting soul of nativeness' within their own style. Mutafov's presentation to the 1929 congress of the Society of Bulgarian Architects (DBA) provoked the participants' decision to systematize local traditional architectural forms and reinterpret them into their practice.

Some architects began by selectively citing decorative folk elements. By the mid-1930s the modern concepts of space, plan and façade compositions were organically combined with articulations of traditional elements and building materials. This ambivalence took a peculiarly subtle form in the interiors of well-to-do dwellings: built-in cupboards, wall bays and arches, fireplaces, accessories of wrought iron, carved stylization of wood furniture, beams and door and window frames. All these elements updated the spirit of folklore in residential and religious interiors with elegance. Numerous modern provincial residences with their four-hipped roofs, projecting wood eaves, bay windows and balconies, stone plinths and exposed masonry manifested their consideration of the Bulgarian conditions.

After a 1934 military coup d'état, the ensuing authoritarian Bulgarian State called for a neo-national revival of the arts. The term 'native' was gradually replaced with the idea of a 'national architecture'. Consequently, even the neo-classical idiom used in designs for important public edifices in Sofia was 'modernized' with functional plans and unadorned façades. Yet, some traditional iconography visible in the interiors and exteriors, carried memories of the past. By the late 1930s the discussion about a national style was renewed and provoked a response by the prominent modernist Konstantin

1
College of Agriculture, Sofia University
8 Dragan Tsankov Boulevard, Sofia 1421
1925 | 1930
Georgi Ovcharov & Genko Popov

Dzhangozov. He stressed that architects could satisfy the 'great need for national identification through architecture' only by adjusting the universal modernism to the contemporary mode of life in Bulgaria.

The Modern Movement spread in Bulgaria throughout the 1930s and even during the 1940s. The diversity of designs was due to the influence of different centres in western Europe where Bulgarian architects have studied. Simultaneously with their commitment to avant-garde ideas, they made conscious attempts to express a regional character appropriate to the economic conditions in the country and related to traditional building practices. This combination of these two aesthetic systems demonstrates a particular local interpretation of the Modern Movement.

As a universal style and a symbol of technical progress, modernism made a come back in Bulgaria during the post-Stalinist period. Very soon it evolved into a bearer of those concepts which have always spawned innovative creations – the influence of climate, cultural traditions, technical potentials and materials. Somewhere in between these two extremes – the ideology of universality and the ideology of the original national particularities – lies the fruitful breeding ground for those architectural creations, which are inspired by 'the spirit of the site' or architecture as a spatial and cultural indicator of its time.

The DOCOMOMO working group has prepared this presentation in connection with our group research project, 'Regional reflections of the Modern Movement in Bulgaria between the two World Wars: the contribution of women.' The main part of this work was conducted between 1997 and 2000 wih financial assistace from the Research Support Scheme of the Open Society Institute in Prague.

Ljubinka Stoilova

The final design differs substantially from their preliminary neo-classical project for the 1924 international competition. It unites expressionist ideas with references to the Bulgarian building tradition. The drawings were prepared in Germany (1925) under the guidance of Professor Paul Bonatz (1877-1951), who was appointed by the jury as consultant. The heavy volumes of rough-cut red brick masonry express a certain medieval massiveness and is evidently influenced by the style of Bonatz. The mystical atmosphere of the main lobby with pointed arch windows, and the brick frames of doors and windows recall Bulgarian late medieval fortified houses.

2
Angel Kantardzhiev's residence
25 Czar Osvoboditel Boulevard, Sofia 1504
1931 | 1932
Ivan Vasiliov & Dimitur Tsolov

3
Mineral Baths with Sanatorium
Bania village, Karlovo district 4300
1934 | 1938
Iordan Iordanov & Sava Ovcharov

The two storey high house, accessible from a front yard, consists of clearly differentiated groups of official, private and housekeeping use. The large living/dining room, and the study, all on the ground floor form a unified space. An official staircase and a domestic back one connect them with three bedrooms and a bathroom on the second level, and the servants' rooms in the attic. The interiors are finished with expensive materials. The original central hot water heating was produced by the former Bulgarian-German Corporation 'Imperial'. The roof is flat. The building was called 'The White Ship' reflecting Le Corbusier's fondness of ship-forms.

The building was recognized as an 'architectural monument of local value' in 1977 by the National Institute for Monuments of Culture. Since 1993 it has been the headquarters of the 'Bonjour' chain of stores owned and operated by Stambouli (Bulgaria) Limited.

The designers won first prize in the 1933 national competition. The spaces for different uses of the natural thermal water are separated in functional groups and are reflected in the façade's treatment. The smaller male (right) wing of changing rooms and baths also included dressing rooms and a pool for the king's family. The architectonic expression of these serene white volumes is due to the sharp contrast between the prismatic form of the main entrance and the horseshoe-shaped volume of the baths intersecting it. This contrast is accentuated by the arched windows of the entrance lobby and the horizontal bands of rectangular windows of the baths.

This fine example of expressionist sensibility, inspired probably by the work of Erich Mendelsohn, was declared a 'monument of national value' by the National Institute for Monuments of Culture in 1987.

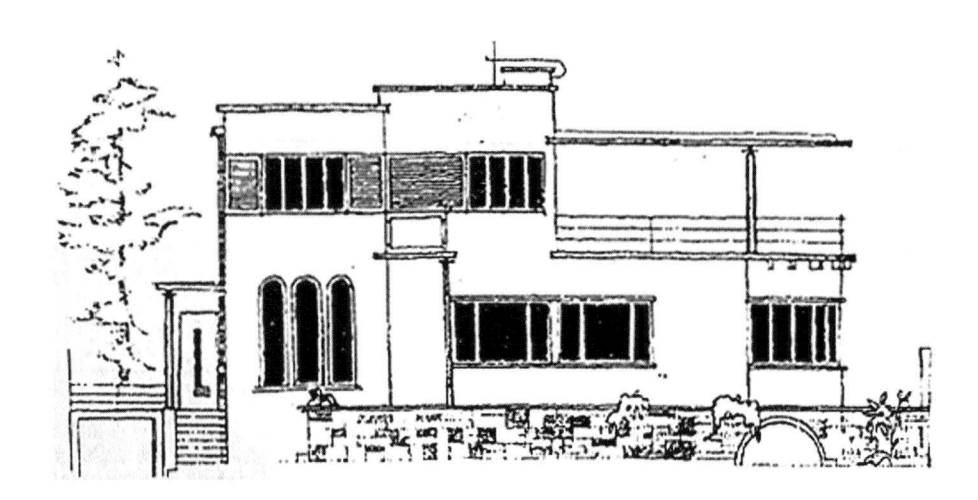

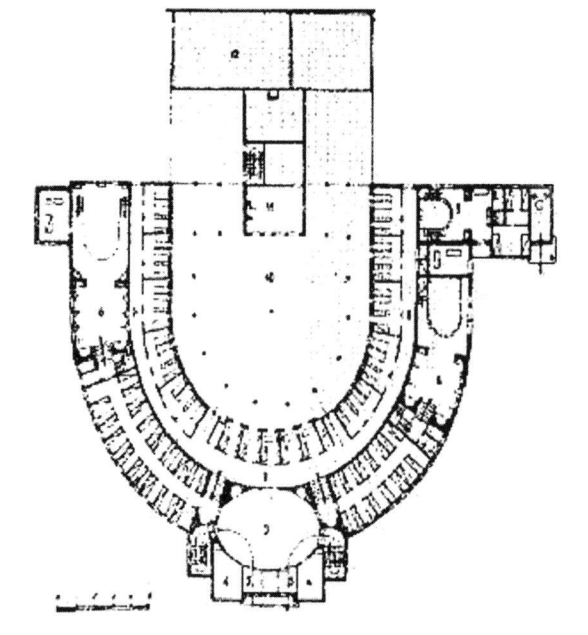

60

4
Association of Financial Employees'
Vacation Building
Nesebar 8230
1936
Krum Plakunov

The building is located on a sloping hill in the contemporary resort part of the town, facing the ancient Byzantine town of Nesebar and the Black Sea. The concave form of the plan follows the line of the seacoast. On the ground floor are located: a reception hall, a kitchen, a canteen, and a spacious living room for common daily use. Above the latter, a roof terrace offers beautiful general views of the sea and the old town. All bedrooms on the upper two floors have balconies and large windows overlooking the sea. Thus, the façade projects a dynamic image reinforced by the continuous tubular railings. The circular windows of the convex living room volume create impressions of a moving ship.

5
Central Trade-Union House and Cultural
Centre of the Transportation Workers
106 Kniaginia Maria-Luisa Boulevard, Sofia
1935 | 1937
Atanas Delibashev & Ivan Boyadzhiev

The plot is a 1935 gratuitous endowment by the Bulgarian State to the Trade-Union of Railmen and Sailors. The building is located at north of the Central Sofia Railway Station. The spaces are separated into functional groups: a cinema on the ground floor, three upper levels with offices, spaces for amateur art activities (dance, theatre, choirs) and for educational courses, as well as for syndicate functions. The volume with office rooms has a plain white façade with rhythmical alternation of horizontal bands of windows. The recessed terrace floor with a flat roof and the shaded passage behind the front columns at the ground floor emphasize the horizontallity of this volume with their dark shadows.

In contrast, the staircase within a semi-cylindrical glass-enclosed volume provides a vertical accent of particular interest. It brings the work of Erich Mendelsohn to mind. The interiors are simple. The Cultural Centre of the Transportation Workers is an excellent example of the influence of expressionism on the authors of this building.

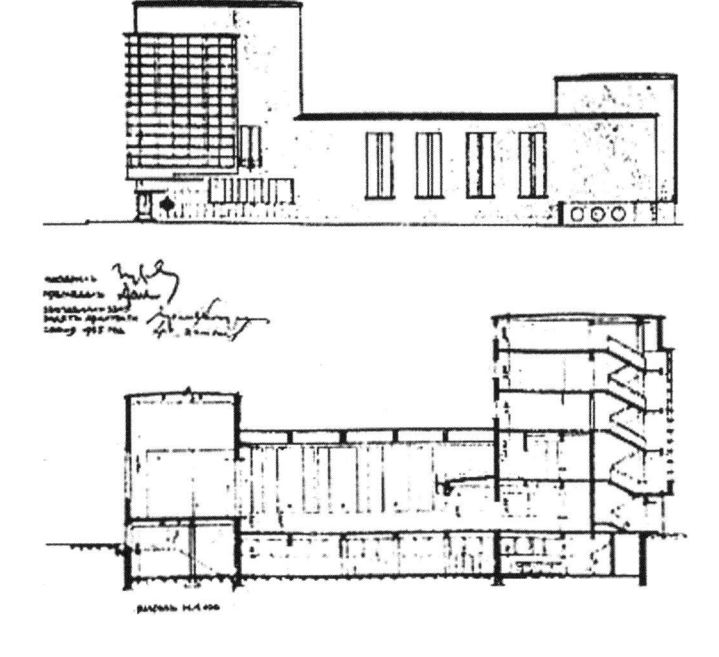

6
Co-operative apartments for Nedkov
48 Vitosha Street
1937 | 1938
and Cooperative apartments for Urumov
59 Vitosha Street
1938 | 1939
Radoslav Radoslavov
& Konstantantin Dzhangozov

7
The Bulgarian National Bank
Alexander Batenberg Street Sofia 1000
1934 | 1939
Ivan Vassiliov & Dimitar Tsolov

Both buildings are eight storeys high with shops on the ground floors. They are situated along the main commercial boulevard of Vitosha Street in Sofia, facing each other at the crossroad with Neophite Rilsky Street. Large entrance hallways in both buildings lead to their staircases and lifts. The spaces for different uses in each flat are separated in clearly distinguished public and private groups around the living room, to which the dining room is widely opened. A winter garden and a balcony to the living room of the corner apartments form a vertical accent. A specially sought after effect of emphatic exterior horizontallity has been obtained by windows in long bands, flat roof terraces with metal tubular railings, and solid balcony parapets.

Both architects had studied in Paris with Auguste Perret. Their buildings are composed according to Le Corbusier's 'five principles.' These two buildings are popular examples of the Bulgarian Modern Movement from the 1930s and have national importance.

The best-known example of 'modernized' neo-classicism, this important building makes a significant mark on the central city streetscape. After consultations with their Professor in Munich, Herman Bestelmayer, the designers incorporated the bank in to one complex with the former Turkish mosque on the site (now an archaeological museum). The asymmetrical plan is reflected in the monumental volumes with simplified classical order. Exquisite symbolic sculptures and stained glass windows decorate the interiors and the exterior walls. The statue of the bankers' protector St Nicole is located above the northwest entrance. The shadow of projecting cornices and clock tower link the bank with the mosque and soften the neo-classical idiom.

8
Southern-Bulgaria Tubercolosis Sanatorium
Raduntsi, Kazanluk region 6100
1939 | 1942
Viktoria Angelova & Maria Zakharieva

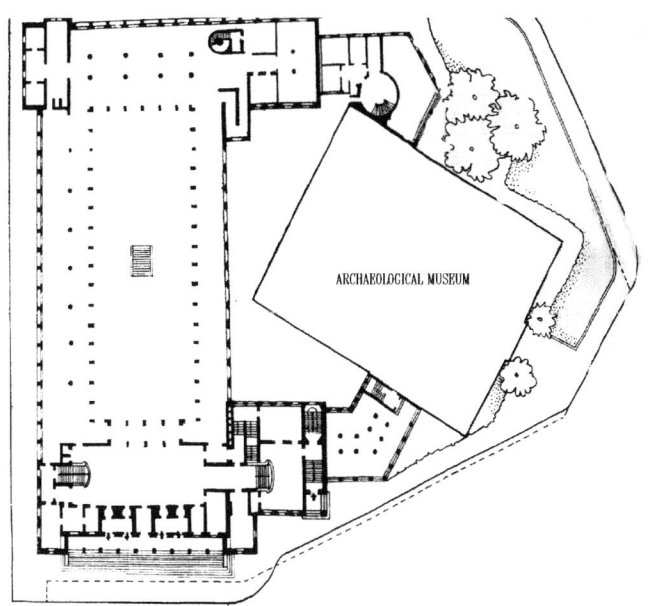

The design won first prize in a 1939 national architectural competition. Construction started the same year on the slopes of the Balkan Mountains. After its completion the sanatorium included 460 beds (200 for men, 160 for women and 100 for children). The central part contains a dining room, a kitchen and the administration on the ground floor with medical services on the first floor. Each of these services is connected on each side to the men's and women's sections. The children's sanatorium is in a separate building with a dining room and a corridor link to the common kitchen. A laundry and the central heating system are located in the lower part of the site, near to the station for easy access to a coal supply. The complex was built in stages. The master plan included a future hotel, villas and buildings for the agricultural needs of the sanatorium. All rooms face south with access to continuous balconies. The horizontal subdivision of the façade is accompanied by the uninterrupted rhythm of the windows.

Selected Bibliography :
Mambriani A
L'Architettura Moderna nei paesi Balcani
Bologna 1970

Stoyanov B
Suvremenna arkhitektura
Sofia 1977

Kazmukov N
'Kooperativnoto Zhilishto Stroitelstvo v Sofia do 1944' in: Tonev L (ed)
Arkhitekturata v Bulgariia 1878-1944
Sofia 1978 pp 82-104

Kovachevski S & Iokimov P
'Konkursnoto delo v Bulgaria 1878-1944' in: Tonev L (ed)
Arkhitekturata v Bulgariia 1878-1944
Sofia 1978 pp 206-236

Anastasov H
'Arkhitekturata v Bulgaria mezhdu dvete svetovni voini' & 'Zhilishti sgradi i kompleksi prez perioda na sotsializma' in: Obretenov A (ed)
Bulgarskata arkhitektura prez vekovete
Sofia 1982 pp 209-235 302-320

'Sources of Socialist Countries' Architecture, 1920s and 1930s'
Architecture and Society special issue
Sofia no 4-5 1985-1986

Stoilova L
'Modernoto dvizhenie v Bulgaria v primerite na niakoi zhilishtni sgradi'
Arkhitektura
Sofia 1994 no 3 pp 32-36

Stoilova L & Iokimov P
'Bulgarskata arkhitektura mezhdu dvete svetovni voini v konteksta na svetovniia arkhitekturen protses'
Arkhitektura
Sofia 1994 no 2 pp 40-44

'Bulgarien – Architektur der Toleranz'
Der Architekt special issue
Bonn 1998 no 1

Illustrations courtesy DOCOMOMO Bulgaria

Czech Republic

The prerequisites for modern architecture began to form in the Czech Republic as early as the turn of the 20th century. The role of the founder of Czech modern architecture was 'assigned' to Jan Kot'era (1871-1923) who embarked on rationalist modernism already before World War I. The movement of Czech architectural cubism – which came into existence in the year 1910 and whose theoretical principles were formulated by architect Pavel Janák 1882-1956) – also affected to some extent, further developments in Czech architecture.

The establishment of the Czechoslovak Republic as a sovereign state in October 1918 gave a strong impulse to the development of a progressive course in Czech architecture. The so-called rondocubism, which represented the decorative variant of cubism, became the national style in the post-war period. In 1920, the Modern Culture Association Devetsil was established in Prague. The Association was headed by Karel Teige (1900-51) who became the main theoretician and critic of the avant-garde. Architects Jaroslav Fragner, Karel Honzík, Evzen Linhart and Vít Obrtel founded a group called The Purist Four, and participated, in 1926, in the establishment of the architectural section of Devetsil called ARDEV. Their architectural works reflecting the spirit of purism, poetism and constructivism followed the example set by Le Corbusier, the De Stijl Movement, the Bauhaus and the Soviet constructivism.

In Brno, the beginnings of modern architecture were associated with the activity of the Municipal Building Authority's Department of Regulation and Architecture headed by architect Jindřich Kumpost (1891-1968) who surrounded himself with young promising designers. Among the most renowned of them was Bohuslav Fuchs (1895-1972) who very soon became the leading personality of Brno's architectural modernism. After making rondocubist designs at the beginning of his career, and after a lesson of neo-plasticism, he began to incline to Le Corbusier's principles and created a distinct variant of emotional functionalism. With the Zeman Café built in Brno between 1925 and 1926, he created one of the first works of the Czech Modern Movement.

In late 1924 and early 1925, the Club of Architects and UP Works organized a cycle of lectures delivered by domestic and foreign architects in Prague and Brno. This cycle decisively encouraged Czech architects to take the positions of functionalism. Of foreign architects taking part in this cycle of lectures, Le Corbusier, W Gropius, A Loos, JJP Oud and A Ozenfant must be mentioned. The declaration entitled 'Our Opinion on New Architecture' published in the journal 'Stavba' became the actual programme of Czech architects.

In the 1920s, centres of modern architecture also began to form in Hradec Králové and Zlín, in addition to Prague and Brno. The Mayor of Hradec Králové, F Ulrich, a man of light and learning, initiated the urban and architectural 'conversion' of Hradec Králové into a modern town. At first, this conversion was based upon J Kot'era's plans, then upon those set up by J Gočár. The dynamic growth of Zlín fully reflected the intentions of Tomás Bat'a, the founder of the world-famous shoe-making combine, with František Lydie Gahura (1891-1958) and Vladimír Karfík (1901-1996) being the most renowned Zlín-based architects of the inter-war period. Thanks to them, Zlín developed to form a prototype of functionalistic town in the spirit of the Charter of Athens of CIAM.

In the late 1920s, the modern course of Czech architecture took firm roots and became stabilized. This was confirmed by the construction of the Exhibition Centre of Brno, in which most of the domestic architects took part, and by organizing the nationwide Contemporary Culture exhibition. One part of this exhibition was formed by the New House housing estate, which represented the first modern housing exhibition in Czechoslovakia and the second in Europe, with the 1927 'Die Wohnung' exhibition having been the first. Modern architecture also began to penetrate into smaller Czech and Moravian towns.

Czech architects were kept well informed about the developments in architecture in Europe and all over the world through domestic journals and their own contacts. Also the leading foreign architects (L Bauer, P Behrens, IA Campbell, Le Corbusier, J Hoffmann, H Lauterbach, A Loos, E Mendelsohn, L Mies and JJP Oud) made designs for Bohemia and Moravia, and their designs were implemented here. Shortly after the Congrès Internationaux d'Architecture Moderne (CIAM) had been established, Czech architects took an active part in its activity. These contacts became reduced, but their activity within this organization was renewed in 1935 thanks to Brno-based architects who initiated the establishment of CIAM-Ost.

The great economic crisis radicalized Czech architects politically, turning their attention to social issues. They focused their main efforts on solving the housing problem. Instead of detached houses, they began to promote tenement houses with small and very small dwellings. In 1930, Teige began to push through the concept of the so called collective house as the only form of proletariat housing. He summed up his opinions on housing issues in a book entitled 'The Smallest Flat' (1932). At the same time, Jirí Kroha exhibited 'the Sociological Fragment of Housing' in Brno, a cycle of panels presenting photomontages as a way of analyzing the housing in Czechoslovakia in the pre-war capitalist period.

The Czech architectural avant-garde developed, on a broad creative basis, the principles of Modern Movement down to the outbreak of World War II. It enriched the rational and scientific basis of the International Style to include specific fine-arts and human elements. However, this successful development was forcably interrupted by the Nazi occupation of Czechoslovakia. Czech architects managed to revive the inter-war tradition after 1945 but for a short period of time only.

Eva Búrilová
Iveta Erná
Jakub Kyncl
Jan Sedlák

1
The Crematorium
Brno
1925 | 1930
Ernst Wiesner

The group of buildings is situated on staggered terraces interconnected by flights of steps. The ceremonial hall of travertine rises above a prism-shaped pedestal with brick lining, the hall being accentuated by pyramid-like pillars around its circumference and covered with a glass hip roof. At the back, business premises around a service courtyard are attached to the hall, with atrium-shaped columbaria being symmetrically attached to the sides. It is one of the most distinctive works of Czech inter-war architecture.

2
The Avion Hotel
Brno
1926 | 1928
Bohuslav Fuchs

A nine-storey row-building situated on a narrow and deep allotment. The reception and restaurant are accommodated on the ground-floor, a café with galleries lining the sides of the space occupy the first and second floors. The hotel rooms are accommodated on the four floors above the café. The 'piano nobile' with the café captures interest by a unique spatial design. It is one of the masterpieces of Bohuslav Fuchs, the leading representative of the Czech inter-war architecture.

3
The Exhibition Centre
Brno
1927 | 1928
Bohumíl ⃞ermák, Bohuslav Fuchs, Josef Gočár, Pavel Janák, Josef Kalous, Emil Králík, Oldrich Stary & others

The Brno Exhibition Centre was opened in 1928 by the Contemporary Czechoslovak Culture exhibition marking the 10th anniversary of the establishment of Czechoslovakia. The area is dominated by the Business and Industry Palace with its rotunda (Kalous-Valenta). Other valuable buildings include the City of Brno Pavilion (by Fuchs), the Brno Trade Fair Pavilion (⃞ermák), the Cinema with a café (Králík), the Academy of Fine Arts Pavilion (Gočár) and the School of Applied Art Pavilion (Janák). The Brno Exhibition Centre was a galaxy of the Modern Movement, significantly affecting the further progressive development of Czech architecture.

4
The Villa Tugendhat
Brno
1928 | 1930
Ludwig Mies van der Rohe

A freestanding one-storey building situated on a slope with its front facing a landscaped garden. Only the top floor made up of the entrance hall, bedrooms, a garage and the housekeeper's apartment is visible from the street. Utilities are accommodated in the basement. A substantial part of the main floor is occupied by the central living space whose subdivision into a reception area, a study, a social area and a dining room is only indicated. Van der Rohe also made the whole interior design. The villa is the most important work of architecture implemented during Mies van der Rohe's European period.

5
The City Baths
Brno-Zábrdovice
1929 | 1932
Bohuslav Fuchs

A public baths complex designed for workers living in Brno suburbs in flats with inadequate sanitary equipment. The complex consisted of two buildings, one designed as Winter Baths with an exterior reminiscent of industrial architecture, and the other one designed as Summer Baths with swimming pools, cloakrooms, playgrounds and sportsgrounds and grass space. The transparent architecture of the Summer Baths made the most of available sun, air and greenery. As one of the most advanced works of Czech functionalism, it made, at the same time, a considerable contribution to improving the social environment in Brno.

6
The Children's Hospital and Clinic
Brno-âerná Pole
1947 | 1954
Bedřich Rozehnal

The urban composition, the layout and the graduation of masses of this complex of interconnected buildings are aimed to fully comply with the requirements to operate this hospital. With its architectural expression, the complex creates, at the same time, a favourable atmosphere for the treatment of patients. The complex is dominated by a four-storey in-patient wing opening with band-shaped balconies to the south, and with verandas to the sides. It is the most significant structure designed by Bedrich Rozehnal who became an internationally recognised expert.

7
The Headquarters of the Railways
Hradec Králové
1927 | 1932
Josef Gočár

Of a great number of buildings designed by Gočár and built in Hradec Králové, this one is the biggest. With all these buildings, he printed a modern urban look on this town. Towards the close of the 1920s, Gočár began to incline toward a special classicist functionalism, which is documented by the symmetrical arrangement and gradation of masses as well as by the simple detail of the official building. The side-wings of the building whose lay-out contains four wings are conceived as gallery halls and reflect the most advanced trends in the Czech inter-war modernism.

8
The Auto/Tatra Company's Business & Residential Building
Kolín
1932
Jaroslav Fragner

One of the examples of a building designed for both business and housing. Designs of that kind frequently occurred in Czech functionalist buildings. The car shop is situated in the two-storey glazed mezzanine with a gallery, with the owner's flat forming the upper glazed-storey. An exterior staircase creates a significant sculptural accent. Designed by a leading Czech functionalist, this building cannot conceal the inspiration from Le Corbusier's houses on piloti.

9
The Prague Trade Fairs Palace
Prague-Holesovice
1924 | 1928
Oldřich Tyl & Josef Fuchs

A freestanding seven-storey block comprising four wings with a recessed top storey. Accommodated underground are utility and storerooms and a cinema while the above-ground floors accommodate shops, restaurants and offices. Offices are situated around galleries interconnected by a transversally positioned passage that divides the ceilinged courtyard into a larger and smaller one. It is one of the first structures representing the Modern Movement in Central Europe.

10
St Wenceslaus' Church
Prague-Vrsovice
1927 | 1930
Josef Gočár

The church is situated on a slope and occupies a deep rectangular site. The open entrance hall is accentuated by a prism-shaped campanile positioned in the middle of this space. Approaching the main altar, the triple-naved space decreases in width and increases, by degrees, in height. Approaching the conceptual centre of the church, the intensity of light increases thanks to the windows placed in the individual degrees of the ceiling and the almost completely glazed presbytery. The church excellently exemplifies the application of the functionalistic morphology in sacred architecture.

11
The Müller Villa
Prague-Stresovice
1928 | 1930
Adolf Loos

A self-contained two-storey cube-shaped house freestanding from a slope. Horizontal and vertical designs alternate in the basement, on the groundfloor and the main floor. The piano nobile level is occupied by an open hall, a dining room with a kitchen, a library and a ladies' room. The second floor comprises childrens' rooms, bedrooms, dressing rooms, a guest room and a servant's room. A minor part of the platform roof is developed to accommodate another two rooms. In this building constructed as one of his late designs, Adolf Loos manifested, in a most convincing manner, his concept of the so-called Raumplan.

12
The General Pension Fund Building
Prague-Zizkov
1929 | 1934
Josef Havlíček & Karel Honzík

A freestanding office building of a cross-shaped lay-out. It comprises a north-south oriented twelve-storey section and a lower eight-storey east-west section. Situated in the area where these sections touch is the central hall with vertical gangways and sanitary facilities. In addition, a two-storey commercial wing is attached in the north while a three-storey residential wing is attached in the south. The Pension Fund Building was the biggest functionalist structure in Prague and became a symbol of the Czech Modern Movement.

13
The Baba Housing Estate
Prague-Dejvice
1928 | 1940
Josef Gočár, Antonín Heythum, Pavel Janák
Jan E Koula, Evzen Linhart, Mart Stam,
Ladislav Zák & others

A model housing estate comprising thirty-nine detached houses and villas was built upon the initiative of the Czechoslovak Building Works Union as an exhibition of modern housing. The houses were designed as individual housing for Prague's cultural celebrities. Here, medium-sized detached houses, one-generation or two-generation villas, the so-called tenement villas and houses with studios can be found. The architectural concept oscillated between the classicizing Modernism (Gočár) and a mature Functionalism (Heythum, Linhart and Zák).

14
The French Schools
Praha-Dejvice
1931 | 1934
Jan Gillar

Designed as a facility to provide education in French, this complex of school buildings combines the monoblock and pavilion systems. It comprises the principal's office, administration, kindergarten and basic school, the 1st and 2nd level of the secondary school, the gymnasium and the assembly hall. The urban design complies with the needs for good access, is in harmony with the relief of the natural ground level and provides for a good illumination of classrooms by natural light. Inspired by Hannes Meyer's school in Bernau and Jan Duiker's Open Air School in Amsterdam, Gillar managed to adapt elements of these models to the special needs of this task.

15
The Miroslav Hajn Villa
Praha-Vysocany
1932 | 1933
Ladislav Žák

This building represents an example of how a single house can reflect the idea of collective housing, in which the architect was intensely engaged. While the groundfloor comprises a continuous space of the hall with a social and dining area, winter garden and a roofed terrace, the upper storey consists of cubicle-style bedrooms. In harmony with the profession of the owner of the villa (aircraft designer), the exterior of the villa is partly reminiscent of an aeroplane, partly of nautical motives popular at that time. It is the culmination of 'villa architecture' in the inter-war Czechoslovakia.

16
The Bílá Labué Department Store
Praha-Nové Mesto
1936 | 1939
Josef Kittrich & Josef Hrubý

The architectural expression of this building is mainly represented by its 20x30m front made of thermolux glass set in a light steel frame. Behind this front are five storeys of sales halls with a continuous space and pathways along the perimeter. In its time, the Bílá Labué Department Store was the most modern department store and the last big functionalist building in Czechoslovakia. It represented a final stage in the architectural development of glass retail sales palaces built from the mid-1920s in Prague and other towns.

17
The Zálesná-Podvesná Housing Estate
Zlín
1926 | 1927
Department of Development of the Firm of Bat'a

18
The Tomás Bat'a Monument
Zlín
1933
František Lydie Gahura

19
The Office Building of the Firm of Bat'a
Zlín
1936 | 1938
Vladimír Karfík

20
The Collective House
Zlín
1945 | 1950
Jiří Voženílek

An example of mass housing development based on the principle of the 'Garden City' characteristic of the inter-war period in Zlín. Built by a continuous assembly-line technology these ensembles of houses gradually surrounded the industrial and social centre of the town. The floor area of one house was 45 square meters and was distributed into two storeys. The houses had complete sanitary equipment. This housing estate saw the stabilisation of the development of the housing standard, which was achieved by means of industrial technologies whose perfection was steadily growing.

This exhibition pavilion called by the architect himself a 'showcase,' was built to commemorate Tomás Bat'a, the founder of the Zlín-based shoe combine, who lost his life in a plane crash in 1932. With its transparency and continuous space, the building is reminiscent of Ludwig Mies van der Rohe's contemporary buildings. It is Gahura's most important work and one of the most advanced designs within the Czech functionalism.

This Bat'a headquarters is a 77.5m high freestanding 16-storey building. A reinforced concrete frame made up of 6.15x6.15m standard modules forms the bearing structure. The core of gangways and staircases and the plumbing unit are shifted to the circumference so that the individual floors are fully flexible. The chief's office sized 6x6m was accommodated in the lift shaft, which is a unique solution. The building became the dominant element of Bat'a works and the symbol of the town of Zlín. This building, was the culmination of the dynamic constructional development of Zlín whereby it became the model functionalist town.

The Czech architectural avant-garde started to be interested in the idea of collective housing in 1930 when the first theories were set up and the first designs made. However, the only two collective houses built were not done till only after the World War II in Litvínov and Zlín. Voženílek's house contains two-and three-room flats whose lay-out can be altered by means of variable partition walls. The space jointly used by all occupants consists of a restaurant, clubrooms, a gymnasium and a day nursery and kindergarten, all of them accommodated in a special groundfloor wing. The building exemplifies the application of constructional technologies designed in Zlín to create new forms of housing.

21
The Czechoslovak Pavilion
Paris
1936 | 1937
Jaromír Krejcar et al.

The pavilion was designed to represent the Czechoslovak state at the International Exhibition of Art and Technology. It was situated on the Goldsmith Bank of the Seine not far from the Eiffel Tower. An overhead terrace reposed on four steel piles, with a glass and steel cube with a set-back roof and a tall flag mast resting on it. Dry-assembly technology was used to build this pavilion, and its construction anticipated the later High-Tech Movement. This 'fragile glass poem on the bank of the Seine' represented one of the most convincing buildings of Czech and European avant-garde architecture.

22
The Sociological Housing Fragment
1932 | 1933
Jiří Kroha

A group of 89 panels with photomontages presenting an analysis of housing in the capitalist era of Czechoslovakia. The work was done at a time when the economic crisis was culminating, thus making housing shortage even more critical. By means of a multi-disciplinary research based upon political and economic studies drawn up by Marx and Engels, Jiří Kroha intended to prove that housing standard is dependent on the social standard of the individual social classes. Along with Teige, Kroha was the foremost Czech theoretician in architecture, and the founder of the scientific approach to housing.

Not illustrated

Selected Bibliography :
Krejcar J
L'architecture contemporaine en Tchécoslovaquie
Prague 1928

Teige K (ed)
MSA 2: Moderní architektura v československsku
Prague 1930

'L'Architecture moderne en Tchécoslovaquie'
L'Architecture d'Aujourd'hui special issue
1933 no 5 (June)

Teige K
Práce Jaromíra Krejcara
Prague 1933

Teige K
Modern Architecture in Czechoslovakia
Prague 1947

Dostál OJ, Pechar J & Procházka V
Modern Architecture in Czechoslovakia
Prague 1967 (second edition 1970)

Burkhardt F & Lamarová M
Cubismo cecoslovacco
Milan 1982

Kotalík J
Tschechische Kunst 1878-1914
Darmstadt 1985

Devetsil.
Česka vytvarna avantgarda dvacatych let
Prague-Brno 1986

Šlapeta V
Czech Functionalism 1918-1938
London 1987

Šmejkal F & Švácha R (eds)
Devetsil. Czech Avant-Garde Art, Architecture and Design of the 1920s and 1930s
Oxford & London 1990

Šlapeta V
Bat'a: Architektura a Urbanismus 1910-1950
Zlin 1991

Kubova A
L'Avant-garde architecturale en Tchecoslovakie 1918-1939
Liège 1992

Novák P
Zlínská Architektura 1900-1950
Zlin 1993

Svácha R
The Architecture of New Prague 1895-1945
Cambridge (Mass) 1995

DOCOMOMO Czech Republic
National Register: 1st Proposal
Brno 1996

Leśnikowski W (ed)
East European Modernism: Architecture in Czechoslovakia, Hungary & Poland between the Wars
London & New York 1996

Dluhosch E & Svácha R (eds)
Karel Teige 1900-1951: L'Enfant Terrible of the Czech Modernist Avant-Garde
Cambridge (Mass) 1999

Photographic Credits & Acknowledgements :
The City Museum of Brno

The National Technical Museum in Prague

Institute for Protection of Monuments in Brno

Denmark

It is no secret that the principles underlying the selection of works for this volume have varied from one country to another. The Danish material bears clear signs of the board members' collective understanding of the history of architecture and its monuments, but, it also illustrates a deep personal knowledge of the majority of the works themselves. So it was natural for us to begin with what was already known. Discussions of how to define what modernism really is occur at regular intervals in the Danish association's board, the pragmatic view being that it is better to adopt a broad definition with the danger of encompassing too much than risk excluding works, by having a narrow viewpoint, which have earned the right to appear on the register. The broad viewpoint plays an important role in creating interest in what modernism is on a nationwide level. The national interest should, in turn, spark a regional awareness that the grounds of modernism can play a role in even local buildings. Does modernism, for example, manifest itself in materials other than concrete?

The association in Denmark has established a database in order to create a more comprehensive registration. This currently covers, for the main part, a number of well known monuments but also a number of lesser-known works which have been brought to notice by local architectural and museum contacts. At present, July 1999, the database contains approximately 150 monuments. The next phase in the registration work is a nationwide follow-up in the form of a questionnaire to local sources regarding modernist buildings in their area. In the first instance the association has sent out a publication showing examples of 25 buildings entitled 'Houses of Modernism. 25 Danish examples'. The text is by Inge Mette Kirkeby and the photography by Aage Lund Jensen. The work was made possible by a kind contribution from the Aalborg Portland and Concrete Element Association. Unfortunately the association does not have the resources to distribute a printed questionnaire and a copy of the replies. Therefore, we have chosen initially to put the database on the internet under our own domain name. It is an interactive database where visitors on one hand may search and sort the registered monuments in several ways. On the other hand they might also send suggestions for more registrations to the board of DOCOMOMO-Denmark. This has been possible since late January 1999. It is all in Danish even though we would like it to be in English as well.

Mich Ottosen

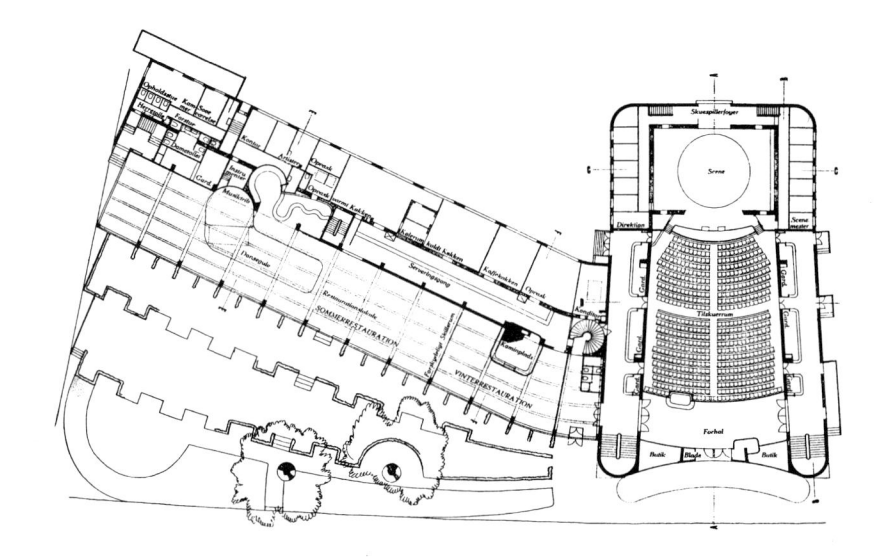

1
The Bellevue Theatre
Strandvejen 451
2820 Gentofte
1935 | 1936
Arne Jacobsen

2
Femvejen 2
2920 Charlottenlund
1934
Georg Jacobsen

Bellevue is first of all designed as a summer theatre – the ceiling can be opened so when the weather is clement, you can see theatre in the open, and the blue-white canvas which has been fastened to the walls with bamboo canes resembles summer awnings. The original asbestos fabric, of course fire-resistant, has been replaced later. The chairs are bentwood (plywood) with a small shelf in front of each 'so that beer bottles or the like do not distract you during the performance'. The building south of the theatre was originally a restaurant but later it was converted into flats.

The main construction of the house is reinforced concrete combined with a 31cm cavity wall. It is plastered and white-painted. In spite of the right angles and horizontal cut-offs characteristic of the period, the theatre has many curves which are already visible from the entrance. The tiers of seats were at one stage removed and dispersed but after Flemming Hertz and Jes Kølpin bought the theatre in 1978, they succeeded in getting them back.

The painter Georg Jacobsen designed this house for the artists, Ellen and Adam Fischer while they all were living in Paris. In Copenhagen the young architect Johan Pedersen, later city architect of Copenhagen, was responsible for the architectural drawings. He was, however, directed to follow instructions from Paris. He was definitely not allowed to change the dimensions as the house has the Golden Section with its centre through the living room. The house is traditionally brick-built with a 30cm cavity wall, but because of the headroom of the studio, its walls are solid.

The house has a concrete floor and iron windows. It says in the correspondence that the house was to be limewashed in a tone between 'Naples yellow and lemon – not as penetrating as lemon and not as warm as Naples'. It is now chalk-white. From both the road and the garden, the house appears like a composition of purely cubic elements. The house, designed by an artist for artists, was later bought by another painter, Victor von Brockdorff, and so still today the studio is full of paintings and easels.

3
Gotfred Rodes Vej 2
2920 Charlottenlund
1928 | 1929
Arne Jacobsen

4
Copenhagen Airport 1939
Flyvervej 22, 2770 Kastrup
1939
Vilhelm Lauritzen

When Arne Jacobsen designed a house for himself, he created a villa characteristic of the period: white and with right angles. The house is relatively closed to the north but it opens up to the garden on the south and the west sides The society 'Better Architectural Tradition' (Bedre Byggeskik) praised the house as 'one of few modern villas which is real functionalism and good architecture according to its form decided by use, room, orientation and building technique.' But the text continues, 'Modern architecture, without established rules of form, calls for an artist´s instinctive creativity, it is not craftsmanship.' In spite of the architectural signals, it is a traditionally brick-built, white-washed house with joists and, however, with steel windows.

The new conception of space entailed an opening of the aspect, especially corner windows and a closer contact between in and out. The house has several protected terraces. Stairs from the terrace above the dining room lead to the garden. The designs shown are taken from the 1936 report of 'Better Architectural Tradition' because unlike the presentations of 1932 in the magazine 'The Architect', they show the wooden joists in design and sectional elevation.

As mobility and means of transport played a steadily more important role in Danish life, they were specially favoured by architects because the edifices connected hereto were seen as a clear sign of development and progress. The design work was not burdened with the requirements for any particular architectural language and factual considerations could speak for themselves. Lauritzen argues the formal rationality, 'When you wished to have the possibility of landing over the building, it had to be low, and as so many of the rooms had to face the airfield, the house had to be long.' The house has free standing concrete columns, partitions. Outer walls are light constructions of timber frame faced with asbestos slabs. Lauritzen wished, however, the hall to be of double height without columns. So it got a 12cm thick, wave-shaped concrete roof with a free span of 12m. The roof of the hall is characteristic from the inside as well as from the outside. The building has many curving forms. The stairs in the hall stand as a free sculpture, and the heavy brass banister emphasizes their soft, curved movement.

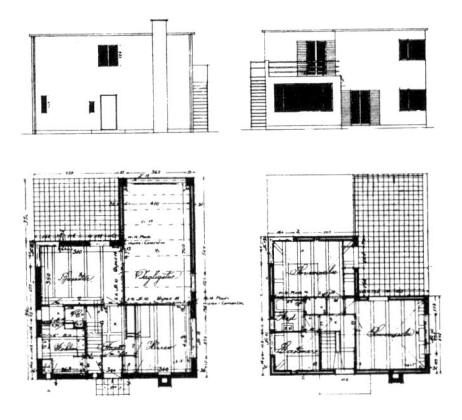

5
The Radio House
The Headquarters for Denmark's
Broadcasting House
Rosenørns Allé 22, 1999 Frederiksberg
1937 | 1945
Vilhelm Lauritzen

6
Petrol Station
Kystvejen 24, Skovshoved, 2820 Gentofte
1939
Arne Jacobsen

The Radio House consists of several buildings, each with its own content: the offices, the concert hall and the studios. Flexibility was a popular concept and the offices have bearing window parapets in reinforced concrete and a ribbon window with broad posts, being able to take a cross wall, if needed, every 90cm. Lauritzen designed all the furniture, too, and the materials are very consciously chosen. An example is the floor made of birch and teak in stripes. The building has load bearing concrete walls, mainly concrete, but covered with many materials according to the acoustics. Outside it is faced with pale yellow ceramic tiles (50 x 30cm). The concert hall is roofed by a concrete shell of double curvature, only 12cm thick. Due to the acoustics there is another ceiling hanging down, 6cm of ferro-concrete, whose surface dissolves into waves. Later, other acoustic modifications have been carried out. GN Brandt designed the roof garden with the canteen; in the background the roof of the concert hall is to be seen. The fine materials and the use of balconies give the concert hall its own intimacy. The elevation of the concert hall shows the construction of the roof with its lowered, wavy ceiling.

Motoring caused among other things a demand for petrol stations and garages, for checking and repairing the vehicles. Already in 1939 Arne Jacobsen designed this small building with the characteristic canopy. Everything is worked out carefully, and the simple forms make a deep impression. The construction is concrete with 12cm thick walls and a 10cm roof; the heated room is insulated with 4cm cork slabs. On the outside the house is faced with very light Meissner tiles, 30 x 125cm. The elliptical canopy was carried by a single, round column. The station stands out by its sharply cut geometrical forms without a footing.

7
The School by The Sound
Samosvej 50, 2300 Copenhagen S
1937
Kaj Gottlob

8
Stelling´s House
Gammel Torv 6, 1304 København K
1937
Arne Jacobsen

The school consists of two parts, the main school and the school for delicate children, having joint administration and services. At that time the building of a school with a central, open space in the middle became common, and the school has three floors with the class rooms connected around an open, main hall. The main school is washed in red and light grey and has white windows. The low wings of the school for delicate children are gathered round a protected yard. To the south there are six octagonal class-rooms. A ramp leads up to a continuous open-air shelter with the façade formed as one big, wavy window because light, fresh air and hygiene were essential elements of the care. A light entrance links the two solid wings.

Stelling´s Art Shop has several floors on a very small corner site. Arne Jacobsen argues for the choice of reinforced concrete because in this way you had the thinnest wall and the biggest floor space. The upper floors are corbelled 20cm. This gave important square metres, too. The authorities demanded that the corner was cut off, so Jacobsen rounded it off and designed an elegant, curved entrance. The house is built as a construction of plate girders with slim columns. Fireproof gable and short walls give the necessary buttresses. The upper floors are faced with grey ceramic slabs. They are carried by fillered metal anchors, and the shop itself produced a special pointing putty in order to eliminate damage from seeping water.

The two first floors of the shop, no longer Stelling´s, are faced with green-washed iron plates. The height of the façade is thoroughly proportioned to the neighbouring houses. The plates not only follow the curve of the corner but there are also plates with the rounded off edges to meet the neighbouring buildings, the next lower floor, and the top.

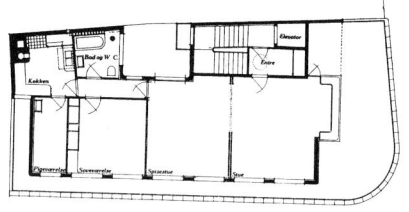

Upper Floor.

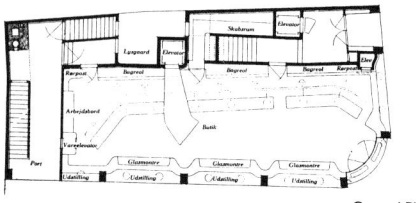

Ground Plan.

9
Sølystvej 11
2930 Klampenborg
1939
Mogens Lassen

Mogens Lassen built three very different houses on the dismantled Christiansholm´s Fortification and all are to a large extent proportioned to the big differences in the level of this ground. Sølystvej 11, which was built for the publisher Iver Jespersen, is cut into the steep slope so that one floor faces the street and two floors face the garden. The house is divided into three independent blocks each with its own form of roof: the kitchen-living room in split level and the sleeping rooms for children and adults are divided into two small blocks due to the tree then existing. The colours are white, redbrown, and a light green which Lassen had seen used by Le Corbusier.

The big windows have parapets with insulation of cork, asbestos cement plates and raw glass just as Lassen used it in the 'House of System'. Foundations, floor division, the convex and flat roofs to the street are made of reinforced concrete, the rest is common brickwork. From Sølystvej you go into the upper floor of the house. The lower floor of the house is on the same level as the garden. The tree at the entrance and the tree which decided the design of the house have been cut down.

10
Århus Town Hall
8000 Århus
1938 | 1942
Arne Jacobsen & Erik Møller

In 1937 Århus was growing fast and the city wanted a new and bigger city hall. The city council arranged a competition which Arne Jacobsen and Erik Møller won. Before the city was able to accept the sober project, it had to be more monumental: the main entrance was worked up and the façades were faced with marble from Prosgrunn, Norway, and the 60m high tower with bell and carillon was added. Bays of 3.15m give an outer, measured impression, and the short walls are movable without changing the construction – once again a sign of flexibility. Outer walls and floor divisions are concrete and main partitions are constructions of concrete in order to ease piping arrangements and installations. The cast balconies and outer columns are made of white concrete with aggregate of calcinated flint. The roof is copper-covered, the window Oregon pine and the frame teak. The inner walls and wainscots are of beech and the floor of the hall is bog oak. The building is designed very carefully in all details, as the City Hall Square with the raised entrance to the City Hall. The functional differentiation is mirrored in a division into three: 1) main wing with hall, city council hall, and wedding ceremony hall, 2) the administration wing with panoptic corridor, and 3) registration office and payments office with its own entrance, 'the tower entrance'.

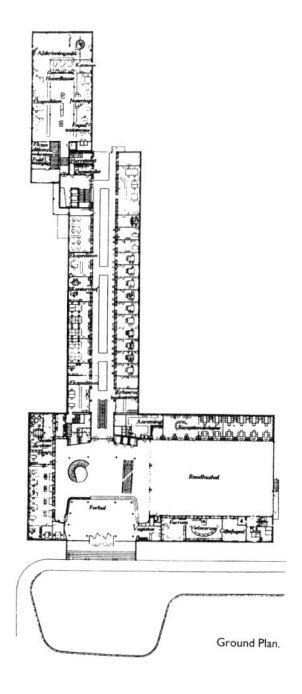

Ground Plan.

11
Aarhus University
8000 Århus C
1932
Kay Fisker & CF Møller

Århus got its university in 1928, and in 1931 a competition was arranged for a university on a ground which falls from north towards south and which runs down to the city. Kay Fisker, CF Møller, Povl Stegmann, and CT Sørensen won a project respecting and taking advantage of the characteristic ground. The buildings are situated to the sides, and most of the broken configuration is laid out as a park with a simple choice of materials: grass, oaks, and water. The main building to Ringgaden with main hall and administration constitutes the protective back of the university to the north, later being expanded to the west with the Library of the State (Statsbiblioteket) and the big tower of books. The houses are yellow bricks with roofs in the same material.

This was a change in comparison with the competition project which had almost flat copper roofs. The choice of materials and the form of the roof give the blocks a precise, sharp-cut form and connect them. The university still expands with yellow brick buildings on varied themes, in the manner which caught on in the thirties. Today the oaks are big and play an important part of the picture.

Selected Bibliography:

Sorensen A
Funktionalisme og Samfund
Copenhagen 1933

Rasmussen SE
Nordische Baukunst
Berlin 1940

Finsen H
Ung Dansk Arkitektur 1930-1945
Copenhagen 1947

The Architecture of Denmark
Book version (1949) of
Architectural Review special issue
London November 1948

Hiort E
Ny Dansk Arkitektur
Copenhagen 1950
English translation as:
Danish Architecture of Today
London 1950
Hiort E
Housing in Denmark since 1930
Copenhagen 1952

Pedersen J
Arkitekten Arne Jacobsen
Copenhagen 1957

Faber T
New Danish Architecture
Stuttgart & London 1968

Guldberg J (ed)
Tema: Funktionalisme
Odense 1986

DOCOMOMO Denmark
Modernismens Huse: 25 danske eksempler
Copenhagen 1998

Wedebrunn O (ed)
Modern Movement Scandinavia
Copenhagen 1998

Illustrations courtesy DOCOMOMO Denmark

Estonia

In the 1920s Estonia was an impoverished state on the edge of Europe with a population of one million; it had recently gained its independence from Russian and German rulers and was in the process of catching up on all fronts. Within a decade, a professional community of architects was established who had received their education in Riga Polytechnical Institute and in various German technical universities at the beginning of the twentieth century; they ousted the previously dominant engineers and technicians and integrated local architects of Baltic-German origin.

The first half of the 1930s saw the extensive application of functionalism. There were practically no academic architects of the older generation who would oppose it. All the leading architects of the middle generation (Johanson, Habermann, Jacoby, Soans, Kuusik) as well as the younger generation (Lohk, Kotli, Matteus, Volberg, Bölau) were carried along by the enthusiasm which was also felt by engineers and technicians who sometimes interpreted the modernist views in a comical and clumsy way. The new architecture was sometimes called cubism or constructivism, although the term most often used was functionalism. The wider public also believed in the advantages of the new style and criticism of these 'box-like' buildings was not heard until the second half of the 1930s.

Since the labour movement in 1920s Estonia was weak, the leftist parties, trade unions and co-operatives as yet being underdeveloped, the discourse of low-cost housing was not as strong as elsewhere in Europe. Even so, there was debate in the press in the late 1920s, and in 1929 a competition for building low-cost houses was held in Tartu, although the results were never actually realised.

One type of building which lent itself well to the modern style was the school. Literacy in Protestant Estonia was widespread and the idea that a modern society can only be built by educating its population was widely accepted. Thanks to reforms in education, a large number of new schoolhouses were built, supported by the new governmental loan policy. While the majority of country schools were in the modernised vernacular style and only a few featured functionalist elements, most of the city schools built in the 1930s were functionalist.

The health resort of Pärnu is sometimes regarded as the summer capital of Estonia, and it is definitely the capital of Estonian modernism. In the 1930s when the resort town was being redeveloped, Olev Siinmaa was the municipal architect. He was one of the most original Estonian functionalists who, on the one hand, expressed his pleasure at Le Corbusier's ideas not being rashly introduced in Pärnu but who, on the other hand, designed the most radical buildings in the Baltic states.

The most original examples of Estonian modernism are the limestone buildings designed by Herbert Johanson. As head of the Tallinn municipal design office, he started designing functionalist buildings of rusticated limestone in the 1930s. At first glance it seems that natural limestone cut by hand was an elitist building material and as such quite incompatible with the principles of modernism. But the fact is that Tallinn and the whole of North Estonia are situated on a limestone cliff, and so it was the cheapest and the most readily available building material.

After the coup d'etat in 1934 Estonia became increasingly authoritarian under the leadership of Konstantin Päts. There was a shift towards more traditional architecture. Although there were no official specifications, the architects were oriented to Germany and adopted a more traditional approach. In the second half of the 1930s, otherwise functionalist villas were capped with high roofs and apartment houses in the city centre were built perimetrically and their façades embellished with a granite finish or dolomite, whereas on the courtyard side curved projections with large windows and balconies were preserved.

In the 1930s Estonia was a small rapidly developing peripheral country where a strong functionalist school of architecture was established which was inspired by ideals of progress, which attempted to follow everything that was happening in the world, and was able to digest and interpret the new architecture in the local context.

Mart Kalm
Piret Lindpere

1
Urla House shops, offices and flats
Pärnu maantee 6, Tallinn
1932 | 1933
Eugen Habermann

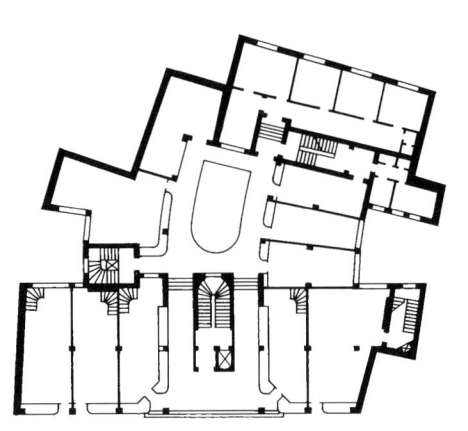

This is one of the few city-like buildings in Estonia. It stretches over a whole block and was erected on the site of the medieval town wall. A new feature in Tallinn architecture was the arrangement of the shops on the ground floor around an inner courtyard. In the middle of the courtyard there is an oval opening for light and ventilation which serves the lower courtyard with its garages. The multi-level courtyard is a development of the motif used at 10 Pärnu maantee by Eliel Saarinen. The offices on the first floor are projecting, and for that reason the building was compared to a chest of drawers with the second drawer from the bottom slightly open. The spacious flats on the Pärnu road side have a clear plan, those within the depth of the site are jagged.

2
Art Hall
Vabaduse väljak 8, Tallinn
1933 | 1934
Anton Soans & Edgar Kuusik

3
The Lender Secondary School
Kreutzwaldi tänav 25, Tallinn
1933 |1935
Herbert Johanson

Sponsored by the Culture Foundation, this building was an improved version of the prize-winning design by Anton Soans in the 1933 architectural competition. It houses KU-KU, a well-known artists' club on the basement floor, shops and shared studio premises on the ground floor, exhibition halls on the first floor, offices on the second floor and studio apartments on the top floors. The circular windows on the first floor were replaced by niches for sculptures in the process of construction and in 1937 two statues by Juhan Raudsepp, 'Work' and 'Beauty' were placed in them. This change shows that there was a lack of belief in the modernist means of conveying the idea of an art hall and that in the authoritarian Estonia of the 1930s there was a shift towards traditionalism. After the Arts Foundation building (1953) was completed, with an extension for the exhibition halls, the Art Hall turned out to be the lowest building on the north side of the square and so a new floor was added in 1963 (Kuusik). The façade and the exhibition halls were restored in 1995 as part of George Steinmann's process art entitled 'The Revival of Space' supported by the Swiss Ministry of Education.

The architectural highlight here is the glass stair tower in the classroom wing on the Kunderi street side. Although the spiral staircase might pose dangers for children and it is highly impractical to heat a glass tower in the Estonian climate, the architect was keen to introduce a popular motif from machine aesthetics and placed an emergency exit there. Initially the space between the windows was painted in a darker colour to create an illusion of strip windows. The assembly hall cum gymnasium has ornamented windows because of its dual function. The classroom wing was expanded in 1957-1959 (design by Wendach). Since the war the building has belonged to the Russian-language Secondary School Number 6.

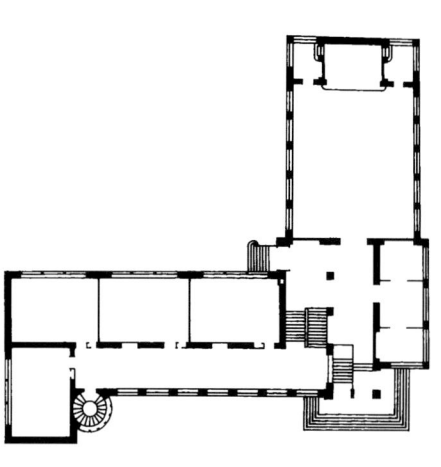

4
Fire Station
Raua tänav 2, Tallinn
1936 | 1939
Herbert Johanson

5
Villa
Rüütli tänav 1a, Pärnu
1931 | 1933
Olev Siinmaa

One of the best examples of Estonian limestone functionalism, the rusticated limestone here conveys the idea of fireproofness. It occupies an entire block. On the site, which is shaped like an isosceles triangle, the main building is placed on the hypotenuse, with the lower wings turning onto the catheti and the tower positioned at a right angle. This symmetrical solution reveals the architect's interest in elementary geometry. The garages open onto the service courtyard, and the fire engines have to pass through double gates to reach the street. As well as the firefighters' quarters, the building contained the Union rooms (a board room, a museum, a shop, classrooms, a gym) and flats on the top floors.

The tower (for drying hoses) should serve the function of the corner of the Politseiaed Park, but is narrowish as it is squeezed between blocks of flats.

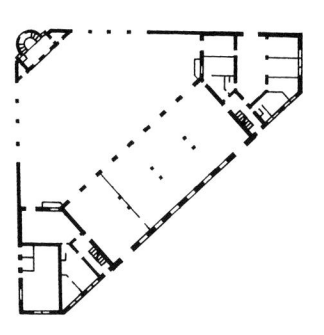

One of the houses that most reformed the traditional way of life in Estonia. The municipal architect built his own house on an uncomfortable triangular corner site which had long been neglected of 158m^2. The functions of the courtyard have been transferred to the basement, where a laundry with a rain-water storage tank, a workshop, a shed etc open into a central room with a well. On the ground floor, a study, a sitting room and a dining room form a freeflow space. The dining-room, which is located next to the fire wall, gets some additional light from an inner window. This house has the only built-in modernist kitchen with movable furniture. The built-in serving turntable inside the cupboard has been preserved.

The sitting room is higher, reminiscent of Raumplan. The rooms were furnished in eclectic style, as the architect had made the furniture himself earlier, the built-in bedroom furniture reflects the influence of de Stijl. On the roof terrace, which replaces the attic, there are hooks for clothes lines. The site-inspired triangular projections make the house restlessly expressionist. It was undergoing restoration in 1998.

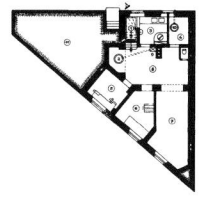

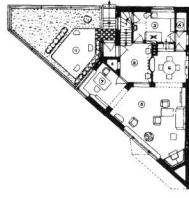

6
Uus Tare housing scheme
Maasika and Vaarika tänav, Tallinn
1931 | 1932
August Volberg, Erich Jacoby, Elmar Lohk
Edgar Kuusik & Franz de Vries

The only functionalist model housing scheme or Mustersiedlung in Estonia. The idea came from the architect Konstantin Bölau, then a civil servant in the Ministry of Transport. In 1931 the town council organised a competition for low-cost houses where mostly functionalist solutions won awards and in 1932 the co-operative 'Uus Tare' was established to make use of the competition designs which were later improved. The semi-detached houses at 3/5, 7/9, 11/13 Vaarika Street (Volberg) have flats spreading over two floors, an idea which was not successful in Estonia. There is no attic as the roof is flat, and there is a special room for drying laundry.

In the cubic semi-detached houses at 3, 5, 7, 9 Maasika Street (Kuusik and de Vries) two flats are located one above the other. The traditionalist shutters create an illusion of strip windows, which shows the architects' disbelief in the expressive means of modernist architecture. The one-storeyed houses at 4 and 6 Maasika Street (by Lohk) have a projecting utility wing which extends the back garden. On the other hand, 8 Maasika Street/6 Vaarika Street (Jacoby) utility rooms are placed at the back of the building.

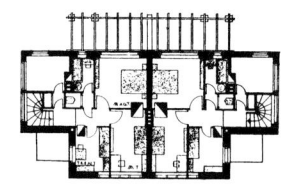

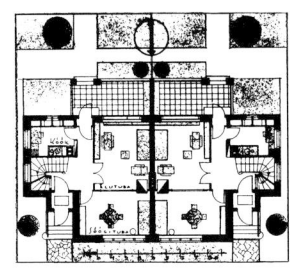

7
Villa
Lõuna tänav 2a, Pärnu
1933 | 1936
Olev Siinmaa & Anton Soans

The image of this elegant villa has repeatedly symbolised rapidly developing Estonia. It is located on the north side of the site. The walls separate the front gardens, the back gardens and the utility yard. In the interior, the motif of an inner window has been used repeatedly to provide light and a visual connection to the rooms at the heart of the house. The built-in furniture has been well preserved. The design of the building is characteristic of Siinmaa and it seems that Soans's contribution was his signature, which he lent to the municipal architect who could not take private commissions. It houses a children's welfare centre.

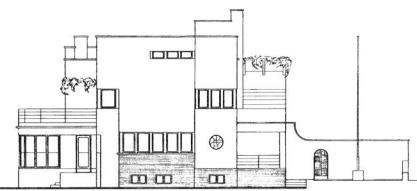

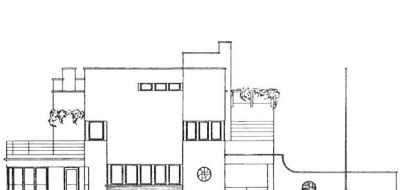

8
The Rannahotell
Ranna puiestee 5, Pärnu
1935 | 1937
Olev Siinmaa & Anton Soans

In 1934 an architectural competition was organized and the award-winning designs contributed to the final appearance of the hotel. It was built by the municipality on a state loan. The rooms look out onto the sea; the appearance from the land is determined by the narrow strip windows in the corridors. To allow people to walk around the house, the utility yard and the garages were concealed behind a wall. The rounded end of the wing on the entrance axis, which leads to the sea, is appropriately the metaphor of a steamer. The interiors did not contrast with traditionalism but modernised it as was common in the second half of the 1930s. In 1992-1995 the hotel was freely renovated.

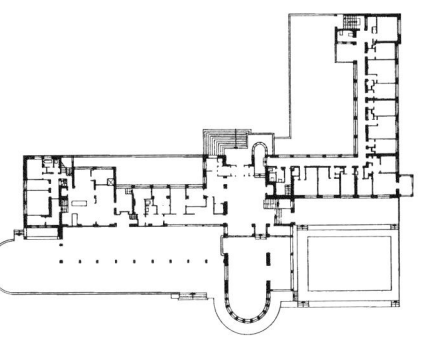

87

9
Rannahoone
Ranna puiestee 3, Pärnu
1938 | 1939
Olev Siinmaa
Tarmo Randvee & Heinrich Laul (engineers)

The building was erected to celebrate the 150th anniversary of the resort, although the transit of visitors to the 1940 Helsinki Olympic Games was also a consideration. It consisted of a one and a half-storeyed café of reinforced concrete and silicate and a wooden wing of cloakrooms with a viewing tower (now demolished). In front of the cafe there was a mushroom-shaped balcony of reinforced concrete, which instantly became the symbol of the city. One of the first public buildings where the texture left by the reinforced concrete moulds was exposed. In accordance with the atmosphere of the late 1930s there was a so-called Estonian room adjacent to the main hall. In the course of renovation in 1992-1996, it was partially restored.

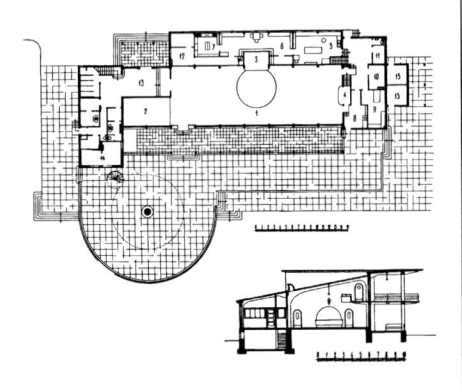

Selected Bibliography :
Bölau K, Kuusik E & Kotli A (eds)
Eesti arkitektide almanak
Tallinn 1934

Kompus H (ed)
20 aastat ehitamist Eestis 1918-1938
Tallinn 1939

Kesa E
'Pärnu suvituslinna uuemaist ehitustest'
Varamu lisa Eesti Arhitektuur
1940 no 2-3 pp 17-28

Hallas K, Kalm M & Kodres K
Tallinn im 20 Jahrhundert: Architecturführer
Tallinn 1991

Kalm M
'Functionalism of the 1930s: The Estonians in the Modern World' in:
Toisin. Funktionalismi ja neofunktionalismi Viron arkitehtuurissa
Helsinki 1992 pp 4-24

Künnapu L
Estonian Architecture: the Building of a Nation
Helsinki 1992

Hallas K
'Arhitektuurimälestiste kaitse ajaloost: 1920-1930 aastad' in:
Vana Tallinn VII (XI)
Tallinn 1997 pp 75-123

Kalm M
Eesti Funktsionalism: Reisijuht / Functionalism in Estonia: Guidebook
Tallinn 1998

Photographic Credits :
Eesti Arhitektuurimuuseum

Tallinna Linnamuuseum

Eesti Ajaloomuuseum

Tallinna Linnavalitsus

Finland

The Finnish DOCOMOMO working group was formed in 1989 when a few professionals within architectural preservation saw the advantages of an international network interested in modern architecture. The number of active members in the group has been 10–15 but the information spread as the seminars held and programmes carried out have reached a much wider audience. One of the organizational curiosities of the Finnish DOCOMOMO is that it is not a registered association but a group of people who become active when needed. This policy is mostly due to the general situation of building preservation and architectural research in Finland: there are several established organizations dealing with these issues, the most important being The National Board of Antiquities and The Museum of Finnish Architecture. Finnish legislation does not set an age limit to buildings worth protecting so quite naturally the built environment of the twentieth century is included in the programme of many already existing organizations. Hence there has been no need to create a new body with obligatory meetings and records. The Finnish DOCOMOMO is seen first and foremost as a visible and positive means of communication and directing attention to questions of modern architecture.

One of the most interesting tasks so far has been the first selection of notable examples of modernist architecture according to the guidelines of DOCOMOMO International. After several enjoyable and animated meetings, which were kept open for any body who wanted to contribute, the Finnish working group made some basic choices. The chronological starting point was agreed to be the period in the late 1920s when modernism was beginning to manifest itself both in architectural forms and in ideology. Before this decision, all earlier theoretical starting points for modernism as a cultural phenomenon were discussed. The closing date of the modernist period was an even more interesting topic, and in the end, a fairly wide perspective was adopted. Included in the selection are also buildings from the 1960s and even 1970s as far as they fit in the continuum of modernist architecture regardless of how they are presently labelled: 1960s Brutalism, Late-Modernism, etc.

Finnish modernist stock has been examined in relation to DOCOMOMO's two lists and their guide lines. For this book, the Finnish group did not bow to the mystique of numbers but chose eleven internationally notable buildings instead of twenty. The work on the larger, nationally important selection started with constructive anarchism and ended in mutual agreement on 70 buildings or groups of buildings. This selection includes individual masterpieces, but also representatives of particular building types, such as the military architecture of the 1930s or examples related to notable historical events, such as the Olympic Games of 1952. The selection is not the result of an architectural beauty contest, but a first attempt to present an interpretation on the essence of the meeting between modernist architecture and the historical development of Finland. The selection has already been useful because it has generated discussion outside the DOCOMOMO group and many well-motivated suggestions have been made regarding additions to the list.

Timo Tuomi

1
Paimio Sanatorium
Kalevantie 275, Preitilä, Paimio
1928 | 1933
Alvar Aalto

2
The Resurrection Chapel
Turun Uusi Hautausmaa, Turku
1934 | 1941
Erik Bryggman

This main work of Alvar Aalto's earlier period established functionalist architecture in Finnish building and was received as one of the main works of the new European architecture immediately upon its completion. At the time Paimio Sanatorium was a major example for the systematic construction of sanatoria. It exploits the full potential of concrete constructions, eg in the cantilevers of the sun-deck structure. Even today, although altered in many ways, its freshness and progressive approach make a strong impression.

The Resurrection Chapel was the major work of a long, creative career; it is Bryggman's masterwork. None of his later churches had the dignity or power of this place. The anonymous façade leads one to the surprise of the interior with its psychological space of heart-stopping beauty. The Chapel is a highly personal work which is at the same time universal. Here, he united the symbols of his life, the motifs of his culture and the spirit of his time to build a house for death and life. He created a monument to man's ultimate transition, beyond any cultural or chronological specifics. He achieved the timelessness of his motto, Sub Specie Aeternitatis. The complex and its surroundings are part of an ancient, classical, everlasting landscape.

While the building points forward, it is also a partial return to Bryggman's ideals of the 1920s. He incorporated the essence of many periods in the elements of his design. He synthesized those compelling cultural and architectural paradigms that were present in his experience: He grasped the iconic significance of The Crematorium Movement, he integrated Scandinavian Classicism of the 1920s, Italian vernacular landscape-confirming architecture, Finnish medieval stone architecture, and Functionalism. It has been described both as the quintessential monument in the 1940s Romantic Movement and as the culmination of the first 'heroic era' of Functionalism in Finland, and it is to be valued universally as one of the most refined sacral buildings.

3
The Book Tower, Åbo Akademi Library
Tuomiokirkonkatu 2–4, Turku
1934 | 1935
Erik Bryggman

4
Kotka Savings Bank
Kirkkokatu, Kotka
1934 | 1935
PE Blomstedt

5
Nakkila Church
Kirkkokatu 4, Nakkila
1935 | 1937
Erkki Huttunen

The book tower is skilfully situated in a milieu which is historically the most valuable in Finland and it is an essential part of the Åbo Akademi complex in the immediate vicinity of the Cathedral. It is an excellent example of Bryggman's early architecture. Harmonious relations make it a mature example of the new style. It is an unrestrained expression of the features of Bauhausian functionalism, and it is one of the masterpieces of the Finnish white functionalism. It is one of the vertically rising libraries in the world; the related type of library has been used in America, and Sweden in the extension to the University library of Lund. In its refinement this new kind of public building shows how well the styles of different centuries can go together.

Kotka Savings Bank is one of the purest functionalist business blocks realised in Finnish town centres. Blomstedt's modernist bank building was a bold exception in its time. The banks built in the capital at the same time represented a more conservative trend, accentuating the wealth and distinction of business companies. Kotka Savings Bank was a herald of 'the new time'. Several classicist bank buildings which Blomstedt designed in the 1920s were realised, but Kotka Savings Bank is his only purely functionalist business block, wherefore it is a crucial example of his work, even in curtailed form. Its pristine lightness forms a subtle contrast to the Town Hall on the other side of the market square.

The juxtaposition of the bright-coloured tile section of the facade with the very carefully proportioned structures refers to constructivist painting. The ascetic interior of the banking hall represented a completely new way of thinking. Instead of distinction, the architect wanted to highlight pertinence and hygiene.

White, undecorated functionalist buildings were considered to meet the demands of industry and business, of hygiene, internationality and the modern way of life, but church architecture was not generally seen as a field in which the new forms were applicable. Churches representing functionalism are rare in the whole world, and Nakkila church is one of Finland's few functionalist churches. In Nakkila Church Huttunen has achieved an extremely skilful application of modernist forms in a sacral building. The purism of its decorations suits to the tradition of Protestant church building as well as to modernist pursuit for a historicality and universality.

6
Villa Mairea
Noormarkku
1937 | 1939
Alvar Aalto

7
The Olympic Village
Koskelantie 38–56, Helsinki
1938 | 1948
Hilding Ekelund & Martti Välikangas

Aalto was given the opportunity to design an 'ideal' house, on a beautiful place for culturally adventurous clients with wealth. He drew on a deep understanding of vernacular building, classicism, and modernism, and on a love of natural materials, to create a house that is humane, rich and lyrical. The Villa Mairea forms the peak of Aalto's housing design. The living, work, and entertainment space for one family, as well as the space for an art collection, consists, in the entrance level, for the most part of open space divided into smaller parts by movable partitions. The bedrooms and the studio with their balconies are on the upper floor. The wooden parts of the building, which is otherwise rendered with white plaster, are of teak and pine.

The Olympic Village became a model for later suburbs in Finland. It was built on site and prefabricated units, the normal method in later development building, were not used. The repairs which have been made have not marred the harmonious overall appearance of the area. The buildings are distributed rather freely on the varied, wooded ground with rocky slopes between the buildings. The Olympic Village is not geometrically stiff and monotonous as some earlier examples were, and natural vegetation has been preserved. The walls, windows and small balconies with dark painted wood make a lively expression by very simple means. The apartments are small in area, most have two or three rooms and a kitchen.

They approach the idea of the 'existence minimum' which the functionalists believed would solve the problem of shortage of apartments. The smallness of the apartments was compensated by the surrounding nature and open views. The balconies and projecting windows were meant to convey the maximum amount of daylight to the interiors. The Village is not only nationally but also internationally valuable. It is the keywork in the development of Finnish housing architecture. It is one of the earliest functionalist suburbs with an open townplan in Finland. The Olympic Village is to be compared with the Weissenhofsiedlung and Siemensstadt in Germany, and Blidah and Hammarbyhöjden in the Nordic countries.

8
The Serpentine House Apartment Building
Mäkelänkatu 86, Helsinki
1949 | 1951
Yrjö Lindegren

The Serpentine House is a good example of the modest and human housing architecture of the reconstruction period. In the 1940s and 50s housing architecture continued functionalism's practical and rational aims but combined them with vernacular features. The Serpentine House has a strong sense of material and is interesting in its changing points of view and the sense of movement. It is one of the very first Arava apartment houses (state financed) in Helsinki and Finland; it represents functionalism's social attitude which in Finland became strong only after the Second World War. The Serpentine House consists of three alternately curving apartment buildings with from four to seven lamellae, and contains 190 apartments. The solution of the building is technically interesting. The amazing impression of variety is created using only two different types of building block and one stairwell type alternately. This idea foreshadows the prefabricated element technique, which had not been introduced in Finland at that time. The crosswise nature of frame construction allows a flexible use of the depth of the building body so that there is no dead space. The solution cleverly avoids the atmosphere of a barracks: the combinations of fan-like lamellae for diverse sheltered yard spaces. Each apartment has its own individual location and aspects as part of the whole. The building is an excellent example of how simply Lindegren was able to avoid monotonous repetition.

9
Säynätsalo Town Hall
Parviaisentie 9, Säynätsalo
1949 | 1952
Alvar Aalto

The Säynätsalo Town Hall combines the form of a sculpture with the style of an old Finnish brick building. It blends and merges with landscape in a way that is peculiar to Aalto, tangling itself in surrounding grounds like old Finnish castles. And yet the inner courtyard acts as a resting place like an Italian piazza. Many features are reminiscent of a castle; the sturdy tower, the solid walls, the flight of steps leading to the council chamber, the roof structure and the dim light entering from beneath the eaves. The mood is created through beautiful attention to detail. The modernity of the Town Hall is in its functionality, dividing the space into different working units by means of the well lit room-like corridor and the short distances between offices. The red brick complex is built around a central courtyard, thus providing an easy access to the communal administrative offices, the communal council chamber, and the library. The whole complex is dominated by the tower-like appearance of the communal council chamber rising above the remainder of the complex. Originally the complex included housing accommodation and, on the ground floor, business premises.

10
House of Culture
Sturenkatu 4, Helsinki
1955 | 1958
Alvar Aalto

11
Kudeneule Factory
Hopearanta, Lähteentie, Hanko
1953 | 1956
Viljo Revell

The House of Culture is an example of the strong, sculptural forms developed by Aalto since the 1930s. It is the first modern building in Finland especially designed for concert and congress functions. Voluntary work amounting to thousands of hours helped to construct the building which with reason can be considered the most remarkable architectural monument to Finnish working class. Aalto has divided the functions of the complex into two completely different kinds of buildings. The copper-plated office wing is strictly geometrical while the asymmetrical concert hall receives its exterior form by a close adherence to the free form of the interior space.

It is remarkable that the desired building form was achieved by specially designed and produced bricks, stressing Aalto's technical invention. The asymmetrical conchlike form of the concert hall is echoed in the streetside elevation: the free curve required the manufacture of a special kind of wedge-shaped brick. The convex hall is contrasted by the orthogonal office wing; together, they flank the sheltered front court. A long covered way ties the streetside elevation together. Here Aalto creates unity out of disparate elements. The auditorium is one of the best concert halls in Helsinki.

The factory is situated on a seashore area marked by natural beauty on the north-west part of the Hankoniemi headland. The building represents the clear-cut, powerful style typical of Revell's work. Kudeneule is one of the major works by Revell and one of the most significant examples of modern Finnish industrial architecture of the 1950s. Special attention was paid to the planning of the structure and materials. Prefabricated elements were used in a very innovative way. Elements making a good working environment have been taken into account in the design of the Kudeneule factory. According to the architect, one of the principal aims was to achieve 'humane working places for the employees'.

The logical, open and continuous space arrangement reflects the production process taking place in that space. The low height and the large window surfaces connect the building to the surrounding nature. The building combines a clear architectural concept of space, constructivist structures giving a light and elegant impression, rational thinking extending from the overall vision to detail finishing and even to the environment, and conscientious work. The Kudeneule factory is considered to have an internationally significant value in relation to architecture, construction technique and industrial history.

Selected Bibliography :
Finlands Arkitektförbund
Architecture in Finland
Helsinki 1932

Neuenschwander E & C
Alvar Aalto and Finnish Architecture
New York & London 1954

Banham R
'The One and the Few: the rise of modern architecture in Finland'
Architectural Review
London April 1957 pp 243-259

Fleig K (ed)
Alvar Aalto
Zurich 1963

Mosso L (ed)
L'opera di Alvar Aalto
Milan 1965

Ålander K
Viljo Revell: works and projects
Helsinki 1966

Gozak A
Alvar Aalto
Moscow 1976

Gozak A (ed)
Alvar Aalto: arkhitektura i gumanizm. Sbornik statei
Moscow 1978

Schildt G
Alvar Aalto: The Decisive Years
Helsinki & New York 1986

Niskanen A
Osuusliike rakentaa: The cooperative builds
Tammi 1987

Helander V & Rista S
Suomalainen rakennustaide: Modern architecture in Finland
Helsinki 1989

Nikula R (ed)
Erik Bryggman 1891-1955 Arkkitehti-arkitekt-architect
Helsinki 1991

Nikula R, Norri M-R & Paatero (eds)
The Art of Standards
Helsinki 1992

Quantrill M
Finnish Architecture and the Modernist Tradition
London 1995

Tuomi T, Paatero K & Raussske E (eds)
Hilding Ekelund 1893-1984 Arkkitehti-arkitekt-architect
Helsinki 1997

Wedebrunn O (ed)
Modern Movement Scandinavia
Copenhagen 1998

Photographic Credits :
P Ingervo
1
A Vahlström
2
Asko Salokorpi
3
Museum of Finnish Architecture
4
Foto Roos
5
Foto Pallasmaa
6
Ekelund-Välikangas
7
Heikki Havas
8, 9, 10, 11

France

The chosen buildings can be divided into three distinct phases:

Early modernism, represented by three projects either built or designed between 1900 and 1914.

Experimentation with modernism, with ten buildings dating between 1924 and 1939.

Development and diversification of the modernist doctrine, with seven buildings dating from 1945 to 1975.

These phases correspond to the relation between the contextual history and the social conditions of the commissions, and are also directly associated with the history of architectural forms and constructional innovations.

Phase 1 (1900-1914) corresponds first to a shift in social demand towards the problem of modern living accommodation in the city created by Haussmann and towards providing community facilities. Secondly it is a period where architects were looking for ways of using concrete in prestigious projects, which implied the realization of aesthetic formulae for construction which could escape from the accepted forms of stone masonry and decorative traditions. This is the reasoning behind the housing projects of Perret and Sauvage; Perret showed the possibilities of a framework in reinforced concrete in his apartment building at 25 bis rue Franklin, Paris, and Sauvage introduced new concepts of living space, with the stepped building and large individual balconies at 26 rue Vavin, Paris. In both cases, the architects used a ceramic cladding, which demonstrated the aesthetic resources of new products from the industrial arts. The Grange-Blanche Hospital in Lyon is an illustration of the new programmes launched by municipal initiatives, which were able to create modern architecture by commissioning an elite group of progressive architects, in a political context where the elected representatives of the moderate left were able to offer public sponsorship. Tony Garnier, who won the Prix de Rome in 1898 but was at odds with the architectural establishment which dominated France in 1900, is an example of this tendency. The City Council of Lyon, led by Augagneur and Herriot, both mayors belonging to the radical-socialist party, showed confidence in the achievements of modern architecture and in the ability of Garnier, a young progressive architect.

Phase 2 (1924-1939) is a period of maturity of modern architecture. As the art of the built form, enriched by a close relation with contemporary plastic arts, there are many examples: in domestic architecture, in luxury residences (Mallet-Stevens at Croix and Le Corbusier at Poissy), for artists' studio-houses (Lurçat in Paris), for low-cost housing (Le Corbusier at Pessac), or for public housing schemes (La Butte-Rouge at Chatenay-Malabry). Progressive architects conceived innovative architectural spaces designed for modern life (the studio type invented by Pingusson for a tourist hotel, adapted to the new way of life of the elite, sun-worshipping at Saint-Tropez) or the comfort and modern fitting-out of a school for children in a working-class suburb as a response to new educational policies (Lurçat and the Karl-Marx School at Villejuif).

Characteristic features of this period are the attempt to break with the criteria of formalism, in the interest of exploiting spatial possibilities, the exploitation of mechanization and the use of flexible spaces. Two buildings can be set apart from this context: the Maison de Verre, 1927-31, by Pierre Chareau (31 rue Saint Guillaume, Paris) with its refined techniques of interior design and the Maison du Peuple, 1937-39, by E Beaudouin, M Lods and Jean Prouvé (39-41 boulevard du Général Leclerc, Clichy). Both use steel construction, with great emphasis laid on the use of new materials: punched steel sheets, pressed sheet-metal, glass bricks, etc.

Phase 3 (1945-1975) corresponds to the period of post-war reconstruction and growth. In a generally dynamic climate of optimism, new techniques and an increased confidence in the industrialization of building projects led to schemes where modern architects were involved in every aspect of social life and planning: adapting the urban environment to increased private car usage (as in the reconstruction of Le Havre), experimenting in the forms of living accommodation (Marseille and Givors), health facilities (Saint-Lô), religious architecture (Ronchamp), architecture related to the tourist industry (Evian) and state initiative for cultural purposes (the Georges Pompidou Centre). Forms arising from the use of reinforced concrete, the organization of Le Havre and the artistic plastic forms of untreated concrete at Marseille (Le Corbusier) are a counterpoint to the varied appearances of the new art of steel construction (Prouvé, Rogers and Piano). The previous period was characterised by repetitive industrial forms, standardization, research into construction and the invention of building types. These are confronted by individual works, exceptional, unique and moving. Modern architecture has given birth to the architectural forms of modernity.

The French section of DOCOMOMO has selected buildings which illuminate the historic phases of collective creation of modern architecture, to highlight the coherent progress of artistic interpretation and the techniques of new programmes. We have not lost sight of the need to take into account the activity of leading architects who have been in the forefront of this movement, and this selection pays homage to these architects. The role played by foreign architects is noticeable, at a time when the dominant tradition led to giving public commissions in France to French architects.

Gérard Monnier
Fabienne Chevallier
Adriana Buhaj
English translation
Robin Lambert

1
25 bis, rue Franklin
F - 75016 Paris
1903
Perret & Frères

This building by Auguste Perret became a major reference for future constructions. He combined new constructional methods with a new spatial concept. The site was wide but not deep, so he had the idea of grouping the five main rooms on each floor on a front concave semicircle, to give natural light to all rooms while the service accommodations, lift and stairs were at the rear. The reinforced concrete frame made this layout possible. This determined the appearance of the front façade as well as allowing a flexible internal arrangement, punctuated by a series of simple columns and non-structural partition walls. On the main façade, the floor surfaces of the two lateral rooms were increased by projecting bays.

2
Edouard Herriot Hospital or Grange-Blanche
5 place d'Arsonval, F - 69003 Lyon
1909 | 1933
Tony Garnier

In 1909, a municipal commission agreed the construction of a hospital centre on the Grange-Blanche site, south-east of Lyon. Tony Garnier was chosen as project architect; he was aware of progress in hospital design and had visited similar projects in Germany and Denmark. Garnier decided on a layout in separate blocks, instead of one large building, a hospital form which was also current at the time. This layout has its origins in the hospital which he had already designed as part of his 'Cité Industrielle' in 1901-1904. The hospital was to have a capacity of one thousand three hundred beds. Garnier wanted to build a hospital 'with a human face', which led him to adopt the solution of a garden hospital.

3
Flats rue Vavin
26, rue Vavin F - 75006 Paris
1912
Henri Sauvage & Charles Sarrazin

26 rue Vavin is a major building in the history of Parisian architecture: it reflects an intelligent compromise between set-back housing construction and the urban building regulations of 1902. This new typology of a stepped façade was based on better natural light and ventilation on each floor while the white metro tiles conformed with the hygienic standards. The flats diminish in size as they step back and originally were to be completed internally with ateliers and sporting installations. This innovation was applied later to the block of flats at the rue Amiraux, with a swimming pool at its centre that creates a new concept of bourgeois housing. The construction is in reinforced concrete and the blue and white tiles on the façade still maintain elegance.

4
Villa Seurat
1, 3, 4, 5, 7a, 8, 9 & 11 villa Seurat
101 rue de la Tombe-Issoire, F - 75014 Paris
1924 | 1927
André Lurçat - Auguste & Gustave Perret

The street named Villa Seurat was laid out in 1926, and contained a group of villas for artists and private houses, built between 1924 and 1926. The street plan laid out at the time of Haussmann's transformations of Paris had left an unbuilt site here. The Villa Seurat reflected the contemporary migration of artists towards the outer limits of the city. Lurçat designed eight houses, including one for the writer Frank Townshend, one for the painters Edouard Georg and Marcel Gromaire and one for his brother, the painter Jean Lurçat. These houses were to be a standardized design. They conform to standards of comfort and hygiene established in European cities at the time. For the studios, Lurçat abandoned the traditional top-lighting.

5
Quartiers Modernes Frugès
Avenue H Frugès, F - 33600 Pessac
1924 | 1927
Le Corbusier & Pierre Jeanneret

In 1923 Le Corbusier had the opportunity, financed by the enlightened manufacturer Henri Frugès, to test his new urban and architectural theories in an area of workers' housing at Pessac, near Bordeaux. These theories had developed from the Domino prototype (1914) to the Cité Contemporaine (1922) and Pessac was the first extensive laboratory in practice. Through this modular design, Le Corbusier dreamed of a rationalized construction process. But the techniques were difficult and two-thirds of the Pessac project was abandoned. Fifty-one houses were erected in three types. They have reinforced concrete frames with non-load-bearing -walls and most have roof gardens.

6
Rue Mallet-Stevens
1-12 rue Mallet-Stevens, F - 75016 Paris
1926 | 1927
Robert Mallet-Stevens

Mallet-Stevens arranged the purchase of several plots of land at Auteuil for his future clients, so that the street could be laid out as a complete composition. The clients were friends of the architect, artists and collectors of modern art. Originally, the street had five private villas and a house for a guardian. Each villa is composed of a complex massing of volumes with horizontal windows and roof-terraces. The concrete structure is rendered. The villas are all built along the street axis. The specifications for the villas, which were built for artists as well as one for Mallet-Stevens himself, were quite individual. The living accommodation is accompanied by work-spaces: a studio for Mallet-Stevens' architectural practice and studios for artists.

7
Maison de Verre
31 rue Saint Guillaume, F - 75007 Paris
1928 | 1932
Pierre Chareau & Bernard Bijvoet

One of the major technical innovations of the Maison de Verre is the combination of new standardized industrial materials and the one-off pieces of high quality, provided by the craft studio. Inserted into the existing two-storey 18th century urban fabric, the three-storey steel structure was completed with reinforced concrete floors and closed with a membrane of translucent glass bricks on the courtyard and garden facade. This material had never been used so extensively before. It encloses a traditional internal domestic layout, but the most important innovation is the complete transformability of the interior volume by moving elements: pivoting screens and sliding components with every detail considered and refined.

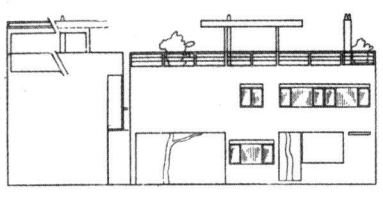

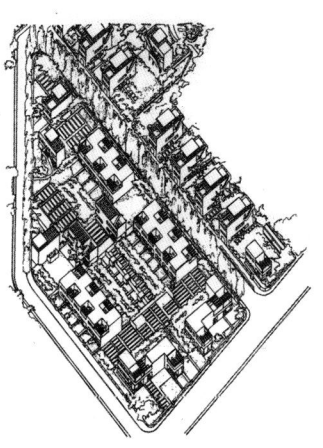

8
Villa Savoye 'Les heures claires'
82 Chemin de Villiers, F - 78300 Poissy
1929 | 1931
Le Corbusier & Pierre Jeanneret

The Villa Savoye was an architectural manifesto, the result of ten years aesthetic and spatial investigation. It expresses with great simplicity the doctrine of 'Five points for a modern architecture', declared in 1927, which acquired a central role in architectural thinking and teaching. Every element here: pilotis, the roof terrace, the long windows, the free plan and the free façade, all exploiting the potential of the reinforced concrete frame. The villa is on three levels. The first and second floors form one composition with a strip window repeated on all four façades. The concept of the 'promenade architecturale' is manifested through the central ramp which ascends in a continuous sweep from the ground floor to the roof and solarium at the apex of the composition.

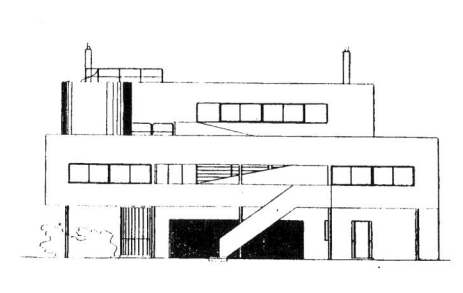

9
Maison du Peuple
39-41 Boulevardd du Général Leclerc
F - 92110 Clichy-la-Gavenne
1935 | 1939
Eugène Beaudoin, Marcel Lods
& Jean Prouvé

The Maison du Peuple is a pioneer multi-functional building where materials and techniques were combined for mechanical flexibility to meet the needs of a complex programme. The building was commissioned by a socialist mayor who wanted to improve the existing market facilities in Clichy and provide accommodation for popular cultural and leisure activities in a rectangular site of 2,000m². The Maison du Peuple, a two storey steel construction, was designed with such versatility that it could be adapted in 45 minutes for use either as a covered market, a meeting hall for 1500 to 2000 people or a 700-seat cinema. Permutations were generated by a system of moveable floors and sliding partitions.

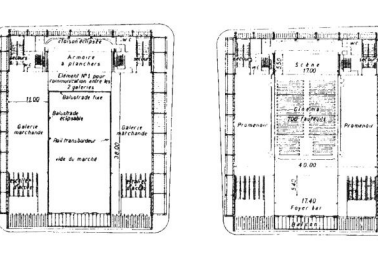

10
La Butte Rouge
Avenue de la Division Leclerc (south part)
F - 92290 Châtenay-Malabry
1931 | 1938
J Bassompierre, P de Rutté & P Sirvin

The Butte Rouge housing scheme was the prototype for a new concept of public construction. For the first time in large-scale social housing, some principles of the modern movement were applied to the aesthetic approach, while early industrial techniques were also used. The first phase of building was from 1931 to 1935, and completed 474 housing units. During the second phase, 1935-38, 1100 apartments were built in a 56-hectare park which had been purchased by the office for cheap housing (HLM). A new kind of housing layout avoided direct views between buildings, and construction combined reinforced concrete with load-bearing walls. Pilotis lifted the main floor above the ground allowing free passage between the gardens.

11
Hotel Nord-Sud
Avenue Saint-François, F - 20260 Calvi
Corsica
1929
André Lurçat

Built on the rocks, facing Calvi citadel, this small two-storey hotel of rectangular plan, a typical building of the cubist period, was one of the first designed for international tourism. The building looks like a ship which has run aground with a rounded superstructure, tubular guard-rails and a mast with a flag. The white rendering and the terraces echo Mediterranean island architecture. In fact, the immaculate aspect of the building is not a reflection of constructional technique: Lurçat, conscious of the technical limits of construction on the island, designed this building, not in reinforced concrete but in masonry load-bearing walls on which white render was used.

12
Ensemble touristique Latitude 43
Avenue du Général Leclerc
F - 83990 Saint-Tropez
1931 | 1932
Georges-Henri Pingusson

The original specifications included a 100 room hotel, restaurant, sports complex (seawater swimming-pool, tennis courts), casino, commercial premises, garages and related buildings. The main building was a slab block, whose length was relieved by an angle. Its outline was varied by superstructures inspired by machine forms (such as a ventilation shaft in the shape of a large inverted cone). The internal layout has closed access galleries to the north, so that each room has an uninterrupted sea view to the north and balcony to the south. Abandoned by its wealthy clientele during the years of economic crisis, the building has since been converted into flats in multiple ownership.

13
Karl-Marx school complex
Avenue Karl Marx, F - 94800 Villejuif
1930 | 1933
André Lurçat

The Karl-Marx school complex was the result of a particular social, political and cultural context. In the inter-war years, social needs took on a new importance in public commissions. For the first time in France, the language of modern architecture, formerly restricted to private projects, was applied to a school programme. The official authorities were aware of innovations in health care, education and architecture and the result was a pioneer school, which became a model for many European countries. A new technique for casting concrete was applied for slabs and walls which achieved a high standard of construction. The building is of two storeys on a rectangular plan. In 1950 the school was extended following André Lurçat's ideas.

14
Villa Cavrois
1 rue JF Kennedy, F - 59820 Croix
1930 | 1932
Robert Mallet-Stevens

In 1930 the industrialist Jean Cavrois commissioned Mallet-Stevens to build a villa; the architect was entrusted with every aspect of the design, including the interiors and the furniture. Prouvé worked with Mallet-Stevens on the design of ironwork details for the interior. In the grounds are a gardener's house, a garage, a swimming-pool set parallel to the house and a small lake. The villa is 90 metres long and 15 metres wide, built for a family of nine. The design concept is a pyramidal construction, formed of isosceles triangles set within a large triangle of the same form. There is a differentiation of volumes but the overall composition is symmetrical. The framework is in reinforced concrete clad in yellow brick.

15
Unité d'Habitation de Marseille
280 boulevard Michelet, F - 13008 Marseille
1945 | 1952
Le Corbusier

Raoul Dautry, Minister of Reconstruction and Planning at the time, commissioned Le Corbusier to build the famous Unité d'Habitation in Marseille in 1945. The programme was a special prototype: Le Corbusier was eager to put into practice his vision of a total planning of the built environment for modern man. The building includes individual apartments, communal services and community clubs for the occupants, shops, office premises, a hotel, a restaurant, a crèche and a private gymnasium on the roof. The Unité d'Habitation is a monumental construction – 137 metres long, 24 metres wide, 56 metres high – built at an oblique angle in relation to the urban network.

16
The France-United States Memorial Hospital
5 route de Villedieu, F - 50000 Saint-Lô
1946 | 1956
Paul Nelson, R Gilbert, Ch Sébilotte,
M Mercier (chief architect for reconstruction)

The building of a new hospital was part of the reconstruction of Saint-Lô. Ninety-five per cent of this small town was destroyed by Allied bombing during the Normandy landings in June 1944. The building was partly financed by voluntary American contributions, with funds raised by former American soldiers. Paul Nelson was an American architect who had studied in France with Perret during the 1920s; afterwards he spent most of his career studying modern hospital construction. Nelson was commissioned to build the 400-bed hospital. The hospital is an eight-storey double block. Nelson used a framework of reinforced concrete with washed concrete cladding. On the south elevations the framework is exposed, painted in primary colours.

17
Reconstruction of Le Havre (city centre)
F - 7600 Le Havre
1945 | 1963
Auguste Perret (chief architect) & members of his architectural practice

After the bombardment of the town centre and several suburban areas by the Allies (5/6 September 1944), Raoul Dautry, Minister of Reconstruction and Planning, commissioned Auguste Perret to direct the reconstruction of Le Havre in September 1945. This Ministry controlled the project, which was financed by the state as part of the reparations scheme for war-damaged areas. Le Havre was the most important example of state intervention in the reconstruction of urban areas in France. The regrouping of land and land-titles by interested parties made the scheme possible. Building work went on for eighteen years. Le Havre was the biggest town-planning scheme conceived and directed by Perret.

18
Chapel 'Notre-Dame-du-Haut'
F - 70250 Ronchamp
1950 | 1955
Le Corbusier

The Chapel at Ronchamp stands on the top of a hill on the foundations of a neo-Gothic church destroyed in the Second World War. It is a singular work in Le Corbusier's œuvre and a site-specific response to the landscape. The temple rises up inviting the pilgrim to a 'promenade architecturale'. The processional walk through the site gives a sequence of axial perspectives, suggesting symbols which are open to interpretation. The chapel was intended to receive thousands of people during religious processions to the open air altar or to hold inside a congregation of two hundred people. From the technical point of view, Ronchamp gave Le Corbusier the opportunity to make the most of the plastic character of reinforced concrete.

19
New Pump Room
Place de la Libération F - 74500 Evian
1957
Maurice Novarina, Jean Prouvé & Serge Ketoff

Novarina commissioned Prouvé to design a new pump room, built in 1957 for patients taking the waters at Evian. Prouvé himself invented a new constructional technique using raking shores. On a rectangular plan, the building is divided into three parts: the pump room, which is distinct from a rest area and a small music room, separated by two screen walls decorated by Raoul Ubac and André Beaudin. A newspaper kiosk and sanitary facilities are in the basement. The structure comprises 12 raking shores in pressed steel, linked by a tubular beam, articulated at ground level to avoid problems of rigidity. On the lower façade, the strainers are round steel bars, attached at the sides: these are set into the structural shapers of the glazing.

20
The Georges Pompidou National Centre for Art and Culture (Centre Beaubourg)
19 rue Beaubourg F - 75004 PARIS
1970 | 1977
Renzo Piano, Richard Rogers & Gianfranco Francini

Georges Pompidou, then President of the Republic, initiated this project for a National Centre for Art and Culture. In 1969, he wrote to Edouard Michelet, Minister of State for Cultural Affairs: 'The Centre must provide not only a great museum of painting and sculpture, but also have special provisions for music, recordings and, perhaps, cinema and theatre research facilities.' In fact, the multi-disciplinary nature of the concept gave rise to an unprecedented cultural programme which was essentially experimental. It combined museum space for modern art, which Paris lacked at the time, and spaces designed for broadcasting, for live performances and for cinema, the 'seventh art'. The Centre was also conceived as a place which would itself generate cultural expression. The building appears like a giant Meccano creation rising from a gently sloping forecourt. The architects' intention was to bring out the relationship between 'master-space' and 'servant-space' in a way which was both playful and didactic. So the ducts and piping for servicing fluids have their own colour scheme. The building is laid out in five levels, each with a free plan, fifty metres long. In recent years, the Centre has been undergoing alteration work, which will improve its functioning and extend the gallery-space of the National Museum of Modern Art.

Selected Bibliography :
Giedion S
Bauen in Frankreich. Bauen in Eisen. Bauen in Eisenbeton
Leipzig 1928
English translation as:
Building in France. Building in iron. Building in ferroconcrete
Santa Monica 1995

Boesiger W (ed)
Le Corbusier: Oeuvre complète
Volumes 1-7 Zurich 1929- & London 1966-

Zahn L
Moderne Pariser Bauten
Berlin c1930

Ginsburger R
Junge französische Architektur
Geneva 1930

Morancé A (publ)
L'Architecture Vivante en France
Paris various nd (c1930-35)

Piccinato G
L'architettura contemporanea in Francia
Bologna 1965

Besset M
New French Architecture
London 1967; in German: Stuttgart 1967

Kopp A, Boucher F & Pauly D
L'Architecture de la reconstruction en France 1945-1953
Paris 1982

Emery M & Goulot P
Guide Architecture en France depuis 1945
Paris 1983

Julien R
Histoire de l'Architecture Moderne en France
Paris 1984

Monnier G
L'Architecture en France: une histoire critique 1918-1950. Architecture, culture, modernité
Paris 1990

Cohen J-L
André Lurçat 1894-1970: Autocritique d'un Moderne
Liège 1995

Photographic Credits :
Gérard Monnier, Paris
Book Art, London
Contemporary Architecture, Moscow

Germany

1
Einstein Tower (Institute of Astrophysics)
Telegrafenberg, Potsdam
1920 | 1921
Erich Mendelsohn

Since the formation of the Deutscher Werkbund in 1907 German architects played an ever increasing role in the development of Modern Movement architecture worldwide. The political situation of that time, and in particular during the 1920s and early 1930s, caused Germany to become a point of attraction for many artists and designers who fled for example, from Soviet Russia. In turn, when German government attitudes became hostile to modernism there was a large-scale emigration outwards. Thus the influence of the ideas and design work which had developed through so many public commissions in the 1920s became spread literally across the globe, influencing every scale of design work from furniture to architecture and city planning. Thus May and Meyer left Frankfurt and Dessau for Moscow and Siberia, taking with them teams of colleagues. Gropius went to America via England and Mendelsohn made the same journey via London and Jerusalem.

In making this selection of works we have tried to show social and aesthetic aspects of these designers' work in their own country, before they took these ideas abroad. At the same time, we have featured two of the most important sites of interchange on German soil between our architects and their foreign colleagues: the Bauhaus in Dessau, and the Weissenhofsiedlung in Stuttgart. Finally we have chosen works which represent both functionalist and expressionist trends within German Modern Movement architecture, since they are complementary and both of central importance to the movement as a whole.

DOCOMOMO Germany

The commission for this small laboratory, a canonical work of the expressionist trend in modernism, came through a contact between Mendelsohn and Einstein's assistant. The building was destined to assist in verification of Einstein's Theory of Relativity. The visible part of the tower is not the whole structure: under ground are certain spaces with controlled temperature and humidity for aspects of the laboratory's work. Although designed to be entirely of concrete, certain parts had to be made of brick due to practical problems in the casting of sculptural forms. Many interior fittings by Mendelsohn still survive, and the whole building underwent preservation in the late 1970s.

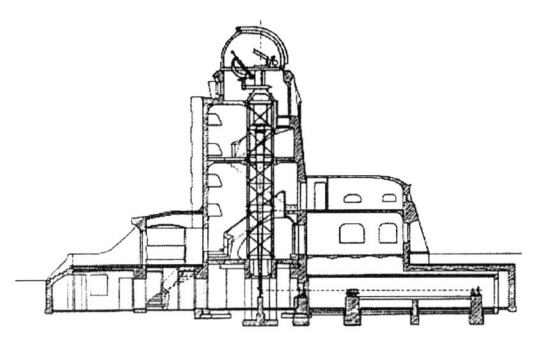

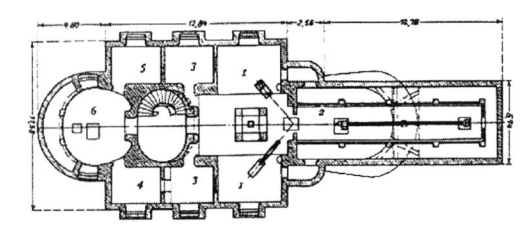

106

2
Hermann-Beims housing estate
Grosse Diesdorfer Strasse, Magdeburg
1925 | 1928
Conrad Rühl & Gerhard Gauger

3
Taut House
Wiesenstrasse 13
Dahlewitz
1926 | 1927
Bruno Taut

With 2100 apartments this was one of the largest housing developments built in Germany in the 1920s. It formed an element within the master plan which Bruno Taut had done, as Magdeburg's director of building and urban planning, for housing within the city. Average size of the apartments was only 65m², all of them arranged on staircases with two apartments per floor. The three-storey buildings are articulated by some perpendicular elements and blocks that form long, well protected courtyards. The ground floors contain certain communal facilities including shops. There is also a kindergarten. Streets are clearly separated into pedestrian access streets and those for vehicular traffic.

This remarkable house by the architect for himself stands comparison with the Melnikov House in Moscow of similar date for its originality as a one-family home where the architect was entirely free to invent solutions for himself. The curved entrance wall which protects the living accommodation from the street is painted black to absorb maximum heat all day from the east and south east. The short wing of service accommodation is to the north. The 'tip' of the house which penetrates westward into the garden has a sun-catching balcony which is actually an outdoor room at first floor and all bedrooms have access to this space. Ingenious circulation on the entrance side gives access from all rooms to the staircase hall. As in Melnikov's house, interiors are coloured, though here in bright tones, all of which were restored in the restoration done between 1992 and 1994.

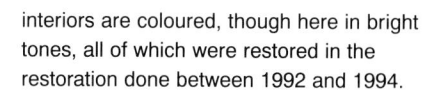

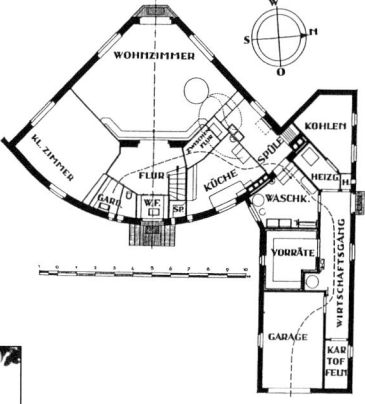

4
The Bauhaus building
Bauhausstrasse 1, Dessau
1925 | 1926
Walter Gropius

The Bauhaus building is an outstanding example of Gropius's work. As an integral part of the historic development of technology-oriented and constructive industrial and glass architecture, the building represents one of the peaks of 'classic modernism'. The glass curtain-wall of the workshop wing, in particular, is taken to its logical conclusion here as never before. The derivation of formal, aesthetic and functional choices from the artistic, educational and social objectives of the then 'Hochschule für Gestaltung' (Design School) lead to the uniquely direct representation of a programme of content in structural form.

In 1932 the Nazis forced the closure of the Bauhaus in Dessau as being a paradigmatic expression of a democratically and humanistically oriented modernity. Deprived of its original purpose, the Bauhaus building was subject to widely varying uses, alterations, superimpositions and damage in the decades that followed. Rough and ready repairs were carried out after the building was almost destroyed by bombing at the end of the second world war. Stylistic and structural alterations followed in the mid-1960s. It was not until 1976 that a partial renovation and reconstruction succeeded to a greater extent in restoring the original appearance. At present, the building is again undergoing complete refurbishment with the aim of securing the original fabric, whilst allowing for the requirements of its use today by the Bauhaus Foundation and Anhalt University. The qualitative standard for this must be the outstanding cultural importance of the building which in 1996, together with the Bauhaus masters' houses in Dessau and the Bauhaus buildings in Weimar, was designated by UNESCO as a World Heritage Site.

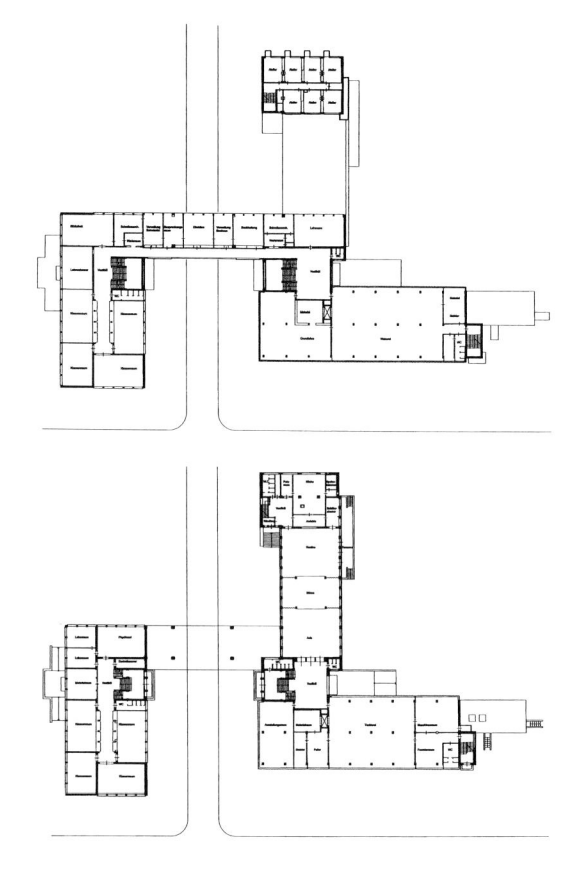

5
Bauhaus masters' houses
Burgkünauer Allee & Ebert-Allee, Dessau
1925 | 1926
Walter Gropius

The masters' houses display what Hans Maria Wingler called 'the consistently supremely high standards of the Dessau complex', which Gropius never quite repeated elsewhere.

The ensemble comprises one single-family house to be occupied by the Bauhaus Director and three semi-detached pairs of houses destined initially for Laszlo Moholy-Nagy & Lyonel Feininger, Georg Muche & Oskar Schlemmer, Paul Klee & Wassily Kandinsky. They were erected at the same time as the Bauhaus building itself, and are aesthetically a fitting extension of their neighbour. The accommodation was conceived on a grand scale, giving the staff comfortable living space and a studio under one roof. Their neighbourliness made possible a level of social and aesthetic interchange which was the downfall of the arrangement between Klee and Kandinsky.

Constructional techniques were progressive and inside were built-in furniture and special light fittings to new designs from the Bauhaus workshops. Like the Bauhaus building itself these houses suffered damage, misuse and structural alterations. Moholy Nagy's house was destroyed by bombing. With the exception of the single-family house the others are owned by the City of Dessau and have been undergoing reconstruction and restoration since the beginning of the 1990s. Completion and opening to the public is expected in 2000.

6
Römerstadt housing estate
Frankfurt
1927 | 1928
Ernst May & team

Ernst May was head of Frankfurt's municipal construction department from 1925 to 1930, and master-planner for the whole series of developments which constituted Das neue Frankfurt: The New Frankfurt, and were documented in the famous journal of that name. Römerstadt was in fact a complete satellite town with a shopping centre and its own school. Its 1220 dwellings stretched along a hill above the Nidda valley. Some were terraced houses with gardens, others were apartment blocks, all arranged along the contours of the hill.

7
Törten housing estate
Dessau
1926 | 1928
Walter Gropius, Georg Muche & Richard Paulick

This estate just outside Dessau was conceived as a demonstration of rationalized construction methods. Houses were located along the line of movement of the crane which delivered and lifted components as in an assembly line. The structures consist of cross-walls with lightweight façades created on site out of blocks. The first batch gave some jointing problems and methods were then modified. Gropius also designed a local shopping building for the complex, but none of this is in good condition today. Even more altered and decayed is the experimental steel house which Muche and Paulick built in 1926-27.

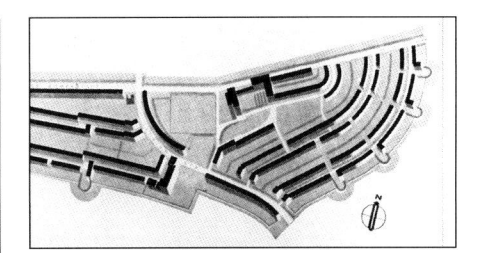

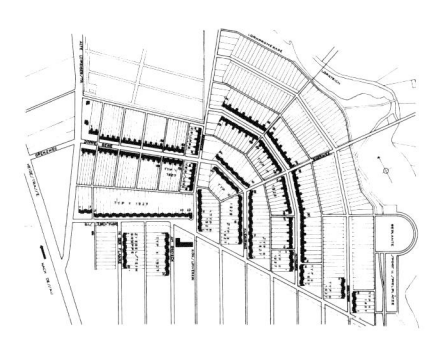

8
Weissenhofsiedlung
Stuttgart
1927
Ludwig Mies van der Rohe et al

In 1927 the Deutscher Werkbund organized an exhibition called Die Wohnung, The Dwelling, whose main part was the group of show houses known as the Weissenhofsiedlung built on a hill overlooking the city of Stuttgart. The city owned the site and financed the project. The Werkbund appointed Mies van der Rohe as aesthetic director and 'dwellings for modern metropolitan man' were executed here by van der Rohe along with Le Corbusier & Pierre Jeanneret (France), JJP Oud & Mart Stam (Netherlands), Josef Frank (Austria), Victor Bourgeois (Belgium), and from Germany itself, Walter Gropius, Ludwig Hilberseimer, Peter Behrens, Hans Poelzig, Max and Bruno Taut, Adolf Rading, Hans Scharoun, Adolf Schneck & Richard Döcker.

Of the 21 original buildings, a mix of 11 houses and apartment blocks survive. The whole Weissenhof settlement was sold in 1938 to the state for demolition and it was bombed by the Allies in 1944. After the war some more houses were demolished. Nevertheless the Weissenhof settlement is one of the most important legacies of the Modern Movement whose influence permeated housing design all over the world. As Leonardo Benevelo has written 'This was a seminal expression of modernism: a coherent plan organization and employment of pristine architectural forms by selected European architects, being demonstrated here for the first time.'

Photograph : Scharoun house

9
Volksschule (Elementary school)
Celle
1927 | 1928
Otto Haesler

Haesler's sketch for the school called 'A healthy mind must live in a healthy body' was selected for construction because it gave the possibility to combine a multi-purpose hall with a house for the school's director. The building has three floors and a rectangular ground plan. It is structured by the horizontal window intervals and the vertically organised windows of the stairwells. The main entrance leads to the two wings with the 18 class rooms and side rooms, which can be reached from four stairwells. This well organised circulation system within the school is further enhanced by the good lighting throughout the building, in particular from the windows to the stairwells and the high-level windows in the inner walls of the class rooms.

The two class-room wings are arranged around a hall, which is the centre of the building. A glass-block roof lets light into what has been described as the 'Baroque inner sanctum' which serves not only as a sports hall but also for film shows. With the projection room used as a stage it also adapts for theatrical performances and concerts. The colour schemes for the external façades and the interiors were done by Karl Völker.

The building was somewhat altered in the 1970s when a wooden framework was installed in the central hall. The whole building is in need of complete renovation.

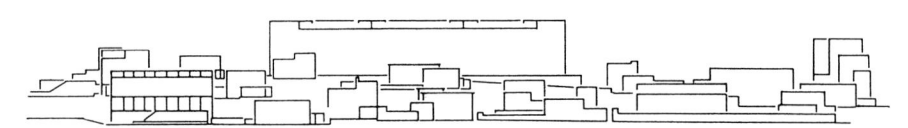

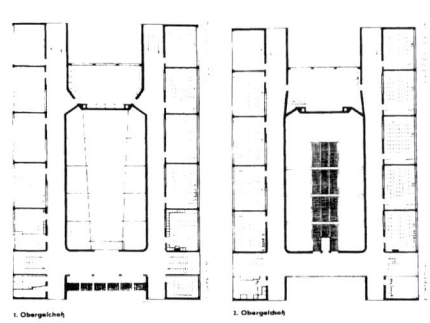

10
Dammerstock housing estate
Karlsruhe,
1928 | 1929
Walter Gropius, Otto Haesler & others

For the first time in modern architecture the terms of the competition for the Dammerstock housing scheme dictated an east-west orientation of the dwellings. The result of the limited competition was that Walter Gropius and Otto Haesler, as winners of the first and second prizes, received the commission to draw up the final scheme. Gropius as aesthetic leader of the project determined the aesthetic scheme for the other architects involved. Two east-west streets are located between the rows, so that one can enter the houses from two sides. The rows range from one to four storeys in height with the highest located on the main road.

The 228 dwellings in 23 blocks were variously designed by Gropius and Haesler, Wilhelm Riphahn and Caspar Maris Grod, Franz Roeckle, Alfred Fischer with Walter Merz, Hans-Detlev Rösiger, Fritz Rössler and Wilhelm Lochstampfer. This model housing scheme was not built by novel or economic construction methods. Only Haesler used steel girder construction: most of the architects built entirely traditionally with brick.

11
Laubenganghäuser
(Gallery-access housing)
Dessau-Torten
1929 | 1930
Hannes Meyer

Soon after the Bauhaus' architecture department was established in 1927 it got a commission from the Savings and Building Society of Dessau which resulted in 1929-30 in construction of 5 gallery-access blocks of very small apartments. Designed under the supervision of Meyer they houses manifested the decline of aesthetic concerns in favour of social criteria which was typical of the architecture that emerged under him as second director of the Bauhaus. Work has been under way since 1996 to restore one model dwelling, but generally furnishing and equipment have been changed. War damage did not affect the brick façade walls and these remain essentially original.

12
Blumenlägerfeld housing estate
Celle
1931 | 1932
Otto Haesler

These dwellings for those 'living on a wage' were built by the Städtische House-building Society of Celle. Two 220m long, 2-storey blocks are steel framed and oriented north-south with tenants' gardens between them. To the south are 2-storey detached family houses with balconies, designed for people with tuberculosis. The paired houses vary from 2- to 6-beds and in area from 34.5 to 51.8m^2. In Haesler's system, living room size depended on the number of bed spaces. The dwellings themselves only have simple washing facilities as a central wash- & boiler house is located at the end of row 1. This scheme needs urgent renovation but present plans propose extremely destructive changes.

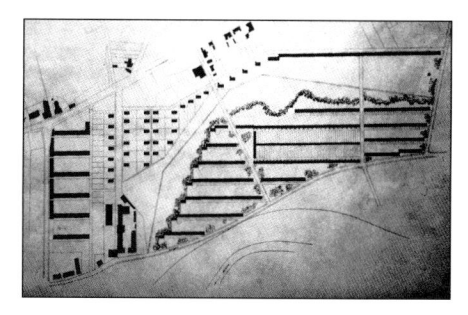

13
Schmincke House
Kirschallee 1b, Löbau
1932 | 1933
Hans Scharoun

This house represents a freeing up of the rigorous modernism that dominated German architectural politics in the twenties. As the house of an industrialist, located close to his factory, it represents an entirely different application of the new architecture to create superb living conditions amongst nature for the affluent. Locked into the ground at one end and ship-like in its glazed projection into the landscape at the other, its double-height spaces and fluid planning embrace such amenities as a studio and winter garden. Since the second world war it has been used by a series of organizations and original aspects like the interior colour scheme have been lost.

Selected Bibliography :
Behne A
Der Moderne Zweckbau
Munich 1926 (new edition Berlin 1965)
English translation as:
The Modern Functional Building
Santa Monica 1996

Deutsche Werkbund
Bau und Wohnung: die Bauten der Weissenhofsiedlung in Stuttgart errichtet 1927
Stuttgart 1927

Fries H de
Junge Baukunst in Deutschland
Berlin 1927

Müller-Wulckow W
Bauten der arbeit und des Verkers
Bauten der Gemeinschaft
Wohnbauten und Seidlungen
3 volumes Königstein-im-Taunus 1929

Mendelsohn E
Erich Mendelsohn: Das Gesamtschaffen des Architekten
Berlin 1930; 1987
English translation as:
Erich Mendelsohn: Complete Works of the Architect
London & New York 1992

Morancé A (publ)
L'Architecture Vivante en Allemagne
4 vols Paris nd (c1930-1935)

Adler L
Neuzeitliche Mietshäuser und Siedlungen
Berlin 1931

Gropius W
The New Architecture and the Bauhaus
London 1935 New York 1936
German edition:
Die neue Architektur und das Bauhaus
Mainz & Berlin 1965

Conrads U
Modern Architecture in Germany
London 1962

Wingler HM
Das Bauhaus
Cologne 1962
English translation as:
The Bauhaus
Cambridge (Mass) & London 1969

Hilberseimer L
Berliner Architektur der 20er Jahre
Mainz & Berlin 1967

Mohr C & Müller M
Funktionalität und Moderne. Das neue Frankfurt und seine Bauten 1925-1933
Frankfurt am Main 1984

Schreiber M
Deutsche Architektur nach 1945: vierzig Jahre Moderne in der Bundesrepublik
Stuttgart 1986

Photographic Credits :
Wolfgang Reuss
1
Roderick Coyne
4, 5, 11
Bauhaus-Archiv, Berlin
7
Karin Kirsch
8
Others courtesy of
DOCOMOMO Germany

Acknowledgements :
Winfried Brenne
Berthold Burkhardt
Christine Hoh
M Kentgens-Craig
Karin Kirsch
Simone Oelker
Andreas Schwarting

Greece

Before any modern building was to rise in Greece, the news of the Modern Movement's existence had been already disseminated by foreign and local technical periodicals, by newspapers and in courses taught at the School of Architecture in Athens.

Hence young graduates of architecture were among its most fervent adherents. They also tried to educate the general public both by publishing articles and by designing and building in the new idiom. Certain factors worked in their favour. One was the 4th CIAM meeting held in Marseille and Athens in 1933, which indirectly demonstrated the links of Greek modernism to the international movement. For this occasion, a local committee worked hard to ensure that the congress would receive sufficient publicity in the local press and to have foreign participants visit a number of locally designed modern buildings.

A pamphlet presenting alternative house types for a then nascent Athens suburb (Filothei, 1931) showed mixed modernist and traditionalist specimens, yet the accompanying text was clearly pro-modern. 'Technika Chronika', the official publication for the Greek Technical Chamber, offered its readers an article by Alberto Sartoris on the new spirit in architecture in 1932; one of its three illustrations was a villa by a young Greek architect, Stamos Papadakis. By 1933, references to modern architecture had obviously increased: four articles appeared in two consecutive issues of 'Technika Chronika'; only one of them was a guarded critique of the movement by Dimitris Pikionis. Included also was a portfolio of ten modern buildings, all apparently built within a four year span (1929-33). Meanwhile Greek modern architecture was being included in Alberto Sartoris' 'Gli Elementi dell'Architettura Funzionale' (Milan l932), in Raymond McGrath's 'Twentieth century houses' (London 1934) and in A. Pica's 'Nuova Architettura del Mondo' (Milan 1938); it was also mentioned in articles in such European magazines as 'Die Form' (11/1932), 'Cahiers d'Art' (4/1934) and 'Der Baumeister' (2/1936).

Partially due to a century-long neoclassical background in Greek architecture, the reception of the Modern Movement was not unanimously favourable. High officials publicly complained of 'the disappearance of Greek character' in new buildings while popular magazines heatedly debated the merits and drawbacks of new forms. Some local architects also openly supported an architecture which combined 'modernism with Greek colour'.

True enough, articles in 1936-37 show the erosion of the initial enthusiasm and an increasing penetration of Fascist propaganda in Greece, by translating German articles of relevant content. In a subtler manner, two exhibitions in Athens (1938-39) showed measured drawings of neoclassical architecture and the work of Ernst Ziller, an eminent 19th century neoclassical architect. When 'L'architecture d'Aujourd'hui' published an illustrated article on the architectural movement in Greece (10/1938), both modern and neo-vernacular examples were equally represented. Finally, Panagiotis Michelis, the foremost theorist on aesthetics, in his book 'Architecture as Art' (1940) held a guarded position on the issue of the Modern Movement, because it did not comply with established laws of composition. By 1939, the full swing of the fascist regime in Greece (established in 1936) was being demonstrated in public buildings – with the marked exception of schools. Worse still, the issue of 'Greekness', raised at the competition for a Concert Hall in Athens (1940), proved the perseverance of a deeply conservative ideology whose goal was the identification with Ancient Greece.

The architecture of the 1930s, often neglected or disfigured, unfortunately received insufficient attention from the Greek state in the past; the first signs of official recognition appeared in 1998.

Panos Exarchopoulos
Maro Kardamitsi-Adami
Dimitri Phillippides

Houses In the 1930s the centres of Athens and Thessaloniki saw a most impressive new development of flats. Exceptional examples of undiluted modernism in Athens were designed by Kyriakoulis Panagiotakos (1902-82), renowned for his 'Blue' apartment house (painted in dark blue and sienna) on Exarcheia square (Athens, 1932-33); by Thucydides Valentis (1908-82) with Polyvios Michaelides on Zaimi Stournara Street (Athens, 1933-34), a landmark of austere modernity. Other major contributors to the same trend in Athens were Kyprianos Biris (20 Bouboulinas Street, 1930-32), Renos Koutsouris (26 Loukianou Street, 1933), Vassileios Douras (30 Stavropoulou Street, 1935-36), Prokopis Vasileiadis (7 P Ioakeim - Irodotou Street, 1937) and Nikolaos Nikolaidis (54 Patission - Metsovou Street). A sideline of these blocks were housing complexes built by the state for refugees, some of them in the

1
Apartment House
1 Zaimi-Stournara Street
Athens
1933 | 1934
Thucydides Valentis & Polyvios Michaelides

2
'Blue' Apartment House
80 Themistokleous-Arachovis Street
Exarcheia, Athens
1932 | 1933
Kyriakoulis Panagiotakos

3
Apartment House
30 Stavropoulou Street
Athens
1935 | 1936
Vasileios Douras

modern idiom (K Laskaris, D Kyriakou by the Lycabettus Hill, 1933-35). Another group of buildings however sported a more reserved use of modern elements combined with traces of decoration and classicist detailing, such as those by Vassileios Kouremenos (17 D Aeropagitou Street, 1932), Konstantinos Kyriakidis (19 Asklipiou Street, 1933-34), Konstantinos Kitsikis (29 V Sofias Av, 1938), and Emmanouil Lazaridis (30 Troias Street, 1935). Private houses also proliferated in the 30s. Stamos Papadakis' best known project is a villa in Athens (Glyfada, 1932-33) published in many pre-war publications. French-educated Panos N Tzelepis (1894-1976) built a number of villas in Athenean suburbs (his personal

4
Apartment House
54 Patission-Metsovou Street
Athens
Nikolaos Nikolaides

5
Villa
62 Papanastasiou-Paparrigopoulou Street
Psychico, Athens
Kimon Laskaris

house, Hellenikon 1929; the Frantzis house, Psychico 1932; the Imbriotis house, Hellenikon 1933-37). Kimon Laskaris (1905-78) also left an imposing villa in Psychico, Athens. Two specimens from other areas could be cited: Nikolaos Mitsakis' villa on the Volos waterfront (1934) and another, by a still unknown architect, in Chora, Andros island.

6
Villa on the Sea Shore
2 P Bakoyanni-D Pavlou Street
Glyfada Athens
1932 | 1933
Stamos Papadakis

7
Private House
281 Dimitriados Street, Volos
1934
Nikolaos Mitsakis

8
Goulandris Private House
Chora, Andros island
1937 | 1939

Public Buildings An ambitious governmental programme for the construction of 4000 new schools in the 30s promulgated 'New Architecture' over the entire country. Many young architects joined the New Schools Programme and designed some of the most innovative and intriguing specimens of modern Greek architecture. Dimitris Pikionis (1887-1968), although not a member of the group, was invited to design an elementary school on Lycabettus Hill (Athens 1931-32) which was duly canonized. Among participants in this programme, the most talented were Nikolaos Mitsakis and Kyriakoulis Panagiotakos; the more prolific was Patroklos Karantinos, who also edited a book on the School Programme (1938).

9
Elementary School
165 Filolaou Street, Athens
1934
Kyriakoulis Panagiotakos

10
Elementary School
67 Distomou Street
Kolonos Hill, Athens
1931
Nikolaos Mitsakis

Mitsakis (1899-1941) was well informed on international currents yet was also attracted by local vernacular architecture. His school schemes range from modern projects – such as two elementary schools in Athens (Kolonos Hill 1931, Koletti Street 1932) and one in Thessaloniki (the Girls' high school 1933) – to mixes with regional idioms such as the gymnasium at Dimitsana (1928-32), the gymnasium and museum on Naxos island (1927) and the Aghia Sofia complex (Thessaloniki 1928-32). Panagiotakos designed two exceptional elementary schools in Athens, on Liosion Street (1931-33) and Filolaou Street (1934) and the high school at Sparta (1932). Valentis' elementary school on Syros island (1930-32) is furthermore a paradigm of contextual architecture as it fits in the midst of a vernacular hill town. Patroklos Karantinos (1903-76) had worked in Auguste Perret's office (1927-28) and his versatility is demonstrated for example by two elementary schools in Athens (Kalisperi Street, 1932; Kallithea, 1931) and a school complex in Marousi, Athens (1932); another elementary school in Piraeus (Taburia, 1932-35) and the gymnasium at Nauplion (1932). His unique Archeological Museum at Herakleion, Crete (1933-58) was an exemplary design to shelter the local Minoan art collection. Aside from schools, the Greek government initiated an extensive Public Health Programme. The hospital 'Sotiria' for

11
School Complex
211 Kifissias Avenue
Marousi, Athens
1932
Patroklos Karantinos

12
High School
Sparti, Peloponnesus
1932
Kyriakoulis Panagiotakos

13
Girls' High School
G. Stavrou-K Dil Street
Thessaloniki
1933
Nikolaos Mitsakis

14
Women's Unit
'Sotiria' Hospital
152 Mesogeion Avenue Athens
1932 | 1935
Ioannis Despotopoulos

pulmonary diseases in Athens commissioned Ioannis Despotopoulos – who wrote on revolutionary city planning and had attended the Bauhaus in Weimar (1924-25) – for a 420 bed women's unit (1932), a functionalist statement of uttermost simplicity. Subsequent annexes designed in 1939 include buildings by Konstantinos Kitsikis (300 bed men's unit) and Periklis Georgakopoulos (laundry and kitchen unit), all distinctly expressive of modern tendencies. The Dodecanese islands, under a long Italian occupation (1912-43), were extensively 'colonized' by a remarkably varied public and private architecture, designed by Italian architects, who used modernism undiluted or mixed with historicist forms.

15
Laundry and Kitchen Unit
'Sotiria' Hospital
152 Mesogeion Avenue, Athens
1939 | 1940
Periklis Georgakopoulos

16
Archeological Museum
Herakleion, Crete
1933 | 1958
Patroklos Karantinos

17
Refugee Housing
Koniari-Gerostathi Street (Lycabettus Hill)
Athens
1933 | 1935
K Laskaris & D Kyriakos

Photographic Credits :
Architecture Archive of the Benaki Museum
2, 6, 7, 9, 12, 13
Tzeli Hadzidimitriou
3, 18, 19
Panos Exarchopoulos
1, 4, 5
Panayotis Tournikiotis
16
Dimitri Philippides
8, 10, 11, 14, 15, 17

Hungary

The twenty buildings we have selected for this book represent the twenty years from 1928 to 1948, a period regarded as the golden age of Modern Movement in Hungary. Although the history of modern architecture goes back to the 1910s and continues after the 1956 revolution, we omitted these periods for their registry is scheduled for the forthcoming years. Since two conservative periods, one in the 1920s, the other between 1949 and 1956, separated three distinct phases in the development of Hungarian modern architecture, it seemed reasonable to focus on the middle one, the production of which is rich enough to make the selection difficult.

To understand the development of the second phase of Hungarian modern architecture we need to discuss its unique characteristics. The most important difference, compared to major European centres of the Modern Movement is that large-scale social housing was practically missing from the Hungarian scene, while the construction of private houses and apartments was considerable. The only significant instance for social housing, built according to CIAM principles, were the Köztársaság tér apartments in Budapest. Another characteristic of modern architecture in Hungary is that is has never been synonymous with straightforward functionalism. The most consistent adherents of modern tenets were the members of the Hungarian CIAM (1929-1938) led by the former Bauhaus student Farkas Molnár (1897-1945) and the social democrat József Fischer (1901-1995), but, because of their leftist stance, they became somewhat isolated within the profession. Their works are the closest to what was later to be called the International Style. Many other architects, however, adopted functional principles but maintained a deep scepticism and reservation towards avant-garde excesses. The diversity of clients' cultural backgrounds and concerns inspired the architects to pursue an amazing variety of modern approaches. Examples range from buildings with an expressionist and decorative overtone to romantic and regionalist attitudes and even modern classicism.

A milestone in the development of residential design was the experimental housing estate in Napraforgó Street, Budapest (1931), which aimed to convince both the public and authorities of the advantages of small houses on tiny plots. Unlike the Werkbund Siedlung projects in other European cities, the Napraforgó colony was not a showcase of avant-garde design. The range of styles went from radical Purism to Expressionism and to more traditional designs. Indeed the same variety was typical of Hungarian villa construction in the 1930s. The 'naked' white cubes of CIAM members, built for enlightened intellectuals, were contrasted by beautiful, often luxurious, villas of Lajos Kozma, Gyula Rimanóczy and others that satisfied the desire of the middle classes for a new way of life. A unique experiment with new technologies and building materials was the house Béla Sámsondi-Kiss had built for his family.

For lack of social housing, speculatively built apartments had to provide the majority of citizens with modern accommodation. By the mid-1930s, a new plan type was developed, and perimeter blocks with gardens in the centre replaced the dense urban fabric of old courtyard buildings. The total area of the apartments became smaller but more comfortable. Modern facilities and devices were common, large balconies and roof gardens opened to the sunshine. The emphasis later shifted to luxury apartments, built by companies and pension funds as a capital investment and indirect advertisement for their firms. The abundance of noble materials, spectacular design of vestibules and staircases and elegant detailing throughout the building aimed to impress both the inhabitants and visitors. In the design of public buildings, Hungarians drew inspiration from contemporary Italian, Swiss and Scandinavian models. The nature of these building types raised the challenge of monumentality, and architects such as Bertalan Árkay, István Janáky and Gyula Rimanóczy had remarkable success in interpreting and re-evaluating the classical tradition within the modernist syntax. Buildings for industry, commerce and transport were more appropriate to a scientific design method. The elliptic concrete shell vault of the Hamzsabégi bus garage was a masterpiece of engineering of its time, as the Stühmer chocolate factory was an early test-piece for solar control and shading devices. The Budaörs airport not only served well the most advanced means of transport but also expressed its function in a symbolic way.

The increasing role of leisure time in modern life resulted in the flowering of new building types such as the cinema, open-air swimming and recreation pools. In Hungary, cinemas were usually built into the courtyard of apartment blocks rather than independently. The design of recreational pools, on the other hand, went far beyond architecture, and merged with garden design and landscaping. The post-war period is represented by one sole building, albeit a very spectacular one: the headquarters of the MÉMOSZ trade union which owes much to the new Brazilian architecture and Le Corbusier.

Although the idea of recording and preserving our recent heritage was pioneered as early as the 1960s in Hungary, the bulk of potential monuments have remained unprotected. This is a serious problem because the position of the Modern Movement in our cultural context is controversial. Most of the public are hostile towards modern buildings for banal architecture and mass production of prefab housing during the 1960s and 1970s discredited modernity for a long time. Sometimes, even professionals are not able to evaluate the modern heritage in an objective way, especially post-war buildings that are the products of a period strongly penetrated with politics.

Modern buildings in our country are more exposed to damage than elsewhere partly because apartments have recently been sold to their former tenants who are not able to spend on careful renovation, partly because the privatization of former state properties menaces valuable modern structure, above all industrial, commercial and office buildings. Therefore, the National Board for the Protection of Historic Monuments decided to extend urgently the national list with a large number of 20th century buildings.

András Ferkai

1
Housing Estate
1-19 & 2-22 Napraforgó utca, Budapest II
1932
Various architects

2
Villa
2/a Lejtő utca, Budapest XII
1933
Farkas Molnár

3
Apartment Block
62-64 Bartók Béla út, Budapest XI
1934
Gábor Preisich, Zoltán Révész & Mihály Vadász

The experimental housing estate is the first example in Hungary as a modern settlement. It was built in order to demonstrate that small plots (360m^2) are suitable for the building of detached family houses. The architects aimed to popularize the modern style.

Baráth & Novák 22
Bierbauer 4
Böhm & Hegedüs 14
Fischer 20
Gerlóczy 19
Hajós 17
Kaffka 3
Kertész 9
Kozma 5 & 6-8
Masirevich Jr 13
Molnár & Ligeti 15
Münnich 10
Quittner 12
Tauszig & Róth 16
Vágó 1 & 11
Weichinger 18
Wellisch 7
Wälder 2

This villa received a prize at the 1933 Milan Triennial. The façade is well-divided but the floor plan is very simple and highly variable. The architect applied ingenious solutions to achieve a flexible floor plan.

A typical block of flats from the thirties with a cinema, the spectacular interior of which has recently been destroyed.

18

13

5

123

4
Apartment Block
10 Kékgolyó utca, Budapest XII
1934
László Lauber

The asymmetrical façade of the apartment block blends into a continuous row of buildings in the street. The staircase is located between the two flats situated on two different levels. The roof garden was destroyed in the war.

5
Villa
88b Szépvölgyi út, Budapest II
1934
József Fischer

One of the architect's best villas designed in the international modern style. The arrangement of the large glass façade and the small window-openings is harmonised with the characteristic curved form of the staircase.

6
Villa
97 Pasaréti út, Budapest II
1934
Gyula Rimanóczy

The fine proportions and a sort of a Latin feeling of this house make it perhaps the best modernist villa of the thirties in Buda. A sun-terrace and loggia stretch the length of the upper storey. Later additions have since destroyed the original asymmetric composition.

7
Apartment Blocks
14 15 16 Köztársaság tér, Budapest VIII
1935
Bertalan Árkay, Sándor Faragó
József Fischer, Károly Heysa, Pál Ligeti
Farkas Molnár, Móricz Pogány
Gábor Preisich, Mihály Vadász

The three rows of eight and six storey apartment blocks are located perpendicularly to the street to afford better orientation and are interconnected by single-storey shopping wings. The complex, built by the Social Security Insurance Institute shows the influence of the resolutions of the Brussels congress of CIAM.

8
Apartment Block and Cinema
55 Margit körút, Budapest II
1936
Lajos Kozma

The building expresses the spirit of modern architecture in a typical way. The façade and interior of the cinema are of high quality.

9
Heart of Jesus Parish-Church
5 Csaba utca, Budapest XII
1936
Aladár Árkay & Bertalan Árkay

The first modern church in the capital. The use of cubic masses, undecorated walls, and raw concrete surfaces were unusual until then in the practice of church architecture. The interior decorations are works of artists belonging to the 'Roman School' fine arts movement.

10
Budaörs Airport
36 Köérbereki út, Budapest XI
1937
Dr Virgil Borbíró & László Králik

Authentic design of a new type of building, very high artistic quality. Structures of reinforced concrete, steel and glass, rubber, etc. dominated. When completed it was one of the most modern airports of Europe.

11
Palatinus Open Air Swimming Pool
Margitsziget, Budapest XIII
1937
István Janáky Sr

A well organised floor plan with simple, sophisticated arrangement of the mass. As in most works of the architect, related arts also play an important role.

12	13	14	15
Apartment Block	Villa	Apartment Block	Office Building
61 Szilágyi Erzsébet fasor, Budapest II	19 Berkenye utca, Budapest II	15-17 Margit körút, Budapest II	75-81 Dob utca, Budapest VII
1937	1937	1938	1939
János Wanner	Lajos Kozma	Béla Hofstätter & Ferenc Domány	Gyula Rimanóczy, Lajos Hidasi & Imre Papp
In contrast to the sometimes quite heavy forms of modern Hungarian buildings this house has a light, smart character. The clichés of modernism, which were widespread in the thirties, are avoided here.	The building containing two apartments is an important work of the modernist period of architect Lajos Kozma. The floor plan is typical for luxury flats. The furnishing of one of the flats, also designed by the architect was destroyed.	An impressive example of the architecture of the apartment block in the thirties. The situation and structure of the building make it possible to provide a very large number of flats with enough light. Two cylindrical glass-walled elevator shafts were considered as a technical tour de force.	This is considered the first large modern public building in Hungary constructed as the Telephone Exchange and Budapest Postal Administration. The involvement of artists from the 'Roman School' gives an Italian novecento neo-classic character to the building.

16
Bus Garage
55 Hamzsabégi út, Budapest XI
1940
Jenö Padányi Gulyás & István Menyhárd

The two huge halls of the garage and the workshop have parabola shaped reinforced concrete shell roofs. When constructed, the shell structure was the greatest span (72m) in the world.

17
Factory
20 Vágóhíd utca, Budapest IX
1941
Aladár Olgyay & Viktor Olgyay

The former Stühmer Chocolate Factory complex is one of the most significant industrial buildings of the era. The complex comprised a factory building, stores and a boiler house. The architects gave careful consideration to functional needs.

18
Apartment Block
12 Petüfi Sándor utca & 6a/b Párisi utca
Budapest V
1943
Gedeon Gerlóczy

One of the largest block of flats with shops in the city of Budapest. The architect made use both of the new techniques of the period and the planning traditions of blocks of flats.

19
Villa
83 Dayka Gábor utca, Budapest XI
1944
Béla Sámsondi Kiss

20
Office Building with Conference Centre
84a Dózsa György út, Budapest VI
1949
Gábor Preisich, Lajos Gádoros
György Szrogh & Imre Perényi

A high quality villa from the beginning of the forties, planned by the architect for his own family. The architect realised his own technical innovations by using multi-purpose box-like columns for the load bearing structure.

The former Trade Union Headquarters is the most important public building from the period of post war construction. This was the short period when modern architecture was finally accepted officially. Right after its completion the political changes stopped the modern architectural style for a long time.

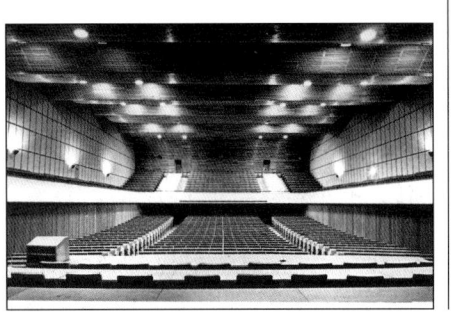

Selected Bibliography :
Györgyi D, Hütl D & Kozma L
Új magyar épitömüvészet
2 vols Budapest 1935 & 1938

Gábor E
A CIAM magyar csoportja 1928-1938
Budapest 1971

Szendrö J
Magyar épitészet 1945-1970
Budapest 1972

Major M & Osskó J (eds)
Új épitészet, új társadalom
Budapest 1981

Gassner H
Ungarische Avantgarde in der Weimarer Republik
Kassel 1986

Ferkai A
Buda épitészete a két világáború között
Budapest 1995

DOCOMOMO Hungary
Modern építészet Magyarországon 1930-49
Budapest 1996

Leśnikowski W (ed)
East European Modernism: Architecture in Czechoslovakia, Hungary & Poland between the Wars
London & New York 1996

Photographic Credits :
Zoltán Seidner
1, 2, 6, 8, 9, 12, 13, 14, 17, 20
Tivadar Kozelka
3, 7, 18
Hungarian Film Institute
4
Olga Máté
5
Budapest Foto Company
10
Hungarian Film Office
11, 15
Gábor Barka
16
József Hajdú
18

Iberia

The initiation of the register of modern architecture in Catalonia was spurred by DOCOMOMO International which delegated to the Mies van der Rohe foundation the formation of the Iberic Committee of DOCOMOMO to compile the register of Modern Movement works on the Iberic Peninsula. The foundation contacted a number of architecture related institutions on the Iberic Peninsula, in Catalonia they contacted the Catalan Architects Association (COAC).

The first phase of the inventory was concluded with its presentation at the third international conference of DOCOMOMO which took place in Barcelona from the 14th to the 17th of September 1994. The register composed by the Iberic Committee included 60 works, 9 of which were in Catalonia.

Immediately following this the Iberic committee agreed on the amplification of the register to include 150 works. The selection of these was completed in November of 1995 including a total of 157 works of which 31 were in Catalonia. The presentation of these remained for the XIX Congress of the International Union of Architects, UIA Barcelona 96, and the fourth DOCOMOMO international conference from the 18th to the 20th of September in Bratislava. Given the need to obtain precise homogeneous and up to date information on the state of Catalonia's heritage of modern architecture, the COAC formed a work group through the culture offices of its branches to select works and create indexes centrally coordinated by the culture office of the COAC. From the exhaustive study of the Modern Movement in Catalonia close to 100 works were selected.

The criteria for the selection of works determines that they must be built (thus excluding un-built projects) and includes their state of repair and alteration. The works must fit in the period of time from 1925 to 1965. The number of works selected for a single author gives a clear idea of the importance of this architect in local Modern Movement architecture. The selected works must coincide with the ideas of the Modern Movement, thus excluding a number of works which may be of clear value but stray from the ideas proposed by the Modern Movement. In the study of the architectural production in Catalonia from 1925-1965 two clear periods emerge. In the first of these which stretches to 1940 and is represented by the GATCPAC, the architecture is more homogeneous to the international style in a clear cubist modality of architecture even if the plan of enclosures is modified to adapt to local conditions of climate, economy, and culture, and a clear preference is expressed for exposed structure and against brick work. The second period corresponds to the years 1950-1965, and manifests a tendency toward a modern regional cultural independence as propelled by the Grupo R which intended to revitalize the rationalist values of the GATCPAC, and at the same time to realistically recover regionalist parameters. Most outstanding as a precedent was the use of manufactured brick as had been seen in Catalan modernism.

The objective of this register of modern architecture in Catalonia is not only the creation of an exact catalogue of the work of the modern movement in Catalonia through extensive field work, which will permit the understanding of the value of the work of the period. It is also is intended that this in depth study will furnish a base to raise consciousness in society at large and in particular institutions and bodies responsible for preservation and management of these works to protect against their degradation and destruction.

Gerard Garcia-Ventosa

1
National Mint of Portugal
Antonio José de Almeida
Lisbon, Portugal
1934 | 1938
Jorge Segurado & Antonio Varela

The building is located on the Antonio José de Almeida Avenue, occupying a whole block. Duarte Pacheco commissioned the building from Jorge Segurado, with the collaboration of Antonio Varela. It occupies the rectangular plot in a diverse and innovative way. The complex consists of an office building and the corresponding mint facilities, which are entered under a long porch on the corner where the two avenues meet. The entrance to the office building is half-way up another road. Two galleries link the mint and the office building. Its clear symbolic meaning adds strength and clarity to the whole. The placing of the columns gives a rhythm to the long mint façades.

The entrance to the mint has a bas-relief and a clock cast into the glazed brick. A clear Art Deco sign reads 'Casa da Moeda' placed above the entrance to the office building. It has had no significant alterations to date, and keeps its coherence and dignity, although the building has not yet been protected.

2
Ugalde House
Caldes d'estrac, Spain
1951 | 1952
José Antonio Coderch & Manuel Valls

3
El Viso Housing Estate
Madrid, Spain
1931 | 1935
Rafael Bergamin, Luis Blanco Soler &
Luis Felipe Vivanco

The plan was worked out according to the instructions of the owner, who wanted to enjoy the local landscape. The plan of the house respects the topographical characteristics of the site, incorporating in its composition the existing vegetation. The view overlooks the landscape, culminating in a platform which projects out of the lowest part of the valley. The final result is a taut design in which the separation of interior and exterior is overcome and the definition of functional space is minimized. This work represents a truly original interpretation of modern architecture and the local tradition of having the building respect for the existing landscape. This is also present in the use of materials, in the paving made of irregularly broken bricks.

The effect of the Casas Baratas (cheap homes) and Casas Economicas (economy homes) law was centred in the extension of Madrid. This residential estate was built in the NE extension of the city. 130 one-family houses were initially planned but eventually, due to high demand and to the convenient use of planning regulations, 242 houses of similar characteristics were built, following a grid of streets parallel and perpendicular to the main axis, Serrano Street. A small sports ground, a few lesser buildings to house a school and a health centre as well as a small group of shops were included.
Despite its relatively small size, its importance has grown.

This housing estate followed the pilot project of El Parque Residencia Estate, in which the same architects had already investigated suburban housing estates. In El Viso they propose a terraced housing plan, that also included detached houses, with a small courtyard as an access from the street and a back garden that can also by accessed by a footpath.

4
Leça de Palmeira Swimming pool
Matosinhos, Oporto, Portugal
1961 | 1966
Alvaro Siza Vieira

5
La Zarzuela Race track
Madrid, Spain
1935 | 1936
Carlos Arniches, Martin Dominguez &
Eduardo Torroja (engineer)

The building is located on the Lega sea promenade in Matosinhos, a town on the outskirts of Oporto. A restaurant was planned to be built near the swimming-pools at a later date by the same architect. The complex consists of a swimming pool on the sea line, integrated with the rocks and waves and closed by rectilinear walls on only three of its sides. Slightly set-back and placed against the promenade wall is the changing area. The building was conceived as a promenade space. Thus, from a open corridor next to the road, successive spaces and functions follow almost informally, in a sequence, until you reach the water. With its compact geometry, it is considered one of Siza's best early works.

In 1935 a competition for the construction of the new Madrid Racetrack was held, in which nine well known Spanish teams took part. The winning entry was by Carlos Arniches, Martin Dominguez and Eduardo Torroja. The building is on a site which has important differences in level. It has three clearly differentiated parts: the tracks, the area for the horses, and the area for the public. The buildings for the public consist of terraces with views over the racetrack, an upper gallery opened to the track and the paddock, where the booking offices and the stairs that go up to the terraces and down to the track are located, and the covered lower gallery.

The structure of the stands is the race track's most innovative and representative element. It is an innovative structure of reinforced cantilevered beams. Torroja – a well-known civil engineer, who was part of the team of the University Campus Technical Office – played an important role in its design. He also took part in most of the land and infrastructure works, viaducts, bridges, schools and sports buildings on the same Campus, very close to the Race track.

6
Colegio Maravillas Gymnasium
Maravillas, Spain
1960 | 1962
Alejandro de la Sota

7
Casa Bloc Housing Unit
Barcelona, Spain
1932 | 1936
GATCPAC, Sert, Suirana, Torres

The Maravillas Gymnasium was built upon a very irregular site which had a difference in level of 12m between the two streets that it faced. This was a very important factor for the project. The building faces south. The lower part is entered from the street and its upper floor from the playground. The interior design of the sports hall tried to achieve, in the words of the architect, 'an atmosphere full of humanity, neutralising the gymnastic coldness through the use of warm and textured materials'. The basement plan houses dressing rooms and a roller-hockey training ring. On the ground floor are a pitch and the coaches room. The first and second floors house meeting rooms for mature students.

The top floor houses the Science Museum, the physics, lecture, games, music and reading rooms. These rooms were introduced using the shape of the gymnasium roof, whose sloped floor follows the lower line of the trusses, thus becoming auditoria. The upper playground is the roof of the gymnasium. In this building, the architecture of de la Sota abandons the superfluous and concentrates on the essential, with a tendency to the minimal, the basic and an expressive will for dematerialization. The building is considered a key work of Spanish modern architecture.

In 1939 a small duplex housing complex, that has since disappeared, was built on a lot adjacent to that selected for the construction of the Casa Bloc. In view of this pilot project success, the construction of a group of 207 duplex apartments was hastily initiated on a larger site of 9.00m². As a reference to its volume its was called the Casa Bloc. The Casa Bloc, a building of an articulated floor plan, integrates perfectly with the urban layout of the Sant Andreu district were it is located. It is composed of five sections, each 10m deep, that delimit two open spaces of 2,800m². Because of its form, the building adapts perfectly to the network of small streets and buildings that define the local urban fabric.

The six storeys of the building that held the apartments were built on a single building type of a duplex unit, with no double height spaces. The construction system combined traditional and modern methods. The structure of the building, formed of two 4xl0m modular patterns, was made of steel beams. The traditional method of brick construction was used as infill for the steel framework, as well as for the vaults of the interior stairways serving the apartments and the exterior walls. The Casa Bloc introduced Spain to the architectural notion of mass production applied to housing, a notion that had recently emerged in European architecture.

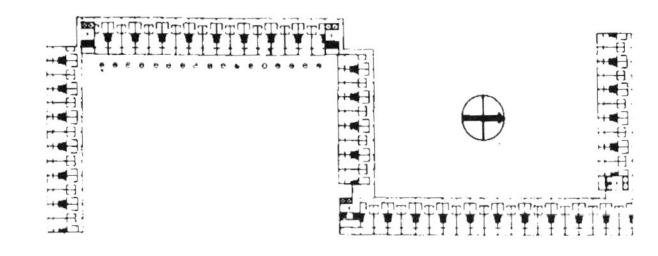

8
San Sebastian Royal Yacht Club
San Sebastian, Spain
1928 | 1929
José Manuel Aizpurua & Joaquin Labayen

9
Antituberculosis Dispensary
Barcelona, Spain
1933 | 1938
GATCPAC, Sert, Torres, Clave, Suirana

The club is situated on an incline, to the left of the Grand Casino. The programme is organized in different sections. Ground floor: hall, library, lounge bar and games room, assembly room, open terrace and general services. First floor: large function room, yachtsman's and swimming quarter, kitchen and general services. Second floor: restaurant, bar and large terrace. The original Club only had only one floor, made of stone walls that were 120cm wide. The concrete structure of the club's enlargement was built on the original walls. The façades are structurally independent, with smooth surfaces that show the geometric features and colour.

The sensibility towards the impressive scenary of San Sebastian Bay inspires a most powerful relationship between architecture and environment. With this in mind the horizontal planes are used as a constitutional element of the work. 'The contemplation of the bay from any point through the large horizontal windows is the most important point in the building' said the architects. This is the reason for the transparency of the building and the shape of the windows. The San Sebastian Royal Yacht Club is the most important work of Basque rationalist architecture and the experiences of avant-garde expressionism, cubism and neoplasticism are present in it.

The autonomous government authorities of Catalonia commissioned this clinic in the 30s during a campaign against tuberculosis aimed at eradicating the illness from the most densely populated and unsanitary part of the old city, which was claiming the highest number of victims. The complex programme adopted a L-shape scheme expanded longitudinally along an east-west axis, making no attempt to align itself to the surrounding site. It opens on to a south-facing patio through which air, sun and light were allowed to enter, providing an environment in which people were able to get back into contact with nature. The treatment rooms in the first floor consist of two consulting rooms with dressing rooms and a shared x-ray area.

The second floor contains a research centre on tuberculosis, a laboratory and a social assistance area. The library and auditorium are located on the second and third floors. The terrace was designed as a solarium for the patients. The metal structure uses brick vaulting set on flagstones. Pre-cast parts are also used extensively in the stairways and floors; stucco is used on the external facades. The Tuberculosis Clinic is a major work of the Modern Movement in the Iberian peninsula. It introduced various technical solutions and processes that can be seen as emblematic devices in the works pioneered by the GATCPAC, while simultaneously respecting the traditional local building techniques.

10
German Pavilion
Barcelona, Spain
1928 | 1929
Ludwig Mies van der Rohe

The building was designed to house the official opening of the German section at the International Exhibition in 1929. The site was a rectangle at the end of a long esplanade from where one of the sides of the building could be seen behind a row of Ionic columns. The travertine paving was laid in 1.1x1.1m square slabs. The travertine walls slabs had a double dimension and had a metal structure. The same structural system was used for the marble walls. The roof was supported by a system of 8 cruciform columns anchored to a network of laminated steel beams freeing the walls from any structural function.

Despite its temporary use, this travertine, glass and marble pavilion became a seminal example of modern architecture that has provided an understanding of enclosure and construction that to a very extensive degree determined later architecture. Extensive research on the original documents in the Mies van der Rohe Archive at the Museum of Modern Art in New York undertaken by the commissioned architects enabled the reconstruction of the building on the original exact site and the closest original materials. Some structural modifications were needed to ensure the permanence of the building.

Selected Bibliography :
Arquitectura Contemporanea en Espana
Madrid c1933

1° Congresso Nacional de Arquitectura
Lisbon 1948

Rafols JF
Modernismo i modernistas
Barcelona 1949

Flores CF
Arquitectura Espanola Contemporanea
Bilbao 1961

Bohigas O
Arquitectura espanola de la segunda republica Barcelona 1970

ODAM **Organização dos Arquitectos Modernos 1947-1952** Porto 1972

Portas N
'A Evolução da Arquitectura Moderna em Portugal' in: Zevi B (ed)
História da Arquitectura Moderna
Lisbon 1977

McKay D
Modern Architecture in Barcelona 1854-1939
Oxford 1985

Portas N & Mendes M
Portugal. Architecture 1965-1990
Milan 1991 Paris 1992

Tostões A
Os Verdes Anos na Arquitectura Portuguesa dos Anos 50 Porto 1997

Photographic Credits :
Giovanni Zanzi
1, 9
Guillermo Landrove
2
Manolo Laguillo
3, 4, 6
Luis Ferreira Alves
5
Pau Maynes
10

Iceland

Until the 1900s Iceland's economy was based on primitive agriculture and fishing. Architecture was limited by the lack of materials for permanent construction. The introduction of concrete around 1900 had special significance in Iceland since for the first time there was an economical way of making permanent buildings out of local materials. After a great fire in central Reykjavik in 1915, in situ concrete became the conventional method of construction though design of the early concrete buildings differed little from that of their traditional timber predecessors.

Mechanization of the fishing fleet caused rapid growth in Reykjavik and other towns during the first decades of the twentieth century. With new prosperity private villas and public housing led to further work for architects. The first to introduce modern architecture into Iceland was Sigurdur Gudmundsson (1885-1958) in a house of 1929 at Gardastraeti in Reykjavik. It has now been altered but when completed in 1930 it was the first building which clearly expressed the aesthetics of the new architecture. This was ten years before modernism became apparent in Icelandic art.

Gudmundsson designed several houses for well-to-do families in the capital between 1929 and 1931. His office became an important training ground for the first generation of modern architects in Iceland. One of these was Einar Sveinsson (1906-1973) who became municipal architect and planning director for the city in 1934. However the social vision of the Modern Movement did not go hand in hand with the new aesthetic. Only in the mid 30s did the ideology of modernism start to manifest itself. This was mainly as a continuation of earlier social efforts in the fields of housing and town planning initiated by a professor of medicine, Gudmundur Hannesson, who wrote Iceland's first book on town planning in 1916. He had been educated in Denmark, where the medical profession had been instrumental in bringing about reforms in urban planning and housing. When massive migration from rural areas into the city created a severe shortage of housing in Reykjavik, Hannesson and the first professional architects in the city campaigned for new solutions. The new garden towns of England and Germany became an important precedent for their reforms. Zoning kept residential areas separate from industry and business. Apartment buildings were limited to three storeys. Great emphasis was placed upon providing sun, fresh air and gardens for all housing units.

The first large-scale state supported housing estate for low-income families was at Hringbraut in Reykjavik, designed and built in stages between 1930 and 1935. As a political vision and a vehicle of social change the project was a great achievement in its time. All units had bathrooms, toilets, electric stoves and living rooms which faced the sun. The urban planning principle was in line with the models from Hannesson's book, with a two-storey perimeter block enclosing a shared garden with playgrounds in the middle. The architectural character of the building was traditional, simple and understated.

In the second phrase of Hringbraut, carried out between 1936 and 1937, the social ambition of the new housing policy merged with the architectural vision of the Modern Movement. This commission went to the young architect Gunnlaugur Halldorsson, who was a leading proponent of the Modern Movement in Iceland. His solution for Hringbraut was in part inspired by housing schemes in Frankfurt and in the Netherlands, which emphasized the concept of Existenzminimum. Detached parallel rows of housing replaced the former perimeter developments. An open field with playgrounds was located in the centre and all private gardens and entrances faced south.

During World War II, Iceland was isolated from Scandinavia and mainland Europe. From 1940 onwards, British and American troops were stationed here. Their activities brought prosperity to the local economy as well as strong cultural influences from Britain and the USA. Housing shortages became worse than ever and after experiments with temporary housing the city authorities started to build free-standing apartment buildings to designs by the architect Einear Sveinsson. These were the earliest examples of a type which became common after the war.

Modern Movement housing reforms were not confined to urban areas. During the 1930s functional and economic solutions were also developed for the farming areas of rural Iceland. New concepts of the farmhouse were developed after careful functional analyses and several types were used as standard designs all over Iceland.

Flat roofs were one aspect of early modernism that was particularly unsuited to local conditions and like roof terraces and metal window frames they soon gave way to more conventional solutions and to use of such local mineral materials such as obsidian, spar, granite gravel and later sea shells, as weather protective coatings on the exterior concrete walls. This became one of the distinctive features of Icelandic modernism where Bauhaus architecture became known as 'the black boxes of the thirties.'

In the 1930s public buildings were less influenced by modernism than the housing. The State Architect's Office remained a bastion of politically-protected National Romanticism in arts and architecture. Only in the next decade did leading modernist architects get their first commissions for larger public buildings. Notable amongst these were the Tuberculosis Sanatorium and Agricultural Bank buildings of Gunnlaugur Halldorsson, dating from the middle and later forties. Despite these, Iceland cannot claim any individual masterpieces on a par with those of other Scandinavian countries. But the movement was adopted very positively by a small isolated culture at a critical moment in its history, when independence was within its reach and vast social transformations were under way.

Conservation of these buildings is now gradually becoming a concern of experts in the architectural heritage field. Research on restoration techniques is under way and a recently approved master plan for Reykjavik till 2016 includes a conservation policy and within that one category of protection covers twentieth century works. The National Conservation Board has recently considered giving the status of national protection to a small selection of Modern Movement works, but much remains to ensure that the importance of this period of Iceland's cultural heritage is recognized.

Petur H Armannsson

1
Asvallagata & Hringbraut
Co-operative housing
101 Reykjavik
1934 | 1935
Thorir Baldvinsson & Axel Sveinsson

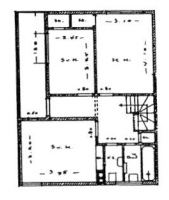

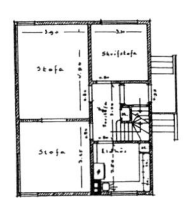

2
Freyjugata 46
101 Reykjavik
1931 | 1932
Sigurdur Gudmundsson

The most progressive developments in housing during the modern period in Icelandic architecture can be found in projects initiated by co-operative building unions. A bill was passed in 1932 which gave them the right to a state guarantee on loans. In 1934, the first co-operative union built a group of 33 detached houses in the west end of Reykjavik. The housing consisted of two basic types, a semi-detached house with one apartment in each end, designed by engineer Axel Sveinsson, and a single-family house by architect Thorir Baldvinsson, who was educated in San Francisco. The design of the single-family houses was a clear expression of modernism, with flat roofs and corner windows.

The houses were built of wood and plastered on the outside for reasons of fire protection. Only few of the single-family houses still have the original flat roof and plaster walls and many have been severely damaged with alternations.

The first buildings in Iceland that clearly expressed the aesthetics of modern architecture were private houses of well-to-do families in Reykjavik, most of which were designed in the office of architect Sigurdur Gudmundsson between 1929 and 1931. The houses were built of reinforced concrete and had many of the external characteristics of European cubist architecture of the 1920s: flat roofs, sun-terraces, steel window casings and corner windows. Regrettably, nearly all of the early modern houses have been robbed of their stylistic features almost beyond recognition. One house by Gudmundsson remains where the exterior appearance is more or less intact, Freyjugata 46.

A gently sloping roof has been added on top of the original flat roof and the original window frames have been placed with new ones of wood. The exterior walls of the house were originally coated with a mixture of cement and granite. The exterior coating has recently been restored with minerals in a lighter tone of grey.

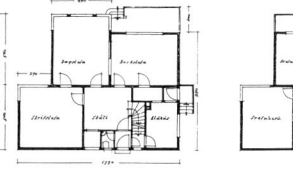

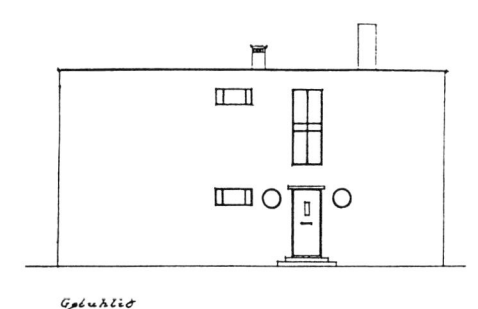

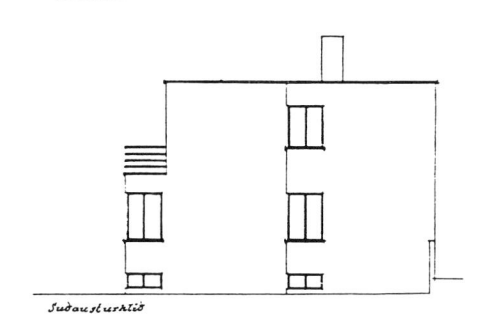

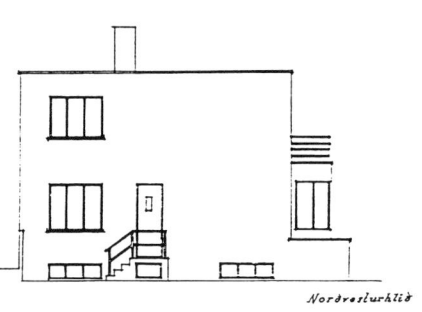

3
Laugarnesskoli elementary school
Reykjavegur, 105 Reykjavik
1934 | 1935 & 1942 | 1945
Einar Sveinsson & Agust Palsson

Einar Sveinsson was the first Icelandic architect to be educated at a technical university in Germany. In 1934, he became the municipal architect of Reykjavik, in charge of urban planning and other building tasks. His first municipal design was Laugarnes elementary school on Reykjavegur for children from the dispersed built-up areas outside the city proper, with boarding facilities for sick children. The original building was completed in 1935, and now forms the east wing of the school. In 1942, Sveinsson proposed a large extension to the school in collaboration with his assistant, Agust Palsson.

The addition, which opened in 1944, was the first school building in Iceland with classrooms arranged several floors high on three sides of a central, open assembly hall. Access to classrooms is from stairs and balconies overlooking the central hall. The main wing tapers slightly towards the south, and the central assembly hall appears correspondingly shallower than when actually entered.

4
Felagsgardur co-operative housing
Havallagata & Tungata, 101 Reykjavik
1935 | 1936
Gunnlaugur Halldorsson

The second group of co-operative housing built in Reykjavik is known as 'Felagsgardur'. The building union organised an architectural competition in 1935, one of the first to be held in Iceland. Most of the houses along Havallagata were semi-detached, built according to a prize winning design by Gunnlaugur Halldorsson. On Tungata, several duplex houses were built according to a design by Einar Sveinsson and Sigmundur Halldorsson, which won second prize in the competition. Also belonging to the group are two single-family houses at Havallagata, one by Halldorsson and the other by Sveinsson. The Felagsgardur houses can be regarded as one of the best examples of pre-war modern architecture in Iceland.

The detailing of walls, eaves and roofs shows clearly the adjustment of the modern vocabulary of design to suit local conditions and construction practice in Iceland. Originally, most of the units were owned and inhabited by middle-class families with regular incomes.

5
Hringbraut workers´ housing
Hofsvallagata, 101 Reykjavik
1936 | 1937
Gunnlaugur Halldorson

6
Ljosafoss hydro-electric power station
Grimsneshreppur, Arnessysla
1935 | 1937
Sigurdur Gudmundsson

Gunnlaugur Halldorsson, educated in Denmark, was one of several young architects who all finished their studies in the early 1930´s and came to practise in Iceland during the depression. In 1936, he was commissioned to design the second phase of the first government-supported workers' housing project in Reykjvik. Halldorsson chose to depart from the rigidity of the perimeter block system prescribed in the master plan for the site. He broke the housing into four separate blocks with open spaces in between. Most of the houses have entrances facing away from the street and towards smaller paths connected to a centrally located playground.

The end row is staggered in order to allow more air and light to enter the apartments. The project is important in the urban history of Reykjavik as the first example of a coherent modernist approach to town planning and architecture.

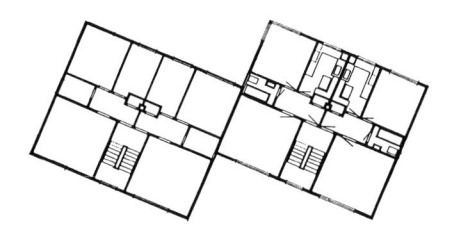

Ljosafoss hydro-electric power station is without question one of the best examples of modern Icelandic industrial architecture. The Ljosafoss station is better preserved than most other buildings by Gudmundsson from the 1930s. In the last two years, the station has been undergoing a very extensive renovation involving both the building and all technical equipment. Minor changes have been made to the building to ensure its structural stability and continuing performance as an active power station. Extra measures have been taken to preserve the integrity of its architecture.

In the early 1950s, Gudmundsson and his partner, architect Eirikur Einarsson, designed buildings for the second phase of the River Sog hydro project, a station at Irafoss along with a canteen building and housing for the staff. The last station in the series was Steingrimsstod, designed in 1958. The simple, formally powerful buildings at Sog interact impressively with the surrounding landscape.

7
Hringbraut 37-47 apartment blocks
107 Reykjavik
1942 | 1943
Einar Sveinsson & Agust Palsson

8
Nes Church
Hagatorg, 107 Reykjavik
1944 | 1957
Agust Palsson

Early in World War II, a serious housing shortage developed in Reykjavik when a contraction in construction coincided with heavy migration from rural areas. After experiments with temporary housing, the municipal authorities asked Einar Sveinsson to design two large terraces of 48 flats each on Hringbraut, at what was then the edge of the city. The buildings formed part of Sveinsson´s new plan for Melar district, with rows of detached multi-residential houses on open ground replacing the urban grid of streets with unbroken rows of houses. Sveinsson´s design was partially based on studies of the correlation between daylight zones and the width of buildings. Every room in each flat has access to daylight and direct ventilation through an outdoor window.

The Hringbraut apartment blocks were the earliest examples of a type which became a common housing solution in Reykjavik after the war. The original exterior mineral coating has recently been restored on one of the two buildings.

The Nes church was the first chuch in Iceland to be designed in the spirit of the Modern Movement. The project of architect Agust Palsson won first prize in an architectural competition held in 1942. The nave rises on platforms to reach a peak above the choir, which is the focal point of the interior space. A large crucifix, placed above the choir, forms the peak of the composition since, according to the architect, there was no functional need for a belltower in a modern church. Using diagonal walls and aisles located alongside the central axis on the nave, Palsson succeeded in unfettering the space from the stiff, symmetrical oblong structure which had typified earlier Icelandic houses of worship.

In his design, he gave priority to the natural transmission of sound and daylight. The church design was a subject of great controversy and conservative voices considered the project to be a disgrace. The realized building was slightly smaller than the original competition project.

9
Reykjalundur Tuberculosis Sanatorium
270 Mosfellsbær
1944 | 1945
Gunnlaugur Halldorsson & Bardur Isleifsson

The Reykjalundur Sanatorium is the first institutional building group in Iceland where both site planning and building design reflect the theories of the Modern Movement. The architects took advantage of the location out in the open landscape, creating an informal, functional layout of buildings oriented towards sun and view. Surrounding the main building of the sanatorium were groups of workshops and individual houses for patients and staff, all designed in an understated modernist manner. The writer Halldor Laxness described Reykjalundur as being much like his own vision of what the farming areas of Iceland should look like in future, with clusters of smaller houses for families and a large building in the centre for collective activities.

The exterior walls of the main building and the smaller houses have recently been clad over, eliminating many important details. This has caused significant damage to the integrity of the original architecture.

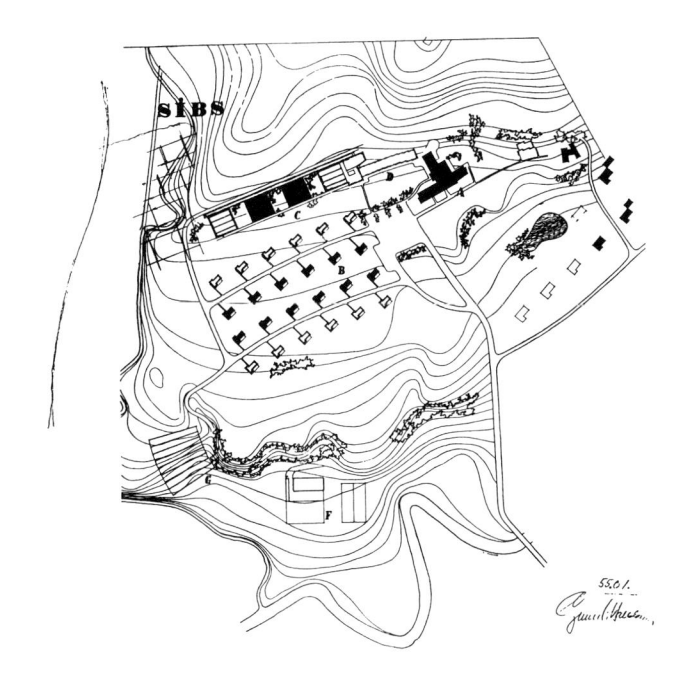

10
Agricultural Bank of Iceland
Austurstræti 5, 101 Reykjavik
1945 | 1948
Gunnlaugur Halldorsson

In the Agricultural Bank in Reykjavik, Halldorsson used a concrete column structure to create a free plan and a non-load-bearing glass façade. The site was very narrow and deep, connecting two parallel steets across a city block. This enabled the architect to develop a new and democratic concept for a modern banking hall which was bright and open and encouraged the man in the street to pass through. The building was a modern design in every detail, such as furnishings and lighting fixtures. Original furnishings in the banking hall were designed by Skarphedinn Johannsson and chairs in the director´s office were by the Danish designer Børge Mogensen.

Progressive Icelandic artists of the time, painter Jon Engilberts and sculptor Sigurjon Olafsson, were brought in by the architect to do wall paintings and decorations. The elevation towards Austurstræti is still intact and important parts of the banking hall interior have survived.

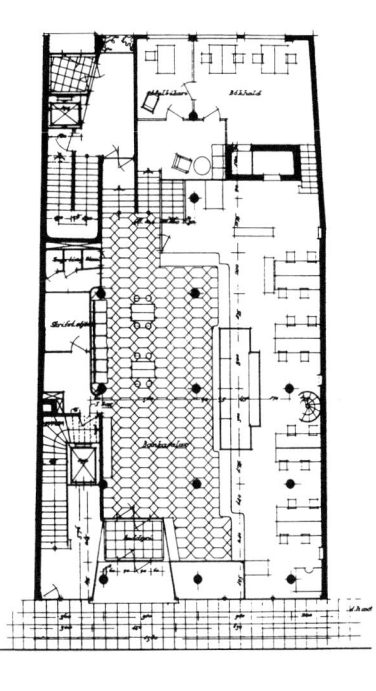

Selected Bibliography :
Hannesson G
Um skipulag baeja. Arbok Haskola islands
Reykjavik 1916

Agustsson H
Gunnlaugur Halldorsson arkitekt: foreword to exhibition catalogue
Reykjavik 1989

Armannsson PH
Einar Sveinsson arkitekt og husameistari Reykjavikur
Reykjavik 1995

Wedebrunn O (ed)
Modern Movement Scandinavia
Copenhagen 1998

Illustrations courtesy DOCOMOMO Iceland

144

Israel

In the short period between the two world wars the land of Israel, then the British mandated territory of Palestine, witnessed a remarkable cultural phenomenon. This was the evolution in what had been a remote corner of the Ottoman Empire of a modern architecture based on the International Style, its acceptance by the small local Jewish community as the architectural norm, and its transmutation by consensus into a modern, architect-designed vernacular of almost universal applicability in the future development of the country. This was an architecture to be found all over Israel, in its towns, villages and communal settlements, but it was most concentrated in those areas of rapid urban growth, where traditional constraints were at a minimum, and where there was a high degree of ethnic homogeneity.

Consequently, while the development of the Modern Movement was manifested to a lesser degree in history-laden Jerusalem or in ethnically-mixed downtown Haifa, it found fertile ground in the modern town of Tel Aviv and its environs, in the new Haifa neighbourhoods on Mount Carmel and the Bay Lands, and in the progressive 'kibbutzim'. In the 1920s this modern architecture was still an emergent phenomenon within a traditional context of indigenous or eclectic buildings. By the mid-1930s, however, it had become the established and dominant idiom. In application it was widespread, ranging from economic public housing schemes to the homes of the middle class, from rural settlements to comprehensive urban design, and from the buildings of industry and commerce to the major public monuments of the Zionist institutions. The architecture of this period was remarkable for its stylistic consistency, and for the quality of its finer monuments.

The Modern Movement in Israel was a predominantly Jewish movement, adapted to the pressing needs of the Zionist venture, seeking to provide the physical infrastructure of the Jewish homeland at a time of substantial immigration in the face of growing anti-semitism in Europe. It was a popular architecture, with both clients and designers accepting the avant-garde as the natural expression of a new architecture for a new society. The role of distinguished architects of international repute, such as Eric Mendelsohn, Adolf Rading or Alexander Klein, was an inspiration, and the influence of Bauhaus-trained architects such as Arieh Sharon was important. Nevertheless, fundamentally, it was not a development imposed from the top, but rather a grass-roots movement generated from within the body of an architectural profession consisting mainly of young European-trained immigrants, highly motivated, at once pragmatic and idealistic, imbued with a sense of mission, and responsive to the challenges of time and place. Outside the heartland of Europe, elite pioneer groups of avant-garde architects in culturally-peripheral countries, such as South Africa or Brazil, also adopted and crusaded to disseminate the credo and forms of the International Style at this time. Israel, however, was unique in the sense that modern architecture became the norm rather than the exception, where the newly-designed physical fabric of life – whole streets, complete neighbourhoods, planned rural settlements – were as consistently modern as the Weissenhofsiedlung or in 'das neue Frankfurt'. It was also unique in that the entire spectrum of the physical environment, ranging from individual buildings to urban projects such as that for Dizengoff Circle in Tel Aviv or Kingsway in Haifa, through the neighbourhoods designed by Patrick Geddes, Alexander Klein or Richard Kauffmann, up to the regional planning of Patrick Abercrombie for the Haifa Bay lands, was at the cutting edge of modern planning theory and architectural practice.

In our endeavour to present the richness of our heritage, we have tried to reflect the differences between the main urban centres of Jerusalem, Tel Aviv, and Haifa; the contrast of urban and rural areas; the geographic diversity of this small land. We have concentrated on architecturally or historically significant buildings and projects, expressive of their time, examples which are either still in good shape or, if showing the ravages of neglect, are still not beyond redemption. Sadly, there are great achievements of the past which we have been unable to present. Some of these are buildings which have been demolished, and others, including such icons as Mendelsohn's Government (Rambam) Hospital, and the former Teltsch Hotel on Mount Carmel, are works whose essential character has been changed by radical alteration. Most of our examples stem from the golden age of the Modern Movement in Israel, which ended in 1939 with the outbreak of World War II. There followed a long period of relative inactivity in architectural terms, a period fraught with human tragedy for the Jewish people in Europe and political uncertainty and violence in Palestine. It was only in 1948, with the end of the British Mandate and the establishment of the State of Israel, that building activity on a massive scale was resumed. It was characterized by a brief revival of the Modern Movement, an architectural Indian summer. In a crisis situation fuelled by economic austerity and an unparalleled influx of immigration, and therefore probably more for pragmatic than ideological reasons, the architectural forms and practices of the 1930s for a short while continued to cast a long shadow, imprinting their genetic code on the emerging architecture of the new state.

Gilbert Herbert
English translation
Nir Buras

1
Beit Hadar
Tel Aviv
1935
Carl Rubin

2
School
Degania
1928
Richard Kauffmann

3
Dubinsky House
Tel Aviv
1936
Lucien Korngold

Carl Rubin's plan was chosen in a limited competition held by the developer of Beit Hadar, the first building in Israel to have a steel structure. The building is functionally divided into three wings, which are expressed in its massing as three independent volumes. The transparent commercial floor at the base of the rounded volume is separated from the upper floors by a projecting canopy above which the upper mass appears to float. In the 1950s, a floor identical to those below was added. Rubin was born in Galicia, studied in Vienna, worked for Richard Kauffman in Jerusalem and in 1931 for several months for Mendelsohn in Berlin. Mendelsohn's influence is evident in this building's expression, volumes and details.

The school at Degania was generated by the special requirements of a kibbutz school and belongs to a building type specially developed by Richard Kauffmann for the hot Syrian-African Rift Valley. Kauffmann designed slots over the first floor windows on either side of the building to induce cross-ventilation. More significantly, he protected the entire building from the scorching sun by a second roof, the broad eaves of which were extended to shade the walls. This lightweight roof was raised on wood columns to create a space between the roofs which was screened to make a covered rooftop porch. The air which flowed between the two roofs relieved the sun's impact and the space served as an outdoor classroom, and as a sleeping porch on summer nights.

One of the most complex and imposing blocks of flats in Tel Aviv, it expresses the principles of architecture as space and the free elevation in an almost 'De Stijl' organization. The separation of the building envelope from the structure was realized by setting back the columns from the wall plane, by extending the wall planes beyond the junctions of surfaces defining the volumes, and by means of narrow slots in the walls indicating separate functional volumes. The building is composed of three masses from which beams project to define outdoor spaces. The volumes are organized around a central stairwell offering varying perspectives. Round windows and water spouts serve as both decorative and functional elements.

4
Engel Apartments
Tel Aviv
1933
Ze'ev Rechter

The Engel apartment building was built to offer a high standard of rental accommodation compared to the characteristic development and construction trends of the 30s. The building comprises three blocks. The western, facing Rothschild Boulevard, is raised on pilotis. This principle of an open storey extends the space of the street visually and enables the free flow of air. This became a norm in Tel Aviv. Rechter was deeply influenced by Le Corbusier, from whom he adopted the principle of raising the building from the ground on pilotis. This is the most Corbusian Israeli building of the period, in its strip windows, projections and reveals of the rectangular window 'boxes', the free composition of the elevations and the concrete pergolas.

5
The Geddes Urban Plan
Tel Aviv
1929
Patrick Geddes

The urban plan of 1929 established Tel Aviv as a modern city. Sir Patrick Geddes developed a hierarchical system of streets, paths and open spaces and determined the direction of the main north to south axes based on his understanding of the city's climate. Thus the city developed parallel to the sea which graces its west. The plan recommended the construction of freestanding buildings on 560m^2 plots to a height of 15m and a maximum site density ratio of 30% in contrast to typical European row houses. During the 1930s, thousands of white stuccoed blocks of flats were built in a modernist idiom referred to locally as 'Bauhaus' style, and Tel Aviv acquired its poetic name 'The White City'.

6
The Glass House
21 Bar-Giora St., Upper Hadar Haifa
1938 | 1941
Theodor Menkes

The Glass House provided minimal bachelor apartments. The layout is L-shaped, with a long axis against the topography, with views from and through the building. The entrance stairwell was originally enclosed within a 'curtain wall' of iron and glass. Outer walls of the apartments, along the corridors, were made of glass blocks to admit daylight into the kitchens and bathrooms. The multiple forms of glass used gave the building its name. The service areas in the apartments were ventilated above the outer corridor through openings in a double ceiling. The balconies in each apartment are reminiscent of Gropius's student hostel at the Bauhaus. Communal facilities included a central dining room, a dumb-waiter, and a swimming pool.

7
Kibbutz Masterplan
Ein Hashofet
1938
Arieh Sharon

The Kibbutz, a collective rural social and economic structure, presented architects of the 1930s with new challenges. Arieh Sharon, founding member of the kibbutz movement, studied at the Bauhaus and returned to Tel Aviv where he opened an architectural practice and designed cooperative and public buildings including Ein Hashofet. Sharon's book 'Kibbutz + Bauhaus' presents his principles and beliefs. For Ein Hashofet Sharon proposed a 'clear and simple solution of central lawn-piazza, leading to the various public buildings, consisting of dining hall, administration, club and reading rooms. The central area would radiate centripetally: the residential and children quarters, the farm buildings and the small, organic children's society.'

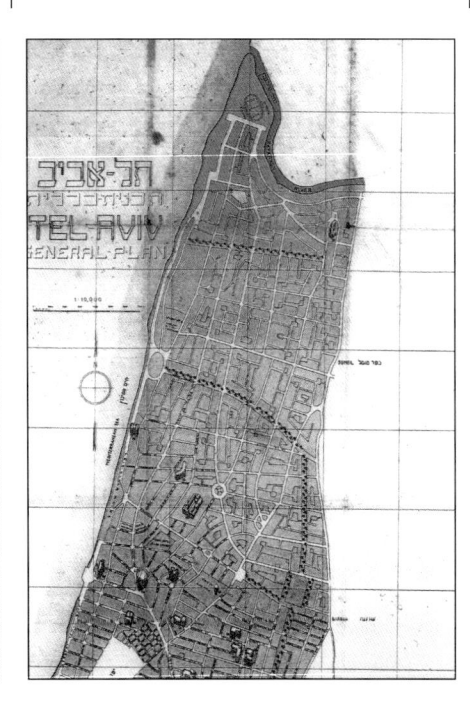

8
Hadassah Medical Center
Mount Scopus, Jerusalem
1938
Eric Mendelsohn

9
Israel Museum
Jerusalem
1965
Al Mansfeld and Dora Gad

10
Kingsway North
Downtown Haifa
1934 | 1937
Clifford Holliday &
RPS Hubbard

The Jerusalem Medical Center was built by the Hadassah Organization adjacent to the Hebrew University campus on Mount Scopus. The building's architect, Erich Mendelsohn, escaped from Nazi Germany in 1934, after having obtained international stature. Upon his arrival in Israel, Mendelsohn applied his concepts of dynamic functionalism to the new context. The building is composed of long, parallel masses perpendicular to the rise of the hill. At its end a rounded element faces the sublime landscape of the Judean Desert and the mountains beyond. The stylized domes of the entrance pavilion make reference to the building's location and Mendelsohn's concepts of racial harmony, an uncommon diplomatic approach.

A relatively late building, the Israel Museum, built to house collections of Israeli and Jewish art and archaeology, is considered one of the Israel's most significant modernist buildings. It is composed of cubic units, roofed by hyperbolic paraboloid shells, supported on central columns. Clerestory windows close the gap between the walls and the roofs. The units were combined to make a cubist composition using organic planning principles. It refers both to the picturesque Arab village of the nearby landscape and to such influential modernist buildings as Mies van der Rohe's brick villa project of the early 1920s. Al Mansfeld studied under Auguste Perret and Dora Gad was educated in Vienna. They immigrated to Israel in the 1930s.

The design of a uniform façade for Kingsway North was an initiative of the British administration, and the culmination of the reclaimed area and the construction of the Haifa Harbour project. This complex of offices and shops was one of the major urban design projects of its day. It created a horizontally banded modern façade some 1500m long, broken by sweeping curves leading to the harbour. The cantilevered canopy along the façade suited the local climate and accentuated horizontality. Stone cladding towards the road, and other details were fixed by Holliday to regulate design. He was a British architect who had been Civic Advisor to the City of Jerusalem and Architectural Advisor to the Town Planning Commission.

11
Kupat Holim Center & Pharmaceutical Stores
8 Beilinson Street, Tel Aviv
1937 | 1939
Josef Neufeld

On a site concentric with nearby Dizengoff Circle stands a unique Tel Aviv building which manifests both Mendelsohnian dynamic functionalism and a Renaissance sensibility. Neufeld worked in Mendelsohn's office from 1927 to 1930 and the influence of the Schocken store in Chemnitz and the Columbus Haus in Berlin is evident. However, the rotational dynamic of this building is unparalleled. The building was designed to contain two functions: the Labour Unions Sick-Fund pharmaceutical stores and its administrative offices. A smooth stucco cylinder punched with windows contains the stores and laboratories in its ground floor and basement. Each interior gallery contributed functional space and utilized natural light.

12
Frederick Man Auditorium
Tel Aviv
1951 | 1957
Ze'ev Rechter & Dov Karmi

The first and largest concert hall in Tel Aviv, this modest cultural monument represents a civic ambition for equality and emancipation. The emphatic horizontals, glass surfaces and thin concrete beams testify to the influence of the International Style. The structure's modest entrance and the grey hues of the stone cladding contribute to its modest character. The sculptured mass of the auditorium rises above the flat volume of the building and a transparent round lift tower has recently been added along the side of the building. The auditorium, a single room clad in wood, contains a stage and 2,700 seats. In spite of its size the space has an intimate feel and is recognized for its acoustics. It is linked to the adjacent Helena Rubinstein art pavilion.

13
Settlement Plan
Nahalal, Jezreel Valley
1921
Richard Kauffmann

Kauffmann planned over 100 settlements in Israel. Nahalal, his first, was also the first 'moshav ovdim', workers' collective farm. This settlement was part of an overall plan undertaken by Kauffmann for the Jezreel Valley and its settlements. Family lots of equal size radiate from a circular centre containing the public institutions and the houses of teachers, artisans and other non-farming members of the settlement. One of the main design sources for Nahalal was the idea of the garden city promulgated by Ebenezer Howard. Kauffmann also adopted tenets of cooperation and equality, whereby the ownership of the land was divided equally.

14
Meonot Ovdim 'Hod'
Tel Aviv
1934
Arieh Sharon

Four Meonot Ovdim workers' housing complexes were built in Tel Aviv in the 1930s. They were influenced by the Karlmarxhof in Vienna and other examples of socialist and cooperative building. Sharon designed three of the workers' housing projects as blocks of apartments around spacious courtyards and gardens. Above the ground floor rise three floors of bright, well ventilated 2-room and 3-room apartments. Sharon located communal functions on the periphery of the courtyard which characterized the community of Meonot Ovdim as a 'fortress of Labor' and set it apart from the surrounding city. Sharon studied at the Bauhaus during the years 1926-29 and until 1931 was the manager of Hannes Meyer's office in Berlin.

15
Haifa Power Station Shell (Paz) 1923 original
design: Eric Mendelsohn
1924 alternative: Richard Kauffmann
1925 executed final project: Palestine
Electric Corporation; Pinhas Rutenberg

16
The Schocken Library
Jerusalem
1934 | 1936
Eric Mendelsohn

17
Talpyoth Market
Hadar-Hacarmel - Haifa
1937 | 1940
Moshe Gerstel

Rutenberg had obtained a concession from the British Government for the development of electricity in Palestine in 1921. In 1923 he invited Mendelsohn to design the Haifa power station. Mendelsohn's design showed a bold composition of cubist masses reflecting the functional divisions of the halls for dynamos and transformers, the workshops and the water tower. In its general appearance it had a pronounced horizontal character. The design was rejected by the acting High Commissioner as being 'too European'. An alternative design, prepared by Kauffmann in 1924, was very similar in form to the Mendelsohn prototype in its composition of masses, its long horizontal windows balanced by verticals, and its use of sun-shading hoods.

The famous department stores which Mendelsohn built for Salman Schocken in Germany were frequently quoted as stylistic examples internationally. However, the library he planned for his old client in Jerusalem, after both of them had fled Hitler's Germany, is a passionate tribute to regional and cultural identity, the architect's homage to the Holy City, a house of books for the 'people of the Book'. Built of bright Jerusalem limestone the library follows the simple cubic character of the vernacular. A semicircular bay window projects from the south façade in a typical Mendelsohnian signature, an expressionistic hint in counterpoint to the archaic background. Mendelsohn's sense of elegance highlights the second floor interior.

Violent disturbances in downtown Haifa and Palestine in 1936-39 caused difficulties in the provision of fresh produce to the Jewish neighbourhood of Hadar-Hacarmel. The objective of Va'ad Hadar-Hacarmel (the ad-hoc local council) was to circumvent this problem by establishing a permanent Jewish market in the neighbourhood. Gerstel won the competition of 1937. He efficiently solved difficult problems of access and servicing caused by the steep slope. The architectural expression is striking: external horizontal banding evoking the flowing lines of the early Mendelsohn. The interior space rising to full height in the centre is covered by a roof of concentric rings of glass blocks, enclosed by a curve of galleries.

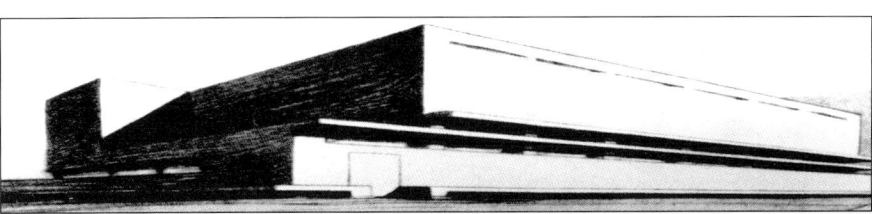

18
Kibbutz Tel Yosef
Dining Hall
1933 | 1936
Leopold Krakauer

The architectonic solution proposed by Krakauer for the Tel Yosef dining hall sets it apart from the other kibbutz dining halls designed by him and others of the Modern Movement. The building is located at the top of a palm-lined grassy slope flanked by dwelling houses. Its cubic mass is topped by another mass rotated 45°. These combine with the staircase at the southern corner of the building to create a pyramidal structure featuring an intriguing interplay of geometric shapes. The upper cube serves to illuminate and ventilate the dining hall. Narrow strip windows in a projecting frame, occupy the entire length of the wall with a bow-like effect. They permit fresh air flow without admitting excessive light or direct sunlight.

19
Weizmann Residence
Rehovot
1934 | 1936
Eric Mendelsohn

The Weizmann Residence was designed for a president-to-be in a state-to-be. This was Mendelsohn's first built project in Israel. It was conceived as a building of national significance and conveys clear aesthetic and political messages. It can be seen as a realization of the architect's intention of an east-west synthesis, which he envisioned to be the platform of Jewish Renaissance and a bridge to peaceful coexistence. Mendelsohn translated his credo into forms that are different from his German vocabulary. Solid walls replace extensive strip windows, there is introvert contemplation instead of extrovert expressiveness, cubic serenity instead of dynamic tension, and vertical permanence instead of horizontal suspension.

Selected Bibliography:
Barkai S & Posner J
'Architecture in Palestine'
L'Architecture d'Aujourd'hui
Boulogne 1937 no9 (September) pp 2-34

Schiffman Y
'The New Palestine'
Architectural Review
London October 1938 pp 142-154

Sharon A
Kibbutz + Bauhaus
Stuttgart & Massada 1976

Harlap A
New Israeli Architecture
East Brunswick NJ 1981

Levin M
White City: International Style Architecture in Israel
Tel Aviv 1984

Heinze-Mühleib I
Erich Mendelsohn. Bauten und Projekte in Palastina 1934-1941
Munich 1986

Taschen B (publ)
Functional Architecture 1925-1940
Cologne 1990

Kroyanker D
Jerusalem Architecture: the period of the British Mandate 1918-1948
Jerusalem 1991 (in Hebrew)
English summary appears in his:
Jerusalem Architecture
London 1994

Herbert G & Sosnovsky S
Bauhaus on the Carmel: Architecture and Planning in Haifa during the British Mandate
Jerusalem & Haifa 1993

Enis R & Ben-Arav J
Sixty years of Kibbutz gardens and Landscape 1910-1970
Tel Aviv 1994 (in Hebrew)

Photographic Credits:
Kalter
1, 4, 11, 12, 14, 19
Peter Szmuk
3
Zionist Archive, Jerusalem
5, 13
Architectural Heritage Research Centre
Faculty of Architecture, Technion
6, 10, 15
Nir Buras
8, 18
Arie Sivan

Italy

In selecting the buildings to illustrate here, our aim has been a narrative one. We have sought to tell the story of twentieth-century architectural development through examples which show the complexity and peculiarity of Italian architecture in achieving the status of modernity.

Three major concerns have guided the selection, summarized as follows:

Buildings that have already become models and true icons of modern architecture.

Buildings that have marked a discontinuity or a critical reconsideration of a presumed 'orthodoxy' of modernism, much too commonly associated with the best results of the thirties.

Buildings that are significant for their symbolic and evocative meanings well beyond their architectural reputation.

The selection covers almost fifty years of Italian architectural history and building production, from mid Teens to the Sixties. This is a significant period which covers the poor years following the first world war, the subsequent rise and then decline of the Fascist regime, the years of the second world war and the early phase of the economic boom during reconstruction. The prevalence of buildings realized in the thirties signals the centrality of the inter-war period for the Italian approach to themes evidently related to international modernism. Before and after that decade the selected buildings testify to the intention to interpret as extensively as possible the Italian critical attitude toward modernism in terms of an architectural vocabulary, including the early attempts as well as developments.

The selection also documents architects who are representative of various schools and tendencies, without pretending to be exhaustive: Vaccaro, Terragni, Michelucci, Ponti, Ridolfi, Moretti, Gardella, Piccinato, Figini, Pollini, Libera, Nervi, BBPR are undoubtedly among the 'masters' of Italian modern architecture. Furthermore, the selection represents a wide spectrum of typologies and functions.

Listing the buildings under these headings, we can isolate the following examples:
Industrial buildings (the Fiat Lingotto Factory in Turin and the Olivetti Office Buildings at Ivrea); Hospital (the Anti-tuberculosis Building in Alessandria); Post Office Buildings (in Rome and at Sabaudia); Seaside Colony (the A.G.I.P. Colony at Cesenatico); Railway Station (the Santa Maria Novella Station in Florence); Fascist Headquarters (the Casa del Fascio in Como); Multifamily Housing (the Rustici Apartment House in Milan and the Girasole building in Rome); One-family Villas (the Figini Villa in Milan and the Malaparte House at Capri); Multifunctional Building (the Torre Velasca in Milan); Sport Facilities (the Fencing Academy in Rome); Convention Centre (the Congress Palace at the E42 in Rome); Engineering Work (the Exhibition Hall in Turin); Exhibition Centre (the Triennale building in Milan); New towns (Sabaudia). Finally, the selection cannot avoid emphasing the major importance assumed by some cities compared to more provincial towns. It is possible to talk of places with a high degree of modernity. About one third of the selected buildings are located in Northern Italy. Here, the regions of Piemonte and Lombardia represent the early nucleus of the modernist vocabulary. In Piemonte, cities such as Turin, Ivrea, and Alessandria became the banner of Italian industrial tradition par excellence. Milan, and the small town of Como, where Terragni lived and worked together with a large group of artists, represent the true cultural milieu of Italian modernism, well beyond architecture. The Fiat Lingotto Factory, per se a memory of the Futurist technological credo, soon assumed an international status as a symbol of the new spirit, recalling Le Corbusier's enthusiasm expressed in 'Vers une architecture'. The technical appraisal received by the Lingotto Factory could be extended in the late forties to the masterly designed Salone B at the Torino Exhibition hall by Nervi with its innovative use of ferro-concrete. The Officine Olivetti and the Dispensario Antitubercolare indicate the attention paid to social attitudes from 'progressive industrialists, following the nineteenth-century mercantile tradition. The Torre Velasca in Milan illuminates the debate of the early fifties about the 'dialogue' between new monuments and the historical continuity in city centres. The so called Modern Movement had dramatically cut off that dialogue.

The largest amount of modern buildings is to be found in central Italy. They are significant examples of the policy of consensus that the Fascist regime attempted to reach in the late twenties and very early thirties. The buildings realised in Rome and in Lazio need very little comment. Rome is the true stage, during the two decades of the Fascist regime, of the three major construction sites: the Sport Facilities at the Foro Italico, the new University La Sapienza, and the EUR neighbourhood for the World Exhibition scheduled in 1942. A similar attitude of suspended symbolism could be seen in Il Girasole, an apartment block deeply imbued with abstract monumentalism. One single building has been selected in Southern Italy: the Malaparte House at Capri, which achieved the status of the modern model of the Mediterranean villa through its critical reception as well as through the success of Godard's movie 'Le Mépris' (1963).

Maristella Casciato
Rosalia Vittorini

1
Fiat Lingotto Works
Via Nizza 294-295, Turin
1916 | 1930
Giacomo Matté Trucco
Vittorio Bonadé Bottino (structure)

2
Palazzo dell'Arte
Via Alemagna 6, Milan
1931 | 1933
Giovanni Muzio

The Lingotto complex, built for the Fiat auto industry, is a huge site with a number of separate buildings. The most important are the clearing workshops (Officine di Smistamento), the new workshops (Nuove Officine) and the office building (Palazzina Uffici). The long main front, stretching out for 780 metres, is one of the most distinctive features of industrial Turin. The load-bearing structure of the complex consists of reinforced concrete frames, a system already well tested by the building company Società Porcheddu, the Italian licensee of the Hennebique patent. The clearing workshops cover a rectangular area and consist of one-floor sheds, divided into 15 aisles, with regular crossings. The production-based features of construction, space and organization make the new workshops a true symbol of modern industrial architecture. The five-floor building is topped by the famous test circuit on the roof. The preservation plan for the building, now used as a business centre and auditorium, was drawn up by Renzo Piano and his studio, with the exception of the office building, which was renovated by the architects Gabetti and Isola.

The Palazzo is the headquarters of the Triennale, a cultural institute set up in the early 1930s to promote architecture and the decorative arts. The building, which is in the Parco Sempione, near the Sforza castle, is a 130-metre long, three-floor parallelepiped with an exhibition area of more than 5,000m². It consists of two main parts, distinct one from the other in terms of both form and structure. One, a monumental building, includes the office section and the reception areas: the entrance hall, the monumental staircase, the atrium and the impluvium, the reception halls, and the portico which looks onto the park. The other part, more often used for exhibitions, consists of two symmetrical wings, with galleries one above the other, surrounding the central core and meeting in the apsidal space next to the theatre. The vast windows, 16 metres in the galleries and the 24 in the theatre hall are made possible by the load-bearing structure in reinforced concrete. The use of special materials such as clinker bricks and granite confer an air of great importance to this perfect 'display machine'.

3
Santa Maria Novella Railway Station
Florence
1932 | 1935
Gruppo Toscano

The building comes from the controversial win in a national competition by the Florentine Giovanni Michelucci and a group of his young students. Mussolini himself was firmly on the side of this intensely modern architecture, of which he spoke enthusiastically: 'Florence station is beautiful and the Italian people . . . will love it'. An airy concourse, with the vault supported by large reticulated beams concealed by a boxed vault, receives and disperses the passengers; the longitudinal building which forms the northern limit of the square provides a number of services around the atrium, including the left-luggage office, the first and second-class buffets with decorative tempera landscapes by Rosai, and the waiting rooms.

4
Sabaudia
1933 | 1934
Guido Cancellotti, Eugenio Montuori
Luigi Piccinato, A Scalpelli

Planned as part of the vast reclamation operation for the Pontine marshes, the new town of Sabaudia is located in an area of great beauty, between Lake Paola and the Circeo promontory. Here the regime intended to demonstrate, even on the international level, that it was modern and efficient. It was designed as a model town. Thus the buildings are connected by squares and street façades; the relationship with the landscape is never lost, but filters into carefully studied vistas; the architecture blends into the very structure of the town. The result is a unified architectural statement. The fulcrum is the tower of the town hall: it plays a symbolic and commemorative role, standing in the square that is dominated by the buildings of civic power.

5
Post Office Building
Piazza Bologna 39, Rome
1932 | 1935
Mario Ridolfi

An important example of the Roman version of modernity, the building was constructed after a design competition for four new post offices in suburban areas. Even though this was Ridolfi's first experience of design, he created a successful blend of formal aspects, functions and forms. The building, with its expressionist effect created by the concave-convex line of the ground plan, plays a powerful urban role, giving the square a note of distinction and setting itself up as a modern civic centre. The compact volume is marked by projecting cantilever roofs, by the short but taut flight of steps, the dark entrance opening, the measured rhythm of the windows, but especially by the elegant and all-embracing travertine stone that dresses the façade.

6
House at the 'Journalists' village'
Via Perrone di S Martino 8, Milan
1933 | 1935
Luigi Figini

Atelier house, designed by Figini for himself and his family, in the garden-city which was being constructed north-west of the central station in Milan. The crystalline volume of the house rises on a grid of reinforced concrete pillars 4.34 metres high. The two-floor building is inscribed within a golden-section of 18 x 5.5 metres. A single-ramp external staircase at the side connects the garden with the first floor, which is divided into three zones: the living room in the middle, with the kitchen and the maid's room on one side and the terrace on the other. On the floor above, the bedroom and bathroom open onto two terraces for relaxation and gymnastics: there are sandpits, sports equipment, a little swimming pool and small bushes.

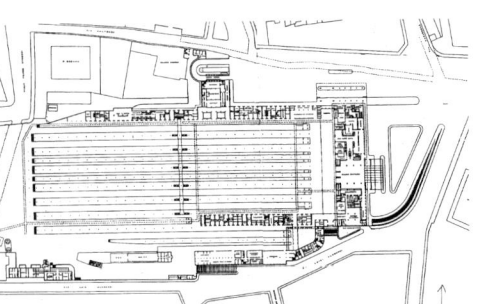

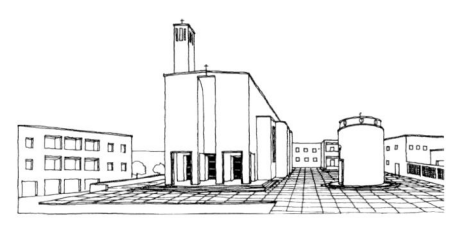

7
Casa del Fascio
Piazza del Popolo 4, Como
1928 | 1936
Giuseppe Terragni

Universally considered to be the masterpiece of modern Italian architecture, this building is the result of a complicated succession of events. Called upon to design a building with considerable symbolic content, in which the regime celebrated itself while displaying its efficiency, Terragni went beyond his original, traditionalist project to effect an original design and construction experiment which was a symbol and summary of the development of Italian architecture in the inter-war period. The building takes its figurative references from the local culture of Como, other references from international experience, and others still from a continuum with Mediterranean tradition, but allows the site as a whole to become a real experimental laboratory.

8
Fencing Academy
Via dei Gladiatori 4, Rome
1933 | 1936
Luigi Moretti

Created as the Casa del Balilla (the Fascist Youth Movement building), the regime's edifice for the physical and ideological training of young people, it was, an exemplary collection of formal, technical and typological features for future projects. At a particularly favourable moment for modern architecture, Moretti brilliantly combines rationalist requirements and references to tradition. By following his own well-established formula, he creates a clear-cut building consisting of two orthogonal blocks around a core of corridors. The reinforced concrete frame is enveloped by the facing of chamfered, veined, statue-marble slabs from Carrara and the gilded mosaic by Canevari, even by the glass membranes.

9
Rustici Apartment Building
Corso Sempione 36, Milan
1933 | 1936
Giuseppe Terragni & Pietro Lingeri
O Hoffmann (structure)

The irregular lot is taken up by two distinct buildings connected on the line of the main façade by superimposed flying cantilever roofs/balconies. This distinguishing feature creates a subtle play of light which adds to the multi-material and polychrome nature of the building. Traditional materials such as white marble are used together with modern materials such as steel and reinforced concrete and glass tiles or Ital-pomice for infills. The symmetry of the façade is broken by the left-hand block, which is chromatically and figuratively separate. A vast, airy atrium on the main axis of the building, protected by an articulated cantilever roof with glass tiles and projecting ribs, serves both the independent stairwells.

10
Antituberculosis Dispensary
Via Don Gasparolo 2-4, Alessandria
1933 | 1938
Ignazio Gardella

The building consists of two levels above ground and a basement. The off-centre external stairs on the façade lead up to the raised floor, which is open to the public and contains the large waiting room and out-patients' departments. A staircase for the staff leads up to the offices, the director's office and the caretaker's apartment on the upper floor. This floor also includes the large open-air space of the sun terrace for heliotherapy which is connected to the small in-patients' ward for those under temporary observation. The structure of the building consists of a regular grid of square pillars in reinforced concrete, including eight bays on the main fronts and two bays, with a lateral projection, in the other direction.

11
Montecatini Office Building
Via Turati, Milan
1935 | 1938
Gio Ponti with A Fornaroli & E Soncini

The modern office building, with the spare and subtle geometry of its façade, is the head office of Montecatini, which had become the largest chemical corporation in Italy. The articulate and imposing H-shaped volume is based on a carefully studied plan of distribution and displays an elementary lexicon: the windows on the tranquil façade reveal the modular arrangement of the load-bearing structure in reinforced concrete; this, at regular 4-metre intervals, divides the interior into minimal office spaces on a contemporary plan. Built in the years of autarchy, the building exhibits the level of progress reached by Italian industry and represents a process of integrated planning that was without precedent in Italy at this time.

12
AGIP Seaside Colony
Viale Carducci 181, Cesenatico
1937 | 1938
Giuseppe Vaccaro

When the seaside colony on the Romagna coast for the children of the staff of the Italian petroleum company was built, it was named after Sandro Mussolini. Its construction, like that of other seaside and mountain holiday homes, built in the decade from 1930 to 1940, was part of a wide-ranging social programme set up by the regime. The main body, which rests on a raised pier system, runs parallel to the sea; it is distinguished by an uninterrupted arcade on the side facing away from the sea, which connects the various parts of the complex. The dormitories are on the first floor of the main building; in this case, the design of the façades has been constrained by their particular orientation,

13
Villa Malaparte
Capo Massullo, Capri
1938 | 1943
Adalberto Libera & Curzio Malaparte

The history of the house that the writer Curzio Malaparte had built for himself on one of the most charming promontories of Capri is itself worthy of a novel. Libera, the architect, was present only in the early creative stage, sketching the key elements of the final building: an elongated rectangular block on the flatter side of the rocky spur. This theme was taken up by the writer, and developed very much according to his own ideas. The layout has given rise to a number of simple nautical analogies, such as the blade of an oar (Heyduk) and broader nautical metaphors, drawn from the genius loci: a houseboat stranded on the rocks, with its sail (the wall of the sun terrace) visible (Venezia), or the command post of the helmsman in the aft study (Tafuri).

14
Congress Centre
Piazzale JF Kennedy, Rome
1937 | 1943. 1953
Adalberto Libera
Carlo Cestelli Guidi (structures)

A Congress Centre which is representative of the E42 Quarter built for the Universal Exhibition of Rome (1942 - though it never took place because of the War). Closing the slightly rising square, this hermetic building, right from its 14 tall columns in Alzo granite which give rhythm to the façade, is a modern interpretation of monumental classicism. This is borne out by extensive use of marble, much of very high quality. From the solid basement with its large glazed atriums on the two opposite sides facing outwards, rises the cube of the reception hall covered by a metal cross-vault which provides natural light through four lunettes. At the rear stands the congress hall, on the roof of which a theatre in stone has been created.

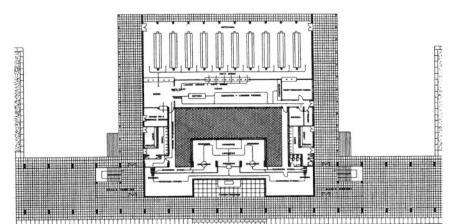

15
Salone B at Turin Exhibition Hall
1947 | 1948. 1953
Pier Luigi Nervi

The works reveal the expressive potential of an original building technique, conceived and perfected by Nervi from the 1940s, based on prefabricated units and on ferro-concrete. The building was part of a permanent exhibition complex in the area of the Valentino Park: it was designed by Nervi to a layout and volumetric plan provided by the client. Construction work was completed by his building company in just nine months, in 1947-48; it was later enlarged in 1953. It consists of a main area covered by a large, 120-metre long, thin, undulating vault spanning 80 metres, which terminates in an apse with a half-dome with crossed ribbing supported by thin pilasters and surrounded by a flat ring-shaped slab roof.

16
Apartment Building Il Girasole
Viale B Buozzi 64, Rome
1949 | 1950
Luigi Moretti

One of the most significant post-war works, it is a sort of abstract formulation of the Roman building. It is the result of a research project, with constant reference to classical architecture, emphasizes figurative elements with the addition of refined quotations and elements taken from Baroque and abstract art. This can be clearly seen in the juxtaposition of natural and naturalistic elements, in the composition, divided floors, in the play of shadows, and in the choice of materials. With its surfaces broken by, the volume projects outwards, breaking out from a high base, and is cut axially by the sharp, dark central slit which rises up to the stylized, asymmetrical tympanum and dilates in an unexpectedly sinuous manner in the courtyard.

17
Serpentine housing
Ina-Casa quarter for 4500 in Forte Quezzi
Via Loria, Genova
1956 | 1957
Luigi Carlo Daneri

Low-income housing project which was part of the reconstruction programme set up by the state to promote the country's renaissance after the defeat. The architects Daneri and Fuselli coordinated the construction work which was designed to create a line of houses laid out along the contours of the southern slope of the hill, creating a harmonious union with the landscape. Daneri worked mainly on the longest building, nicknamed the "biscione" (grass-snake) after its long, sinuous shape. This building consists of six-floor apartment blocks separated at mid-height by an open gallery-corridor reached by lifts. From this level, which acts as a promenade, meeting place and scenic terrace, staircases lead up and down to the apartments.

18
The Velasca tower
Piazza Velasca 5, Milan
1950 | 1958
Studio BBPR
Arturo Danusso (structure)

Multipurpose building with 29 floors above ground level and two below, divided into sectors on seven levels: shops on the ground floor with showrooms on the first; nine floors of company offices; seven of offices and homes; one transitional floor, eight floors with a total of 72 apartments of various sizes, each with its own loggia or veranda. The copper-sheet facing connects the top floor with the service areas. The tower is built around a central core containing the servicing ducts. The main elements of the volume are: the load-bearing pilasters which accentuate the verticality of the structure, the brickwork construction perforated by the serrated sequence of windows and loggias, the apartment floors which jut out over the floors below.

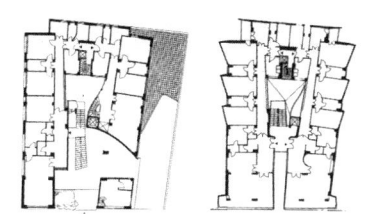

19
Veritti House
Viale Duodo, Udine
1955 | 1961
Carlo Scarpa

The recurrent motif of the project is the circle which, in the completed version, is transformed into two semi-circular elements. The first is the semi-cylindrical wall which encloses the house on the northern side, while the second is the south-facing pool. To the west, an elongated winter garden stretches away from the circular plan of the building. The distribution of space, articulated by reinforced concrete pilasters, places the day area on the ground floor, reached by a passageway across the pool that reflects the eastern façade of the building. The bedrooms, bathroom and other work areas are on the first floor, while the attic contains a studio next to a sun terrace.

20
Olivetti ICO factory
Via Jervis, Ivrea
1934 | 1962
Luigi Figini, Gino Pollini, Annibale Fiocchi

Series of buildings constructed over 30 years as additions to the original Olivetti factory built in 1908; a long period in which the name of Adriano Olivetti is inextricably linked to those of the two Milanese architects, Figini and Pollini, who were responsible for the project. The first building, originally on two floors but later raised to three, is an L-shaped construction with a modular structure in reinforced concrete. The long glazed wall on Via Jervis is broken up by T-shaped piers which contain the drainpipes and the mechanism for closing the curtains. Two enlargements were completed in the years 1939 to 1955: the extension of the glazed façade on Via Jervis and the construction of a building on the adjacent Via Monte Navale.

Selected Bibliography :
Libera A
'Arte e Razionalismo'
La Rassegna italiana
Milan March 1928

Fillia L (ed)
La nuova architettura
Turin 1931

Albini M
'Modern italy: the national style and the international style'
Architectural Review
London January 1937 pp 15-19

Pica A
Architettura moderna in Italia
Milan 1941

Moretti B
Case d'habitazione in Italia
Milan 1947

Figini L & Pollini G
'Les origines de l'architecture moderne en Italie'
L'Architecture d'Aujourd'hui
Boulogne June-July 1952

Kidder Smith GE
Italy Builds
London 1955

Rogers EN
'La tradizione dell'architettura moderna italiana'
Casabella-Continuità
Milan no 206

Sartoris A
Encyclopédie de l'architecture nouvelle vol 1
Milan 1957

Koulermos P
'The work of Terrangi, Lingeri and Italian Rationalism'
Architectural Design special issue
London March 1963

Persico E
Scritti di architettura 1927-1935
Florence 1968

Photographic Credits :
Archivo Storico Fiat
1
Archivo Triennale
2
Franco Panzini
4, 14, 16
Grazia Sgrilli
5
Archivo Figini-Pollini
6
Archivo Terragni
7
Archivo Vasari
8
Andrea Canziani
9, 11, 18
Archivo Gardella
10
Archivo Vaccaro
12
Archivo Talamona
13
Archivo Nervi
15
Giovanna Franco
17
Maura Manzelle
19
Archivo Olivetti
20

Acknowledgments :
Daniela Bosia
Andrea Canziani
Ferruccio Dilda
Giovanna Franco
Claudio Greco
Cristiana Marco
Sano dell'Erba
Sergio Poretti
Luca Veresani

Japan

Modernism, as characterized by ideological rationalism, an aesthetic of pure lines, planes, and volumes, and a commitment to the betterment of society, was introduced into Japan in the 1920s. New architectural thought, consciously intended to supersede modernism, came to the attention of Japanese architects in the 1970s. The twenty buildings, selected to represent Japan's modernism, are from the period between 1920 and 1970.

To Japan's architects, modernism was, above all, a revolution of aesthetics. Although in the 1910s they had realized that function and economy should be the key factors for a new architecture, they did not try to assimilate and express these characteristics in their designs; such a notion was too vague to determine a canon of form. They needed a new aesthetic that seemed appropriate for the new vision. It was the Japanese Secessionists who, in 1920, first acclaimed a beauty of pure lines, planes and volumes rather than the Classical Orders or other historically based ornament. They sympathized with German Idealism and their first proposals derived from Expressionism. Expressionism in Japan, however, soon waned, and simpler forms gradually dominated in the architectural scene. Japanese modernists so quickly absorbed this new aesthetic that, of foreign architects, Le Corbusier by the late 20s already had become the most notable figure. The aesthetic affected even the design of a headquarters building of one of the most prestigious companies.

Some architects were interested in determining architectural elements by using meteorological data. They tried to determine the depths of eaves by solar angles, and the sizes of the openings by analyzing alternate patterns for efficient ventilating. Grade school buildings in Tokyo are good examples in which to trace such approaches. 'Health' was the keyword. Architecture should be a science whose data could justify the shape end dimension of every opening.

But the war soon hampered construction activities. Buildings related to social reform were not much realized other then those apartments built by the semi-governmental organization. Modernism began to bloom again in Japan in the 1950s. Although cities had not recovered from the war and the economy was in turmoil, Architects at that time could believe in a bright future in which a better society based on democracy and modern technology would emerge. Leading architects thought that they were responsible for realizing the future through new architectural design developing from modern production systems.

Their first task was the design of small houses. These were wooden buildings influenced by American houses and characterized by free space with a utility core. Some architects worked out a well-organized structural system and succeeded in reconciling it to their design concept. Such structural systems related to planning and space composition can also be seen in grade school buildings. Wooden structures were so popular in Japan that not a few architects proposed to renovate the type on a widespread rationalistic basis.

At the same time Japan's architects began to search for ways to relate function with form.

Some took the naive view that each 'function' should respond to a specific form without reference to some larger ideal. The group led by Kenzo Tange (b1913) criticized this naive view. They addressed the more dynamic and ambiguous aspects of 'function' and submitted designs that could permit multi-purpose use, and exploring enabling structural innovations. Since earthquakes are a severe threat to buildings in Japan, long spans and large open spaces posed a special challenge. Thus progress in structural engineering seemed to promise Japan's architects a new architecture.

Easier and more economical construction methods were also one of their chief concerns. Prefabrication was welcomed and modular coordination, which relates each part of a building with a module, was introduced. Prefectural halls become the typical vehicle for experimentation with these methods in the 1950s and 60s. Prefectural halls were thought, after the war, to symbolize democracy. They gave architects a chance to design high-rise buildings, a type not then popular in Japan. And since this building-type was a complex of different functions, including offices and an assembly hall, architects could study how to compose volumes as direct responses to functions. And the architect become concerned not only with the building itself but also with the characteristics of the space surrounding it. Thus in the 1950s and 60s, in complexes like the prefectural halls mentioned above, a different volume and exterior design was often assigned to each function in the composition. Increasingly architects were interested in planning building mass and plaza design. Japan's modernists had early and often asserted that Japanese traditional architecture 'resembled' modern architecture in character and aesthetics. They argued that simplicity of plan and structure, absence of applied ornament, exploitation of the beauty of materials, and asymmetry are a part of a 'real' Japanese architectural tradition. As examples they cited not temples but shrines, houses and tea houses as the most 'Japanese,' temples being considered 'Chinese.' They also insisted that the compositional beauty of lines and planes emphasized by modernism was characteristic of Japan's traditional designs.

Such an interpretation of architectural tradition became popular among Japan's architects in the 1930s just when modernism began to spread. Some said they were surprised to find characteristics of modern architecture in their own traditional buildings. But as one architectural critic pointed out, this was a predictable coincidence; they simply looked at their traditional architecture through the filter of modernism; they were seeing in the past what they wanted to see. It is actually easy to point out different features from modernistic disciplines even in the same type of architecture.

After the war, 'free space' was added as one of the characteristics of Japanese architectural tradition. This addition from the influence of modernistic concepts of the time. Some architects insisted that their slender pillars and fully glazed openings were related to the Japanese architectural tradition. Many architects abroad shared such recognition of Japanese architectural tradition. Japan's traditional architecture, especially the traditional house, attracted them chiefly because it seemed to them that Japanese traditional architecture not only resembled modern architecture but also implied ways to humanize modern architecture by making much of human-scale and natural materials.

Such attention to Japanese traditional architecture tells us how strongly modernism affected the architectural thought then. Metabolism emerged in 1960, and was the last stage of Japan's modernism. It was the first Modern Movement acknowledged by architects worldwide as original to Japan. Introducing biological metaphor and the concept of 'time,' it proposed an architecture and urban design that could respond to 'changes.' Metabolists distinguished 'major-structure' and 'sustainable parts' from 'minor-structure' and 'easily-replaced parts,' sorting them in accordance with their lives. Constant renewal, corresponding to needs and lives, was the theme. The Metabolists, like Archigram, their counterparts in Great Britain, tried to respond optimistically to the advent of the consumer society. Their urban design projects feature such views.

Urban design become a major concern of Japan's architects after the war, although urban reform projects were carried out in large cities like Tokyo where a major earthquake in 1923 had caused enormous damage. Such reforms meant chiefly widening roads and land readjustments. They were the fields for city planners in the national and local governments. With a few exceptions, projects for 'ideal cities' had not been proposed by architects before the war. Even Le Corbusier's apprentices such as Kunio Maekawa (1905-86) and Junzo Sakakura (1901-69) were not involved in such projects before the war. But in the 1960s more and more architects proposed their 'ideal cities.' Tange's 'Tokyo 1960' was among the best-known; the Metabolists too were eager to submit their urban projects.

Doubts about modernism were already being expressed in the 1960s. Modernism had stressed sophistication, abstraction and systematic thinking. But unrefined shapes, vernacular materials and construction methods, and rough textures began to look like a more reliable approach to some architects. Hiroshi Oe (1913-89) criticized modern architecture by advancing a unique interpretation of Japanese architectural tradition. According to him, buildings traditionally had two different kinds of parts; those seen, and the essential but unseen supportive elements. The former solely relates to expression independent of structural concerns. He regarded role-sharing as important to a better architecture, criticizing the modern architectural tenets that require a close relationship between the expression and the underlying structure. Modernism thus began to lose its legitimacy and from the 1970s on was gradually replaced by a new thinking proposed by younger architects like Arata Isozaki (b1931), who advocated autonomy of forms. Few of Japan's architects practicing today still fully believe in the dogma and canons of modernism, but it is still regarded, nevertheless, as the most influential contribution to architectural thought in Japan's recent architectural history.

DOCOMOMO Japan

1
Dojunkai Apartments
Tokyo 14 sites, Yokohama 2 sites
1924 | 1934
Dojunkai Building Department

The first group of reinforced concrete apartments, built by a public organization in Japan, which was to have influence all over the world. 'Dojunkan' was the foundation established to aid the Great Earthquake victims of 1923 with the financial support of the Japanese Government. Among its enterprises, the construction of reinforced concrete structure apartments was highly evaluated. The first one was built in Nakanogou in 1925 and the last was in Edogawa in 1934. During these 9 years, Dojunkai developed 16 housing complexes and constructed 109 ridges including 2,788 houses. The sites are widely spread: 14 areas in Tokyo, 2 in Yokohama. The buildings were surrounded by courtyards which encouraged families to share facilities.

2
Sumitomo Building
Kitahama, Chuo-ku, Osaka
1926 | 1930
Eikichi Hasebe & Kenzo Takekoshi

A masterpiece of modern architecture, the client was a Japanese 'zaibatsu' who had started a banking business in 1900. They required a new headquarters building to expand their business. To this end Sumitomo established its own in-house architectural department led by two young architects, Hasebe and Takekoshi of the Tokyo Imperial University (the architectural department developed to Nikken Sekkei). They were sent to Europe for one year, in order to study the architecture of similar buildings. The design motif of the building was to integrate Western classicism and modernism. The northern part of the building, facing the river, was completed in 1926, and the rest in 1930.

3
Chochikukyo
Ohyamasaki, Otokuni, Kyoto 618-0071
1929
Koji Fujii

On a site of 33,000m² near Kyoto, this is the last of a series of the experimental houses that investigated a type of Japanese dwelling, that was designed to relate to the new modern life style and also Japanese climate. Scientific research of climate and the utilization of Japanese traditional materials are the basis of the design. The planning is totally controlled within a one metre modulation; the architect included in the design many new environmental details such as an underlaid ventilation system on the floor and the ceiling, the adoption of deep eaves to protect from the strong sunshine and a cloud-wall to maintain the insulation.

4
Tokyo Detention Center
Kosuge, Katsushika, Tokyo 124-0001
1930
Shigeo Kanbara

This was built for the control office in the Tokyo Detention Center, by Kanbara who was an architectural engineer of the ministry of Judicial Office. The front façade of the control office composed of the observation and clock tower, recalls a bird spreading its wings; it is one of the last examples in the movement of Expressionism in Japan since 1920s. He also designed in the Art Deco Style, the details of interior with his own aesthetic. Even though he adopted re-inforced concrete which was introduced in Japan at that time, he could manage to express dynamic form and sublime space, even in the restricted conditions associated within a detention center.

5
Tokyo Central Post Office
Marunouchi, Chiyoda-ku, Tokyo 100-0005
1931
Tetsuro Yoshida

A complex of two functions (central post and business office) is characteristic of modernism in the 1930s in Japan, Yoshida's Tokyo Central Post Office is a masterpiece and is sited in front of Tokyo Central Station. Although the planning of the building was started in 1922, the construction was not executed until 1927, because of the Kanto Earthquake and budgetary cutbacks, it was finally completed in 1931. Immediately, it was appreciated by Bruno Taut and also Japanese modernists as one of the best examples of new architecture in Japan. Yoshida was also famous for Deutsche-philia and published three books in German: 'Das Japanische Wohnhaus', 'Das Japanische Architekture', and 'Das Japanische Garten.'

6
Kameki Tsuchiura House
Kamiosaki, Shinagawa, Tokyo 141-0021
1935
Kameki Tsuchiura

This is representative of modern houses, which experimented with the adoption of the dry wall system. The influence from Walter Gropius is clearly seen in the building. Kameki Tsuchiura who was the owner and also the designer of the building, and worked for Frank Lloyd Wright at Taliesin. Nobu Tsuchiura, his wife, was also an architect and studied under Wright. With his encounter with Czech architect, B Feuerstain who worked for Perret, Tsuchiura developed his design ideas that he started with Wright's style, that later included Perret's, and finally he then arrived at the International Style. He designed 26 modern houses from 1931 to 1939 when he moved to Manchuria.

7
Keio Gijyuku Grade School
Ebisu, Shibuya, Tokyo 150-0013
1937
Yoshiro Taniguchi

8
Ube City Public Hall
Asahi, Ube, Yamaguchi 755-0041
1937
Togo Murano

9
Miyuki-no-ma, Hasshokan
Hirokoji, Showa-ku, Nagoya 466-0834
1950
Sutemi Horiguchi

10
Kamakura Modern Art Museum
Kanagawa Prefacture
Yukinoshita, Kamakura, Kangawa 248-0005
1951
Junzo Sakakura

There were only few architects who considered environmental planning in design practice in the 1930s. Taniguchi was one of them when he designed this grade school based on the theme of function and hygiene. He proposed new environmental engineering, such as adopting a glass curtain-wall to enrich openness, planting grass on the terrace to ease reflecting sunshine, and using a panel heating system. He challenged and created several new concepts, such as the interior facilities when he designed clover-typed desks for the workshop in the science classroom. This school is one of the best examples of a modern school in the pre-war Japan.

The building is dedicated to Yusaku Watanabe and six companies, who developed Ube city from a rural town to an industrial city. Thus the Ube City Public Hall is also a memorial hall and cultural center, in this region, and symbolizes modern industrial utopia. Its symmetrical composition creates a very strong impression, with its simple volumetric shapes, curving, brick-covered front facade, and six tall concrete pylons in front of the entrance plaza. The symmetrical fan-shaped form, rightly follows the three functions which are a stage, an auditorium and an entrance hall. In particular, the entrance hall and second-floor foyer, have equally curved spaces in which their simplicity is underscored by their cylindrical columns.

This was built as accommodation for the Emperor Showa, when he attended the Aichi National Athletic Games. Horiguchi understood that modern architecture was composed of lines and planes as its aesthetic principle and advocated this even in prewar time. He also insisted that the Japanese tradition was also composed of such aesthetics. He had a particular theory, that the Japanese tea ceremony room expresses an aesthetic work within one space, and that the aesthetic composition of pillar, shoji, and tatami mats, are the essence of Japanese architecture. This accommodation space, was designed under Horiguchi's principle of aesthetic composition, which was to apply the motif of traditional architecture, such as that by Katsura Villa.

The Museum was built beside the greenish pond which is located in the precinct of Kamakura Hachimangu Shrine, constructed in the Kamakura era (1192-1333). Junzo Sakakura, who was the prizewinner, studied under Le Corbusier from 1931 to 1936, and returned to Japan because he was granted a grande prix for designing the Japanese pavilion for the Paris Exposition in 1937. He is one of the architects who contributed and gave many influences to the Japanese architectural world, both before and after the war. The building encloses a central courtyard. The block on the first floor, is divided by a masonry wall of Oya stone, and a slender steel frame that supports the exhibition space on the second floor.

165

11
Hiroshima Peace Centre
Nakajima, Naka, Hiroshima 730-0811
1952
Kenzo Tange

This monumental building including landscape, was initially planned as a national competition for the project to commemorate 200,000 victims of the A-bomb. Tange proposed a long rectangular documentation museum raised on piloti, with a central view along the axis through the plaza, the monument, and atomic-bomb dome (world heritage). The project was designed for concern with environmental landscape, to memorize the importance of peace and the abundance of war. Tange gave the presentation of this plan at the CIAM 8 Congress in Hoddesdon in 1951. He proposed the Japanese idea of Core and emphasized the lack of metaphysical centre, such as those in Occidental examples.

12
Hara House
Todoroki, Setagaya, Tokyo 158-0082
1954
Makoto Masuzawa

This is located in a quiet residential zone. The building is rectangular in shape, its dimensions are 7.2 x 13.5m. The free plan without any columns in the interior was realized by quake-proof walls which are well-balanced distributed on its circumference, and a roof truss which is horizontally braced between the ceiling and the roof. Private rooms are placed at the two ends of the building, leaving a central space which is divided into living, dining, and kitchen by a sliding door and a service core independently constructed of concrete blocks. There is a 1.5m height difference between the site and the street level. This realized the open air space. Masuzawa, the architect, was working for Antonin Raymond when he designed this house.

13
Kangawa Prefectural Library and Music Hall
Momijigaoka, Nishi-ku, Yokohama 220-0044
1954
Kunio Maekawa

This is a complex of a music hall and library, located on the hill looking down over the Yokohama harbour. Among several architects who were designated as competitors, Kunio Maekawa was selected as a prizewinner. He studied under Le Corbusier from 1928 to 1930. He worked for Antonin Raymond after his return to Japan, and later established his own office. He is one of the leaders in Japanese architectural world, both before and after World War II. This complex is composed of two volumes accompanied with a clear single path of circulation flow. Maekawa had pursued this order prior to the war. These two buildings were shifted and arranged at right angles to each other and connected by a bridge.

14
Taiheiyo Cement Chichibu Plant
Ohnohara, Chichibu, Saitama 368-0065
1956 | 1958
Yoshiro Taniguchi

The cement company had started the planning of the most advanced plant in the 1950s during the reconstruction period of industry after the war. They imported the production line ideas from Smidth Co. in Denmark, learned the engineering for the production and also the architectural planning. Taniguchi's design concept for this plant, was to realize a clean and bright image, for example, to adopt electrical dust vacuum system, to create a green planting zone including a water fountain. He designed the elevation façade, with vertical panels arranged regularly between pilaster and vault roof with steel frame, in order to diminish the volume of the building. He also considered the connection of each building with the total environment.

15
Hizuchi Grade School
Hizuchi, Yawatahama, Ehime 790-0170
1959
Masatsune Matsumura

This building is representative of architecture designed by Masatsune Matsumura. He studied under Kameki Tsuchiura before the war, and then worked at the Yawata Municipality which is near his home town, after the war. Active as a modern architect in the region, he designed many buildings such as schools or hospitals. The space in this building is consciously composed based on the principles of modernism, rather than on that of a traditional wooden structure. Regarding the planning, the class rooms, corridors and bathrooms are treated as independent elements. By arranging the courtyard between classrooms and corridors, lighting and ventilation are obtained from both sides of the classroom.

16
Kagawa Prefectural Hall
Tenjincho, Takamatsu, Kagawa 760-0017
1958
Kenzo Tange

This building was built in 1958, when many government offices were built in Japan during the 1950s and 60s. It is representative among the works of Kenzo Tange, and symbolizes the concern of the expression of tradition and the collaboration between architects and artists. The functions of the whole building were composed of two volumes, one of them is a high-rise building which includes the Administration division and another is a low building which is for the Congress. The garden is surrounded by these two buildings. With the concern for the spatial continuity between the street and the garden, the Congress building is raised on a piloti. In the late 1950s there was respect for a design methodology, that willingly provided an open public space.

17
Gunma Music Center
Takamatsu, Takasaki, Gunma 370-0829
1961
Antonin Raymond

The concert hall was built for the franchised Gunma City Symphony Orchestra. Antonin Raymond was a Czech architect, who came to Japan with Frank Lloyd Wright to assist in the planning and building of the Imperial Hotel in 1920s. He revolutionized the arts of design and construction and influenced modern Japanese architecture. It was a unique example when the construction of this hall was promoted by the citizens of Takasaki, who donated one third of construction costs. We can say this building was real modern architecture, that represented democracy and supported the ordinary citizen. In 1991 there was a huge renovation to both interior and exterior. However the building has maintained the original design, as well as its great acoustics.

18
National Olympic Stadiums
Jinnan, Shibuya, Tokyo 150-0041
1964
Kenzo Tange

Tange presented his idea of modern architecture and urbanism in the planning of this building. He took into consideration not only the architecture itself but also urbanism and social environment. These National Olympic stadiums include two buildings, the indoor gymnasium and the swimming pool, and the site planning is based on an urban-axis and a core connecting plaza. The stadiums symbolized the rapid economic progress of Japan, with the demonstration of the dynamic space, which was realized by the suspension roof structure. This brought an international success of the representation of the Japanese responses to modernism, in which the structural engineering and its application was emphasized by Tange's works.

19
Inter-University Seminar House
Yuki, Hachioji, Tokyo 192-0000
1965
Takamasa Yoshizaka

The purpose of the building is to facilitate communication among the students from several universities in the Metropolitan area. The architect Yoshizaka who studied at the Atelier of Le Corbusier from 1952 to 1953, was also the great educator at Waseda University, as well as the leader of his own studio Atelier U. Amongst the site of a deep valley forest, there are groupings of several facilities, the main office, the library & seminar space, and six groups of accommodation units, which are each organized in a cluster like an organic living thing.

20
Palaceside Building
Hitotsubashi, Chiyoda-ku, Tokyo 100-0003
1966
Shoji Hayashi & Nikken Sekkei

Each building is designed with a different formal idea, the main building, the symbolic gate, housing an administration office and a dining hall, with the form of a reversed pyramid, the pyramid-like seminar room, the conference room roofed with a paraboloid shell and the accommodation facilities structured by a wooden prefabrication unit raised on a precast floor. The varied designs are the resemblance of a village which represents a community. This contrasting idea between difference and identity, is the key concept of the design of Yoshizaka, which he calls Discontinuous Unity which is also based on his idea 'Ukeigaku' protest against a narrow functional modernism.

Shoji Hayashi, was the chief architect of the architectural office of Nikken Sekkei, during the high growth period of Japan. It was a good idea for him to design a building of very high architectural quality, on the same site of the Readers Digest Building designed by Antonin Raymond (1949-51), which expressed modern architectural design after the Second World War. The overlapping office slabs with twin cores are beautifully sited facing south to the water moat and Emperor's Palace in the centre of Tokyo. Hayashi resolved high complex functions that housed a newspaper company's head office including printing service, a commercial office and a shopping arcade.

Selected Bibliography :
Koike S (ed)
Japan's New Architecture
Tokyo 1956

Ishimoto Y, Tange K & Gropius W
Katsura: Tradition and Creation in Japanese Architecture
New Haven 1960

Kultermann U
Contemporary Architecture of Japan
New York 1960

Seike K & Terry CS
Contemporary Japanese Houses
London 1965

Tempel E
New Japanese Architecture
London & Stuttgart 1969

Stewart DB
The Making of Modern Japanese Architecture
Tokyo 1987

Matsukuma H et al (eds)
DOCOMOMO 20 Japan
Tokyo & Kamakura 2000

Photographic Credits :
Akihisa Masuda
1, 2, 3, 4, 5
Hiroyasu Fujioka
6, 11, 16
Yoshio watanabe
7, 9
Yuzuru Shimizu
8, 14, 15, 17, 19
Fumio Murasawa
10, 13
Shinkenchiku-sha
12, 18, 20

Latvia

The Modern Movement prevailed in Latvian architecture in the 1920s and 1930s. Other stylistic trends – generalised historicism, the search for 'pure' national style and Neoeclecticism – also developed. Historicism was rooted in local traditions of Eclecticism, Art Nouveau and other previous styles. It was especially wide spread in mass-scale housing and construction of economical buildings, dairies, schools etc. in rural areas. Various options in the search for national style reflected in a number of public buildings all over the country. Neoeclecticism, based on monumental expression of classical language, was officially defined as the foundation of a real national style in the second half of the 1930s. Mostly it was used in large scale public buildings, such as Latvian Ministry of Finances in Old Riga (1937-1939 A Klinklāvs), Court Palace in Riga (1936-1938 F Skujiņš), multifunctional 'Unity House' (Vienibas nams) in Daugavpils (1936-1937, V.Vitands) ao.

The question of architectural style gained special attention and was reflected in numerous publications, although in the late 1930s Modern Movement or 'new utility' (German 'neue Sachlichkeit', Latvian 'jauna Lietiškïba') was recognised as more typical and safe trend in the heterogeneity of contemporary Latvian architecture.

Distinct features of MoMo formal language – ribbon-like fenestration, stressed horizontal balconies etc. and technical innovations – reinforced concrete or steel framework structures and great glassed surfaces, already appeared in several Art Nouveau buildings in Riga before World War I. It is the most visible proof of the statement that the contemporary architecture started directly with Art Nouveau. Selection of the Latvian MoMo 8 top structures is based on the following principles. To reflect the innovative characteristics of MoMo in Latvia in chronological order; to record the creations of the best-known Latvian MoMo architects; to depict the scope of the typology of buildings, constructed in Latvia in 1920s and 1930s; to comprise the wide scale of formal vocabulary of Latvian MoMo, both 'canonical' (corresponding to the international archetypes) and 'ordinary' (local reflections of the style).

Among pioneers of Latvian MoMo the most popular and prolific was architect Teodors Hennanovskis (1883-1964). His tenement houses with shops in Riga at Marijas iela 8 (1927, 1928) are considered to be the very first MoMo structures in Latvia, still reflecting several features of Art Deco. Synthesis of the latter with canonic language of MoMo is characteristic for several more buildings, constructed in late 1920s, among them for Central Market halls in Riga (1924-1930). The most fertile soil for implementation of the language of the MoMo was construction of detached houses, containing one or two apartments.

Housing area Teika in Riga presents the largest assemblage of MoMo buildings in Latvia. Tenement house with offices and shops in Riga, at Elizabetes iela 51 (1928 P Mandelstamm) is one of the earliest buildings in Latvia of canonical MoMo formal expresion. The period was especially fruitful for the construction of school buildings. More than 800 new schools were constructed all over the country in the 1920s and 1930s. In the last decade functionalistic language of MoMo totally replaced the previous historicism.

The school in Riga, at Ciekurkalna I. linija (1933 architect A Grinbergs) became a seminal example of a functionally differentiated arrangement of building volumes in the architecture of schools. An harmoniously balanced composition and successful use of contrasts in the horizontal and vertical perforation of walls define this building as a paradigmatic example of MoMo.

In the 1930s building activities also comprised housing, construction of health care institutions, banks, buildings for administration, entertainment, public organisations etc. Significant contribution to the development of social welfare and health service infrastructure in Latvia was sanatorium in Tervete (1930-1934, arch. A Klinklavs, A Kalnins). Its architecture being nearly 'canonical', ie, corresponding to the international archetypes and well adapted to local rural context.

Alongside T Hermanovskis, P Mandelstamm and A Klinklavs, the architects who promoted the development of MoMo in Latvia were A Karr and K Baetge. Their Latvian Stock Bank in Riga, at Kalku iela 13 (1931) is a typical example with the ribbon fenestration, vertical bay windows and rounded corners. The club building of Aizsargi Organisation in the town of Madona (1933 V Vitands) presents a local version of the formal language of MoMo. Functionalism or MoMo architecture in Latvia reflected both influences from abroad and values of local traditions. Its short but prosperous period was completely interrupted by the Soviet occupation in 1940.

Janis Krastins

1
Central Market
Riga, Pragas iela
1924 | 1930
P Dreijmanis, P Pavlovs, V Isajevs, G Tolstojs

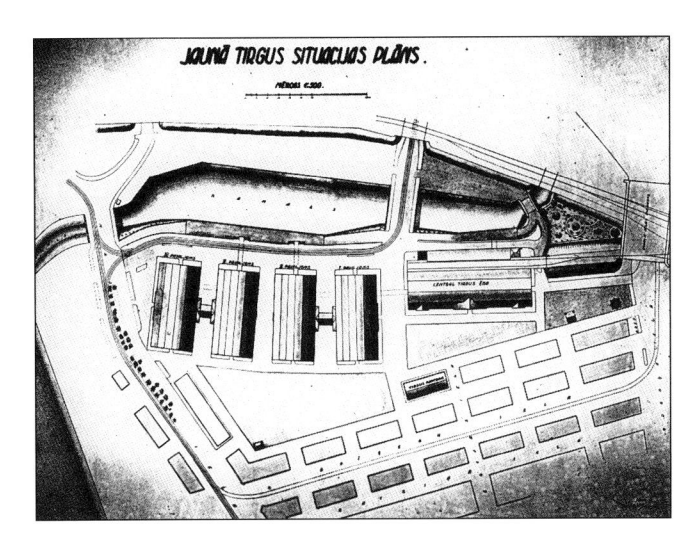

The market complex is considered to be the largest in Europe. After World War I Riga City Municipality obtained metal arched constructions meant for hangars and used them in the construction of the market hall. At that time the market place was one of the biggest and modern structures in Europe. The total area of its 5 halls comprises 16,000m^2. The basements are constructed under each hall and used as store houses. The goods can be brought there through special tunnels under street level. The architecture of the market halls is based on the structural systems used. Some influence of Neoclasicism and Art Deco of the 1920s can be perceived in the details which stress the functional use of the halls.

2
Tenement Houses with Shops
Riga, Marijas iela 8
1927 | 1928
T Hermanovskis

An early example of functionalism, contemporary with the works of MoMo pioneers in the world. The first relatively large private structure in Latvia during the economic recovery period, following the heavy destruction of the World War I. Both buildings are five-storey, double-lauded of a section type, placed on two small neighbouring plots. Both buildings have shops on the two lower floors, connected with inner stairwells, and apartments on the upper floors. Shop levels of both buildings are constructed on a steel frame with the total glazing of the street façades. The architectural vocabulary of the buildings comprises elements both of MoMo and Art Deco as expressed locally.

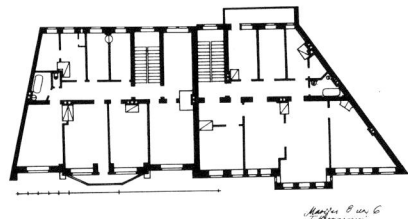

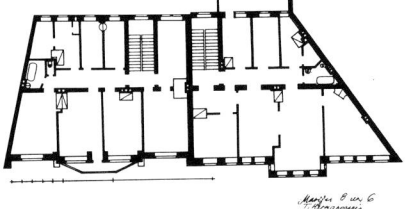

3
Tenement House with Offices and Shops
Riga, Elizabetes iela 51
1928
P Mandelstamm

The building with a horizontal ribbon fenestration and rounded corner of the total volume is considered to be one of the earliest examples of the canonical MoMo formal language in Latvian architecture. Ribbon fenestration and carved, horizontal balconies contrast with glased bay windows. The six-storey building is located on the corner of densely built-up block in the central zone of Riga. Shops and storage of the courtyard side are located on the ground floor of the building. Offices and apartments are placed on the upper floors of the building, arranged in two sections around two staircases. The building has outer brick walls covered with artificial stone plates and reinforced concrete floor slabs.

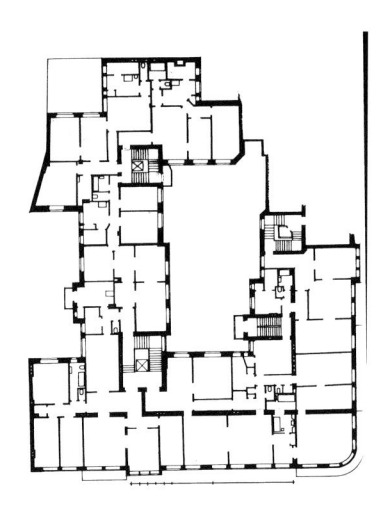

4
Residential Area
Riga, Teikas rajons
1920s
P Bérzkalnis

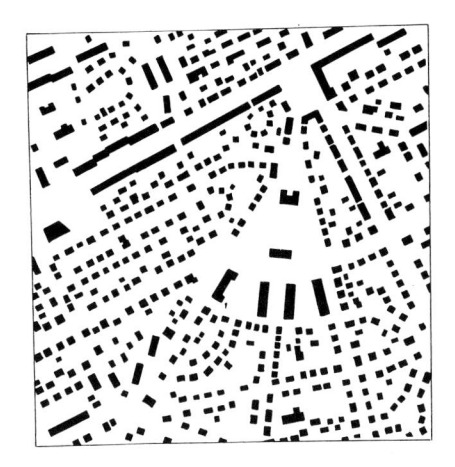

Plan
1 Tenement house with shops, Brivibas iela 308, T Hermanovskis, 1931.
2 Tenement house with shops and cinema, Zemitina laukums 2, T Hermanovskis, 1933.

The shortage of housing was solved in two ways: building municipal tenement houses, co-operative small size houses and private houses. The biggest residential area of this type is TEIKA, the houses mostly designed by architect P Bérzkalnis. Four-storey tenement houses with fourty 2 to 6 room flats each and public buildings in the centre of the area were designed by engineer T Hermanovskis. The construction of the area was consistently carried out and is a good example of town planning and building of that period in Latvia.

5
Latvian Stock Bank
Riga, Kalku iela 13
1931
A Kars & K Betge

A seminal example of functionalism architecture in Riga. The steel and reinforced concrete framework structure is located on the corner of Kalku and Vatou streets and has wide glazing, expressive plasticity of volumes with a dominating horizontality. High quality exterior and interior finish, utilising a variety of materials, such as an artificial stone, glass, iron, timber, ceramics. In 1996 during its restoration, an artificial stone finish was renovated, an operation hall above a large safe in mezzanine was carefully restored.

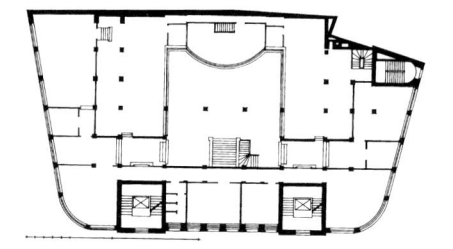

6
Elementary School
Riga, Ciekurkalna I linija 53
1933
A Grinbergs

Characteristic example of 'canonical' functionalism in Riga, which later serves as an pattern for educational buildings in Latvia.
The free-standing of cubic arrangement of volumes is shaped in plan like 'L'. A principal hall is placed in one of the two wings, the second wing accommodates classrooms along a gallery. At the end of this wing is a two-storey volume with service facilities and teachers, apartments. A vertical stairwell is located at the crossing of these two wings. A dining room and cloakroom are located in the basement.

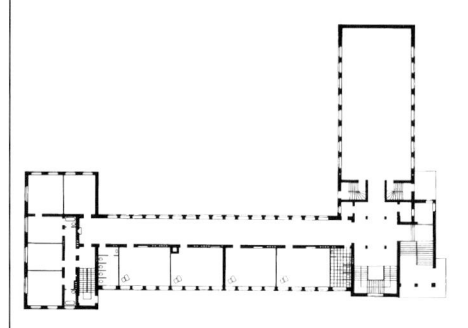

7
House of Aizsargi Organization
Madonas rajons, Madona, Raina iela 12
1933
V Vitands

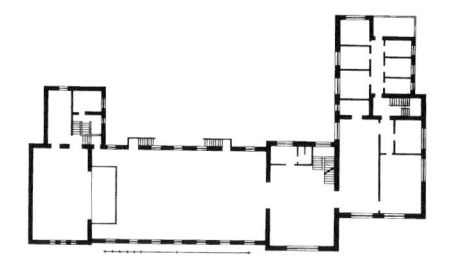

An expressive building now used as a Municipal club house, is a significant example of a local understanding of the functionalist style. An asymmetric composition of cubic volumes, with a massive and higher middle part creates a monumental impression. The monumentalism is achieved without classical details, with an exception – the emblem of the Aizsargu Organisation and the low relief at the main facade. Natural stone tiles are used for the decoration of an entrance portal.

8
Sanatorium
Dobeles rajons, Tervetes pagasts, Kalnamuiza
1930 | 1934
A Klinklavs & A Kalnins

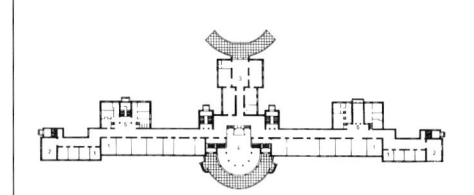

The Latvian Red Cross State Tuberculosis sanatorium is one of the largest buildings of the 1930s in Latvia. It is well set in rural landscape in a pine wood. A building of geometric volumes with a symmetric arrangement of rectangular units in wings and semicircle units in the middle. The south façade is dominated by ribbon fenestration. The functionalist style building is adorned by several reliefs created by the sculptor Karlis Zemdega.

Selected Bibliography :
Rutmanis J
'Arhitektura Latvijs pastavesanas pirmajos desmit gados'
Ilustrets zurnals
Riga 1928 no 11

Rutmanis J
Latviesu arhitektura 19 und 20gs
Riga 1934

Laube E
'Latvijas arhitekturas cels 20 gados'
Latvijas Arhitektura
Riga 1938 no 4-5

Krastins J
Latvijas Republikas bûvmâksla
Riga 1992

Krastins J et al (eds)
Docomomo National Register Latvia
Riga 1998

Illustrations courtesy DOCOMOMO Latvia

The Netherlands

From the very beginning Dutch architects played a vital role in the rise and dissemination of the Modern Movement. As a result of a precarious policy of neutrality the Netherlands had not been directly involved in World War I, but it felt the adverse effects of a certain isolation, military mobilization and economic decline. Nevertheless, the country could benefit from already existing tendencies towards modernization of arts, architecture and society during this war and afterwards.

Hendrik Berlage, master of the Stock Exchange at Amsterdam, paved the way for modern Dutch architecture. He recognized early the significance of reinforced concrete as well as the new developments in American architecture (skyscrapers and 'Prairie houses'). Although one of the first architects to support standardization in public housing, he continued to strive for 'beauty in society' with a contemporary yet ponderous architecture. Instead, Theo van Doesburg, who founded 'De Stijl' magazine in 1917, argued in favour of 'Neo-Plasticism' to express a universal truth by means of 'dematerialization' and four-dimensionality (space-time) in architecture. Therefore he sought collaboration with Piet Mondriaan and young architects like Rob van 't Hoff, JJP Oud and Jan Wils. For some of their works he supplied geometrical colour schemes and stained-glass windows. With Cor van Eesteren he exhibited in 1923 the influential 'Contra-compositions' and models of the Maison particulière and Maison d'Artiste in Paris and he published Gerrit Rietveld's Schröder house which became later the paradigm of De Stijl idiom. During the inter-war period, Van Doesburg, Van Eesteren and Oud used a variety of forums – from 'L'Architecture Vivante' to the Bauhaus – to spread their avant-garde ideas. Even more idealistic were Han van Loghem and Mart Stam who went to the young Soviet Union to build new towns. Partly influenced by the Russian Revolution and World War I, the political climate in the Netherlands began to change in favour of the worker's class: universal suffrage, eight-hour working day and more financial support to public housing. Also demobilization and scarcity of materials made the standardization and industrialization of the building process an inevitable pre-requisite for lowering the building costs and speeding-up construction to overcome the shortage of housing. Municipal experiments with various systems of concrete-built public housing, such as Amsterdam's Concrete Village (1920-28), were intended to address these problems.

Gradually, the number and variety of ready-made serial products for the construction market grew, from pre-cast concrete elements to entire kitchen units. The use of such prefabricated components was strongly encouraged by the Dutch functionalists of the Nieuwe Bouwen who searched for a truly modern architecture, suitable for modern life under the motto of Light-Air-Sun. In 1920 the Rotterdam group Opbouw was founded for this aim by Oud, Stam, van Eesteren and others, followed in 1927 by the Amsterdam group De 8, of Ben Merkelbach, Charles Karsten, Jan Duiker and others. Together they published an audacious manifesto in the new international review 'i10'. In 1932 they started a joint journal, 'De 8 en Opbouw', which proclaimed even more radically their innovative ideas about architecture, industrialization and society. The groups were also heavily involved in the activities of the Congrès Internationaux d'Architecture Moderne (CIAM) and during some years they were joined by the members of Groep '32 who tried to create a New Architecture, both functional and aesthetic.

Apart from housing they applied themselves enthusiastically to designing the unprecedented building types which arose from new cultural, economic, social and technological developments, such as apartment buildings, cinemas, broadcasting studios, sanatoria, (Montessori) schools, high-rise offices and department stores, stadiums, public swimming pools, holiday cottages, multi-storey car parks, signal boxes, discharge sluices and airports. They investigated, after a meticulous analysis of user needs, the technical possibilities of modern construction and convenience, based on a minimal use of materials and 'spiritual economy', as Jan Duiker put it. His Zonnestraal sanatorium (Hilversum), Open Air school and Cineac cinema (Amsterdam) are striking examples of the pure functionalist approach, as well as the Van Nelle factories at Rotterdam by Jan Brinkman and Leendert van der Vlugt. Only functional decoration in the form of neon advertising and names (in sans lettering) was used, while all other – redundant – ornamentation was omitted. The Volharding insurance fund building in The Hague by Jan Buijs, which turned into an illuminated column by night, was one of the first buildings in which advertising was an essential part of its architecture. The question of whether or not to use ornamentation later became as great a source of contention among the associated Dutch Modernists as the question of a possible (left-wing) political stance. But soon World War II made an end to all building activities and prompted study groups to consider reconstruction and the CIAM principles. So a new generation of architects started their career while adopting and transforming the pre-war ideas of the Modern Movement for new needs. Especially in the devastated city of Rotterdam, new prototypes were invented to provide a quick and modern solution for the needs of new business and shopping areas at a large scale: the Groothandelsgebouw and the Lijnbaan by Hugh Maaskant and Willem van Tijen, and by Jo van den Broek and Jaap Bakema, respectively. In the meantime the Amsterdam architect Aldo van Eyck, co-founder of Team X and the review 'Forum', created his intimate Orphanage, expressing his vision on pluriformity and complexity.

When composing its international selection, the Dutch working party decided to concentrate on those works which played a key role in the renewal of architecture, urban planning and civil engineering as well as to search for a satisfactory distribution according to type, place, time and architects. This meant also the inclusion of innovative and influential creations of architects outside De 8 and Opbouw, such as Willem Dudok's townhall at Hilversum, Frits Staal's Skyscraper at Amsterdam and Frits Peutz's 'Glass Palace' at Heerlen. Moreover, three post-war highlights were selected to demonstrate that the Modern Movement continued to inspire architects to strive for innovation and social progress.

Marieke Kuipers

1
Villa Nora (Henny)
Amersfoortseweg, Huis ter Heide
1915 | 1916
Rob van 't Hoff

2
Daal en Berg housing estate
Papaverhof/Klimopstraat, The Hague
1919 | 1922
Jan Wils

Villa Nora, built for AB Henny, was directly inspired by FL Wright's architecture, for which Rob van 't Hoff had made a tour in the United States. The symmetrical villa was one of the first Dutch houses mainly constructed in reinforced concrete and expressing the use of modern materials by means of cantillevered roofs. The outer, seamless walls were white-rendered with horizontal accents in grey, just as the integrated balconies and sheltered terrace with pool. The interiors were finished with wooden or white painted mouldings on ceilings and walls in a geometric pattern. Although the house was provided with a central heating system, with incorporated radiators and pipes, the south-facing living room had a central fireplace.

For the cooperative housing association 'Daal en Berg' Jan Wils designed a 'Wrightian' estate of rather spacious 125 middle-class houses with modern comfort. The core consisted of 65 one-family houses, which were partly constructed with light concrete walls and partly in brick, finished with plaster. Ingeniously, Wils arranged the plastered units – interlinked back to back in pairs – and three-storied apartment blocks in brick around a deep and long public garden. All blocks have flat roofs, conspicuous Stijl colours, integrated flower-boxes and horizontal windows. The original colours on the wooden doors, window frames and front garden fences have been reconstructed during the restoration of 1989, together with an outer insulation layer.

3
Nijverheidsschool (Polytechnic school)
P Driessenstraat, Groningen
1922 | 1923
Jan Gerko Wiebenga &
Leendert van der Vlugt

Jan Gerko Wiebenga, trained as a civil engineer and a concrete specialist, developed his career as the main constructor of the Dutch Nieuwe Bouwen. His collaboration with LC van der Vlugt started with the new Polytechnic School at Groningen, after being appointed as its director. Within six weeks Wiebenga designed a symmetrical, economically laid-out complex, which was already completed after thirteen months and served two separated types of technical education with the higher Nijverheidsschool at the front. The innovative concrete construction allowed long, uninterrupted window strips and freely divisable inner spaces. Freestanding workshops were placed in the centre, covered by glazed sheds under which the noisy machines could be placed.

4
Betondorp (Concrete village)
Schovenstraat, Amsterdam
1923 | 1924
JB van Loghem

Shortage of housing and materials prompted the municipal experiment of 'Concrete Village' in Amsterdam, which started in 1920 in the marshy Watergraafsmeerpolder. Nine architects tested ten different pre-fab systems of various methods (monolith, elements, blocks or frames of concrete, not all reinforced) for 900 dwellings within the setting of a garden village. In this case the new materials led to new forms of architecture (with flat roofs) and the gradual acceptance of standardization. Also new housing types were developed for a maximum of living space for one or two families on a minimal plot. For this purpose van Loghem designed 120 'duplex dwellings' – temporarily meant for two families instead of one – with in-built cupboards and folding doors.

5
Rietveld-Schröderhuis
Prins Hendriklaan, Utrecht
1924
Gerrit Rietveld

The elementary Rietveld-Schröder house resulted from a fruitful collaboration between client and architect. In fact, this house was the first complete architectural achievement of Rietveld, who was trained as a furniture maker. Located at the end of a traditional row of houses, the Schröder house was specially designed for the view over the countryside. Its immaterialised, dynamic architecture with flexible spaces and primary colours has become an icon of the Stijl movement. Flexibility was obtained by sliding doors on the upper floor, while a continuous contact with the space outside was provided by balconies and turning corner windows. Practical details can be found on every spot, including all furniture, which was also made by Rietveld.

6
Coöperatie De Volharding
Grote Markt, The Hague
1927 | 1928
Jan Buijs & Johan Lürsen

The head office of the cooperative society 'De Volharding' (perseverance) is prominently located at the main market street, expressing the power of workers cooperation. The cubistic building functioned as a permanent advertising column, especially by night, and was one of the first examples of 'glass architecture', possible by the inner concrete skeleton. The glass spandrel panels, lit from inside, sported advertising. Originally, the building accommodated shops (for selling Volharding products), offices, stores and a dental clinic. The society was transformed into a medical insurance fund and so the building changed. During a refurbishment for office premises in 1974, the former glass panels were replaced by white tiles.

7
Villa Van der Leeuw
Kralingse Plaslaan, Rotterdam
1927 | 1929
Jan Brinkman & Leendert van der Vlugt

Bachelor Kees van der Leeuw, first director of the Van Nelle factories and later a psychoanalyst, had strong sympathies for theosophy and modernity. He attracted the same architects as for the factories to design his own house, suited for modern, sportive living. Provided with every comfort, the 'electric house' had a garage, services on the ground floor, a double-height winter garden, living rooms on the first floor with a magnificent view over the lake of the Kralingse Plas, bedrooms on the second floor and on top a gymnasium and sun terrace. The use of a steel frame is clearly shown at the glazed garden side, where a balcony and a spiral staircase are connected. In the garden a small cabin was placed near the private tennis-court.

8
Van Nelle factories
Van Nelleweg, Rotterdam
1925 | 1931
Jan Brinkman & Leendert van der Vlugt

This first daylight factory in the Netherlands resulted from a close cooperation between Kees van der Leeuw and the young architects Brinkman and Van der Vlugt. The dynamic, transparent architecture is directly inspired by the Dessau Bauhaus, American efficiency and theosophic thoughts. Much attention is paid to optimal labour conditions, transport, advertising and flexibility. The curved office building is linked with the long, undivided factory buildings. Inside the decreasing volumes, the production process for the refining and packing of tobacco, coffee and tea was organised vertically. The round tea room was added during the building process, just as the diagonal conveyer bridges between factories and dispatch department along the river Schie.

9
Kiefhoek housing estate
Kiefhoekstraat/Eemstein, Rotterdam
1925 | 1929
JJP Oud

By elongated rows of 300 standardized dwellings Oud elaborated the concept of Existenzminimum for low-budget public housing. Most houses were meant for two families and had very compact ground-plans without corridors, while along the short side-streets larger houses were placed for big families. Although Oud had wished to build the estate in concrete, all houses had to be constructed in brick, while foundations were reduced to a minimum, both for economic reasons. The horizontalizing white-rendered exteriors had plinths in yellow brick and were enlivened by primary colours. Two round-cornered shops, a cubic ornament-less church, a hot-water station, playgrounds and small gardens completed the Kiefhoek estate.

10
Townhall
Dudokpark, Hilversum
1924 | 1930
Willem Dudok

In 1915 Willem Dudok became Director of Public Works in the fast growing town of Hilversum, where he began his career as a public architect with both urban housing and public schools. Also a new town hall was planned, but it was not until 1927 that the construction could start. Dudok's new town hall with cubic volumes of yellow brick and a huge tower, reflected by a pond, was to become the icon of Dutch modern architecture, while representing its romantic side. Dudok designed every detail, from building materials and colours to furniture and interior decoration. Besides the council chamber he projected an office room for himself. The building, dominated by horizontal awnings and vertical accents, is logically laid-out.

11
Open Air school
Cliostraat, Amsterdam
1927 | 1930
Jan Duiker

This first open-air school for ordinary children is entirely fit to let in light and fresh air, by means of south-pointing loggias, roof terraces and turning windows for all classrooms in glazed curtain walls. Open-air lessons can be given for two classes on the roof at once, just above all pairs of closed class-rooms, having the black boards placed at the inner walls near the entrances and central staircase. Duiker used a minimum of materials by precise calculation of the concrete construction – with tapered cantilevering beams, narrowing columns – and a maximal attention to practical details. Because of its clear functionalist architecture the white-rendered school building had a compulsary backward location within a perimeter block of brickwork houses.

12
Zonnestraal aftercare colony
Loosdrechtse Bos, Hilversum
1926 | 1931
Jan Duiker

Designed as a 'disposable' complex for tuberculosis patients, the Zonnestraal sanatorium symbolizes both the Dutch labour movement and the Nieuwe Bouwen. The name ('sunray') and architecture of this after-care colony epitomize the ideal of 'Light-Air-Sun', fit for sun and labour therapy. Duiker used reinforced concrete and steel-framed windows for his symmetrically laid-out ensemble, with far protruding cantilevers and sun-oriented terraces where the patients could lie sheltered in open air for their recovery. The V-shaped pavilions flanking the main building had a common meeting room and two floors with private rooms along a corridor, based on a module of 3m. Four wooden workshops were partly built by the patients for the labour therapy.

13
Simon Stevin/Lorentz discharge sluices
Afsluitdijk, Den Oever/Kornwerderzand
1932
Dirk Roosenburg

In 1932 the former Zuiderzee was closed by a 32km long dyke in order to reduce the risk of flooding and to enable reclamation. At both ends three series of five discharge sluices were built with six pairs of huge concrete structures for the machine rooms and steel sluice gates slung-in-between. The welded steel wire gates were the first constructed with this new technique. The control portals of exposed concrete are accentuated by strong vertical profiles and horizontal awnings on top, demonstrating both a aesthetic and technical control over a typical Dutch engineering construction of unprecedented dimensions. Dirk Roosenburg, who as 'aesthetic consultant' of the State Department of Hydraulic works also designed the Zuiderzee pumping-stations.

14
Signal box
Railway yard, Maastricht
1932 | 1933
Sybold van Ravesteyn

Trained as a civil engineer and concrete specialist, Sybold van Ravesteyn started his career with the Dutch Railroad Company, for which he designed dozens of technical buildings and constructions, besides a private practice as an architect. Of ten signal boxes only one has survived. All were variations of an elegant overhanging construction in reinforced concrete and glass to provide unrestricted views. The Maastricht signal box – with one hollow and one massive column, a cross-cantilever under the heavy loaded floor, a w-shaped roof with far projecting awnings for an intricated balance of forces – had to store the 10,000kg weigh of electrical equipment within a very limited space: a truly functional combination of construction and form.

15
Bergpolderflat
A Kuyperlaan/Borgesiusstraat, Rotterdam
1932 | 1934
Willem van Tijen, Jan Brinkman &
Leendert van der Vlugt

The Bergpolderflat was the first highrise project in the Netherlands specifically meant for working class-families. The galleried flats, surrounded by a collective garden and provided with three shops, arose amid perimeter blocks and became the proto-type of many post-war towerblocks. Mainly constructed with a steel skeleton, also pre-fab elements of concrete were used. The basement served for storage, laundry and a central heating installation. Besides the glazed stairwell a lift, stopping halfway the stores, could be used to reach the galleries and from there the individual entrances. Originally, each unit had a very economic plan, fit for day and night use by means of a glazed sliding wall, as well as a shower and a west-facing balcony.

16
Landlust housing estate
W. de Zwijgerlaan/K Doormanstraat
Amsterdam
1933 | 1936
Ben Merkelbach & Charles Karsten

Urged by the founders of De 8, Merkelbach and Karsten, the Landlust district became the first 'open row' housing estate in Amsterdam instead of the initial layout of perimeter blocks. The project received the support of the three housing corporations involved Het Westen, Labor and AWV and became a pilot for Cor van Eesteren's Amsterdam Extension Plan (AUP), which was in 1933 still under development. The parallel blocks had communal gardens with playgrounds in between and at the short north and south ends low shops and houses for the elderly, respectively. A service road intersected the blocks with rectangular gates. Due to radical renovation not all original architectural details survive, but the modern spirit is still recognizable.

17
Department Store Schunck
Bongerd/Nassaustraat, Heerlen
1933 |1936
Frits Peutz

In the historic heart of his birthplace the Heerlen architect Frits Peutz realized a new commercial concept for the commissioner Peter Schunck: an indoor clothing market and department store, with workshops and a roof-top house for the owner. Located between two squares at different levels near a Romanesque church, the high building is constructed as transparent as possible with varied, tapering mushroom columns (round in the lower floors and octagonal on the higher floors) and free hanging glazed curtain walls at 50cm distance from the concrete floorings. So, in combination with the hatches in the roof, the 'Glass Palace' had an experimental system of natural ventilation. Radically rebuilt in the seventies, the building is now under restoration.

18
Groothandelsgebouw
Stationsplein, Rotterdam
1949 | 1951
Hugh Maaskant & Willem van Tijen

The nine-storied Groothandelsgebouw (whole sale complex), symbol of Rotterdam's post-war reconstruction, was the first Dutch megastructure and directly inspired by American multi-company buildings. The huge inner space of 446,000m^3 was meant for a flexible use, varying from office to showroom, workshop or storage with uniformly detailed units grouped around three inner courts with an internal road system, underground parking and roof-top cinema. The reinforced concrete frame, constructed with the innovative use of sliding forms, is clearly shown at all sides and combined with glass. The accentuated entrances, stairwells and undulating shapes of the upper parapet demonstrate a more ornamental use of concrete.

19
De Lijnbaan shopping centre
Lijnbaan, Rotterdam
1951 | 1953
Jo van den Broek, Jaap Bakema &
Frans van Gool

20
Burgerweeshuis (Orphanage)
IJsbaanpad, Amsterdam
1955 | 1960
Aldo van Eyck

The Lijnbaan, built in Rotterdam's devastated city heart, became the international prototype of traffic-free shopping centres. The revolutionary concept combines 65 shops along two intersecting, broad pedestrian streets with separate towerblocks, public gardens and service roads behind. Most shops are provided with basements and two levels (with three service levels at the back). Concrete frames and partition walls of brick allow a flexible subdivision, while also the width can vary, though on a module of 1.10m, because of the precast concrete elements of the façades. The horizontalism of the flat roofs, awnings (and balconies of the flats) is continued by several arcades, while kiosks, flowerboxes and a special pavement define the public space.

Amsterdam Orphanage, laid out like a kasbah with domed units around patios, refers to non-Western cultures. Its structuralist architecture reflects the 'Habitat' ideals of Team X and the influential Dutch review 'Forum' led by Van Eyck. Here he visualized his 'Story of Another Idea' by means of 'twin phenomena' like open/closed and inside/outside. Originally, the building provided a home for about 125 children of eight different age groups. Besides common spaces, each group had its own zone, with an open square or patio and marked by a larger dome and a series of smaller domes on four round columns, all made of concrete. The interior had a variety of details and surprising effects, but underwent several changes.

Selected Bibliography :
Oud JJP
Holländische Architektur
Munich 1926

Morancé A (publ)
L'Architecture Vivante en Hollande
2 vols Paris nd c1930-1935

Loghem JB van
Bouwen Bâtir Building
Amsterdam 1932

Berlage HP et al
Moderne Bouwkunst in Nederland
20 monographs, Rotterdam 1932-1935

Bakema JB
'Dutch architecture today'
Architects' Year Book
London no 5 1953 pp 67-82

Fanelli G
Moderne architectuur in Nederland 1900-1940
's-Gravenhage 1978

Casciato M, Panzini F & Polano S
Olanda 1870-1940. Citta, Casa, Architettura
Milan 1980

Bock M
Van het Nieuwe Bouwen naar een Nieuwe Architectuur: Groep '32 1925-45
's-Gravenhage 1983

Rebel B
Het Nieuwe Bouwen, het Functionalisme in Nederland 1918-1945
Assen 1983

Photographic Credits :
Netherlands Architecture Institute
Rotterdam

Netherlands Department for Conservation
(RDMZ), Zeist

Nederland in den Vreemde

Architectenbureau Van den Broek en Bakema
Rotterdam

Vrijhof, Rotterdam

Municipal Archive Utrecht

Acknowledgments :
Wessel de Jonge
Mariet Willinge
Arjan Doolaar
Birgitta van Swinderen

New Zealand

Modern architecture in New Zealand is mostly a post-World War II phenomenon. The economic depression of the 1930s caused a massive down turn in building activity, though the Hawke's Bay earthquake of February 1931 necessitated the rebuilding of the neighbouring towns of Napier and Hastings during the depression years. This reconstruction was mostly modest Art Deco in style, but precipitated a strong interest in new approaches to structural and construction issues.

A Labour Government was elected to power in 1935, coinciding with the start of economic recovery. To improve living conditions the new government initiated a state-funded housing programme. It built almost 30,000 state rental units nation-wide between 1937 and 1949 when it was voted from power. Most of the units were detached houses in a conservative cottage style, built in schemes of up to 300 and more. The state housing programme did, however, also include a number of experiments with higher density accommodation in terraces and high-rise slabs in Auckland and Wellington, the largest cities. These buildings were in a much more contemporary, international style.

The late thirties saw another important development. A number of European architects emigrated to New Zealand, bringing direct experience of mid-European modernity with them. Mostly employed in government agencies where many young architects and students worked, they had an impact beyond their small numbers. The most notable of these emigres was undoubtedly Ernst Plischke, who arrived in 1939, and stayed in Wellington till 1963 when he returned to Vienna. He did important town planning work for the government, a series of fine private houses – notably the Sutch House completed in 1956 – and with Cedric Firth designed Massey House in Wellington (1955-57), the city's first contemporary curtain-wall high-rise.

Plischke was also an important commentator, writing a book titled 'Design for Living' that was published in 1947. This was but one of a number of post-war initiatives to promote modern architecture in New Zealand. Notable in this regard was the foundation of the Architectural Centre Inc. in Wellington in 1946, which held exhibitions devoted to planning issues, and published the journal 'Design Review' from 1948 till 1954.

A parallel organization in Auckland founded the same year was the Architectural Group. Its members were under the strong influence of their teacher Vernon Brown, who by the forties was building a simple domestic architecture of shed roofs, direct planning, and creosote and white paint. The Group published a manifesto, 'On the Necessity for Architecture', that called not only for a modern architecture but also for one that was specific to New Zealand. Like other architects in New Zealand with similar views – notably the Christchurch architect Paul Pascoe – the Group were aware of emerging patterns of regionally inflected modern architecture elsewhere in the world. Group participants were to go on to build a number of remarkable houses in the 1950s and beyond with slab floors, timber framing members pushed to the limits of their structural performance, long and low pitched roofs, and woody open plan interiors.

A key post-war architect who had an early association with the Group and its members was John Scott, who turned the general fifties interest in the local toward the traditions of Maori architecture. His most important achievement is Futuna Chapel.

The concern with local vernacular led in Christchurch to the emergence by 1960 of a mode of architecture based in robust concrete block walls (left unpainted or painted white only), fair-face concrete frames, and complexly structured timber roofs. This was influenced by English and Scandinavian architecture of the period. The principal protagonists were the firm of Warren and Mahoney, and the more romantic Peter Beaven. In domestic work, this language was worked through simplified cottage forms. But it was also employed for inventive institutional buildings like the Christchurch Town Hall (completed 1972) and Christchurch College (completed 1967) – both by Warren and Mahoney – which are notable for their rigorously organised plans, robustly expressed structure, and picturesque massing.

The 1960s witnessed an increase in office building construction for the burgeoning bureaucracy of the welfare state and for private business. Apart from Plischke and Firth's Massey House, important early high-rise office buildings are Shell House in Wellington (1960), designed by Cedric Firth for the local office of the Australian firm Stephenson and Turner and the AMP Building in Auckland, by Thorpe, Cutter-Pickmere & Douglas (completed 1962). After the death in 1959 of the Government Architect Gordon Wilson, the quality of official work dropped. But the Auckland City Council architect Tibor Donner did a fine design for the Auckland City Administration Building (1964-66).

Small buildings by Ian Athfield and Roger Walker started appearing in Wellington in the late sixties that were a reaction against both the banality of most of the commercial work being done in New Zealand cities and the equal banality of the spreading suburbs. Both architects produced work that took advantage of the spectacular topography of Wellington's hills and extended the vernacular references of New Zealand domestic design using a rich melange of differing materials and colours, small building volumes, and complex roofscapes. Walker developed this into larger scale buildings, notably the Wellington Club of 1972, unfortunately demolished in 1985 for a weakly post-modern office block. Athfield meanwhile has expanded the idiom of his work to include a wide array of references – including modernist ones – so that the output of his office is currently New Zealand's most interesting and inventive architecture.

DOCOMOMO New Zealand

1
Savage Crescent State Housing Scheme
Palmerston North
1938 | 1945
Reginald Hammond
Department of Housing Construction

2
State Fire Insurance Building
Lambton Quay & Stout Street, Wellington
1939 | 1941
Gunner & Ford

Savage Crescent is one of the many state housing schemes built up and down the country by the first Labour Government between 1937 and 1949. It was named after the first Labour Prime Minister, Michael Joseph Savage, who died in 1940. The individual houses are representative of those built by Labour, but the scheme as a whole is distinguished by its oval planning around a school, park and playing fields. The designer, Reginald Hammond, was an architect who had trained in town planning in England and had a particular interest in garden suburb ideology. This is reflected in the layout of many of the state housing schemes, with much attention being given to the design of roads, cul-de-sacs, pedestrian paths and public recreation areas.

The State Insurance Building is an eight-storeyed reinforced concrete framed commercial building with a basement below street level. Many of the high rise commercial buildings built in New Zealand in the 1930s belong to a period of transition between Neo-classicism, Art Deco and Modern Movement. But the State Insurance Building has been singled out from the mainstream. It is almost devoid of applied ornament, and is distinguished by the rippled surface of its two street façades. As a result of this detailing, the building has been compared to Emil Fahrenkamp's Shell Building, Berlin. Upon completion the State Insurance Building was described as a 'new note in modern architecture which will probably be the forerunner of many of its kind.'

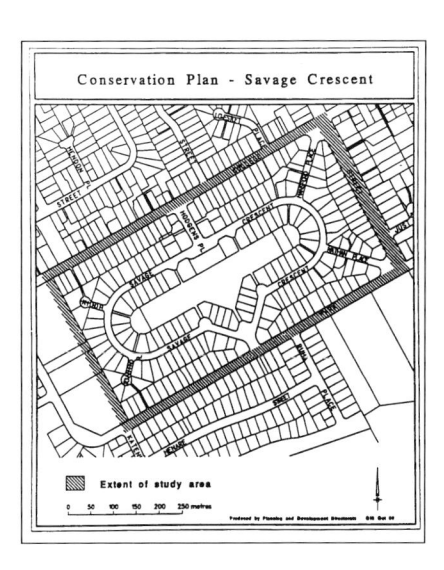

3
Kahn House
53 Trelissick Crescent, Ngaio Wellington
1941 | 1942
Ernst Plischke

The Viennese Plischke designed his first house in Wellington for a German couple, Joachim and Gertrud Kahn, who had founded a chemical company in Petone in 1937. They were recent immigrants, and, like him, refugees from Nazism. Collectors of modern art, they customarily staged theatrical and musical events at home. They wanted only two bedrooms, but an expansive living area with a stage at one end. The site was a windy hill top with panoramic views. Plischke used an innovative construction system in this house. He opted for a wooden skeleton and flat roof, allowing a glass infill on the sunny side of the house where the living areas were concentrated.

4
Haigh House
76 Bell Road, Remuera Auckland
1941 | 1942
Vernon Brown

This is a small scale domestic dwelling, the timber frame construction of which is clad in weatherboard and finished in creosote. The plan reflects wartime restraints on size and materials but includes a large central living room off which other spaces and services are arranged. The house was designed in the period in which Brown first joined in partnership with Robin Simpson, an architect highly attuned to European modernism. Simpson's impact on Brown is to be felt here, in Brown's most modernist work to date. Brown later became a lecturer at the Auckland School of Architecture and the Haigh House became highly influential on the development of a later school of New Zealand modernism.

5
Dixon Street Flats
Wellington
1940 | 1944
Gordon Wilson
Department of Housing Construction

The Dixon Street Flats, a ten-storeyed monolith just over 30m high, was New Zealand's first slab apartment block. Its scale, planning and aesthetics were unprecedented in this country's domestic architecture. Clearly the architects were following European precedents. The building is not typical, however, as its rectilinearity is compromised by the reduced height and stepped appearance of its south end, a consequence of the city's height by-laws. It was built by the same Labour Government that built the Savage Crescent State Housing Scheme, and continues to operate as state rental flats. It comprises 115 one-bedroomed flats and one two-bedroomed flat (originally reserved for the caretaker).

6
First Group House
Northboro Road, Takapuna Auckland
1949 | 1950
Group Construction Company

In 1946 some second-year architecture students agreed a constitution for an Architectural Group, produced a spirited manifesto (enthusiastically endorsed by Richard Neutra, then president of CIAM), and published a magazine ('planning 1', the first and only issue). On emerging from the School of Architecture, some of them set up Group Construction Company and built houses in Auckland (see 'The Architects' Journal' 22 March 1951) until the interest they aroused enabled them to work as Group Architects. This is their first house. Open plan, light timber construction, rafters at 4' 6" centres with diagonal marking over for exceptional rigidity and a beautiful ceiling finish, glass fixed and windows and doors hung directly on the framing.

7
Roxburgh Hydro-Electric Power Complex
Clutha River South Island
1949 | 1956
Frederick Newman
Power Division Ministry of Works

8
Massey House
126-132 Lambton Quay Wellington
1952 | 1957
Ernst Plischke

The signature structure of this complex is a 150m high concrete gravity dam spanning 750m. This mass is punctuated vertically by three massive concrete control gate structures and the slender mass of a glass and concrete lift enclosure. The skewed axis created by the gates, crowning the dam, is carried forward into the spillway structure. Running past the powerhouse and administration complex rectilinear forms are articulated to generate tension and rhythm, while the 10m wide penstock pipes punctuate the dam side of the power house with extraordinary force. Both space and light in the powerhouse are regulated by means of the building's structural elements, the portal frames, which are further delineated by the almost classical geometry.

Plischke's building for the Dairy Board and Meat Producers' Board, with its eight storeys of reinforced concrete and glass and radical U-shape, announced the importance of primary industries in the capital's main street in post-war New Zealand. Fronting, the former foreshore, and backing on to The Terrace, the site was notorious for drainage problems and made treacherous by underlying seismic thrusts. Yet the load-bearing large round columns still soar white and free-standing, exposed at the top and bottom of the building and prominently visible behind the glass curtain walls of each façade. Boardrooms and offices were lavishly appointed with native timbers and the foyer with rose-coloured Italian marble.

9
Dorset Street Flats
Christchurch
1957
Warren & Mahoney

10
War Memorial Hall
Queen's Park, Wanganui
1956 | 1960
Newman, Smith & Greenhough

11
Futuna Chapel
Friend Street, Karori Wellington
1958 | 1961
John Scott

12
Alington House
Homewood Crescent, Karori Wellington
1960 | 1962
William H Alington

Designed by Miles Warren on his return from London and the LCC, these flats introduced a new kind of detailing to New Zealand domestic architecture, based on English New Brutalism. The building consists of two offset groups of four flats, each group bisected by a clearly articulated stair with open risers. The construction is of fair-face concrete beams set on white concrete block walls. Low-pitched, timber framed roofs covered in corrugated iron are designed without eaves. Ground level flats open onto walled courtyard gardens; upper level ones have balconies. Conceived as small 'bachelor' flats, the interiors each have an open plan with an inserted bathroom box articulating three subspaces around for kitchen, living, and bed.

In the best tradition of international modernism, the War Memorial Hall is a clean, white block floating on piloti. Within, the main spaces — foyer, hall, auditorium and supper room — are each unique and powerful. While their individual identities are maintained, they are unified by the building's simple rectilinear form. The building assembles materials and rooms in a controlled and consistent plan, so that walking through it is to experience a succession of beautiful and dramatic spaces. Perhaps New Zealand's finest example of modernist-inspired public architecture, it serves as a persuasive reminder not only of optimism but of how to make civic buildings which endure both functionally and as emblems of our social and cultural experience.

Futuna Chapel is a Catholic retreat chapel and, as far as religious architecture in the Pacific is concerned, a rare synthesis by architect, sculptor and brother-builders. Indeed, it has been described as a 'New Zealand architecture … a rich characterization of Maori and Pakeha values in a natural setting'. The square plan is divided into four. This division is expressed in the steeply pitched roof: two opposing quarters are hipped and the other two are half-gables. One of the four quarters is given over to the entrance, resulting in an L-shaped interior. Central to the building is a hewn pole with branches supporting the exposed timber roof structure. Small in scale, the chapel is rich in theological and architectural references.

The Alington House, built for a family with three children, is a small (126m^2) pavilion house set in native forest on the edge of the city. It was designed after the architect/owner had spent time studying New Zealand colonial houses, the wood post and beam house of one of his contemporaries, James A Beard, some small traditional Japanese houses and the work of Mies van der Rohe. The house has a symmetrical plan with a reinforced concrete cork-covered floor. The insulated walls are timber framed with wood exterior sheathing and modulated interior plasterboard linings. The regular post and beam roof structure forms a 3:1:3:1:3 plan pattern to the house. The insulated roof is flat, wood sarked and sheathed with aluminium welted trays.

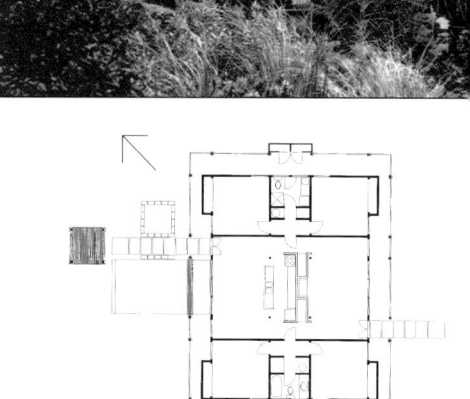

13
Christchurch Memorial Garden Crematorium
Christchurch
1962
Warren & Mahoney

This crematorium employs the white painted concrete block walls with timber trussed roofs that these architects used in many fine institutional buildings during the sixties and seventies. Here the roof is an asymmetrical butterfly form: the shorter wing provides a covered entry to the chapel over which the longer wing soars. The chapel's glazed sides look into walled garden courts. At the front of the chapel, behind the black terrazzo catafalque, a dramatically vertical concrete slab rises well above roof level. This composition makes the focus of a memorial garden, carefully articulated into a series of semi-enclosures by walls of the same height and construction as those of the building proper.

14
Lyttelton Road Tunnel Authority
Administration Building
Christchurch
1964
Peter Beaven

The Lyttelton Road Tunnel Authority Administration Building is a powerful, strongly articulated building, located adjacent to the inland mouth of the road tunnel that connects the city of Christchurch to its port town of Lyttelton. It has two main floor levels, and basement and penthouse, with an exposed concrete column and double beam structure. Enclosing walls are glass and painted precast concrete panels. All levels are literally and visually connected by a dramatic interior stair. The upper, principal administration floor has a form reminiscent of a ship's hull. This is achieved through the plan shape of the floor plate which at that level cantilevers beyond the column grid, and through the form of the precast exterior wall units.

15
Auckland City Administration Building
Greys Avenue, Auckland
Designed 1954 |1957 Built 1964 | 1966
Tibor Dormer Auckland City Council

Originally conceived as a prominent part of a greater civic centre scheme, this narrow (40x16m), nineteen-storied high-rise is steel-framed and clad in glass and aluminium with end walls of pre-cast concrete panels. Its style, building form and material use were then unusual in New Zealand. Many of the components and the technologies used – including the seismic design and analysis – were especially developed for the building. In construction fine tolerances were achieved. The design evidences an application of new technology, attention to design abroad, and a design elegance, that typified the work of Donner's office through the 1950s and 60s. At the time of design, this was the tallest building in New Zealand.

16
Synagogue and Community Centre
Auckland
1969
John Goldwater

This institution contains a principal synagogue seating 750 and another for 100. The larger has an elongated octagon plan, features a high pagoda-like roof with clerestory windows at three levels, and is girdled by an arcade. Accommodation is also provided for a kindergarten, administration, and social activities. The latter focus on a rectangular hall with a roof supported by wonderful, Aalto-esque trusses. In plan, this mix is held together by a central courtyard about which the other key spaces are disposed. Passers-by can glimpse the interior of the complex and the community it serves through a lofty entry porch which connects to the courtyard. The consistent use of buff-coloured brick and fair-face concrete surfaces throughout adds further order.

17
Hocken Building, University of Otago
Castle Street, Dunedin
1975 | 1979
EJ (Ted) McCoy

18
Brake House
Titirangi Auckland
1977
Ron Sang

19
Buck House
Te Mata Hawke's Bay
1980
Ian Athfield

McCoy and Wixon solved the problem of accommodating three Departments, the Law Faculty and a major research library within one building by dividing the structure into three separate blocks. To cope with expansion, the width of the building is spanned by beams for the suspended floors which allows flexible internal planning. Like the perimeter structural frame and the walls these are all concrete, so warming natural light and ventilation were maximized by keeping the structure narrow. Elongated in plan with mansard roofs clad with cement slates, the tall structure acknowledges the architecture of one of the original University buildings nearby, referring to its signal forms in a radically simplified fashion.

In the 1970s Brian Brake, a New Zealand photographer with an international reputation for his photos of Picasso, India and more, then working in Hong Kong, commissioned Ron Sang to design his house in steep lush Auckland bush. The basic concept was soon agreed: a long narrow house across the site with a Japanese influence. New Zealand architects respond to the elegant austere qualities of Japanese architecture: timber structures that flex but do not fail in earthquake. Brake was receptive but particular, and fine tuning, required 18 revisions by correspondence. The result is open but private, and simple but infinitely complex.

Sitting in rolling, vineyard country this fine house's picturesque composition of hips and gables, dormer windows, verandahs and high chimneys, is reminiscent of New Zealand's ad hoc colonial vernacular. As such it could be taken as the end of a line of inquiry concerned with establishing a particularly local architecture, but in modern idiom. This inquiry began in New Zealand domestic architecture in the 1940s. However, the references the design of the Buck House makes are not only to this. The white plaster with which it is covered has an altogether different quality. This has been hypothesized as referring to a particular tradition in the locality of large, white houses. But it is consistent with Athfield's penchant for multiple reference.

Selected Bibliography :
Architectural Group Manifesto
On the necessity for architecture
Auckland 1946

Plischke E
Design for Living
Wellington 1947

Firth C
State Housing in New Zealand
Wellington 1949

Illustrations courtesy DOCOMOMO New Zealand

Norway

The ambition of DOCOMOMO Norway is to continue working for documentation and conservation of major modernist buildings. We will aim our work towards our national authority for antiquities to activate its awareness of and responsibility for our modernist heritage. The Norwegian working party is relatively small, consisting of architects and art historians. The main effort has been watch-dog actions to prevent major historical buildings from being demolished, beside the work done in connection with the DOCOMOMO international register of buildings from 1920 to 1940.

What really got the Norwegian working party going was the tragic demolition of the Candela shell in 1993. The Candela shell was built in 1965 after the design of the Mexican architect Felix Candela, in connection with the landscape exhibition 'Form and Flora'. The wish to take away 'disturbing modern elements', so that the park could be completed according to the sculptor Vigeland's classicist plan was decisive for the demolition. In spite of the working party's protests the Candela shell and a tennis hall in Oslo from the 1920s designed by architect Lars Backer have been demolished.

Fortunately we did succeed in saving the interiors of Klingenberg cinema designed in 1938 by the architects Blackstad and Munthe-Kaas. The cinema is now listed and restored according to its original plans. The 'Vestkant' bath from 1932, designed by Bjercke and Eliassen is an indoor bathing complex in the centre of Oslo, with an interior of high architectural quality. We recommended protection by law to prevent the swimming hall from being converted into a conference centre. The interior is not listed, however it is now carefully restored, and we look forward to the reopening of the bath.

It seems today that the older a building is, the greater is the general approval for protection. In 1993 the Directorate for Cultural Heritage decided to protect 67 buildings by law in connection with its project 'Listed buildings from the 20th century'. Out of 67 only 11 buildings date from after the Second World War. DOCOMOMO-Norway is now engaged in recording the buildings from the period after the Second World War. Thereby we are hoping for increased focus on buildings and sites from the post war period of modernism. In the selection process we study buildings built between 1945 and 1970. The registration work that now is in full swing will give us an outline of the buildings that might be the architectural monuments of tomorrow.

DOCOMOMO **Norway**

1
Oslo Town Hall
Ridhusplassen 1, 0160 Oslo
1950
Arnstein Arneberg & Magnus Poulsson

The two architects Arnstein Arneberg and Magnus Poulsson received a prize in an ideas competition held in 1916 for a new town hall in Oslo. The architects worked out several propositions until the final project was approved in 1930. The town hall consists of two office towers, respectively 66 and 63 metres high. A lower volume, between the two towers, contains the representative rooms as well as the city council hall. Built in reinforced concrete, the building is faced with handmade bricks with detail in granite. The two architects designed most of the interior and made extensive use of marble inside. For the decoration with sculpture and mural paintings, the elite among Norwegian artists were employed.

Stylistically Arneberg and Poulsson's Town Hall developed from a romantic project, with influences from the town halls in Copenhagen and Stockholm, to a functionalist project with details from national motifs. The Town Hall and the area surrounding represent some of the most pronounced and dramatic changes in the history of urban development in the capital of Norway.

2
Semi-Detached Houses
Professor Dahlsgate 31 & 33, 0353 Oslo
1931
Frithjof Reppen

In 1928-30 the architect Frithjof Reppen designed some semi-detached houses at Professor Dahl's street in Oslo. The buildings were finished in 1931. In order to capture as much sunlight as possible, the architect curved the buildings; therefore they are often referred to as the Banana-Houses. Being laid out in a sloping terrain, the buildings display an elegant solution of a difficult building task where the wish for sufficient sun-light was decisive. The layout of the plans is good and has later been used as a model for other flats. The design is simple, yet well proportioned and with a certain discreet tension in the use of a few repetitive elements. These houses are among the finest early examples of functionalism in Norway.

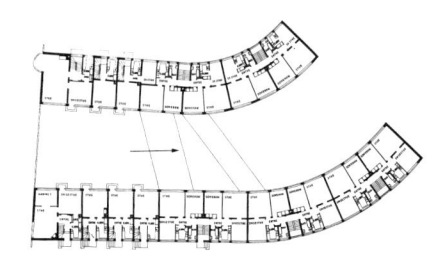

3
Klingenberg Cinema
Olav V's gate 4, 0161 Oslo
1938
Gudolf Blakstad & Herman Munthe-Kaas

In 1938 the Klingenberg Cinema was opened, designed by the architects Gudolf Blakstad and Herman Munthe-Kaas. The building fills up an entire row of houses between Klingenberg Street and Roald Amundsen's Street with the cinema placed in the backyard between two office buildings. The curved entrance of the cinema leads the spectators past multicoloured neon lights and mirrored walls to a foyer placed underneath the upper part of the cinema auditorium. The interior of the auditorium displays elegantly curved walls in artificial leather and peau de pêche, a curved acoustic panelled ceiling in plaster rabitz and dynamically formed light fittings in aluminium. This cinema has been looked upon as one of the important, functionalist cinemas in Europe. It is still in use and stands out among other cinemas even today. In 1995 the interior was listed and during 1996 it was totally renovated.

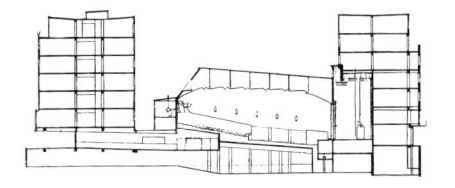

4
Ingierstrand Bath
Ingierstrandveien 30, Svartskog 1415
Oppegird
1934
Ole Lind Schistad & Eivind Moestue

The architects Ole Lind Schistad and Eivind Moestue designed Ingierstrand Bath, finishing it in 1933-34. The bath is magnificently situated, facing west in a terrain sloping down to the Bunnefjord, about 12km east of Oslo. The Ingierstrand Bath includes about 0.25km^2 of green areas, smooth rocks and a 400-meter long shore. The elongated restaurant building, partly resting on concrete columns on the hillside, conveys a pure composition of volumes. There used to be a roof terrace with table service. This restaurant was connected to a room with an open fireplace, and windows which were pulled up to expand the area. The complex is amazing in its interaction between landscape and architecture. Particularly the angular diving tower and the circular dancing platform, balancing on a centric column are examples of outstanding design and engineering. Ingierstrand Bath represented, when it was built, a bath complex of dimensions formerly not seen in Norway. Ingierstrand Bath is also a manifestation of the great social changes in the 1920s and 30s in Norway. When it was built the Ingierstrand Bath received attention and recognition both at home and abroad.

5
The Kalmar House/ Kalmarhuset
Jon Smørsgate11, 5011 Bergen
1939
Leif Grung

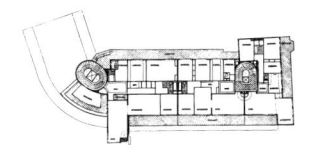

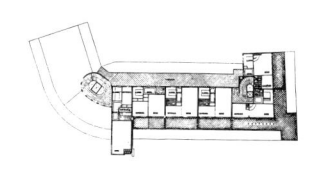

This building was designed for the Aeolus Insurance Company in 1935-37. It was finished in 1939 and contains a petrol station, shops on three levels, offices, a hotel/pension and flats. The demanding building site, the complex content and its dynamic form show the architect's abilities as a designer. The building is also characterized by its strong vertical elements and its dark parapets, and by its different functions being expressed in the façade. Although being ten storeys high, the building mingles elegantly with the surroundings. Its dynamic design and composition of volumes are among the most distinguished of that period, not only in Bergen but also in Norway.

6
Villa Stenersen
Tuengen allé 10c, 0374 Oslo
1939
Arne Korsmo

The architect Arne Korsmo designed the Villa Stenersen in 1937-39 as a residence for a stockbroker and art collector Rolf Stenersen and his family. The rectangular building is three stories high and placed on a small hill with half of the building cut into the terrain, and the other half elevated above the ground on columns. A circular garage with a gate at each end so that the driver can go straight through cuts off a corner of the ground floor. The whole building is composed as a rectangular volume but with circular forms. A concrete skeleton runs through the whole building defining the basic proportions of both exterior and interior. The porch, the fireplaces, the outdoor stairs and the whole constructive system of the building are based upon the circle, while the rest of the rooms lie in the rectangular part of the building. The living room is on the first floor having characteristic glass brick towards the garden. The second floor recedes in blue glass plates, blurring the transition between the house and the sky on days with blue sky. The obvious skeleton of the construction and the open plan represent a synthesis of order and liberty. The elegance and the perfection in detail make Villa Stenersen a highlight of Norwegian functionalist villa architecture. In 1974 Rolf Stenersen donated Villa Stenersen to the Norwegian government as a residence for the prime minister. It was restored in 1995 and is now used for entertaining by the Norwegian government.

7
Geir Grung's Own House
Jongskollen 27, Sandvika, Bærum
1963
Geir Grung

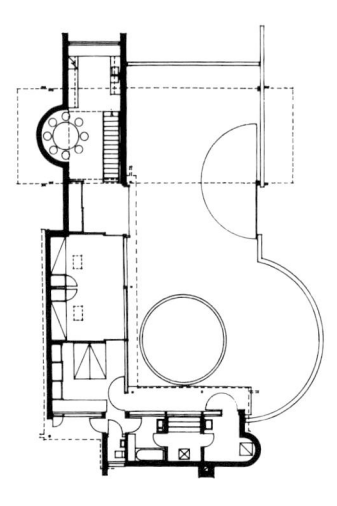

The house which Geir Grung designed for his own family is situated with a magnificent view on a hill in a reidential area in Bærum County outside Oslo. In 'Byggekunst', 63/8, he wrote 'The house was based on the family's idea of living. With both the totally open room and the totally closed room, sliding walls make the façades changeable according to the climatic demands of the season and environmental regards. I took the main principles from the log cabin, which has a pure composition of materials, leaving each unit free play in the architecture. The intention was to build a house with today's constructions and materials. Culture is not man living for old objects, culture is when objects and house fulfill the needs of man today.'

8
Norwegian Hydro Administration Building
Bygdøy allé 2, Oslo
1960
Erling Viksjø

Erling Viksjø (1910-71) became one of the most influential architects of his generation. The Norwegian Hydro Administration Building was built in 1960-63 and stands as a well preserved example and a worthy representation of the rationalist tradition in Norwegian and Nordic architecture. The building stands like most of Viksjø's buildings as a monolithic structure in an open, green area in the centre. It was built in so-called natural concrete, developed and patented by Viksjø in co-operation with the engineer Sverre Ystad. This concrete is made with riverside pebbles filled into a form-work covered with concrete. Afterwards the concrete gets sandblasted to uncover the pebbles and give it a beautiful surface. In order to integrate architecture and artistic decoration Erling Viksjø worked together with different artists. In this building he co-operated with the artists Carl Nesjar, Odd Tandberg and Jacob Weidemann.

Selected Bibliography :
Norberg-Shultz C
Modern Norwegian Architecture
Oslo 1986

Wedebrunn O (ed)
Modern Movement Scandinavia
Copenhagen 1998

Illustrations courtesy DOCOMOMO Norway

Quebec

In Quebec, the modernization of society came about relatively late, when, at the international level, capitalist expansion was embarking on its second phase of development. Taking place after Canadian Confederation in 1867, it was carried mainly by British investments at first and then by American investments after World War I. The industrialization of production took place during the second half of the 19th century, resulting in a gradual urbanization of the population. By 1915, Quebec was a mainly urban society and Montreal was the metropolis of Canada. Architectural practice and design was modernized by the end of the last century, coinciding with the founding of the Province of Quebec Architects' Association in 1890. Architectural training became available at McGill University in 1896 and new building techniques and types of buildings, including tall buildings, were imported from the United States. However, architectural language remained dependent on styles of the past until the 1920s, when there was somewhat more openness to rationalist ideas and the European avant-garde.

The first modernist buildings were erected in the mid-1930s, when the country was slowly making its way out of the Depression. These were modest residential projects, houses built in the finest areas of Montreal or the capital, Quebec City, and designed by local architects who had spent time in Europe or had emigrated from Europe. The Depression years, aside from being a relatively long dry spell for building construction, were in fact years spent challenging convictions. In terms of mentalities, it was a time that could in a manner of speaking be compared to the first world war in Europe.

And architectural education felt this impact. In Quebec City, the architecture section of the École des beaux-arts closed its doors in 1937 and in Montreal, plans were made to shut down the Architecture Department at McGill University. In Canada in general, and in Quebec in particular, certain educational institutions played a vital role in the advent of architectural modernity.

A new generation took the helm at McGill University in the early 1940s. John Bland (1911), a Montrealer and a McGill graduate himself, had just returned from London where he had studied urban planning at the Architectural Association's school and had worked for the London County Council's urban planning department. He undertook a complete redesign of the architecture programme: he defined a new vocation for teaching, and consequently for architectural practice which he directed toward issues of housing and urban planning. He introduced a basic Bauhaus-inspired design workshop. At the École des beaux-arts de Montreal, the reform took place 10 years later and benefited from the employment of new professors including André Blouin (1920), a student of Auguste Perret. The first graduates of this modernized programme designed the first postwar modernist buildings for public and commercial clients.

At the federal level in Canada, state modernization occurred earlier than in Quebec. With the exception of the Second World War years, when the Liberals were in power, the Quebec government was extremely conservative and consistently in favour of free enterprise.

However, the end of the 'Grande Noirceur' as the Maurice Duplessis regime (1936-1940, 1944-1960) became known, resulted in a period of political and cultural effervescence carried by the strength of the postwar economy.

Church and state played a major role in modern architectural production in Quebec, the latter by commissioning numerous facilities when it broadened its intervention in different sectors of social life, particularly in the 1960s which were known as the 'Quiet Revolution' in Quebec.

Another major player was big business. In the early 1960s, Montreal was a city in great demand by major real estate developers, although its status as Canada's metropolis was definitely challenged by the construction of the Seaway in 1954-1959, which displaced Montreal as an ocean port and continental railway junction. From then on, Toronto's standing as the country's major economic and financial centre was inexorably confirmed. Nevertheless, some very ambitious service and commercial complexes were built in Montreal, financed largely by foreign interests.

In 1967, Montreal hosted the World's Fair, an event at which architects including Otto Frei, Carlo Scarpa, Carlos R Villanueva were represented. DOCOMOMO views Expo '67 as the outer limit for its inventory work. This date has been pushed back a few years, however, to 1973, the year that the Van Horne mansion was demolished and when awareness began to grow about the heritage value of 19th century architecture, which is inseparable from the rejection of modernity, considered responsible for the destruction of the historic city.

The selection published here reflects the current state of knowledge about architectural modernism in Quebec. Furthermore, the relevance of the illustrations taken mainly from archival sources, for essentially practical reasons, can be discussed, given the conception of heritage that it implies.

France Vanlaethem

1
Grain Elevator 5
Port of Montreal
1903-1906, 1913, 1922-1924, 1957-1958

2
University of Montréal Campus
Montreal
Main Pavilion 1927 | 1943
Ernest Cormier
Women's Residence 1962 | 1964
Papineau, Gérin-Lajoie Leblanc
Garage Louis-Collin 1967 | 1970
Ouellet Reeves et Alain

3
Maisons Jarry
Outremont
1936
Marcel Parizeau

One of the industrial constructions praised by the European avant-garde was the Port of Montreal's concrete Grain Elevator 2, built in 1910-12, under direction of John S Metcalfe. Its 'belles formes' were illustrated in the magazine 'L'Esprit nouveau' (1920) and the 'Jahrbuch des Deutschen Werkbundes' (1913). Elevator 5 survives as a reminder of the rich past of the city and its industrial architecture. Elevator 5 was built in several phases: the first phase (1903-06 steel) and the second (1913-15 concrete) can be attributed to Metcalfe; the third and final phases were constructed in 1922-23 and 1958 respectively. Its demolition appears to have been forestalled since 1988, when authorities and heritage groups held a symposium on its future.

The University of Montreal's main building has been hailed for its modernity, nevertheless tempered by the classicism of both its composition and restrained ornamentation. Its architect, Ernest Cormier (1885-1980), was an engineer who did further studies at the École des beaux-arts de Paris and in Rome. He drew up the first site plan (1924-1927) for the new campus. In the 1960s, as the university expanded, his plan was revised by the firm Lahaye et Ouellet, a pioneer in urban planning. Of the new blocks built during the 50s and 60s, the most interesting are the women's residence and the Louis-Collin Garage, both remarkable for their 'brutalist' handling of concrete. Smooth and exposed, the material's plasticity is used to underscore the functionality and verticality of the so-called 'tour des vierges' or 'tower of virgins'; by turns grooved and edged, the openworked and articulated mass of the parking garage, set within Mount Royal's flank, constructs the landscape.

In 1945, Father Marie-Alain Couturier published a short monograph on the lifework of his friend, the architect Marcel Parizeau (1898-1945). Among Parizeau's achievements is a double house built shortly after his 1933 return from a long period of study in Europe. The building stands out for the novelty of its compact layout, the spatial generosity of its interior, its unornamented façades and the use of modern materials such as reinforced concrete and steel for the structure, as well as metal framing and glass brick. Along with the Swiss-born architect Blatter's Bélanger (1929) and Bourdon (1934) houses (now demolished) in Quebec City, Parizeau's house ranks among the first examples of architecture free from the past.

4
Laval University Campus, Sainte-Foy
Science Pavilions 1958
Lucien Mainguy
Parent Residential Pavilion 1963
André Robitaille
Comtois Agricultural and Food Sciences
Pavilion 1966
Gauthier, Guité, Roy

5
Habitations Jeanne-Mance
Montreal
1954 | 1961
Rother, Bland & Trudeau (urban plan)
Greenspoon Freedlander & Dunne
Jacques Morin (consultant architect)

In the mid-1940s, Quebec City's Laval University decided to relocate outside the city limits. The site plan of the new campus (1948-49) was drawn up by Édouard Fiset (1910-94), a graduate of the Écoles des beaux-arts of Quebec and Paris. The classical spirit of his axial composition contrasts with the modernism of university blocks built at the end of the 1950s. A vast, functionally articulated megastructure, the two blocks of the Science Faculty met the call for monumentality, heard within the modern movement since 1944. The ceramist Bonnet's large-scale mural vigorously affirmed this tendency. Also remarkable are the five slab blocks of student housing, as well as the Agricultural and Food Sciences Building.

In the latter project, concrete is utilized in a less abstract manner, its materiality affirmed by the rough texture of forms cast in situ and the great plasticity of prefabricated siding. During recent years, as the campus has become more densely built up, the once-forceful effect of the slab block has waned.

Collective housing has not been in wide favour on this side of the Atlantic; consequently, large-scale public housing is rare in Canada. The Habitations Jeanne-Mance were an operation run by the Central Mortgage and Housing Corporation, a federal agency born of the National Housing Act. But, unlike those erected in Toronto or Halifax, this housing project was set in the heart of the city. Its site plan applied the principles of CIAM as revised by the London County Council, which favoured mixed development. On either side of an exterior common space, the complex consists of five subsets, each dominated by a high-rise building giving onto a parking lot, a playground and a rest area, for a grand total of 796 units housing 3,200 people.

This project has retained its social calling, but the parking lot has encroached considerably on the green spaces, and the buildings themselves have undergone minor changes.

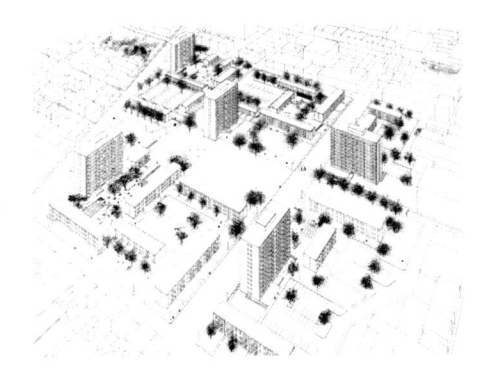

6
St Marc's Church
La Baie
1955 | 1956
Paul-Marie Côté

Religious architecture was a major vector for architectural modernity in a society where the Catholic Church was still quite powerful. The rebirth of religious art has been at the core of cultural debate since the 1930s, when the architect and monk Dom Bellot won many admirers. St Marc's Church was built in a small industrial city in Saguenay-Lac-Saint-Jean, a northern region far from the larger centres, by the young architect Paul-Marie Côté. The church`s architecture reveals astonishing formal and technical boldness. Its layout shows more than a passing resemblance to Dombellist architecture: it is rationalist, angular, yet not strictly traditional. A single vast volume, its nave is entirely covered by a wide, folded-concrete skin roof.

7
Church of Our Lady of Blessed Love
Montreal
1955 | 1956
Roger D'Astous
Robillard, Jetté Beaudoin
(consultant architects)

8
Place Ville-Marie
Montreal
1957 | 1966
IM Pei & Associates
Affleck, Desbarats, Dimakopoulos, Lebensold
Michaud, Size (local architect)

Place Bonaventure
1963 | 1967
Affleck, Desbarats, Dimakopoulos, Lebensold,
Michaud, Size
RT Affleck (project architect)

In the 1950s, suburban development led to the creation of new parishes. The parish of Cartierville offered young Roger D'Astous (1926-98), just returned from Taliesin, one of his first contracts. With its diamond-shaped layout and its roof structure solidly anchored to the ground, the architectural scheme of the church shows affinities with the First Unitarian Church (1949-50) built by Wright at Madison. The wide, overhanging concrete roof, supported by eight pillars finished in long, thin bricks, shelters the nave in the form of a Greek cross; the resulting space is single, compact, and inward-looking.

Along with this simple geometric exercise comes a more shaped – yet still structured – articulation in the treatment of the walls. The church and its adjacent rectory have retained most of their architectural integrity.

Place Ville-Marie (PVM) and Place Bonaventure are two components of a vast operation undertaken in 1910 by one of the largest Canadian railway companies, which decided to construct a huge commercial complex to mark the implantation of its terminal in the city centre. In 1955, the operation was relaunched, and the ambitious New York promoter Zeckendorf was called in. His team of architects, directed by Pei, proposed a new site plan synthesizing the experience of modern urban planning as conceived by Le Corbusier and Victor Gruen, and also by Jacques Gréber. Reserving for itself the development of the northern quadrangle, Webb & Knapp built the PVM, remarkable for design clarity.

Its wide plaza is a fine example of modernist urban space, while its cruciform tower, finished in aluminum, and its interior public spaces are excellent examples of International Style. As for Place Bonaventure, its huge mass of rough concrete, mostly blind-walled, presents a far different, brutalist esthetic. These commercial buildings have both had to weather the effects of fashion and vocational change.

9
Place Victoria
Montreal
1961 | 1965
Luigi Moretti
Pier Luigi Nervi (engineer)
Greespoon Freedlander & Dunne
(local architect)
Jacques Morin (consultant architect)

Its promoter's intention was to build the tallest office complex in North America. A first version of the plan had three 51-storey towers; later consultations reduced the towers to two. In the end, only the Stock Exchange Tower was built, the highest concrete-framed skyscraper of its time. It and the block adjoining it were erected under Italian supervision. Its concept is quite sophisticated: slim pillars on each corner are protected from temperature extremes by panels of pre-stressed concrete, with a heated technical space separating shaft from siding. In addition, the tower's volume is not a simple rectangle: its sides are slightly convex and faintly inclined, with recesses for the mechanical floors giving rhythm to its verticality.

10
Westmount Square
Montreal
1964 | 1969
Mies van der Rohe
Greenspoon, Freedlander & Dunne
(local architect)

Ludwig Mies van der Rohe drew up five large-scale projects for Montreal: the first was Westmount Square. This complex, bringing out the great themes and details of Miesian architecture, is nevertheless unique in that it was planned to encompass all major urban needs. On a vast plaza, set down with exquisite feeling for the surrounding city context, are two residential slabs, an office tower and a pavilion destined to house a department store, along with an underground gallery of boutiques, including a cinema, parking lot and metro station offering residents every modern convenience. This complex has somewhat failed to withstand the effects of business competition and technical ageing.

11
Intercommunity Campus at Cap-Rouge
Saint-Augustin-de-Maures
1962 | 1966
Jean-Marie Roy

The campus was designed to provide education for members of several religious communities. The buildings and those devoted to community life were set out independently on vast acreage along the Saint Lawrence; care was taken to respect topography, vegetation & the river view. A unity was sought using treatment of volumes, materials, and colours. Several architects were associated with this project. Roy, aside from coordinating the project, designed seven of the buildings, including the Redemptorist Fathers' residence, typical for its interrelationship between private & public concerns: its residential slab block, supported on piles, appears to slide out over a lower block intended as religious and collective space.

12
Montreal Metro System
Peel Metro Station
1962 | 1966
Papineau, Gérin-Lajoie, LeBlanc

In Montreal, the construction of a metropolitan transit network was one of the great projects of the Quiet Revolution. Hailed at the time as 'the most beautiful metro in the world', its general design adopted the best of several European experiments: it integrated the arts (Stockholm), adopted a modern aesthetic aspect (Milan), and employed a rubber-tyre/concrete track system (France). But the Montreal metro was not merely the gathering of proven successes; it was also an opportunity to innovate. The network's main novelty is architectural: resolutely modern, each station was treated differently. Each was designed by a different architectural firm, in league with one or several artists.

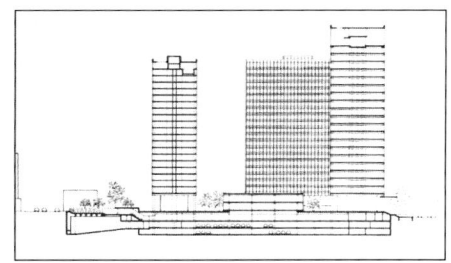

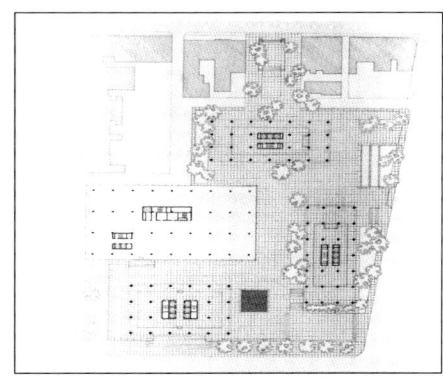

13
Expo '67 Montreal. Habitat '67
1963 | 1967
Moshe Safdie & David, Barrot, Boulva

14
Nun's Island Housing Development, Verdun
Johnson, Johnson & Roy
Ann Arbour (urban planner)

Esso Service Station
1967 | 1968
Mies van der Rohe (consultant architect)
Paul H Lapointe (local architect)

The modernity of Montreal's Expo '67 centred mainly around the processes of circulation and production. Its site plan, supervised by Fiset, stressed the various means of transportation. Projects for several pavilions exploited the potential of geometry and prefabrication. Some of these structures have escaped demolition, and of these, the most interesting are Habitat '67 and the former United States Pavilion. The residential complex was designed as a model of clustering and prefabrication. As for the geodesic dome, it is a nearly-complete sphere, unique in Fuller's production. Unfortunately, the sphere's acrylic envelope was destroyed by fire in 1970.

The structure was recycled in 1994 as an interpretation centre for the Saint Lawrence River, according to a plan drawn up by Blouin and his associates. Its structural integrity was respected, and the structure can still be regarded as a cultural heritage, as long as conservative notions of heritage are not adhered to.

The development of Nun's Island, a large unspoiled territory just outside Montreal's downtown core, became cost-effective when the highway network was modernized in the late 1950s. It fell to a Chicago company to develop the island in several phases, ending in 1978. The principle of 'cluster planning' oriented the urban project, which consisted of diversified and grouped housing served by dead-end streets. Close to Metropolitan Structures, Greenwald's successor Mies was involved in several aspects of this operation. He was consultant for the site plan, architect of the apartment buildings constructed along the river, and architect of the first service station on the island. The latter project, a prototype, is unique in Mies' œuvre.

Selected Bibliography :
Bergeron C
L'Architecture du XXe siècle au Québec
Quebec 1989

Miron JR
House, Home and Community: progress in housing Canadians 1945-1986
Montreal 1993

Photographic credits :
FVL
1, 7
Canadian Centre for Architecture
Ovellet Reeves & Alain
2
Marcel Parizeau Architecte
3
Archives de l'Université Laval
4
Gestion de documents et archives
Ville de Montreal
5, 8, 9, 12
Église Saint-Marc Archives
6
Chicago Historical Society
10, 14
Archives nationales du Québec
11

Russia West Moscow & St Petersburg

Russia West **Moscow**

In 1918 the young Soviet government moved from St Petersburg (Petrograd) to Moscow and after 200 years this city again became the capital. As such it was the centre of professional activity and debate in which the adherents of modern architecture formed their societies – the Rationalists first in 1923 with their Association of New Architects, ASNOVA, and in late 1925 the Constructivists with their Union of Contemporary Architects, OSA.

Working and teaching alongside them were other architects who worked in modernist idioms but without such self-conscious pursuit of a new theoretical and ideological principles. Many of these remained loyal to the city's pre-revolutionary professional organization, the Moscow Architectural Society, MAO.

This was the body mainly responsible for running the vast number of architectural competitions which became one of the main forcing grounds for Soviet Modern Movement ideas. Moscow itself was full of state, commercial and social organizations that sought a new show piece headquarters, but even more of the nationwide competitions were for such buildings in rapidly growing cities across the whole continent. Moscow was thus at the centre of a nationwide network of experimental design activity, just as it was at the centre of educational and theoretical innovation. It was also a melting pot of young and old, and many schemes reflect this in their design teams.

Moscow work was relatively very widely published compared to that of other Soviet cities, which is why Modern Movement work elsewhere in Russia is still so little known.

Moscow's privileged position in this respect was certainly merited by the quite exceptional levels of innovative design talent working in the city, who were in close touch with their Western colleagues, received their publications, had visits from some of them. But it was also because of its own energetic publishing activity. The Constructivist group's journal Sovremennaia arkhitektura (Contemporary Architecture), was the country's only publication comparable with avant-garde architectural journals in the West; it included work by Le Corbusier, the Germans and Dutch with whom they sympathized. The Moscow City Soviet's journal Stroitel'stvo Moskvy (Construction of Moscow) complemented SA by extensive publication of other modernist architects like Melnikov and Golosov.

The buildings shown here represent both the work of these different trends and the range of socially innovative building types being pioneered in the city. Notable among these are the clubs for political education and entertainment of working people, mostly built by individual trade unions or factories for their own members. They also include various forms of housing, ranging from the unique single-family house which Melnikov built for himself to the semi-collectivised Narkomfin complex and the fully collectivised Textile apprentices complex built by members of OSA. Even the new types of office building, a workers' department store and the planetarium were ideologically charged new types in their time.

Irina Chepkunova
Catherine Cooke

1
Izvestiia newspaper building
Pushkinskaia Square 5
Moscow,
1925 | 1927
Grigory & Mikhail Barkhin
(engineer Artur Loleit)

A building of unusually high technical quality for this time in Russia due to its prestige client: Izvestiia was the newspaper of the Communist Party's Central Committee. Some handsome bronze details etc thus remain, though elevational typography has unfortunately gone. The original project had a twelve storied tower but height limits introduced into central Moscow in 1925 forced a redesign. The complex comprises two blocks: editorial offices on the front and a parallel printing house behind, with link block containing stairs, lifts, staff facilities. Barkhin was an established architect, already practising before the 1917 Revolution and did not join the avant-garde groups of the twenties. This is typical of his sound and undogmatic modernism.

2
Gostorg building
Miasnitskaia Street 47
Moscow
1925 | 1927
Boris Velikovsky with Mikhail Barshch,
Georgy Vegman & Maria Gaken

Like Barkhin's Izvestiia, this headquarters for the State Trading organisation was originally designed with a central tower that fell foul of the 1925 regulations. Velikovsky was also an established architect, here working with some of his Constructivist students. Staircases inside were open and glazed in a manner genuinely evoking transatlantic modernity with two internal courts lighting the offices. Higher ground and first floors contained display spaces for state produced goods. The bold frame, maximal glazing, and attractive curves and portholes at the top caused Alfred H Barr to describe it on his visit of 1928 as 'easily the finest modern architecture in Moscow, very Gropius, with steamboat balconies etc'.

3
Mostorg department store
Square of the Krasnopresnensky Gates 2/48
Moscow
1927 | 1928
Leonid Vesnin with Alexander & Victor Vesnin

This fully-glazed facade was a bold statement of accessibility to the new proletarian customers who were never admitted to such stores before the Revolution. It was also a demonstration of western-style economical construction with its calculated concrete frame. The slender steel glazing bars against bold planes of masonry display the confidence of this already well experienced trio, and of all the Constructivists' built works this one best indicates what their earlier unbuilt competition schemes such as the ARCOS, Orgametal and Russgertorg buildings would have been like.

4
Workers' Club named for I V Rusakov
Stromynskaia Square 6
Moscow
1927 | 1929
Konstantin Melnikov

This ingeniously planned building on a tapered, wedge-shaped plan comprised a main auditorium with three smaller spaces, in the protruding wedges, that could be linked to or separated from it as required. A club for municipal employees, it was typical of this new Soviet building type in being located on the city's outskirts amongst workers' housing. Its boldly sculptural form was therefore originally felt more powerfully as it stood alone on an empty site. External staircases and balconies on the main front created the interaction with street life which previously typified the fairground pavilions or balagany common in old Moscow streets. The original low-relief lettering with the club's name on the three protruding walls has unfortunately gone.

5
Melnikov House
Krivoarbatsky Lane 10
Moscow
1927 | 1929
Konstantin Melnikov

This house was unique in the twenties as the only such prestige, single-family house comparable to those commonly built for themselves or others by pre-revolutionary Moscow architects. That element of self-aggrandisement was officially lessened by proposing this ingenious double-cylinder form, with hexagonal window spaces created in the underlying brick coursing, as a model for terraced development as mass workers' housing. Internal spaces at ground floor are a jigsaw of wedge-shaped rooms, whilst first and top floors have bold and handsome volumes for living space, studio and bedroom. Internal walls were coloured in various pastels to Melnikov's scheme.

6
Workers' Club named for S M Zuev
Lesnaia Street 18
Moscow
1927 | 1929
Ilia Golosov

The composition of this dramatic building is based on the intersection of a cylindrical glazed staircase and a stack of rectangular floor planes behind which move from open foyers to sequences of club rooms, and up to a rectangular 850-seat auditorium. Bricking-up of various windows to those spaces has turned a highly perforated cubic mass into a more solid box, but the drama of cylinder against flat planes remains immensely powerful. Like Melnikov, Golosov was an enthusiast for expressive, dynamic form rather than the logics of Constructivist design methods. The photogenic corner was widely published and made this club an iconic work of Soviet avant-garde architecture abroad.

7
Moscow Planetarium
Sadovaia-Kudrinskaia Street 5
Moscow
1927-29
Mikhail Barshch & Mikhail Siniavsky

In the 1920s there was world-wide interest in the German Zeiss company's invention of optics for a projecting the night sky as a planetarium. In the Soviet Union the type was widely developed as an educational facility, not least to support anti-religious campaigning. The Moscow building was conceived as an educational complex linked to the zoo behind, a natural science museum and library but only the planetarium was built. In the original scheme of these two young Constructivists the ferroconcrete outer dome followed the dumpy hemispherical profile of the German 'Netzwerk' sky inside. This was 'harmonised with Moscow architecture' by their Constructivist artist colleagues the Stenberg brothers.

8
Narkomfin semi-collectivized housing complex
Novinsky boulevard 25 (korpus B)
Moscow
1928 | 1930
Moisei Ginzburg & Ignaty Milinis
(engineer SL Prokhorov)

Perhaps the most elegant and important of all Russian Modern Movement buildings, this is now in tragic disrepair. It was conceived as 'a building of transitional type' (dom perekhodnogo tipa), not fully collectivized by elimination of family structure like the communal house (dom kommuna) but prompting social change through minimizing kitchens etc and providing extensive communal facilities in the separate pavilion linked by a bridge. Here the Constructivists first demonstrated the new minimal apartments they designed for the state construction body, Stroikom, including the famous Type-F split-level units and internal corridor-street which inspired Le Corbusier's later Unités d'habitation. The project was also a demonstration of economical construction.

9
Tsentrosoiuz building
Miasnitskaia Street 39
Moscow
1928 | 1936
Le Corbusier & Pierre Jeanneret
with Nikolai Kolli

After an extended competition Corbusier finally started on site with his largest building to date under supervision of site architect Kolli, from the Constructivist group, but he personally never saw it finished. The design demonstrated the principle of natural ventilation between a double glazed curtain-wall that he called 'respiration exacte', but crude workmanship and the vicissitudes of completion after Modernism fell from favour produced a seriously flawed result. While the volumes are magnificent with flying ramps and airy foyers inside, the dark pink tufa facing stone makes a heavy impression outside, worsened by enclosure of the ground floor around the hitherto open pilotis.

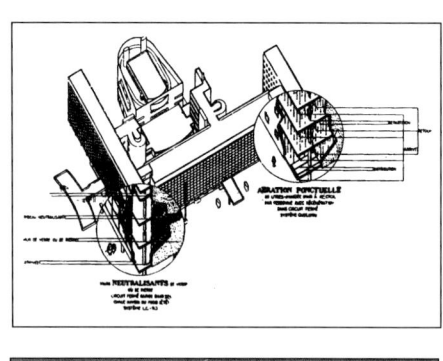

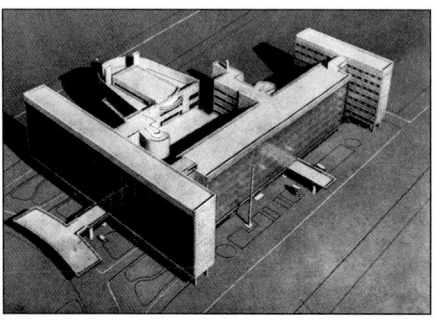

10
Communal house for Textile Institute students
Ordzhonikidze Street 8/9
Moscow
1929-30
Ivan Nikolaev

Where the modestly sized Narkomfin complex is 'transitional' this vast building by another Constructivist demonstrates the fully collectivised dom kommuna. The 2000 adult apprentices shared 1000 6m² cabins in a 200 meter-long eight-storey block. A rich mix of dining rooms, and recreational spaces were located in the low block that forms one side of the open court, where its curved porte cochère creates a subtly sculptural accent. The scale of the half-round stair towers and the vast rectangular volumes is at once brutal but superbly judged. It is a truly Corbusian achievement of 'the masterly, correct and magnificent play of masses in light' whose community life was imagined by Nikolaev in equally Corbusian sketches.

Russia West **St Petersburg**

Soviet Modern Movement architecture always comprised many trends, and Leningrad in particular represents this diversity. (The city took this name in 1924.) All the three main avant-garde groups has their representatives here: the Constructivists with their 'functional method', the Rationalists and Suprematists with their different compositional principles. While differing in their methodologies and varying in their theoretical aims, they interacted and became entangled in real practice. Meanwhile Leningrad architecture of the twenties and early thirties remained greatly influenced by neo-classical reminiscences. These evoked the city's historic role as Russia's capital, which it lost to Moscow in 1918, as well as prefiguring the socialist classicism that would return nation-wide in the mid-1930s.

The first major symptoms of the Modern Movement in St Petersburg date back to the beginning of the twentieth century when industrial and commercial buildings appeared with reinforced concrete frames, and sleek, undecorated, facades. Enlightened workers' housing schemes became forerunners of future experiments by Soviet architects.

Active construction began again in Leningrad in 1925, after the post-war collapse. Technically it was at a low level. Extensive use of old materials and artisan technologies prevented the realization of many original design ideas or caused them to be simplified. Steel beams and reinforced concrete were replaced by the timber used for tram rails. Large areas of glass were difficult, and the motif of uninterrupted horizontal windows was often simulated by dark-coloured piers between windows.

By the later twenties however there were buildings that fully exploited the latest technology, like the four factory-kitchen complexes of which two are presented here, whose structures are reinforced concrete frames.

When serious building started again in the second half of the twenties, Leningrad modernism was distinguished by particular attention to the aesthetic problems of form. Suprematism was one influence, as Malevich was working and teaching here. The other influence was German Expressionism.

This tendency was especially strengthened by the erection in Leningrad of the Red Banner factory by Mendelsohn, which began on site in 1926. The influence of this was particular direct upon architects like Noi Trotsky, for whom revolutionary symbolism had not died out. We see it reflected even in such apparently functionalist buildings as Nikolsky's School named for the Tenth Anniversary of the Revolution, whose functionally zoned plan is subordinated to the figure of the hammer and sickle. Meanwhile Neo-classical allusions remained in the work of many Modernists until the end of the twenties, only to re-emerge more strongly after 1932.

These are the regional peculiarities of Leningrad architecture between 1925 and 1935 which are represented in the selection of buildings presented here.

**Boris Kirikov
Maria Makogonova**

1
Palace of Culture named for AM Gorky
Stachek Square 4
St Petersburg
1925 | 1927
Alexander Gegello & David Krichevsky

This compact but heroically scaled building, with sectoral plan around a 2200-seat auditorium, was the first of Leningrad's great civic Palaces of Culture. These had similar educational, entertainment and assembly functions to the Moscow workers' clubs but served for a whole district not just the workers of a single trade union or factory. The revolutionary Putilov Plant nearby held a 'Palace' competition here in 1919 but it was set aside and repeated in 1925 when the adjacent housing areas were being completed. Alexander Dmitriev won but Gegello and Krichevsky simplified his expressionistic scheme. Like the nearby school the Palace was ceremonially opened on the revolutionary anniversary of 7 November 1927.

2
Secondary school named for the
10th anniversary of the October Revolution
Stachek Prospect 11/5
St Petersburg
1925 | 1927
Alexander Nikolsky

Leningrad's first post-revolutionary school and one of the first built works by the city's leading Constructivist, this complex was designed around the new programme of a special Leningrad commission for school construction, to foster maximum independence and scientific enquiry in pupils – hence the observatory, numerous laboratories, libraries and studios. Maximum sun, daylight and cross ventilation were a priority. Within the limits of the period, quality of materials as well as design was the highest possible, with extensive wood panelling inside and natural stone trim to the entrances. This was conceived as a 'school-palace' for children of the revolutionary workers and opened on the tenth anniversary of the Bolshevik takeover.

3
Red Banner knitwear factory
Pioneerskaia Street 57
St Petersburg
1925 | 1937
Erich Mendelsohn

Leningrad Textile Trust commissioned Mendelsohn for this extension to an existing plant after failing to get a usable design locally and visiting his hat factory at Luckenwalde of 1921-3. An extensive complex for 8000 workers was designed with dying and bleaching plants, a 500m perimeter of four-storey production and administration space, and a power plant on one corner. Only this and a few minor portions were built. The commissioning of a foreign architect without a competition caused widespread professional protest. The expressionist forms of the built part had profound influence on the formal language of all subsequent Modern Movement buildings in the city.

4
Secondary school for the Tkachei district
Tkachei Street 9 & Babushkina Street
St Petersburg
1927 | 1929
Georgy Simonov

At 1540 pupils, this was Leningrad's largest school and formed the educational and social heart of a new workers housing district in the Tkachei Street and Palevsky areas. Spaciously planned on an open, green, corner site, three parallel blocks are linked by a perpendicular corridor block raised on pilotis. Started as the Nikolsky school approached completion, this followed the same principles: the two teaching blocks served different age groups whilst all had access to extensive laboratories, studios, library, observatory, as well as a dining hall and central sportshall with outdoor games area beyond – all used by adults too.

5
Public baths for the Lesnoe district
Karbysheva Street 29a
St Petersburg
1927 | 1930
Alexander Nikolsky with Vladimir Galperin, Nikolai Demkov & Alexander Krestin

This is a simplified version of Nikolsky's well known unrealized design for a circular public baths with central swimming pool under a dramatically glazed dome. Here the annular structure provides two floors of bath facilities and specialist treatment rooms designed to serve 2100 people a day. Entrance is through a double-height rectangular block with stairs to upper and lower levels. The compact circular form was seen as minimizing energy loss and the two lines of small windows are linked visually by ridged panels which give the impression of horizontal bands of fenestration to lighten the solid outer walls.

6
Viborgsky district factory kitchen
Bolshoi Sampsonevsky Prospect 45
St Petersburg
1928 | 1930
Armen Barutchev, Isidor Gilter, Iosif Meerzon & Iakov Rubanchik

The factory kitchen was among the most important 'new types' of early Soviet architecture because its public feeding provision was the key to liberating women and enabling shift workers with bad housing to get reasonable food. Leningrad authorities commissioned research from a team of mass feeding specialists and these four young architects who formed the Rationalist (ARU) group in the city. This first complex was designed in 1928 and it was immediately decided to construct three more across the city (see Kirovsky, below). Feeding options ranged from full canteen meals to cafe-type snacks and ready-prepared meals for cooking at home. The curved elements made a dynamic composition typical of this group.

7
Kirovsky district department store and factory kitchen
Stachek Square 6
St Petersburg
1929 | 1931
Armen Barutchev, Isidor Gilter, Iosif Meerzon & Iakov Rubanchik

This largest of the city's four factory-kitchen complexes was designed to produce fifteen thousand meals a day for the populations of two new workers' districts, the Kirovsky around it and the Moskovsky to the south. Stretching deep into the site around a rectangular courtyard the vast cooking facility fed a series of dining spaces, with a main semi-circular dining hall opening onto a garden at the right side. In this complex the front block on Stachek Square was a department store, adding a purely glazed vitrine element to the dynamic composition which otherwise strongly echoes its Vyborsky district prototype.

8
Bread factory
Levashevsky Prospect 26
St Petersburg
early 1930s
Alexander Nikolsky & studio

Mass bakeries or 'bread factories' were central to raising Russia's handicraft food production to Soviet levels. This design used the common bread-making system devised by Moscow engineer Marsakov but here and on another site in north Leningrad, Nikolsky's team shaped the building very literally around the process. In the cylindrical main volume the bread descends on a spiral route from the top with completed loaves emerging ready to pack in the adjoining ground floor spaces, whence they are transferred into lorries backed up around the perimeter. A rich composition of interlocking cylinders thus results directly from the function.

9
Headquarters of the Kirovsky District Soviet
Stachek Prospect 18
St Petersburg
1930 | 1934
Noi Trotsky

District Soviets (Councils) were the core of Soviet local administration. This building combined all usual municipal functions with public amenities including banking and post office. On the green-field site of this new district the fifty-meter tower created an accent on the long Prospect after the historic Narva Triumphal Arch. The long main facade forms the south side of a public square for parades etc perpendicular to the Prospect, to which the short half-round wing forms a closure. In 1935 a larger wing with 1000-seat auditorium was added behind the tower. Changing tastes over the construction period made final detailing less sleek than originally designed.

10
Communal Housing (dom kommuna) of the Society for Tsarist Political Prisoners and Deportees
Troitskaia Square 1
St Petersburg
1929 | 1933
Georgy Simonov, with Pavel Abrosimov & Alexander Khriakov

In the Soviet period those who were imprisoned for subversion under the old regime had hero status and this prime site on the Neva Embankment looking to the river and the Fortress reflected that. The Society typically favoured partially communal life. Thus the two perpendicular blocks facing the river and the former Revolution Square comprised tiny individual apartments, each with a balcony but no kitchen. Private space was supplemented by extensive communal eating facilities, lounges and reading rooms, library, meeting rooms, mostly on the fully-glazed ground floor. The roof terrace had a solarium and viewing areas.

Selected Bibliography :
Modern Movement in USSR

Morancé A (publ)
L'Architecture vivante en URSS
Boulogne Automne 1930 Hiver 1930

El Lissitzky
Russland: die Rekonstruktion der Architektur in der Sowjetunion
Vienna 1930
Republished as:
Russland: Architektur für eine Weltrevolution
Vienna 1965
English translation as:
Russia: an Architecture for World Revolution
London 1970

Kopp A
Ville et revolution: architecture et urbanisme sovietiques des années vingt
Paris 1967
English translation as:
Town and Revolution. Soviet architecture and city planning 1917-35
London & New York 1970

Kroha J & Hrůza J
Sovetská architektonická avantgarda
Prague 1973

Senkevitch A
Soviet Architecture 1917-1962: A Bibliographical Guide to Source Material
Charlottesville 1974

Kopp A
Architecture et mode de vie: textes des années vingt en URSS
Grenoble 1979

Khan-Magomedov S
Pioniere der sowjetischen Architektur
Dresden 1983
English translation as:
Pioneers of Soviet Architecture
London 1987
Russian edition as:
Arkhitektura sovetskogo avangarda
Moscow 1996

Cohen J-L
Le Corbusier et la mystique de l'URSS: théories et projets pour Moscou 1928-36
Liège 1987
English translation as:
Le Corbusier and the Mystique of the USSR
Princeton 1992

Cooke C
Russian Avant-Garde: Theories of Art, Architecture and the City
London 1995

Moscow

Starr SF
Melnikov: Solo Architect in a Mass Society
Princeton 1978

Cooke C
'Map Guide to Moscow 1900-1930'
Architectural Design
London 1983 no 5/6 pp 81-96

Khazanova V (comp)
Iz istorii sovetskoi arkhitektury 1926-1932: rabochie kluby i dvortsy kul'tury: Moskva
Moscow 1984

St Petersburg-Leningrad

Kirikov B
'Die Architektur der Leningrader Avantgarde. Besnderheit ihrer Stilentwicklung' in:
Schädlich C & Schmidt D (eds)
Avantgarde II 1924-1937: Sowjetische Architektur
Stuttgart 1993 pp 34-43

Kirikov B & Makagonova M
'The Modern Movement in Leningrad: problems of the register' in:
Proceedings of the Third International Conference of Docomomo
Barcelona 1994 pp 65-8

Cooke C
'Leningrader Avantgarde'
Kirikov B
'Avantgarde und Konstruktivismus' (guide)
du
Zürich 1998 no 12 (December) pp 63-72

Photographs courtesy of : Catherine Cooke

Russia East Ekaterinburg & Novosibirsk

Russia East **Ekaterinburg**

The massive scale of the construction programme which the young Soviet government brought to the Urals in the mid 1920s was a function of its programme of national industrialisation. In 1923 the classical city of Ekaterinburg was designated Soviet Russia's first 'Oblast (regional) Centre'. In 1924 it was renamed Sverdlovsk (reverting to Ekaterinburg in 1991). Major replanning began especially in the centre, where the main East-West boulevard was opened up at various points with key buildings to create a chain of open spaces designed as the foci of new functional and cultural zones.

The selection of Sverdlovsk as location for the country's massive new heavy-machine building plant consolidated its national role. While this socialist town (sotsgorod) of Uralmash grew on its northern edge, the new Sverdlovsk itself was treated as an exemplary project, a city of the future. Funds were generously allocated for architectural and building activities here. The city could draw upon the best architectural talents whilst having its own lively professional life with frequent competitions and numerous creative groups.

Through these major national competitions, ideas and people were imported from Moscow, where the Constructivists' Union of Contemporary Architects (OSA) was very active, and from Leningrad. There was also an established group of local architects who adopted Modern Movement ideas enthusiastically. Meanwhile graduates of the Tomsk Technical School who up a branch of OSA in the city and followed its theoretical principles.

Distance from the capital and relative autonomy made this a fertile land for the Modern Movement and Ekaterinburg's heritage today is large, amounting to some 140 works. Some of these have been heavily altered and their quality is not uniform, being the work of three quite different groups of architects.

Typologically, however, they represent the whole spread of industrial, residential and public architecture. In this small selection we have stressed this diversity by including a medical complex, legal centre, sports facilities and utilities buildings as well as the well-known 'new types' of Soviet modernism like the workers' club and various semi-collectivist forms of housing.

The backwardness of building technology and the quality of building materials in the Urals at that time made it inevitable that the pure Modern Movement principles of spatial composition were sometimes treated superficially, even sceptically. Analysis of archival drawings shows how often original intentions were modified due to enforced speed and the rigours of climate. Rugged foundations and relatively solid walls were thus typical, with plans often compartmentalised in the interests of function, though flowing spaces were not infrequent in the public buildings. On some sites however major Moscow contracting organisations like 'Tekhbeton' and 'Standart' were working here in collaboration with the architectural avant-garde of Moscow, which made it possible in many cases to erect large works ranking with capital-city ones in their architectural and technical quality.

Ludmilla Tokmeninova

1
Water tower for the socialist town (sotsgorod) of Uralmash
Prospect Kultury 1
Uralmash, Ekaterinburg
1928 | 1929
M V Reisher

The tower was a competition project constructed as part of the new socialist town by the specialist concrete construction organisation from Moscow, Tekhbeton, using advanced technologies of the time. It was the first such tower designed specially for the 'Inza' type of tank. Besides providing a water supply it served as a viewing tower on a main axis of the town where it met the parkland and forest near the lake. Famous locally as 'the white tower', the combination of functionality and expressive form achieved by this Tomsk-trained member of the local Constructivist group has provided an identifying image to the whole area.

2
Institute of Physiotherapy and Occupational Diseases
Lenin Prospect 2 & Moskovskaia Street 12 & 14
Ekaterinburg
1929 | 1930
Georgy Golubev

Golubev came to Ekaterinburg from St Petersburg in 1920 and made a great contribution to development of modernist architecture in the Urals. This Institute was designed to investigate working conditions, to diagnose and treat occupational diseases and conduct preventative work in industrial enterprises. It was part of a large-scale new 'medical village' flanking the city's main artery at its western end. The administrative, treatment and residential building forms a courtyard intended as a garden for patients. Other buildings in the parkland site were variants on the same vocabulary, many boldly glazed and of vigorous composition.

3
House of Justice (Dom iustitsii)
Malyshev Street 2B
Ekaterinburg
1929 | 1930
S E Zakharov

This building formed a focal element of the area of new social facilities created from the mid-1920s on a raised site on the western end of the city centre. The medical area is nearby and the city prison stands on an adjacent site. This legal centre contained advice and information services for workers, educating them to their legal rights under the new social order, and magistrates courts and other assembly spaces in the circular tower facing down the long axis of Malyshev Street. Its simple structure and elevational treatment make this one of the boldest statements of modernism in the city.

4
Urals Worker publishing house
('House of the press')
Lenin Prospect 49
Ekaterinburg
1929 | 1930
Georgy Golubev

The dramatic sweeping corner used here was already something of a leitmotif on corner sites across the city, adopted by modernism from the classical vocabulary of old Russian cities. This scheme had somewhat mixed authorship, but the essential scheme remained Golubev's original concept. As headquarters for the main mouthpiece of the new regime and society in the area, publishing a vast range of popular, political and educational books and the 'Uralsky rabochii' newspaper, this building again demonstrated the extent to which the new regime identified itself with modernism in architecture.

5
Housing complex for the Urals Region Economic Council (Uraloblsovnarkhoz)
Malyshev Street 21 and Khokhriakov Street
Ekaterinburg
1929 | 1931
Moisei Ginzburg & Alexander Pasternak
(engineer S L Prokhorov)

This complex was one of several regional schemes which applied the same units and approach developed by Ginzburg and the Constructivist group in their housing research and in the Narkomfin building in Moscow. Here the main scheme comprises 4 rectangular blocks arranged around a planted courtyard on a pin-wheel plan. Three blocks use Stroikom family apartment types A-2, A-3 and A-4, one having a rooftop kindergarten. The 8-storied block on Malyshev Street is a communal hostel with a variant on the split-level type-F units, whose 'indoor street' access galleries are visible on the facade. The top floor here was originally open forming a terrace to the communal dining room behind, and the ground floor contained offices.

6
Workers' club for the Builders' Union
Lenin Prospect 50
Ekaterinburg
1929 | 1933
Iakov Kornfeld

This large complex on a prominent corner site was seen as a part of the city-centre ensemble of large public buildings that transformed old Ekaterinburg into Soviet Sverdlovsk. Besides the usual club facilities for entertainment and events, it was a training centre for builders. Spatially, it forms two functionally distinct parts. The club is itself in two volumes linked by a passageway: a 3-storied block along Lenin Prospect and a 2-storied block running perpendicular. The second part, with auditorium for public events, lies along the cross street. Pergolas on the flat roofs made solariums and viewing platforms. The scheme is a rich example of Constructivist planning by one of OSA's Moscow founders.

7
Dinamo sports complex (Dom fizkultury)
Eremina Street 12
Ekaterinburg
1929 | 1934
Veniamin Sokolov

This five-storied concrete-framed building of sports hall, training rooms and athletes' accommodation stands on the tip of a peninsula in the centre of the City Lake. Consciously conceived to evoke a ship, it is a prominent landmark visible to all citizens who promenade around the lake. It was originally a centre of land and water sports belonging to the military. Rowing boats were originally moored alongside and behind it is a running track and field-sports stadium.

8
Residential quarter for members of the Cheka (Gorodok chekistov)
Lenin Prospect 69
Ekaterinburg
1929 | 1936
I. P. Antonov, Veniamin Sokolov & Arseny Tumbasov

This project was won in a closed competition run by the Cheka and its high technical and design standards reflected the prestige of its inhabitants. Conceived as a self-sufficient area for the secret police employees, the district was a precursor of the later Soviet micro-district concept. Apartment blocks are located around the edge enclosing a landscaped area with kindergarten, polyclinic and sports ground. The 10-storied half-cylindrical building which forms a major landmark on the city's main street was a single-person hostel organised on 'dom kommuna' lines with shops at ground level. A club and administrative block links to this by a bridge to the east.

9
Housing district for workers at Uralmash
Ilich Street & Square of the First Five Year Plan
Uralmash, Ekaterinburg
1930 | 1931
Petr Oransky

This low-rise area of workers housing stood across the vast square from the great Uralmash plant, the Urals Factory of Heavy Machinery, which was located here as the 'factory of factories' to produce complete factory installations for Stalin's industrialisation of the Soviet Union under the early Five Year Plans. Oransky, as chief architect to the socialist town, created a number of buildings around the square including the technical college for workers, the Uralmash laboratory building, nearby public baths and this area of housing. Some blocks consists of small family apartments. Others are collective housing for single people. Though simple, the area is typical of housing in Sverdlovsk of the twenties in its attractively human scale.

10
House of Communications (Dom sviazy)
Lenin Prospect 39
Ekaterinburg
1931 | 1933
Kazian Solomonov

In the early 1930s this was one of the showpiece buildings of the new socialist Sverdlovsk. Its dramatic composition of cubic volumes and linear fenestration, vertical and horizontal, demonstrate the confidence with which the city projected itself through the architecture of modernism. The public entrance to postal and telegraph facilities is at the corner, marked by the tower. Right of this, at upper levels vertical perforations mark the telephone exchange equipment and a parallel block to the rear accommodates further office and administration, sorting facilities etc.

Russia East **Novosibirsk**

At the time of the 1917 Revolution the present city of Novosibirsk was a small railway town of under 70,000. During the 1920s/30s, however, it was urbanised at an even faster rate than other Soviet provincial cities, and by 1937, its population had grown, as a result of Soviet development of Siberia's resources, to 400,000. It became the administrative capital of Siberia and was known throughout the Soviet Union as 'The Siberian Chicago'.

The Modern Movement thinking in Novosibirsk is manifest not just in its architecture but also its planning. The 1925 Garden City inspired plan of engineer Ivan Zagrivko, the Greater Novosibirsk plan of 1929 by Professor Korshunov and the socialist town (sotsgorod) plan of 1930 for Novosibirsk's Left Bank, are the most interesting and innovative events in the urban history of the Siberian region and represented a very important contribution to Russian city planning as a whole.

Local interpretations of the new architecture can be found in all buildings constructed in Novosibirsk between 1925 and 1935. The selection presented here shows some of the key buildings of this period. Siberian industry and trade are represented by the Club for employees of the Soviet Trading organisation Sovtorg, the commercial building called Delovoi dom and the local headquarters of the state industrial bank Prombank. Pioneering Soviet medical facilities for the growing population are represented by the First City Polyclinic, located in the city centre and the Sibzdrav (Siberian Health) regional hospital complex built on what was then the city's northern periphery. The massive operations of local government and Party leadership for the affairs of this rapidly growing region are represented by the Krai-ispolkom building, whose long façade dominates a stretch of the city's main street. Among the city's social show pieces of that time were the many new areas of workers housing with their compact apartments and communal facilities on site. The Dinamo complex represents the city's new facilities for sports and recreation.

There are naturally differences in design quality and approach between those buildings constructed in the city by experienced Moscow and Leningrad architects who came to Siberia through architectural competitions and those by local architects of the region. But the social, constructional and aesthetic innovation are common to them all. It is also very important that at this time, as never before or since in the region, the general public was involved in the architectural process, with all newly proposed and constructed buildings being the subject of vigorous local discussion. Such involvement can once again have a most positive influence on the democratisation of decision making in architecture, urbanism and management of the cultural heritage.

For Novosibirsk, whose heritage is almost entirely recent, these Modern Movement monuments have a highly important role to play in the future development of the city. In symbolic as well as practical respects, their reintegration into the contemporary situation can be most fruitfully linked with the revival of Novosibirsk's role as the capital of Siberia.

Ivan Nevzgodine

1
House of Commerce (Delovoi dom)
Krasnyi Prospect 25, at Lenin Square
Novosibirsk
1926 | 1928
Daniil Fridman

In 1925, the Moscow Architectural Society, MAO, which organized most Soviet architectural competitions at that time, ran a closed competition for 'commercial' buildings for the rapidly growing Siberian capital of Novosibirsk. Others invited along with Fridman were Panteleimon Golosov, David Kogan and Sergei Chernyshev. This building, containing a department store and a hotel, was a version of Fridman's own competition design with assimilation 'of the most successful elements of the ground plans by architects Chernyshev and Golosov.' This building was the first in Siberia to use a concrete frame without brick walls to protect it from the harsh climate. With its bold glazing it formed a visible symbol of the city's modernity.

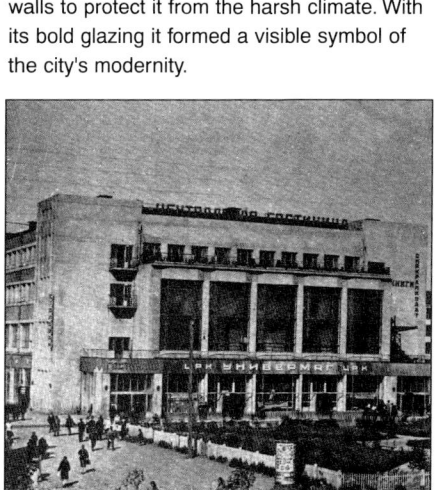

2
First City Polyclinic
Serebrennikovskaia Street 42
Novosibirsk
1927 | 1928
P Shchekin

A competition was held for this site in 1927 and Shchekin from Moscow received first prize, beating the experienced local stalwart Kriachkov into second place. The building's concrete frame and Shchekin's new system for planning such a building with rooms connected through waiting halls, and corridors eliminated, made this modestly sized building one of the best local examples of the new architecture. The single-storey part, extreme right, was the clinic for children.

3
Regional Hospital complex
Zalesskogo Street
Novosibirsk
1927 | 1928
Alexander Grinberg with N Gofman &
Alexander Klimukhin

In 1927 the Siberian public health service, Sibzdrav organised a closed competition to design an 850-bed regional hospital for Novosibirsk. Those invited were Nikolai Markovnikov, Nikolai Ladovsky and Grinberg from Moscow, Lev Ilin from Leningrad and Andrei Kriachkov from Tomsk. Grinberg won and brought in two collaborators for executing the building. The hospital was noted for its highly functional planning, its careful handling of orientation in relation to the northern sunlight, and its system of underground passages whereby people could move easily between different buildings of the complex even in coldest periods of the Siberian winter.

4
Club for workers of the
Soviet Trade organisation (Sovtorg)
Lenin Street, 24
Novosibirsk
1928
Ivan Burlakov

One of the most interesting regional examples of this building type which was among the 'social condensers' of the revolutionary period. The building consists of a foyer, bold staircases, a 600-seat hall and a 'small hall' for 200, a library and a set of club rooms. Its volumetric composition was generated by the necessity to organise this range of functions on a triangular site and create something which distinguished itself from the pre-revolutionary building of the Business Men's club opposite, dating from 1911-14. As socialist realism took hold, the designers of the Sovtorg club – both Burlakov and his technician N Lavrushenko – were brought to justice for 'the low architectural quality' of their building.

5
Communal housing complex
for railway workers
Lenin and Cheliuskintsev Streets
Novosibirsk
1928 | 1933
Ivan Voronov, Boris Gordeev, Sergei Turgenev
& Nikolai Nikitin

The initial plan comprised four L-shaped buildings standing on the perimeter of the block. Only two buildings were erected but these were the first in Siberia to be fitted with built-in cupboards. The resulting housing quarter had been designed to have its own laundry, boiler house and canteen, but only the latter was built. In 1930, however, the quarter was redesigned to operate on a communal basis. A purpose-built dom kommuna was added as the third residential block and a children's facility comprising crèche, kindergarten and polyclinic. A community centre was designed with 300-seat theatre-cinema, a 250-seat dining hall, a 150-seat auditorium, a gymnastics hall, library, club rooms and 25 individual rooms for study, teaching etc.

6
State Bank building (Gosbank)
Krasnyi Prospect 27, at Lenin Square
Novosibirsk
1930
Andrei Kriachkov

In 1928-9 the national open competition for the design of this Siberian Regional Office of the State Bank was won by the Moscow architect Grigory Barkhin. Second prize went to another Moscovite, Moisei Ginzburg. The Bank's directors then decided to reduce the building's volume to less than half that specified by the competition brief. The experienced Siberian architect Andrei Kriachkov was then commissioned to redesign the scheme and he used Ginzburg's scheme for the office part of the ground floor. The result has none of the bold sweeping half-round corner of Barkhin nor the cool logic of Ginzburg, but with the House of Commerce it forms an ensemble of modernity on the main square of the rapidly growing Siberian capital.

7
Housing for Kuzbass Coal Trust
(Kuzbassugol)
Krasnyi Prospect 49-51
Novosibirsk
1931 | 1933
Dmitri Ageev, Boris Biktin & Boris Gordeev

This housing complex for the construction cooperative of the Kuzbass coal workers was designed to form a new type of enlarged city block whose core was a group of eight four-storied 'Zeilenbau' buildings for which two types were designed, one with split-level apartments. These would be framed on the Krasnyi Prospect edge of the site by two five-storied buildings with shops, kindergarten and other services at ground level, and a school building at the back of the site. As with so many other developments, this was never completely finished and only six apartment buildings and the school were built.

8
Regional Supply Committee building
(Obl-Snab)
Krasnyi Prospect 11
1931 | 1934
Novosibirsk
Sergei Turgenev, Boris Gordeev & Nikolai Nikitin

Universally known in the city as 'The house with the clock' (Dom s chasami), this six storied building was the last one erected in the region before World War II on the principle of 'socialisation of the household'. From one elevator in the corner tower of the L-shaped block, all the minimal apartments are reached by long semi-enclosed access galleries. At street level there was a food store, rooms for children's activities and the community facilities while administrative offices of the client organisation, the Regional Supply Committee, occupied the first floor.

9
Regional Executive Committee
of the Communist Party (Krai-ispolkom)
Krasnyi Prospect 18
Novosibirsk
1931 | 1933
Boris Gordeev, Sergei Turgenev,
Andrei Kriachkov & Nikolai Nikitin

This building typifies a whole series of large administrative buildings erected by the national government at this time as a manifestation of Soviet power. The final building emerged from a competition, won by the young architects Gordeev and Turgenev despite strong competition from experienced architects like Alexander Grinberg who had several such buildings to his credit. Kriachkov therefore represented local experience, and engagement of the young Nikitin to design the concrete frame launched the career of this talented structural engineer. The vast building contains a range of administrative offices with grander chambers and auditoria for meetings of Party bodies.

10
Dinamo Sports Club
named for V R Menzhinsky
Kommunisticheskaia Street, 60
Novosibirsk
1932 | 1933
Boris Gordeev, Sergei Turgenev & Nikolai Nikitin

In the original design this complex comprised a sports club, a swimming pool with water tower, a cultural club (with 75-seat hall, dining and club rooms), two buildings containing 87 apartments, and a 'children's combine' or kindergarten. The sports club was designed with heated bridges to the swimming pool and cultural club but only the sports club and the apartment buildings were executed. The sports hall was designed for the Siberian climate with a circular gallery inside for running which could be transformed into viewing galleries for competitive events. The great nailed timber arches which originally roofed the sports hall were a unique construction devised by the innovative Nikitin, but were destroyed by fire in 1989.

Selected Bibliography :
Urals and Siberia

Kazus I
'Architektur-Avantgarde im Ural und in Siberien' in: Schädlich C & Schmidt D (eds)
Avantgarde II 1924-1937: Sowjetische Architektur
Stuttgart 1993 pp 54-65

Ekaterinburg-Sverdlovsk

Volodin P
Sverdlovsk
Moscow 1948

Shelushinin A
'K istorii arkhitektury Sverdlovska' in:
Iz istorii khudozhestvennoi kul'tury Ekaterinburga-Sverdlovska
Sverdlovsk 1974 pp 72-82

Alferov N, Beliankin G et al
Sverdlovsk: stroitel'stvo i arkhitektura
Moscow 1980

Bukin V & Piskunov V
Sverdlovsk: perspektivy razvitiia do 2000 goda
Sverdlovsk 1982

Tokmeninova L
'Sverdlovsk – a city unique in its heritage of Constructivist architecture' in:
Proceedings of the Second International Conference of Docomomo
Dessau 1992 pp 241-3

Starikov A, Zvagel'skaia V, Tokmeninova L. & Cherniak E
Ekaterinburg: istoriia goroda v arkhitekture
with supplement:
Ekaterinburg: katalog pamiatnikov arkhitektury
Ekaterinburg 1998

Photographs courtesy of :
Ekaterinburg City Archives
Catherine Cooke

Novosibirsk

Belogortsev I
Arkhitektory Novosibirska
Novosibirsk 1945

Ashchepkov E
Novosibirsk (Arkhitektura gorodov SSSR)
Moscow 1949

Kriachkov A
Arkhitektura Novosibirska za 50 let
Novosibirsk 1951

Ogli B
Novosibirsk: ot proshlogo k budushchemu
Novosibirsk 1973

Balandin S
Novosibirsk: istoriia gradostroitel'stva 1893-1945
Novosibirsk 1978

Vasileva N et al (eds)
Novo-Nikolaevsk–100–Novosibirsk
Novosibirsk 1993

Nevzgodine I
'Experiments in Siberian Constructivism during the 1920s' in: Botta M (ed)
Vision and Reality: Proceedings of the Fifth International Docomomo Conference
Stockholm 1998 pp 194-8

Photographs courtesy of :
State Archive of the Novosibirsk Region (GANO)
Ivan Nevzgodine

Scotland

Perhaps because of the relative social and political stability of the country throughout the twentieth century, Scottish modern architecture developed during this period in a steady manner, without revolutionary innovations or schisms. From c1900 to 1960, the concept of modernist innovation in the aesthetic, social and technical spheres steadily developed. This process paralleled the wider movement of the rise of the state, and the increasing emphasis on the unified nation as the main source of social and economic initiative, despite the fact that the country was incorporated in a larger, multi-national United Kingdom for the whole of this period.

The emergence of modernism in Scotland was divided into a phase of tentative and highly variegated preparation, up to the 1940s, during which modern ideas were largely filtered through variants of classicism, and an accelerated phase of innovation in the 1940s and 1950s, reaching a climax in the 1960s in a sudden ascendancy of both Modern architecture and state initiative across all areas of Scottish national life.

From the late 1960s and 1970s, there was widespread public and professional disillusionment with this materialistic modernity. All these phases were conditioned by the longstanding geographical polarisation within Scottish urban culture, between the more thrustingly modern 'West' (centred on Glasgow) and the more traditional, introspective 'East' (centred on Edinburgh, the capital).

During the earliest period of Scottish modernism, around 1900, there were two mainstream movements and one avant-garde – all seeking to distance themselves from the mass-produced nineteenth century eclecticism. Dominant in Edinburgh was the 'Traditionalism' represented by R Rowand Anderson and Robert S Lorimer, emphasising the 'home' and 'domestic' values and culminating in the crafts masterpiece of the Scottish National War Memorial (1923-7). In the West, the predominant tendency was a rationalist Beaux-Arts modernity led by JJ Burnet, especially esteeming the great public building and the modern office block; its climax, though built in Edinburgh, was Burnet, Tait & Lorne's St Andrew's House (1937-39), a stepped classical headquarters for devolved Scottish government. Alongside these more sober movements, Glasgow also witnessed one of the pioneering examples of avant-garde artistic modernism, in the branch of Jugendstil led by CR Mackintosh. While Mackintosh was mainly interested in innovative interior work, his friend James Salmon II adapted elements of his style to multi-storey concrete construction in the office tower 'Lion Chambers' (1907).

The triumph of modernism in the 1940s came in the wake of the mass planning and co-ordination of war; there was a belief that the same disciplined consistency, led by architect-planners such as Robert Matthew, could make it possible to build complete new communities on rational lines. The sharp divergence from the muddle of the past was symbolized above all by the vertical form of the multi-storey tower, as signalled in Matthew's university redevelopment of Edinburgh's George Square (from 1960), the new headquarters tower of Lanark County Council in Hamilton (1959-64), and, more obliquely, the soaring new Forth Road Bridge (1958-64). The same principles of rationalistic design could also be applied in a more muted fashion in sensitive or landscaped contexts, as at the new Stirling University (from 1966) or Edinburgh's Commonwealth Pool (1967-68). Other modernist designers, such as Gillespie, Kidd & Coia at the St Peter's Seminary community (1959-66), drew instead on the poetic, artistic strand of the movement, first established by Mackintosh.

The final phase of high modernism – the post-war discontentment of groups such as Team X or the Situationists with CIAM rationalism, and their attempts to devise more complex or flexible modernisms - were most directly represented in Scotland by the building of Cumbernauld New Town (from 1959), with its dense residential areas tightly clustered around the futuristic, megastructural town centre. However, the megastructural ideal, with its concept of the rigid frame and ever-changing interior, was realised even more fully in an area which was, strictly speaking, outside the field of architecture – the 1970s programme to build large numbers of oil production installations in the North Sea, such as Ninian Central Platform (1974-78).

Miles Glendinning

1
Lion Chambers
Hope Street, Glasgow
1907
James Salmon & John Gaff Gillespie
LG Mouchel & Partners (engineers)

This multi-storey office tower, in central Glasgow, was an early example of reinforced concrete building, exploiting the Hennebique system of construction to maximise lettable accommodation on a restricted site. Commissioned by a practising lawyer and patron of the arts to accommodate his own offices and artists' studios, Lion Chambers attempted to adapt a 'national' or primitive-vernacular version of classicism to 'the age of reinforced concrete'. (Salmon 1908)

2
St Cuthbert's Co-operative Society
Bread Street, Edinburgh
1935 | 1938
TP Marwick & Sons
David Harvey & Philip McManus

This structure was a classic 1930s extension to an existing co-operative store to provide a furniture showroom. The daring street façade consisted of a great glass curtain wall (Scotland's first) which originally floated clear of the internal structure. Lighting along the soffit of the curtain wall floodlit the glazing from inside, enhancing its separation and transparency, and provided a new and astonishing concept in a city with a tradition of solid stone street architecture.

3
Lanark County Buildings
Hamilton
1957 | 1964
DG Bannerman (county architect)

The Civic Council headquarters, splendidly located in the rolling landscape of the Clyde valley, consist of two large linked buildings set on a raised landscaped podium; a monumental seventeen storey slab block with glazed curtain walling, and a circular council chamber. This symbol of post-war local government pride and power was Scotland's foremost example of late international modernism: a characteristically modern expression of different functions boldly juxtaposed in a precise and refined manner.

4
Forth Road Bridge
North and South Queensferry
1958 | 1964
Mott Hay Anderson (engineers)
Sir Giles Scott Son & Partners

At its completion, this was the longest suspension bridge outside the USA, and the first to break decisively from the solid, monolithic aesthetic of structures such as Mackinac Bridge (1957) and Verrazano-Narrows (1963) towards a new, soaring lightness; the depth-to-span ratio of the road deck, 1:999 at Mackinac was reduced to 1:178. Twin towers of high tensile steel, 156m in height, support a twin-truss suspended structure. The main span is 1,006m in length. The picture below shows the 1940s scheme for Forth Road Bridge with a heavier structure.

5
Dysart Housing Scheme
Phase 1 2 and 3, parts 1 2 and 3
Dysart, Fife
1958 | 1977
Wheeler & Sproson

This redevelopment provided an overall plan of medium density low rise housing within the core of the 16th and 17th century town structure. The quasi-vernacular architectural forms of this scheme culminated in the harled and pantiled mini Scottish tower houses (utilised as maisonette housing) of phase three. Wheeler & Sproson's Dysart development introduced a new wave of vernacular inspired small housing projects in the historic burghs of Fife.

6
Residential zone
Cumbernauld New Town
Seafar, Kildrum Park, Muirhead & Carbrain
Cumbernauld
1959 | 1974
Cumbernauld Development Corporation

A pioneering attempt to design a community which would satisfy the Modernist demands for hygienic rationalism while evoking some of the dense togetherness of older towns: this was the first time that the postwar reaction of younger designers against CIAM functionalist planning was put into practice at the scale of an entire new town. Cumbernauld's housing was disposed not in segregated neighbourhood units but in a cellular layout clustered around the futuristic town centre.

7
St Peter's College
Cardross
1959 | 1966
Gillespie, Kidd & Coia
I Metzstein, A MacMillan
WV Zinn & Associates (engineers)

One of the key monuments of post-war Scottish architecture, Cardross was designed as a vast megastructural extension (housing 100 priests) to an existing 19th century mansion. This brutalist design was critically acclaimed prior to its official opening in 1966, but the ambitious project only functioned as intended for a short time; in 1980 it closed, and soon after began its long decline into decay and ultimately ruin. Despite increased state protection, Cardross Seminary remains a ruin today.

8
Edinburgh University redevelopment
Faculty of Arts and Social Sciences
George Square, Edinburgh
1960 | 1967
Robert Matthew Johnson-Marshall
& Partners
Percy Johnson-Marshall (planning consultant)

Basil Spence's 1954 plans for the university's extension involved the partial redevelopment of George Square; 18th century town houses surrounding a large central garden. The 14-storey David Hume Tower, commissioned in 1958, incorporated with adjoining faculty buildings in a multi-level complex in Percy Johnson-Marshall's detailed amendments in 1961, was pivotal to the redevelopment and an example to other universities anxious to retain their central sites.

9
Cumbernauld Town Centre
Phases 1 and 2
Cumbernauld
1963 | 1967
Cumbernauld Development
Corporation Architects
Geoffrey Copcutt (group architect)

A massive multi-level, multi-function town centre building set on an elevated ridge, straddling a dual carriageway through-road, and crowned by a bold line of penthouses supported on slab supports. Significant as the international exemplar of the 'megastructure' idea — a late1950s / early 1960s conception of a single, agglomerative building mass containing multiple, flexible, easily-altered functions.

10
Royal Commonwealth Pool
Edinburgh
1967 | 1970
Matthew, Johnson-Marshall & Partners
John Richards (partner in charge)
Ove Arup & Partners and Steenson, Varming
Mulcahy Partners (engineers)

The Royal Commonwealth Pool, a regional recreational and educational resource, was completed for the Commonwealth Games of 1970. The characteristic problems of swimming pool design (heat loss, condensation and glare from windows) were solved by enclosing the main pool halls with smaller rooms, circulation and services. Careful management of building height, restrained architectural expression and selection of materials aided the insertion of a large public building in a low-density residential area.

11
Ninian Central Platform
Shetland North Sea
1974 | 1978
John Howard Engineers (UK) &
Doris (France) engineers

An artificial island in the North Sea, carrying oil and gas production facilities, Ninian Central is a concrete gravity platform weighing over 620,000 tonnes. A concrete tower incorporating well slots and storage tanks is mated to a steel deck 40m above the water. Modules stacked on the deck contain production and service functions with accommodation, catering and recreational facilities for 340 workers. The entire assembly was constructed on the west coast of Scotland and towed to its mid-ocean site, realising the avant-garde 1950s and 60s projects of Archigram and others for 'a city of components on racks [and] stacks, plugged into networks and grids.'

Selected Bibliography :
Willis P
New Architecture in Scotland
1977

'Cumbernauld Town Centre'
Architectural Design
London May 1963 pp 206-225

McKean C
The Scottish Thirties: an Architectural Introduction
Edinburgh 1987

Glendinning M & Muthesius S
Tower Block
New Haven & London 1994

Edwards B
Basil Spence
Edinburgh 1995

Cowling D
An Essay for Today: Scottish New Towns 1947-1997
Edinburgh 1997

Glendinning M (ed)
Rebuilding Scotland: The Post-war Vision 1945-1975
East Lothian 1997

Watters DM
Cardross Seminary: Gillespie Kidd & Coia and the Architecture of Post-war Catholicism
Edinburgh 1997

Photographic Credits :
Keith Gibson
2
de Burgh Galwey
6
Bookless
7
Henk Snoek
8, 10
Bryan and Shear
9

Acknowledgements :
Forth Road Bridge Joint Board
Sir Anthony Wheeler
Professor Isi Metzstein
RMJM
Chevron UK

Research :
Miles Glendinning
Diane Watters
David Whitham

Slovakia

The Slovak architectural scene of the first half of the 20th century was determined by several key events at the same time. Up until 1918, Slovakia was a part of the Austro-Hungarian Monarchy. It did not have its own school of architecture or professional periodicals published in the Slovak language. The cultural life of that time was dominated by an effort to reach national emancipation. After World War I, the Czechoslovak Republic was created, unifying Slovak and Czech lands. This event was crucial to the cultural climate in Slovakia. For a certain period of time, Slovak culture escaped the trauma of the national issue and could freely develop towards authentic modern values. However, the democratic- and plurality-oriented new republic created opportunities for universal contact with European centers of culture. The period of the 20s and 30s is thus decisive in terms of social and cultural modernization in Slovakia. These years witnessed also the breakthrough of modernism in Slovak arts and architecture. In that period, specific social conditions were created, allowing of the growth of many unique persons in all the fields of art. In these years, even architecture in Slovakia matched up with European movements for the first time and became their integral and equal part.

The year 1930 was the milestone for the Modern Movement in Slovakia, when many outstanding functionalist constructions were created. A hanging facade was implemented for the first time in Slovakia. The fashionable ship-like aesthetics were materialized in fantastic buildings of sports clubs. Several important international competitions were organized in Slovakia, boasting of the participation of the top European architects. In 1930, an architecture-social discussion about new housing fully developed. The Arts and Crafts School started working too. The School's orientation was influenced by two decisive factors. First, there was an effort to improve local production with high quality education of craftsmen. Second, the school was influenced by an effort to approximate the progressive European tendencies, as, for example, the German Bauhaus. The school invited the most remarkable representatives of modernism, including László Moholy-Nagy or Hannes Meyer, as lecturers to Slovakia. The Modern Movement even strengthened its position in Slovakia with the help of two professional magazines that were launched in 1930. The trilingual German-Slovak-Hungarian magazine Forum had a wider artistic focus, featuring articles on arts, architecture, movies, and theatre. The more technical magazine Slovensk Stavitel (Slovak Constructor) was published in Slovak and was oriented exclusively at the art of construction. In the plurality atmosphere in Slovakia in the 1920s and 1930s, several artistic clubs and associations actively worked. Architects were involved in associations like Umelecká beseda slovenská (Slovak Artistic Forum), Kunstverein (Artistic Union), Klub architektov (Architects' Club), Klub inzinierov (Engineers' Club), or Svaz inzinierov a architectov SIA (Association of Engineers and Architects). The Slovak architectural production of that time is manifold and plural, being determined by various influences melting together in this cultural environment. The Modern Movement in Slovakia represents a unique combination of internal, autochthonous impulses (a regional determination, an interesting confrontation between innovative and conservative features, the modernization uniquely combined with the original folk culture, etc.), and external influences. The most important external factors included the education of future Slovak architects in Brno, Prague, Vienna, Budapest, Munich, or Zurich; the arrival and domestication of Czech architects in Slovakia (Alois Balán, Jiří Grossmann, Klement Šilinger, Jindřich Merganc), or the implementation of the constructions created by remarkable Czech and European architects in Slovakia (Peter Behrens, Bohuslav Fuchs, Jaromír Krejcar). The structure of construction activities in Slovakia in the 1920s and 1930s was dominated by government orders (schools, administrative buildings, and housing for state officials), the investments of the health insurance companies (sanatoriums, offices of the insurance companies), and urban buildings (social housing). Orders coming from the high class of the society were quite rare. This fact was caused by the structure of the society in Slovakia. The challenging designs of the exclusive architecture of villas are therefore reduced in Slovakia.

Slovak architects emphasized the utility value of a work. The artistic side and style were not primary to them. First, this attitude was caused by an environment that was not ready enough for the ideas of avant-garde affecting the social demand. Second, the refusal of things that are new and a priori better is typical to the prudent nature of Slovak people as residents of Central Europe. There is no doubt that this social situation was one of the reasons why architects in Slovakia did not create any state-of-the-art works. However, this architectural approach, being moderated and limited by the real possibilities of clients and practice, created in Slovakia unique works of regional modernism that became an inevitable part of the Modern Movement in Europe. The main criteria we applied while selecting the representative sample of the MoMo constructions included: (a) the top quality of the design and implementation, understood as a shape composition, the purity of the layout, as well as the quality of construction materials and the craft work, (b) the work's originality and uniqueness, (c) the breakthrough character of a work (we preferred earlier works), (d) a good authentic state of a construction substance (meaning the durability based on a high quality design and implementation), (e) the maintenance of the original function of a building, (f) a high quality reconstruction performed in accordance with original architecture and materials used,(g) a proportional representation of individual construction kinds and authors, responding to the situation in Slovakia of that time. In addition, our selection emphasizes the specific values of the Slovak Modern Movement in the context of European architecture. The values include a refusal of a dogmatic avant-garde, a humane approach, a high quality of craft works, an inclination to smaller, more easily handled designs, and healthy pragmatism. We tried to reflect some concrete typical features as well, as certain monumentality or a unique material scale (travertine combined with ceramic tiles, brick, or white plasters). All the chosen works illustrate the specific situation of the Modern Movement in Slovakia during its most valued period.

Henrieta H. Moravãíková

1
Slovak Artistic Club
Bratislava
1924 | 1926
Alois Balán & Jiří Grossmann

2
Spa Building Palace
Sliac, Central Slovakia
1925 | 1937
Rudolf Stockar

3
University Dormitory & Mensa Lafranconi
Bratislava
1927 | 1933
Klement Šilinger

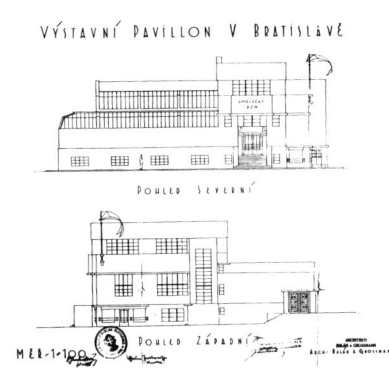

Slovak Artistic Club (UBS) was founded in 1921 and united all arts. In the year 1924 it organized an architectural competition for the design of its own exhibition and club building on the embankment of the Danube. Two young Czech architects living in Bratislava won this competition. The pavilion consists of two exhibition halls – a big one for painting and a small one for sculpture exhibitions. There used to be archives, stores and a small session hall in the basement. On the UBS building we can see the development from the classical to the functionalist architecture. While the entrance hall has still heavy traditional ceiling, the big exhibition hall is constructed of simple ferroconcrete skeleton with framed-glassed ceiling construction.

The spa was bought by state in 1922. In 1924 the Ministry of the Public Health Care announced a competition for a complex of restaurant and social rooms, which architect Stockar won. The grand concept of Stockar respects the natural scenery of the spa slope into which the building with two vertical dominants is composed. First is a hotel of four storeys with 249 rooms. A second two storey building houses a bar and café with a gallery, stores, offices, performance hall and restaurant. A long colonnade connects these two buildings. The construction of the 240m long complex consists of a reinforced concrete monolithic skeleton. The building composition is based on alternating open and closed areas, exterior and interior.

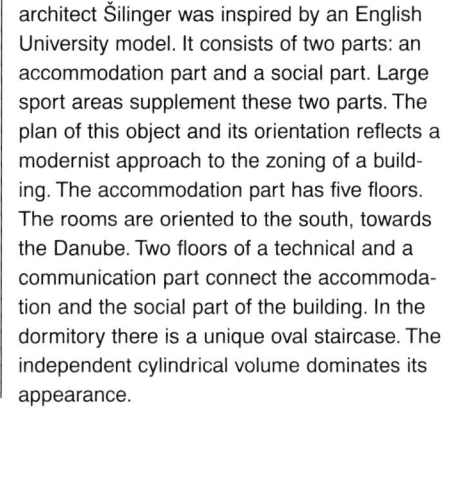

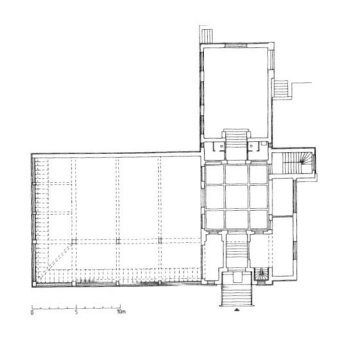

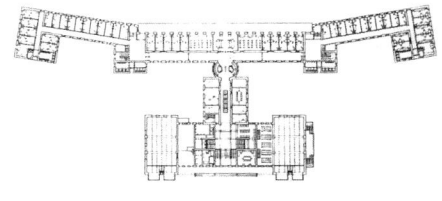

The building of the university dormitory and academic canteen Lafranconi is the first of its type in Slovakia. In designing this project, architect Šilinger was inspired by an English University model. It consists of two parts: an accommodation part and a social part. Large sport areas supplement these two parts. The plan of this object and its orientation reflects a modernist approach to the zoning of a building. The accommodation part has five floors. The rooms are oriented to the south, towards the Danube. Two floors of a technical and a communication part connect the accommodation and the social part of the building. In the dormitory there is a unique oval staircase. The independent cylindrical volume dominates its appearance.

4
Cure House Eden and Hotel Excelsior
Piešťany, Western Slovakia
1928 | 1930
Pavel Weisz

Two different investors gave a commission to the architect for two edifices at the same time on neighbouring sites in the centre of a spa town. They were to be of a hotel character and almost of the same volume. Height was six floors in both cases. The buildings have one underground floor and flat roof topped them both. The result seems to be successful as a unit, though both buildings act independently and are architecturally fully autonomous. The Excelsior basic ground floor plan is L-shaped; typical floors are arranged as a two-part disposition. Architecturally, the front façade, which gradually runs back by two floors, deserves special attention.

5
Neologic Synagogue
Žilina, North Slovakia
1928 | 1931
Peter Behrens

The building is situated at the corner between two streets, close to the historic city core, on a slightly sloping site. The main hall, crowned by the dome and equipped with galleries and serving rooms, represents the core of the whole disposition, based on the square. On both southern and northern sides of it, the attached transverse longitudinal entrance halls transform the ground plan into a rectangle. The predominance of horizontal lines (terraces, flat roofs, and attics) supports the impression of stability and massiveness of the whole building. At the same time, the block character of the central part, the rhythm of the narrow vertical windows and massive dome show associations with the Orient. The building is unique of its kind in Slovakia.

6
Arts & Crafts School
Bratislava
1928 | 1937
Jiří Grossmann

The Arts and Crafts School was established on the model of German Bauhaus in the year 1930. The former evening vocational school (1928) thus became an important avant-garde arts school. Its goal was to improve the arts and crafts quality of the domestic industrial production. For purposes of this school, architect Grossmann designed a large building developed from the central courtyard along the street with the wings leading into the inner block. The four storey high central wing dominates the edifice. The layout is organized in two-part disposition. The hygienic spaces and staircases are placed at the junction of the two wings. The bearing structure was built as a pre-cast concrete frame with flat roof.

7
Finanial Palace
Žilina, North Slovakia
1928 | 1931
Michal Maximilian Scheer

This building of the former finance office stands in the town center on a narrow sharp-angled site. It was build according the winning competition design. Its layout consists of two wings, which follows the street line precisely. The glass-roofed half-cylinder-shaped staircase with the main entrance situated into the narrow building front creates the architectonic dominant of the building. It recalls some designs by Soviet constructivists. The former four storey high building was shortly after its completion raised by one floor. This caused a loss of dynamic expression of the cylindrical corner. There are offices in the building, rationally organized in two-part disposition. The building is among the best of Scheer's architectural work.

8
City Savings Bank
Bratislava
1929 | 1931
Juraj Tvarožek

9
German Rowing Union Donau
Bratislava
1930 | 1931
Josef Konrad

10
Sanatorium Machnác
Trencianske Teplice, Central Slovakia
1930 | 1932
Jaromír Krejcar

If we sought the most revolutionary Slovak building in its time, it would be the City Saving Bank in Bratislava. The basement and first two above-ground floors occupy the whole site. The four other floors are split into two independent blocks. In the ground floor a passage enters the building in the centre. On the 1st floor there is an impressive deposit hall and offices; above that are flats. The front façade of steel construction filled with opaque glass is typical for this building. It is one of the first in Slovakia with the expressive attributes of functionalism. The technical solution (ferroconcrete skeleton, curtain wall) was considered to be extraordinary progressive. The façade solution resembles the Moravian Bank by Fuchs & Wiesner in Brno.

The building of a former Rowing Union Donau is situated on the Danube river bank, in a leisure zone which has been a rowing centre since the beginning of the century. The form of building follows the fashionable boat-like aesthetics of the 20s and 30s, which was symptomatic for the European Modern Movement. The Rowing Union uses a combination of smooth white, big glass areas and stylish horizontal railings. The vertical core of the whole composition is the high glass prism of a staircase. The floors of the building come out from this place, like boat decks. The horizontality of so-called decks is also supported by two rows of windows. They create, especially in curved corners, a very effective and stylish detail.

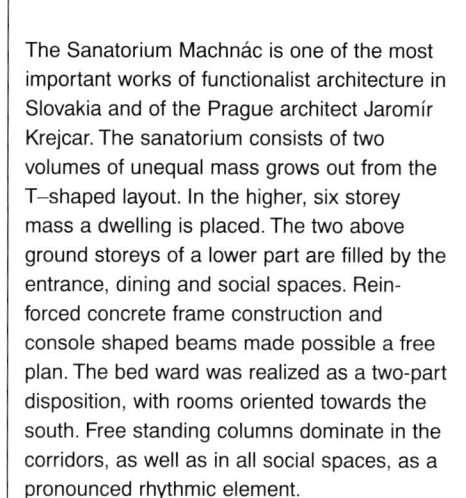

The Sanatorium Machnác is one of the most important works of functionalist architecture in Slovakia and of the Prague architect Jaromír Krejcar. The sanatorium consists of two volumes of unequal mass grows out from the T–shaped layout. In the higher, six storey mass a dwelling is placed. The two above ground storeys of a lower part are filled by the entrance, dining and social spaces. Reinforced concrete frame construction and console shaped beams made possible a free plan. The bed ward was realized as a two-part disposition, with rooms oriented towards the south. Free standing columns dominate in the corridors, as well as in all social spaces, as a pronounced rhythmic element.

11
Catholic Church
Bratislava
1930 | 1932
Vladimír Karfík

This functionalist three-nave church is one of the first projects made by Vladimír Karfík after his return from the USA under Frank L Wright. The church is built in the construction system which was used by the Baťa company for building industrial architecture. It has a simple three-nave basilica-like composition. Above the entrance there is a slight extension, which symbolizes the traditional bell-tower. A skylight window of a pyramid-shape illuminates the altar. The whole building represents the rational spirit of so called Zlín architecture: the ideas of unification and standardization are strongly expressed here. The pillar module of the main nave is 6x8m; the aisles are 3m wide. The parish office and chaplain's flat are also part of the building.

12
Colonnade Bridge
Piešťany, Western Slovakia
1930 | 1932
Emil Belluš

Unique in Europe, this functionalist roofed bridge was one of the architect's favourite works. The bridge connects the town of Pieťrany and the spa island. Formerly both the pedestrians and cars used the bridge. Today pedestrians use it only. The bridge had to be connected with colonnades on the embankment; that is why it is called colonnade. Though essentially only a bridge, it is an extraordinary architectural work. It proves the ability of the modern architecture to create a utilitarian technical work with a noble human dimension. The bridge is accessable from both sides by simple gates. Small shops cover both ends of the bridge. The bridge is not only roofed; there is glass-covered wall protection against winds.

13
Convalescent Home Morava
Tatranská Lomnica, High Tatras
North Slovakia
1930 | 1933
Bohuslav Fuchs

This Trade Union Convalescent Home by Moravian architect Bohuslav Fuchs was built by an insurance company. It is situated inside the park of the spa town Tatranská Lomnica. The dramatic natural scenery expressively influenced the convalescent home architecture. The building consists of two functional components – the residential ones and the social ones. The higher, five-storey dwelling part has a transverse supporting system, in the module of 3.65m. In the three-part disposition the rooms are laid oblique, oriented directly towards the south. It causes the tooth-sectioned form of the façade. The contrasting lower part, serves the social functions, demanding undivided spaces.

14
Housing Block Avion
Bratislava
1931 | 1932
Josef Marek

The housing block Avion represents an interesting approach to the solving a dwelling problem in the beginning of 30s. The architect combined a compact ground floor with functionalist linear organization of the higher floors. The wings on the sides have six, and the middle one, seven storeys. The compact base consists of 25 shops. The 6 individual dwelling blocks are two-part disposition with 118 flats of maximum 4 rooms. Avion is made of a pre-cast reinforced frame with double span. The architecture of the block is of simple purist character.

15
New Age Housing Complex
Bratislava
1932 | 1942
Friedrich Weinwurm & Ignác Vécsei

New Age (Nová doba) housing complex in Bratislava's, Vajnorská Street was built as a housing project of small size flats for private employees and workers. It comprises three almost identical residential blocks built in three stages from 1932 to 1941. It is one of the most interesting examples among numerous constructions aimed at reducing insufficiency of flats in the 30s. The architects tried to combine the advantages and intimacy of a freestanding detached house with the effectiveness of a residential rental house. The orientation of the flats to the inner courtyard removes inhabitants from noise in humming streets. The neighborhood consists of three identical complexes. Each is a five storey high simple white box with 160 flats.

16
Sanatorium Vyšné Hágy
Vysné Hágy, High Tatras, North Slovakia
1933 | 1938
František Libra & Jiří Kan

The most frequent cause of death in 1930s Czechoslovakia was tuberculosis. For that reason for Central Social Insurance Company built in Vysné Hágy a big modern sanatorium and hospital for respiratory diseases and TB. Completion of the whole complex was prevented by the second world war. It consists of 13 buildings – the main therapeutic house, an infection pavilion, central furnace, a power station, workshops, a laundry, garages, a greenhouse, a reception building, and four buildings for the staff. The main building is constructed as a reinforced concrete skeleton filed with bricks, isolated by the cork and covered by the ceramic facing bricks.

17
Villa of Dr Dvořák
Bratislava
1933 | 1934
Jindřich Merganc

This villa is a unique example of the Corbusian white villa in Slovakia. It was built for the doctor Dvořák and his wife writer Zuzka Zguriřka. The hall with a gallery and a staircase runs through two floors and forms the basic motif of the composition. All the diverse rooms of the house are placed in relation to this centripetal element, creating an architecture of sliding and overlapping planes. The street façade is characterized by a long strip window, which lights the main living space. The building is a mature functionalist work, in a cultivated way using the modernist conception of space and at the same time still stressing the practical functioning of the house.

18
Cooperative Buildings
Bratislava
1933 | 1939
Emil Belluš

This complex of three buildings with a cinema, shops and bank in the partèrre, offices and dwellings in higher storeys, was designed by Emil Bellus for the Agricultural Cooperatives in the very central part of Bratislava. The corner building (No 15), a bank Union of Agricultural Mutual Treasurer, was built first. It was called Farmer's House and there were deposit hall, shops and passage in the ground floor. Nearly parallel was built building No 13 where the Central Cooperatives were located. In its partèrre there is a passage with an extraordinary oval skylight. The Cooperative Headquarters and underground cinema were housed in it. First two floors of the complex have stone facing; upper floors a ceramic one.

19
The Open - Air Pool Green Frog
Trencianske Teplice, Central Slovakia
1935 | 1937
Bohuslav Fuchs

This organic shaped functionalist architecture with a sensitive relation to surrounding nature is one of the best works of Moravian architect Bohuslav Fuchs. The swimming pool was built in the time of spa Trencianske Teplice's growth, on a southern slope above the spa town. The programme comprised three objects. In the first were all main working spaces, including an open-air pool 33.3x12m. The second was a skittle-playing room and the third an area for children with a circular pool. With high creativity the architect solved the task of enriching the quite strict functionalist forms. Using pure but noble means he succeeded in creating a work that is functionally clear and organically linked with surrounding nature.

20
District Social Insurance Office
Bratislava
1936 | 1939
Alois Balán & Jiří Grossmann

This is one of the best examples of modern health service architecture in Slovakia. It has an irregular H-shaped ground plan. The rounding of southern wing supported by columns vitalizes its cubic shapes. It presents the first evident influence of Le Corbusier in Slovakia. In the centre of the plan there is a hall running through three storeys, illuminated through the glass and concrete ceiling. Around the hall, in two storeys of galleries, there used to be offices. Today these are surgeries. Horizontal windows, creating an illusion of striping divide the clear façade. The expressive glass vertical lines of staircases are added. The left wing was used by surgeries, the right one for offices. Each part has its own staircase and entrance.

Selected Bibliography :
Kusy Martin
Architektura na Slovensku 1918-1945
Pallas, Bratislava
1971

Kusy Martin
Architektura na Slovensku 1918-1945
Pallas, Bratislava
1971

Foltyn Ladislav
Slowakische Architektur und Tscechische Avantgarde 1918-1945
Verlag der Kunst, Dresden
1991

Dulla M (ed)
Architekt Emil Bellus Reional Modernism
SAS Bratislava
1992

Slachta S
Fridrich Weinwurm –
Architekt der Neuen Zeit
SAS, SNM, Bratislava
1993

Dulla M, Moravcikova H (ed)
DOCOMOMO **Architektura & Urbanisms 29**
1995, 1-2

Photographic Credits :
DOCOMOMO Slovakia Archive
1, 3, 11, 17, 20
Archive of the Slovak Institute of Memorial Care
2, 4, 6, 7, 10, 12, 13, 14, 15, 16, 18, 19
Archive of Ladislav Foltyn
5
The Literary Archive of Matica Slovenská
8
Forum 2, 1932, 168
9

Sweden

DOCOMOMO Sweden was first founded in the autumn of 1990 soon after the international conference in Eindhoven. The initiator and organizer was architect Eva Rudberg, attached as a researcher to the Museum of Architecture in Stockholm. We are primarily a working-group, composed of architects, antiquarians and architectural historians in Stockholm with contacts to universities in other parts of Sweden. The group has concentrated its efforts partly on broad outward-looking activities and partly on helping to save threatened buildings by writing articles and statements, putting forward arguments and providing information to those involved. Sveaplans Gymnasium, upper secondary school for girls in Stockholm, built by the City of Stockholm in 1936, and the Helsingborg Concert Hall built in 1932, are two of the many buildings with which the group has been successfully engaged. As to the outward-looking activities, the working-group has held two large conferences in Stockholm. The first one in 1992 was on the Functionalism of the 1930s, and the second one in 1995 on the Modern Movement of the 1950s. Both conferences were well attended and each of them attracted around 150 participants. The group prepared a publication for the first conference 'Functionalism värd att vårda', 'Functionalism worth taking care of', which was very well received. Other important outward-looking activities have been lectures and articles in both newspapers and professional journals.

The greatest undertaking, however, was the 5th International DOCOMOMO Conference, 'Vision and Reality', which the Swedish DOCOMOMO group organized in conjunction with the Swedish Museum of Architecture and in collaboration with the other Scandinavian groups. It took place in Stockholm over four days in September 1998 and attracted 270 participants from 25 countries. For this event the five Scandinavian DOCOMOMO groups also presented their book: Modern Movement Scandinavia (published by Århus in Denmark).

The group has also compiled a register of important modernist buildings built in Sweden from around 1925 to 1960. The list covers buildings still in existence and in a relatively damaged condition. The exact physical state of every building has sometimes been difficult to ascertain and some of them may have been changed while the register was being prepared. There are also buildings which should have been included in the register, primarily from recent decades, but our limited time did not permit us to research and include them. Our ambition is, however, to extend the register. The buildings in this publication are a representative selection from our present register. The facts have been researched and the descriptions have been compiled by members of the Swedish DOCOMOMO group.

Only one of the buildings in our register is on UNESCO's World Heritage List, namely Gunnar Asplund's and Sigurd Lewerentz's Skogskyrkogården, crematorium and cemetery in Stockholm, 1916-1940. It is a work which includes buildings of both Classicism and the Modern Movement. A small number of buildings in the register have been declared Listed Buildings and a few others are declared as Buildings of National Interest. The former classification provides buildings with strong protection while the latter is a strong recommendation to municipal and local authorities, who grant building permission, and to the owners, managers and administrators of the buildings in question to preserve the buildings and to proceed with great caution in connection with alteration and extension work. Furthermore, Part 3, Section 10 of the Swedish Planning and Building Act states that 'Alterations to a building must be carried out with care, thus paying attention to distinctive features as well as to constructional, historical, cultural, environmental and architectural values'.

Eva Rudberg

1
Woodland Cemetery Skogskyrkogården
Sockenvägen 492, 122 33 Enskede
1916 | 1940
Gunnar Asplund & Sigurd Lewerentz

An architectural response to a social need for new, practical and hygienic ways to handle burials in an expanding society and a growing population. Modern architecture is used as a subtle and sensitive way for expressing new ideas in a new ritual situation in connection with burial reform. The cemetery and its buildings form together a whole of unusual architectural power. After an international competition in 1915 the cemetery was planned and developed over a long period. Woodland Chapel by Asplund (Skogskapellet) was built in 1920, a service building in 1924, Resurrection Chapel (Uppstandelsekapellet) by Lewerentz 1926 and the three Crematorium chapels by Asplund with the Main Chapel, The Chapel of the Holy Cross (Heliga korsets kapell) in 1940.

The site, originally a Scandinavian pine forest, is carefully brought to an intense spiritual landscape by means of architectural work. From an exedra-formed main entry and a narrow passage between boundary walls of heavy stones, a wide serene landscape opens up. To the west a high knoll rises with a circle of trees to form a place for meditation. To the east a walled-in area for urns and columbarium walls stretch uphill along the edge of the forest towards a sequence of three chapels, the last of which has an open hall, a large portico in front. Beside this hall a tall cross of stone is placed. The two minor and the main chapels are joined together by small walled-in gardens adjacent to a waiting room for each chapel. The façades of the minor chapels are light and four-sided in white marble. Behind the huge portico, where pillars and beams merge together into a simple form and an even surface, the Main Chapel extends into a sofly rounded form. In front of the open hall a mirror pond is placed in the green fields. Further south areas follow with graves in grass under tall pine-trees. To the east the small Woodland Chapel is placed among the trees in a separately walled precinct, with increased density of forest and natural forest soil. Completing an axis from the Meditation grove at the top of the knoll lies the Resurrection Chapel, a tall, slim classicist building with just one window facing south. The entrance portico with decorated tympanon faces north.

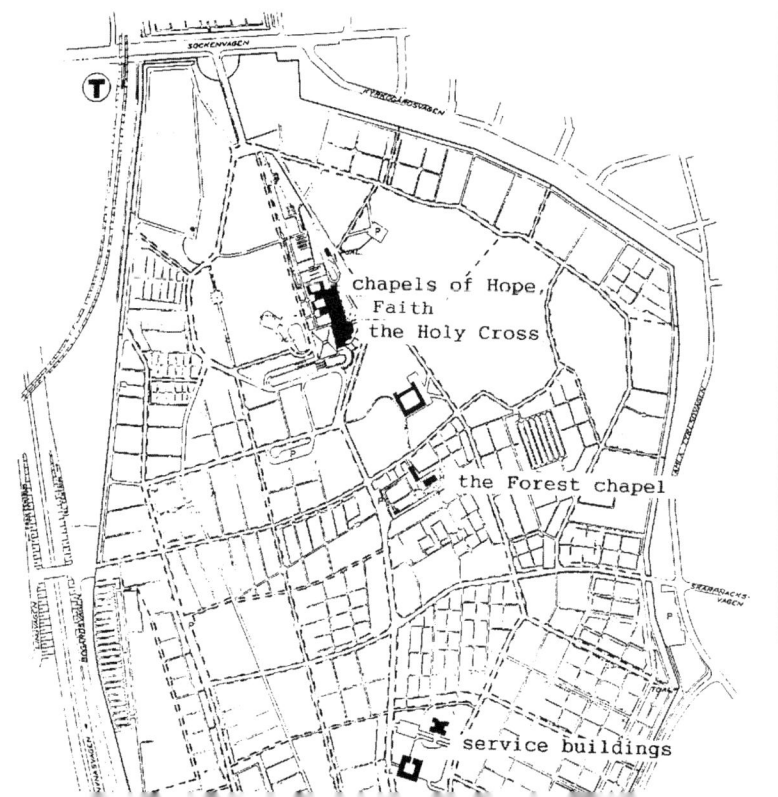

2
Hammarforsen & Krångforsen
Hydro-Electric Power Stations
The river Indalsälven 840 70 Hammarstrand
The river Skellefteåälven
25 km upstream of Skellefteå
1926 | 1928
Osvald Almqvist

These two power stations represented the break through of the Modern Movement in Sweden in both their functionalist planning and their style It would previously have been normal to collect all functions into one building volume and give it an effective, symbolic form. But Almqvist separated the three functions of water intake, machinery hall and distribution plant into three different buildings. He took up the engineer's plain aesthetics, them a new grace and refinement and composed the three elements into one ensemble where the three buildings mirror the movement and power of the water. No Swedish architect had done that before. Hydro-electric power stations are a key building-type in Sweden, and these two are newly listed as outstanding examples.

3
Housing & Industrial Area Kvarnholmen
Tre Kronors väg, Havrevägen, Vetevägen, Rågvägen, Siktvägen 131 31 Nacka
1927 | 1934
Eskil Sundabl, Olof Thunström,
Artur von Schmalensee, Olof Hult
& Anders Ekblad

Some of the first modernist buildings in Sweden, the mills, factories and the storage buildings were built on this little islet by Kooperativa förbundet, which played an important role in the growth of the Swedish welfare system. They also built housing for the factories' employees. The storage house (1927) by Sundahl and Thunström and mill by Schmalensee (1928) are built in concrete. Terrace houses in four rows have small gardens and two 3-4 storey buildings provide 94 flats. All are small, though above current Swedish average, with maximum daylighting and standardization of elements. Such integrated developments of industry and housing had not been seen in Sweden since the eighteenth century.

4
Helsingborg Concert Hall
Drottninggatan 19, 252 21 Helsingborg
1929 | 1932
Sven Markelius, Mogens Mogensen &
Artur von Schmalensee

Two competitions were held 1925 and 1926 and all entries were neo-classical. The final winner was Sven Markelius who developed his scheme into a pure Modern Movement building after his visit to Germany where he was deeply influenced by the new architecture at Bauhaus and the Weissenhofsiedlung. When finished in 1932, it was regarded the most outstanding Modern Movement building in Sweden. Collaboration of Gustave Lyon from Paris gave the hall superb accoustics. Its walls are covered with Sapeli mahagony. It contains 1000 seats and can be divided into two rooms. Today the entrance and the big windows are changed into more clumsy solutions but the ambition is to restore its original state.

5
Housing Area of Södra Ängby
Carl Larssons väg, Zornvdgen a o
168 50 Bromma
1933 | 1939
Edvin Engström & Björn Hedvall

The townplan from 1933 can be regarded as a garden city. The area contains more than 500 residential houses. The municipality of Stockholm and the city planning office commissioned the plan but the houses were built by private building contractors. This is a residential area with more than 500 houses in Modern Movement style. The houses all have their own individuality but the area gives a very orderly impression through common use of white plastered, cubic forms with mostly flat green sheet iron roofs. Internationally such a large area of co-ordinated Modern Movement buildings is rare and this is by far the most extensive of such areas in Sweden.

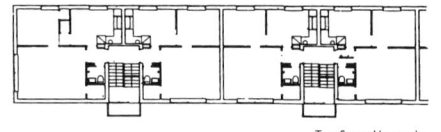

Two-Storey House, plan.

6
Collective Multi Family House
John Ericssonsgatan 6, 112 22 Stockholm
1934 | 1935
Sven Markelius

This is the first fully developed collective house in Sweden. The idea behind it was to release employed, married women from childcare, cooking, laundry and so on. The initiative was taken in 1932 by an association of working women. The Social Democrat and later peace politician Alva Myrdal was one of them and a strong supporter. Originally the project was much larger but economics dictated a six-storey building of 55 flats. These are very small, most of them two rooms, with a food lift to order meals up from the restaurant. On the ground floor was a nursery with garden. In 1991 the house was carefully restored and then also got its warm yellow colour back. The nursery, food lifts and restaurant are still working.

7
Sveaplan Upper Secondary School for Girls
Cederdaisgatan 10-20, 113 47 Stockholm
1934 | 1936
Nils Ahrbom & Helge Zimdahl

This building was both architecturally and socio-politically a milestone. In 1927 the Swedish government decided to let girls into state secondary schools. This school was built as a result of this reform. A competition was held in 1931, and these two young architects won. The project underwent some changes, and the assembly hall got a new form compared to the winning contribution. The school is divided into four parts, each in its own building and all connected by the staircase hall. Standard windows etc kept down the price. Daylight dominates the whole building, especially the staircase hall where also a fresque by Bo Beskow describes women's life. The building was carefully restored and slightly altered in 1996 for use by Stockholm University.

8
Kungliga tekniska högskolans kårhus
Student union building
Drottning Kristinas väg 15-21, Stockholm
1929 | 1930
Sven Markelius & Uno Åhrén

One of the earliest strictly functionalist, official buildings in Sweden. Ribbon windows, flat roof and framed construction are combined with solid brickwalls facing Drottning Kristinas väg.

9
Riksförsäkringsanstalten
National Insurance Office
Adolf Fredriks kyrkogata 8, Holländargatan 15
Wallingatan 1, Stockholm
1930 | 1932
Sigurd Lewerentz

Seen from the street side a powerfully expressive cubic volume creates a secretive exterior. The façades enclosing the central courtyard with the main entrance are a complete contrast, as the horizontal strips of windows open up the whole interior.

10
Ålstensgatans radhus (Terrace-houses)
Alstensgatan, Bromma
1932
Paul Hedqvist

11
Gyttorp multi-family
and terrace houses and centre
Gyttorp
1945 | 1954
Ralph Erskine

12
Vällingby New Town
Vällingby
1954
Sven Markelius
(Stockholm City Planning Officer)
Sven Backström & Leif Reinius
(centre buildings)

The zig-zag shaped plan is made up of houses like cubes, two-storey, plaster covered. This was one of the first terrace-house areas in Sweden where a fully developed Modern Movement architecture was carried through.

The Gyttorp project involved the design of an entire small industrial community with the local Nitro-glycerine industry as the client. Concrete shell constructed terrace houses have vaulted roofs and plastered façades in different colours.

Vällingby represented a key stage in the development of Swedish post-war new town building, developing ideas previously applied in Årsta (started in the latter half of the second world war) and leading in its turn to the development of Farsta in the later 1950s. The town was designed around three functions: work, housing and the community oriented centre. Being larger than Årsta it had a more solid economic base, with more employment alternatives than its predecessors. The town centre was planned to serve surrounding communities as well as the population of Vällingby itself. This two- and three-storey area created a community focus with its lively shopping centre, as well as offices, banking, restaurants, etc. It had extensive car parking but its central building was also located directly above the underground station, the whole expressed in an architecture that combined exposed structure with a festive lightness. The industrial zone was located to the east. Building height was differentiated by zones. The central area was punctuated with tower blocks. Further out were three- and five-storey apartment blocks grouped around well planted traffic-free open spaces. The outer zone contained detached houses and some terraced units.

13
Göteborgs konserthus (Concert hall)
Götaplatsen, Göteborg
1932 | 1935
Nils Einar Eriksson

This is one of the masterpieces of the Swedish Modern Movement and particularly well suited to the context of the classicistic Götaplatsen Square. A functionalist plan is superbly enriched by its sophisticated interior colouring.

14
Badhus i Eskilstuna (Public baths)
Eskilstuna
1930 | 1931
Paul Hedqvist

Cleanliness of the function here is expressed in a white, plastered building of geometrically distinct forms with huge glass windows.

15
Eslövs medborgarhus (Community hall)
Södergatan 29, Eslöv
1957
Hans Asplund

An outstanding example of post-war Modern Movement architecture in Sweden, this community building is immaculate both in details and as a whole with elegant interiors of marble, oak and brick.

16
Gävle krematorium (Crematorium)
Skogskyrkogården, Gävle
1957 | 1962
Alf Engström, Gunnar Landberg
Bengt Larsson, Alvar Törneman (ELLT office)

This slender, well-maintained construction of glass, concrete and wood is beautifully composed to complement the surrounding pines. The crematorium consists of three chapels and a bell-tower made of steel girders.

17
Biografen Draken (Cinema)
Drottningholmsvägen 25-29
Fridhemsplan 25-29, Stockholm
1938 | 1939
Ernst Grönwall

This beautiful wooden auditorium with characteristically fine carpenters work. The foyer has a marble floor inlaid with patterns and intarcia doors. Typical neon signs of this period completed the façade.

18
Telefonaktiebolaget LM Ericsson (Factory)
Telefonplan, Stockholm
1938 | 1940
Ture Wennerholm

Here a long industrial complex is articulated with expressive glass stair-towers. The structure is reinforced concrete throughout.

19
Villa Claëson (Summer residence)
Rostockervägen 1, Falsterbo
1924 | 1927
Josef Frank

This brick house at the seaport Falsterbo in southern Sweden was one of the very first functionalist buildings in Sweden.

Selected Bibliography :
Ny Svensk Architektur
Stockholm 1939

Rasmussen SE
Nordische Baukunst
Berlin 1940

'Sweden'
Architectural Review special issue
London September 1943

Kidder Smith GE
Sweden Builds
London & New York 1950 (revised 1957)

Svenska Arkitekters Riksförbund
Modern Architecture in Stockholm: Guide
Stockholm 1959

DOCOMOMO Sweden
Functionalism – värd att vårda!
Stockholm 1992

Wedebrunn O (ed)
Modern Movement Scandinavia
Copenhagen 1998

Illustrations courtesy DOCOMOMO Sweden

Switzerland

The choice of Modern Movement architecture presented in the following examples tries to respect the fundaments of the different areas of influence.

Switzerland's modern architectural heritage is linked to the cultural institution of the Polytechnical school (later on Swiss Federal Institute of Technology) in Zürich with teachers like Gottfried Semper and Carl Moser. They formed in a time segment of fifty years between the end of the century and the twenties. An avant garde group of architects under them included for example H. P. Berlage.

In the Italian and French oriented cultural regions of Ticino and Vaud/Geneva the development of modern architecture was influenced by a vigorous exchange, a sort of import-export dynamism which we can better define with names like Mario Chiattone or Charles-Edouard Jeanneret.

But the main stream of exchange was oriented to Germany with an important contribution by the Swiss Werkbund group for the Weissenhof settlement in Stuttgart and a year later by the nomination of Hannes Meyer as the director of the Bauhaus. Strengthened by a qualified education and an upcoming industrial technology, Swiss architects found attractive working possibilities in foreign countries. Thanks to the cultural relations established in the CIAM Congresses with catalytic figures like Helène de Mandrot and Sigfried Giedion the fleeing German intellectuals, under them many Bauhaus teachers, could find their first refuge after the exodus in peaceful Zürich.

Swiss Modern Movement architecture reflects all the aspects of this dynamic interchange. Nonetheless, it was very important in the choice to give a synthethic view of currents like pragmatic modernism, which due to topographical, meteorological and geopolitical conditions could not develop to abstract functionalism but more to a 'pretentious modesty' based on collaborative research. The early Modern Movement finds its end in 1939, when the National Exhibition in Zürich was characterized by the prevailing mood of the incoming 'Heimatstil' and by the outbreak of World War II.

Documentation and conservation of the architectural heritage of this period began in the 1980's. Nearly every city and Canton established registers, which assured the identification of an architectural work defined in jurisdiction as an 'architectural witness of social and cultural importance for the period'. The identification does not imply protection, which can only be given if an intervention on the building is planned and advised to the building police. Preservation is therefore always a delayed reaction and lacks active support by the law which considers a preservation act as a restriction of property rights.

DOCOMOMO **Switzerland**

1
Brigde Saiginatobel
Kantonsstrasse
Schiers GR
1928 | 1930
Robert Maillart

The highest and widest spanning bridge is a three-hinge arch of box-section in a form typical of Maillart's work, in which the spandrels are omitted leaving triangular openings. It is one of his finest constructions in terms of material, economy and elegance.

2
Community house Biel
Bahnhofstrasse 11
Biel BE
1929 | 1932
Eduard Lanz

This monument of Neues Bauen is a witness to a design method with fixed components appropriate to their function with tower, staircase, hall, rotunda arranged for optimal harmony with the site. The whole is an impressive example of urban modernism.

3
Hotel Monte Verith
Via Collina 84
Ascona TI
1926 | 1928
Emil Fahrenkamp

The white, angular building is distinguished by precisely incised openings, the ground level terrace, and the steel and glass façades of the living room and the 2 floors of bedrooms. It was build in conjunction with the Monte Verità movement.

4
Shop Wohnbedarf AG
Talstrasse 11
Zürich ZH
1932
Marcel Breuer & Robert Winkler

For the distribution of functional, mass-produced, reasonably priced furniture for small apartments a new type of shop was created in an existing building: an open space with a glazed frontage as an expression of modern approaches to living.

5
Sports house Ortstock
Braunwaid - Alp GL
1930 | 1931
Hans Leuzinger

The building shows a carefully empathizing approach to the circumstances of the site. Because of the natural facts of the materials Leuzinger chose a wooden structure, which underlines his attitude to adjusting the degree of modernity to the budget and the Alpine climate condition.

6
Swimming-bath Heiden
Kohlplatz 5, Heiden AR
1932 | 1933
Beda Hefti (engineer)

This generously dimensioned facility was built as part of the 'health and welfare' aspirations of the 1930s although it was not so much the social aspects that were uppermost in the minds of the private initiators.

7
School and museum of arts and crafts Zürich
Ausstellungsstrasse 60
Zürich ZH
1930 | 1933
Karl Egender & Adolf Steger

This early manifesto of Neues Bauen was celebrated as a witness of the social awakening. It is composed of three parts and with its extremely pragmatic interior organisation is reminiscent of cubic abstract Bauhaus geometry, but also of industrial architecture.

8
University institute of Bern
Bühlstrasse 20 / Sahlistrasse o.Nr.
Bern BE
1928 | 1931
Otto Rudolf Saivisberg & Otto Brechbühl

In terms of town planning this is a convincing extension of the existing chemistry building: the complex is orientated inwards and the 'comb system' formally binds the autonomous institutes together, but is also enriched by the motif of rhythmic repetition.

9
Trade school Bern
Lorrainestrasse 1, Bern BE
1934 | 1939
Hans Brechbühler

From the point of view of the old city the school, creating a bridge-head situation, seems to be the starting point of a new city development. It is structured in autonomous volumes which are differentiated in the construction, the façades were developed on 'tracées regulateurs'.

10
Library of the Canton Ticino
Via Cattaneo, Lugano TI
1937 | 1940
Rino Tami & Carlo Tami

This Library has two aspects, the modern one with the structural composition and the design of the front elevations, and the expressionist one with the handling of the corners, which reveals its function. The formal choices are typical of Tami's architecture.

11
Settlement Freidorf
St Jakobs Str, Freidorfweg & Schanzweg
Muttenz BS
1919 | 1921
Hannes Meyer

Based on the model of the garden city and organized as a cooperative the 150 houses are arranged in rows with a few, precisely employed elements as spatial variations: circulation roads, compost ways, squares of various sizes and flower and vegetable gardens.

12
Settlement Neubühl
Nidelbad, Ostbühl & Westbühlstrasse
Zürich ZH
1928 | 1932
Artaria & Schmidt, ME Haefeli
Hubacher & Steiger, WM Moser & E Roth

With this cooperative estate the initiators aimed at promoting social contact. They created conditions for a new form of communal life by means of residential roads and various communal facilities.

13
Dwelling block Ronde
1-19 rue Charles-Giron, Genève GE
1927 | 1930
Maurice Braillard

The semicircular monolith, with the powerful rhythm of the articulations of the secondary system and the enhancement of the courtyard as a support for community life, forms a strong structural element of the urban area.

14
Dwelling block Clarté
2-4 rue St Laurent, Genève GE
1927 | 1932
Le Corbusier & Pierre Jeanneret

The immeuble Clarté is a living machine and a living laboratory in the sense understood by the avant garde of the twenties. New themes of the 'cellules de 14m^2' and the 'maison à sec' are added to the 'five points' of Le Corbusier.

15
Dwelling block Zossen
St. Alban-Anlage 37-39, Basel BS
1934 | 1938
Otto Heinrich Senn & Rudolf Mock

This free-standing block, constructed as steel frame with delicate stone cladding, with luxury town apartments, is organised in three functional zones for living, cooking and sleeping, all of them executed with great elegance.

16
Apartment houses Doldertal
Doldertal 17 und 19, Zürich ZH
1932 | 1936
Alfred & Emil Roth & Marcel Breuer

The two apartment blocks correspond to the formula of 'light, air, open space' for the concept of 'liberated living'. They follow Corbusian principles with the free-standing ground-floor, the 'plan libre' and the habitable roof space.

17
Villa Schwob
167, rue du Doubs, La Chaux-de-Fonds NE
1916 | 1918
Le Corbusier

The villa is a remarkable achievement for the construction with the walls, the slabs, the pillars in reinforced concrete and the yellow brick facing, which has Mediterranean connotation. It was also the first attempt by Le Corbusier to apply the 'tracés régulateurs'.

18
Petite Villa
21 Route de Lavaux, Corseaux VD
1923 | 1925
Le Corbusier

In this small detached house, which is standing on a strip of land reclaimed from the shoreline, a peripheral circulation route leads through the line of rooms. This leaves the south side free for an 11-metre panoramic opening facing the lake.

19
Ribbon building Rotach
Wasserwerkstrasse 27 29 & 31, Zürich ZH
1927 | 1928
Max Ernst Haefeli

As one of the programmatic works of 'Neues Bauen' in Zürich, the relatively low building evidenced architectural and constructional innovations such as flat roof, double-glazed aluminium windows and sliding partition walls.

20
Dwelling house Schaefer
Sandreuterweg 44, Riehen BS
1927 | 1928
Paul Artaria & Hans Schmidt

This row house prototype is distinguished by its spatial qualities. The cross-shaped ground plan made it possible to relate the living space to the garden, whereas the bedrooms are situated along the street side of the house.

Selected Bibliography :
Bill M
Moderne Schweizer Architektur 1925-1945
Basel 1944

Roth A
'Swiss architecture, yesterday and Today'
Architects' Year Book
London no 3 1949 pp 106-114

Smith GE Kidder
Switzerland Builds: its Native and Modern Architecture
London 1950

Curjel H et al
'Swiss Architecture'
Architectural Design special issue
London September 1962

Schmidt H
'The Swiss Modern Movement 1920-1930'
Architectural Association Quarterly
London vol 4 no 2 April-June 1972 pp 32-41

Gubler J
Nationalisme at internationalisme dans l'architecture moderne de la Suisse
Lausanne 1975

Gubler J
ABC Architettura e Avanguardia 1924-1928
Milan 1983

Charollais I & Marchand (eds)
Architecture et la Raison. La Suisse des années vingt et trente
Lausanne 1991

Ingberman S
ABC: International Constructivist Architecture 1922-1939
Cambridge (Mass) 1994

Illustrations courtesy DOCOMOMO Switzerland

United Kingdom

The number of Modern Movement buildings dating from before the Second World War in the United Kingdom (which in this context means England and Wales) is relatively small. In the optimistic post-war period of reconstruction, however, modernism became the dominant ethos in British architecture. Significant numbers of pioneering architects had acquired positions in municipal offices and architectural education. They had a powerful influence across the whole spectrum of new buildings, for public housing, education, medicine, industry, in urban planning and the design of new towns.

Most of the significant pre-war works resulted from the migration of foreign-born architects to England in the early 1930s. Some 'modern' buildings were erected by native architects but many of these had more connection with Britain's industrial and nautical past than with the ideological intentions of a functionalist architecture or with the International Style, both of which came to Britain from continental Europe. Indeed the exhibition of International Style architecture in New York's Museum of Modern Art in 1932 included only one British example: the new headquarters of the Royal Corinthian Yacht Club built on the banks of the River Crouch in rural Essex by Joseph Emberton, completed the previous year. This was typical of its period in being commissioned for an obscure site by a small group of discriminating private clients whose friends generally considered their taste eccentric.

Emberton was British, but most of the innovators were immigrants. Connell and Ward came from New Zealand in 1924. Lubetkin arrived from Russia via Germany and Paris in 1931. Mendelsohn and Gropius came from Germany in 1933 and 1934. The Hungarian Goldfinger arrived in England from Paris in 1934. Chermayeff was born in the Caucasus though educated in England. Coates was born in Japan and brought up in Canada while Moro who came in 1937 was a German partly trained in Switzerland. This community of talent found relatively few sympathizers in the British public or profession. Due to the international editorial strengths of the leading British journal, the 'Architectural Review', however, neither group were ignorant of European or Scandinavian work, but their preferences lay elsewhere.

Thus French Art Deco had a strong influence, notably in buildings for entertainment and in newspaper headquarters. The brickwork of Dutch architects like Wils and Dudok was widely admired. Le Corbusier's 'Vers une architecture' was ably translated by the progressive architect Frederick Etchells as 'Towards a New Architecture' and published privately in an edition of 1000 copies in 1927. Only after the second impression appeared in 1931 did it really attract professional attention. By then, the UK climate was becoming more favourable to modern architecture in both its European and its American forms.

The English architect Fry recognized the importance of both these sources of new ideas. Fry's teacher Professor Charles Reilly introduced another of his students to Crabtree to work on the Peter Jones department store in London's fashionable Chelsea, which in 1936 became the first curtain wall building in the country and remains one of its most distinguished.

Clients for pre-war modernism were generally progressive thinkers in some field: a research anatomist at London Zoo and an educationalist at Impington Village College were typical. With their friends who ranged from abstract artists and designers to academic philosophers, such people joined the architects in various modernist groups. Most notable were the Twentieth Century Group (1930-33), Unit One (1933-34), the MARS (Modern Architectural Research) group (1933-57) which was the main link with CIAM, and the more politically engaged ATO (Architects' and Technicans' Organisation, 1935-38). They constantly propagandized through publications and exhibitions. In 1937 a group covering all these broader interests launched the international Modern Movement annual 'Circle', but it only appeared once.

Another generation of Modern Movement architects emerged after the war. By then they were numerous and the buildings shown here represent only the tip of a wave of forward-looking design that swept the UK in the post-war period. New buildings for the 1951 Festival of Britain in London were a showcase of design recalling the 1930 exhibition in Stockholm. There is no space here to include the sophisticated Hertfordshire Schools programme, for example, or schemes from the vast New Town and reconstruction programmes, nor indeed any of the industrial projects such as the Brynmawr Rubber factory by the Architects' Co-Partnership in Wales.

By then some of the eminent foreigners who came to Britain in the 30s had left. In the immediate post-war period, architectural education in the UK's two most progressive schools, the Architectural Association School in London and at the Liverpool School, was dominated by modernists and many of these were also of foreign origin. Among them were Arthur Korn from Berlin, Felix Samuely from Vienna in London; the Polish Lucjan Pietka and the Czech Arnost Wiesner in Liverpool. Major municipal offices like that of the London County Council under Leslie Martin, a co-editor of the 1937 'Circle', became natural extensions of the studios in these schools. Meanwhile numerous private offices developed which produced distinguished modern solutions to a whole new generation of building tasks. Yet another, more radical generation led by James Stirling, James Gowan and the Smithsons charted new directions and helped set up the reforming group of CIAM which called itself Team X.

In January 1970, thirty seven Modern Movement buildings from 1919-39 were added to the UK's statutory lists of buildings 'of special, architectural and historic interest.' Fifty had originally been proposed by a sub-committee of the Historic Buildings Council which included the German historian of modernism, Sir Nikolaus Pevsner. He invited the present author and the modern architectural historian Tim Benton as advisors. Today such Listing is conducted through the state organisation English Heritage which administers protection of all national monuments, with an equivalent in Wales, but the British public's antipathy to modernism changes very slowly.

Dennis Sharp

1
'High and Over'
HighOver Park, Amersham, Buckinghamshire
1928 | 1931
Amyas Connell

2
Royal Corinthian Yacht Club
Burnham on Crouch, Essex
1929 | 1931
Joseph Emberton

3
Boots 'Wets' D 10 Building
Beeston, Nottingham
1929 | 1932
Sir Owen Williams

'High and Over' was the first 'Modern' Movement house in Britain. Amyas Connell, its architect, was a New Zealander, who together with his later partner, Basil Ward, travelled to England in 1924. Two years later in 1926 Connell won the RIBA Rome Prize. While at the British School at Rome Connell met Bernard Ashmole, the School's Director, who subsequently commissioned him to design a modern house sympathetic to the Classical tradition he was in Rome to imbibe. High and Over, designed in 1928, shows many Italian characteristics in its siting and garden layout. The Y-shaped plan however with its three wings projecting at 120 degrees was Ashmole's idea and has a number of precedents in Edwardian 'butterfly' plan houses. Despite this it was also a house in the Corbusian manner, stark, cubic and not so monolithic as it first appears. The house had a concrete frame and brick in-fill and was rendered to simulate the Modern Movement aesthetic as seen at the Weissenhofsiedlung at Stuttgart of a year earlier. Bold, open cantilevered canopies are located on the roof terrace with its play and garden areas. The house was sub-divided into two parts in the 1970s but is still in good condition. A further four Sun Houses (plus a lodge, now spoiled) on the approach road to High and Over were developed after Connell had been joined by Ward. This remarkable group of houses survives virtually intact, while the villa itself is rather hemmed in by later developments.

A building in a nautical context, Emberton's Yacht Club is one of the first public buildings in the modern idiom. The original commission asked for 'a large three-storey ferro-concrete structure of advanced design'. The RCYC was built on land overlooking the River Crouch, a popular sailing venue. Emberton had already shown an interest in the Modern Movement design from France and Germany. The Yacht Club was a new direction in his work, apparently influenced by one of his assistants, George Fairweather. The building has a lightweight, steel framed structure resting on concrete and concrete deck with brick rendered walls. It was the only British building included in 'The International Style' exhibition held at MOMA, New York in 1932.

The architectural engineer Owen Williams was an original innovator who designed numerous major buildings in Britain in the 1930s. They included several newspaper offices and a number of structures for the Boots pharmaceutical company at their Beeston site in Nottingham. The building for 'wet' production was the only part built according to his scheme. As the design developed various alterations were made, such as replacement of a banded black glass exterior with clear transparent glass that exposed the floor slabs. From its inception the Wets building was widely reported internationally. It was a key work of early British modernism and affirmed Williams' place as an engineer prepared to challenge the aesthetic expertise of architects.

4
The White House
(formerly 'Aldings' also known as 'New Farm')
Grayswood near Haslemere, Surrey
1931 | 1933
Amyas Connell of Connell & Ward

Amyas Connell's second house was built for Sir Arthur Lowes Dickinson on a large site near Haslemere. It is a most original design. It has a reinforced concrete frame with non-loadbearing concrete walls. Its unusual irregular plan is related to the general layout of the entry drive and follows a flowing line into the uniquely fan shaped sun-seeking house. The thin wall construction was lined with 'Celotex' insulation board and made the economical use of standardized shuttering possible. Some columns interrupt the plan. Metal windows were made up out of standard sections by the pioneering Crittal company. Hot water central heating was housed in the staircase core and the exterior was originally painted light pink.

5
'Isokon' Flats
Lawn Road, London NW3
1933 | 1934
Wells Coates

This steeply sloping site was purchased by furniture producer Jack Pritchard in 1929, a year before he met Coates. 'Isokon' was the name of a client/architect company set up in 1931. Its purpose was the construction of an experimental project for 'minimum existence' living inspired by German and Russian models. The complex comprised 22 single flats with 4 double flats, 3 studio flats and a penthouse for the Pritchards. It was a concrete structure and a scheme of stringent economy. All the built-in furniture, kitchen fittings etc were designed by Coates. Initially there was a full range of services including meals and cleaning. In 1936-7 the communal kitchen was converted into a club called 'Isobar' by architects FRS Yorke and Marcel Breuer.

6
The Penguin Pool
London Zoo, Regents Park, London NW1
1934
Lubetkin, Drake & Tecton

Commissioned as part of an extensive modernisation programme at London Zoo in the 1930s the Penguin Pool is one of the chief icons of British Modern Architecture. The US historian H-R Hitchcock commented in 1937: 'It was that unique monument, the Penguin Pool by Lubetkin and Tecton, which first dramatically attracted the attention of the world to developments in England.' The original design programme treated penguins as performers. The concrete outer curved walls connected with spectacular theatrical ramps lead down into the pool itself. In John Allan's words, 'reinforced concrete was suddenly revealed as a virtuoso material capable of poetry.' The engineer was Dr. Felix Samuely, an assistant to Ove Arup.

7
Highpoint 1 & 2
North Hill, Highgate London N6
1933 | 1938
Lubetkin & Tecton

Sigmund Gestetner, of duplicating machine fame, was the client for this elegant, ambitious apartment block project. It was his original intention to build it for his firm's employees. However, the apartment block Highpoint 1 soon became a commercial venture. A six storey structure it had a 'double' cruciform plan. There were two plan-types, twin stairs and lifts. Many of the flats enjoy superb panoramic views across London. Two double-height penthouses were included in the south wings. The ground floor, with open common areas and an elegant entrance, is a virtuoso example of architectural spatial geometry. The building is notable for its detail design of fittings and services, many of which were widely published at the time. The monolithic concrete external walls were treated as combined beams and stanchions. They were erected using climbing shuttering lined with thin compressed cork sheets. The spine is also of concrete columns and beams. Aesthetically both Highpoint I and the later addition on the same site (1938) Highpoint 2 have remained unchallenged examples of English modern design. A new freedom of expression was developed by Lubetkin and Tecton for Highpoint 2. Economic constraints meant that fewer flats could be built in this second block and since the site costs were higher they were more tightly planned, with a number of duplex flats. The landscaped gardens and recreational areas were an integral part of the Highpoint ensemble.

8
De La Warr Pavilion
Bexhill-on-Sea, East Sussex
1935
Serge Chermayeff & Eric Mendelsohn

This award winning pavilion was designed as part of a large seaside entertainment complex promoted by the Mayor of Bexhill, Earl De La Warr as a subject of a national competition. The brief included a hotel, cinema, swimming pool and beach access. It was won by Chermayeff and Mendelsohn. Eric Mendelsohn had arrived in England in June 1933 and this was to be his major English public building, although other seaside designs were made for Blackpool and Southsea. The competition result produced considerable controversy at the time and only this central pavilion was built Today it is considered one of the finest of twentieth century buildings. The pavilion has been carefully restored and remains generally popular as a local community building, though it is currently (2000) being transferred into commercial operation. The unique welded steel frame structure was designed by engineer Felix Samuely. External walls had an air space for ventilation. Terrace balconies and roof garden were paved in brown tiling. The entrance foyer and the public staircases were built in reinforced concrete covered with terrazzo inlaid with ebonite. The suspended north staircase is cantilevered to give a free space below. The southern staircase spirals through the full height of the building within an independent wall of glass and is a magnificent reminder of Mendelsohn's imagination.

9
Kensal House
1-68 Ladbroke Grove, London NW
1937
Maxwell Fry
Elizabeth Denby (housing consultant) et al

Kensal House was an innovative working class social housing experiment for London. The project was developed by the site owners, the Gas Light and Coke company. It set out to prove the efficiency and economy of a properly planned and installed automatic fuel service. It was carried out in strict conformity with the terms of the Housing Acts, thus qualifying for generous subsidies. The 68 flats, although rather small, were designed for large families and an adjacent circular nursery school with a playground were built on the site of a gasholder. There was also a clubroom. The wide curve allowed morning light to the bedrooms. The design has an affinity with German social housing in the 1920s which Fry had studied.

10
Peter Jones Store
Sloane Square, London SW3
1936
William Crabtree
(associated architects) Slater and Moberley
with Sir Charles Reilly

One of the most important curtain wall buildings in London its first phase was completed in 1936, with further extensions in 1939 and in the 1950s. Professor C H Reilly the influential head of the Liverpool School of Architecture, acted as a consultant architect to the shop's owners. For this store he recommended the employment of a former student, William Crabtree (1905-91). Crabtree – who had worked previously with Joseph Emberton – is often credited as the sole architect. However, the store was erected by specialist store designers Slater and Moberley, with Reilly as their consultant. It has a steel framed riveted structure with concrete casing and walls and a large concrete cantilevered entrance canopy.

11
Finsbury Health Centre
Pine Street, London ECI
1935 | 1938
Lubetkin and Tecton

Commissioned by Dr Katial, a Finsbury Borough Councillor, the Centre developed as a new building type for the UK, a 'polyclinic' housing various medical facilities, including a dispensary, cleansing station, mortuary, dental clinic, solarium and flat for families during the disinfection of dwellings. The public appearance of the building and its foyer were designed to attract potential patients. The lecture hall in the centre block is a dominant feature. Loadbearing external walls and internal columns contrast with the framed wings. The significance of Finsbury Health Centre is primarily in the attention paid to co-ordination of mechanical and electrical services and their strategic integration into the structural system.

12
1-3 Willow Road
London NW3
1938 | 1939
Ernö Goldfinger

This terrace of three houses was designed by Goldfinger acting as both developer and architect. The largest and central house (2) was reserved for his own family use. The houses, with their Staffordshire brick facings, had concrete floors, metal windows and elegant spiral staircases set in cylindrical drums. Extensive use was made of fixed furniture with cupboards set into walls. Controversy raged over the demolition of on-site cottages and the modern style of the building, which eventually resulted in a careful linking by Goldfinger with the local Georgian terrace tradition. Goldfinger's Willow Road houses demonstrate the way he modified his architectural ideas to match their English context. No.2 is now a house museum dedicated to Goldfinger.

13
66 Frognal
Hampstead, London NW3
1936 | 1938
Connell, Ward & Lucas

Built for a solicitor, Geoffrey Walford, 66 Frognal became a cause celèbre and the subject of a lengthy public enquiry. It proved to be a battleground for a conflict between older local and more conservative architects (notably Sir Reginald Blomfield and Adrian Gilbert Scott), and the radical younger architects. Municipal leaders called the building 'an act of vandalism'. The design architect was Lucas. The first floor was planned as a complete living unit with sound proofed floors and continuously glazed living room. The concrete construction was rendered and coloured with an ochre finish. Dark blue bricks were used at the base.

14
Palace Gate Flats
10 Palace Gate, London W8
1936 | 1939
Wells Coates

This apartment block was designed by Coates using a '2/3 section'. He had devised a unit layout based roughly on earlier designs by Ginzburg in Moscow and Scharoun at Breslau. The flats extended over three floors on one side and over two – with a tall living room – on the other side on the east garden elevation. Palace Gate was somewhat less original than his earlier Lawn Road Flats in Hampstead. Situated on a corner site the block resembles Le Corbusier's Pavilion Suisse in Paris. An underground car park is reached by a curved ramp and, at the top of the seven storey block, a penthouse has generous terraces. Internally a clever access system for domestic staff connects to their own accommodation on the ground floor.

15
Impington Village College
Impington near Cambridge
1936 | 1939
Walter Gropius & Maxwell Fry

The 'Village College' was an innovative building type devised by Henry Morris, Cambridgeshire County Education Officer with the intention of combining a school building with library, adult education and leisure facilities. A brief for a college was devised with Walter Gropius, although his English partner Max Fry and his assistant Jack Howe were to steer it through to completion after Gropius left for Harvard in 1938. Construction was carefully controlled to prevent overspend and completed only at the outbreak of war in 1939. The College became an important image in wartime propaganda for improving education, though important for its social implications rather than for its planning or structural innovation.

16
Royal Festival Hall
South Bank, London SE1
1949 | 1951
LCC Architects Department
Robert Matthew, JL Martin, Peter Moro et al

Although often referred to as the diamond in the crown of the 1951 Festival of Britain, the Royal Festival Hall was an independant concert hall built to replace those lost in the war and is one of the finest UK buildings of the period. This premiere London venue is now a Grade 1 Listed Building which befits its newer role in the South Bank Arts Centre, adjacent to the Hayward gallery and the Royal National Theatre by modernist veteran Denys Lasdun. The Hall's unique features include a large 2800 seat auditorium protected from external noise and suspended like a separated body above the huge interlinked open public foyer spaces, ballroom and bars. The auditorium box rises through the roof surrounded by the ample terraces.

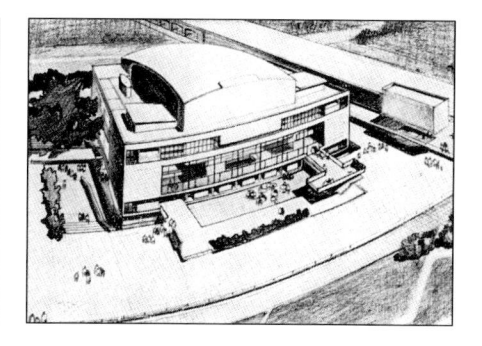

17
Engineering Faculty Building,
Leicester University
1959 | 1963
Stirling & Gowan

Drawing on elements from an earlier period of the Modern Movement (cf: the jutting out lecture halls with those of Melnikov's Soviet Workers' club) the design architects' team (Stirling Gowan and Wilford) combine them with a distinct rhetoric of their own. So much so that this building, above others, was seen as a turning point in British modernism in the 1960s with the emergence too of a new generation of inventive architects. As an iconic gesture it dominated this provincial university campus bringing on site thousands of visitors. It bridged the gap of understanding between engineering and architecture. However, its industrial glazing and blue blocks were part of the chosen aesthetic as much as an adaptation of industrial elements for university purposes.

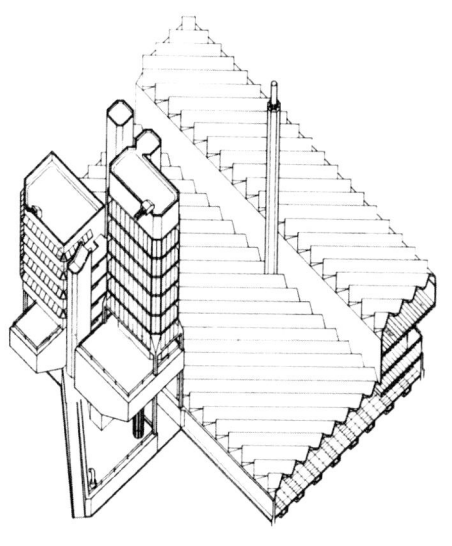

18
St Catherine's College
Oxford
1959 | 1965
Arne Jacobsen

19
The Economist Building
St James's Street London
1959 | 1964
Alison & Peter Smithson

20
Royal College of Physicians
Regent's Park London NW1
1960 | 1965
Denys Lasdun & Partners

One of the few Modern Movement buildings in Britain built by a first rank architect from abroad as a result of a limited competition. Jacobsen later also designed the Danish Embassy in London (1977). A series of elegant constant height concrete framed structures placed around open courtyards which are held in place on site by the buildings' strict rectilinear and repetitive geometry. 'A unique ensemble' as Reyner Banham observed, 'it can be understood in principle in a single sweep of the eye'. There are two parallel 3-storey blocks with, between them, four separate buildings containing common rooms, dining-hall and the library and lecture rooms and auditoria which share a garden space with its bell tower.

A design essay in re-structuring urban space the Smithsons' Economist building was highly influential both for planning and architecture. Its essay style is rooted in the polemics of Team X and its revaluation of city spaces and forms. Avoiding the idea of the block or of a single mass structure they approached the layout as if it were a cell in the body of the city. Three separated blocks are joined on a common plaza each elegantly finished with a common and clearly articulated structure and characteristic clipped off corners. The hard faced north side of the development - incorporated part of the famous Boodles Club, the side bay of which was drawn into the Smithsons' compositional scheme.

Designed to replace the previous college building in London's Trafalgar Square this new HQ building was built on a sensitive site to the south of Nash's Regent's Park. It displays many aesthetic subtleties. The central staircase is a key element in the design. It is directly approached from the high and strongly expressed front entrance from the park. This staircase is connected via a processional route to the Library and the Censor's Room. This part of the College is expressed as a permanent element and finished in a light coloured mosaic. This contrasts with the blue rustic facings of the remainder, which is intended for future extension. Another element, a low block to the south of the site accommodates a 300 person lecture theatre.

Selected Bibliography :
Hitchcock H-R & Bauer C
Modern Architecture in England
New York 1937

Yorke FRS
The Modern House in England
London 1937

Dannatt T
Modern Architecture in Britain
London 1959

Jackson A
The Politics of Architecture: a history of modern architecture in Britain
London 1970

Allan J
Berthold Lubetkin: Architecture and the tradition of progress
London 1992

Sharp D (ed)
Connell Ward & Lucas: Modern Movement Architects in England 1929-1939
London 1994

Benton C
A Different World: Emigré Architects in Britain 1928-1958
London 1995

Photographic Credits :
Book Art Architectural Picture Library
The Boots Company
Dennis Sharp
James Connell-TRIAD
EMAP

United States of America

The Modern Movement took root in the United States through a complex cross-fertilization of American and European architectural ideas which took place between the 1880s and 1930s. Following the pioneering influence of the Chicago School, Frank Lloyd Wright and the American industrial vernacular upon the early practitioners of Modernism in Europe, the principles of this movement returned via a group of young European architects emigrating to the United States in the 1920s and 1930s. Drawn to America by opportunity and its progressive outlook on engineering and technology, the Modern Movement first blossomed in the open cultural climate of Southern California through the work of Rudolph Schindler, Richard Neutra and Wright himself.

In 1932, Henry-Russell Hitchcock, Philip Johnson and Alfred Barr codified the principles of the Modern Movement as they understood it into an orthodox aesthetic, presenting it to America, through the Museum of Modern Art, as 'The International Style.' This had the effect of reinforcing and heightening the awareness of modernism both in the US and abroad, and paved the intellectual path for the eventual welcome of Walter Gropius (Harvard, 1937) and Mies van der Rohe (Armour Institute, later IIT, 1938) to begin the redirection of American architectural education toward the Bauhaus based design curriculum they had established over the previous two decades.

By the end of the 1930s, modernism began to spread and adapt to the diverse regions of the United States. This is first evident in the Bay Region Style developed by William Wurster and others around San Francisco, and in the subtle modifications made by Gropius and Marcel Breuer (a colleague at both the Bauhaus and Harvard) in adapting the white stucco geometries of Central European modernism to the wood building traditions of New England. The 30s also witnessed the beginning of the final phase of Frank Lloyd Wright's career, where at Falling Water, he transforms aspects of the form, language and massing strategies of modernism (specifically of Schindler, his former pupil), into a uniquely American synthesis of nature and technology.

It was not until the aftermath of the second world war however, that a characteristic, pervasive American modernism was accepted on a broad cultural level. Although distinctive local models continued to evolve, regionalism remained primarily apparent at the domestic scale, where houses on both coasts, and collective structures such as Aalto's Baker House dormitory at MIT ushered in a 'softening' of modernism similar to that occurring in Britain and Scandinavia at this time. Meanwhile the larger construction industry began to develop standardized materials and means of production for those building types most in demand such as schools, hospitals, research labs and, most ubiquitously, the office building. In the immediate postwar period, the first all glass and steel skyscrapers were finally realized with the construction of Pietro Belluschi's Equitable Building in Portland, Oregon, and Lever House in New York, by Gordon Bunshaft of Skidmore, Owings and Merrill. It was also at this time (1947-1954) that the design of the United Nations Headquarters in New York, one of the most significant political and cultural icons of the twentieth century, was realized by an international team of architects, including Le Corbusier and Oscar Niemeyer, under the direction of Wallace Harrison. Both Lever and the UN represent early large scale successes of the integration of a slab tower with a larger, low-rise base, a volumetric schema planned (though rarely executed) in modernist projects dating back to the early 1920s.

Concurrently, Mies van der Rohe pursued the relentless refinement of what William Jordy has called the 'laconic splendor of the metal frame' in projects ranging in scale from the week-end house for Edith Farnsworth of 1946-51 (the antithesis of Falling Water in its conscious isolation from nature) to the high-rise Seagram Building on Park Avenue in New York of 1956, to large free span structures such as IIT's Crown Hall of 1956. Here is modernism at its most formal; an apparently rational, neo-classical aesthetic often defying its own tectonics, with a profound, minimalist sensibility for the refinement of detail and the inherent luxuriousness of finely worked stone, metal and glass.

By the 1950s a younger generation of architects were challenging the orthodoxies of the early Modern Movement and beginning again to lend personal, evocative images to their buildings. These often took expressionist themes, as in the work of Eero Saarinen or Paul Rudolph, or were based upon varying hierarchies of function and material, with a strong underlay of formal historical reference, as in the work of Louis Kahn. This infusion of an 'alternative' energy, and a new willingness to look to history for precedent reinvigorated American modernism, and produced, in the works of Kahn, some of the most original and internationally influential buildings of the post war era. However, Kahn's return to the archaic font of form, and the resultant romantic power of his images, would eventually provide a foundation for the rise of the new historicism that would signal the end of modernism's hegemony in the early 1970s.

David Fixler

1
Lovell Beach House
Newport Beach, California
1926
Rudolph Schindler

Elevated over the beach for privacy and views, the house is an artful integration of structure and space with rooms enclosed as required between concrete frames. Main stairs from the ground level lead to a two-story living room overlooked by an upper level gallery. Four bedrooms off the gallery form a horizontal counterpoint to the exposed concrete structure on the main facade.

2
Lovell (Health) House
Los Angeles, California
1929
Richard Neutra

The three-story, steel-framed structure is a pioneering example of modern technology applied to the creation of a residential environment. Walls spanning between the shop-fabricated, lightweight frame are sprayed concrete over an insulation backing and combinations of standard window units. Through its dramatic hillside site and exposed structural system, the house is a recognized monument of the International Style.

3
Philadelphia Savings Fund Society
Philadelphia, Pennsylvania
1932
George Howe & William Lescaze

The PSFS building is one of the most influential skyscrapers of the early Modern Movement and an icon of functional expressionism. With its T-shaped office tower set on a two-storey, podium-style base containing street-level shops and a banking hall above, the building's volumes and subtle changes in finish materials offer a clear and sophisticated architectural expression of the distinct and separate uses contained within.

4
Kaufmann House 'Falling Water'
Bear Run, Pennsylvania
1935
Frank Lloyd Wright

Perhaps the most recognizable private residence in the world, the Kaufmann house appears to spring from the surrounding rock ledges to become an organic part of the waterfall over which it is sited and draws its name. Combining cantilevered slabs of reinforced concrete anchored into the hillside above with a stone-clad core, Wright aimed to create a place of living fused into nature.

5
Johnson Wax Building
Racine, Wisconsin
1936 | 1939
Frank Lloyd Wright

Covered by a glass ceiling and the building's signature tapered concrete columns with lily-pad-like capitals, the main space of the SC Johnson Wax Company building is Wright's most dramatic design for a workplace. The inwardly focused structure, with walls of red brick trimmed with sandstone and topped by a clerestory band of glass tubing, is completed with furnishings also designed by the architect.

6
Gropius House
Lincoln, Massachusetts
1938
Walter Gropius & Marcel Breuer

Gropius' own house was the region's earliest and purest built expression of his European ideas – notably the interpenetration of solids and voids in the building's main volume. The architect also attempted to absorb New England's relevant and living architectural traditions as evidenced by the wood used in construction and a dining room extension reminiscent of an American screened porch.

7
Crow Island School
Winetka, Illinois
1940
Saarinen & Saarinen
Perkins, Wheeler & Will

Recognizing that educational objectives and methods can generate architectural form, the architects here were among the first to carefully analyze the spatial and practical needs of children and teachers. The resulting approach, characterized by flexible classrooms with separate work areas, individual adjacent outdoor yards, natural light, practical materials and a child-sized scale revolutionized elementary school design.

8
Kaufmann Desert House
Palm Springs, California
1946
Richard Neutra

Intended by Neutra to be a machine in the garden, juxtaposing a foreign man-made construct onto a natural setting, the house appears sculptural, contrasting conspicuously against the rugged desert with geometrical forms and low floating planes broken only by a second-storey, aluminum-louvred viewing room. While remaining an object apart, the pinwheel-shaped plan reaches out to embrace the natural landscape.

9
Equitable Savings and Loan Association
Portland, Oregon
1948
Pietro Belluschi

This structure demonstrates the evolution of many construction technologies which have become standard practice in glass-walled office building design. The façades have a crisp, nearly flat, machined-appearance, combining sheet aluminum cladding over the structural concrete frame and aluminum spandrels. The first sealed air-conditioned building in the United States, double glazing with tinted, heat-absorbing glass help to moderate the indoor environment.

10
Baker House Dormitory MIT
Cambridge, Massachusetts
1949
Alvar Aalto
Perry, Shaw & Hepburn

Baker house is the first major building to synthesize modernism with the regional material vernacular of New England. An undulating slab clad in the local rough brick is set along the Charles River. A series of spaces, axially placed toward the heart of the university campus, bisect the slab near its mid-point. The termination of this axis is a two-story dining pavilion, clad in limestone with wood-framed ribbon windows and the architect's signature grouping of circular skylights.

11
Case Study House 8
Eames House and Studio
Los Angeles, California
1949
Charles & Ray Eames

An 'Arts and Architecture Magazine' sponsored project using off-the-shelf, mass-produced, modular materials, these steel-frame buildings enclosed by solid, transparent and translucent panels were a study in living and working space by the influential postwar designers. The house and studio, built against a retaining wall into the hillside and separated by a small patio, along with the interiors, gardens and site are a unified whole.

12
Farnsworth House
Piano, Illinois
1951
Ludwig Mies van der Rohe

Noted for its high cost and transparent walls, the building introduced Mies van der Rohe's ascetic modernism to a sceptical American public. Designed for a woman doctor, it was intended as a weekend retreat in which the ordered minimalism of glass and steel would transform the domestic realm into a space of contemplation.

13
Lever House
New York
1952
Skidmore, Owings & Merrill

The construction of the 24-storey glass and stainless steel Lever House established the suitability of the International Style for office building design. The building is especially dramatic in its setting since the vertical slab is set perpendicular to Park Avenue and appears to float above the one storey base and open plaza.

14
United Nations Headquarters
New York
1954
International committee of architects
Wallace Harrison (chairman)

Recognizable around the world, the UN complex represents in one sense the apotheosis of the design ideals and aesthetics of the Modern Movement. The unique, collaborative nature of the design process perhaps lessened the complex's pure formal qualities, but it remains a significant realization of many fundamental principles and was the largest group of US buildings to be built in the modern idiom at that time.

15
Solomon R. Guggenheim Museum
New York
1956
Frank Lloyd Wright

16
Seagram Building
New York
1959
Ludwig Mies van der Rohe & Philip Johnson
Kahn & Jacobs

17
Dulles International Airport
Chantilly, Virginia
1962
Eero Saarinen & Associates

18
United States Air Force Academy Chapel
Colorado Springs, Colorado
1963
Skidmore, Owings & Merrill

The museum for abstract art is the major New York City work of Wright and considered to be the crowning achievement of his later career. The rectangular base of the exterior conforms to the street grid while setting apart the spectacular independence of the building's upper spiral form from the city. On the interior a cantilevered ramp punctuated by exhibition alcoves surrounds an open, sky-lit central space.

This powerful skyscraper sheathed in glass, a concept Mies van der Rohe first proposed in Berlin in the 1920s, is temple-like in its design with a traditional hierarchy of the principal façade versus the secondary side and back façades, inflexible symmetry in plan, profuse use of marble, accentuated entrance and vast foreground plaza. In detailing and site planning it became a model for both sky-scraper design and urban planning.

Evocative of flight itself, the main terminal building is a part of a unified airport design intended to serve as the international gateway to Washington DC. Pairs of reinforced concrete pylons, higher along the front, support a cable-suspended concrete roof. As was planned for in the original design, the building has recently been extended with additional matching bays.

The chapel is an uplifting departure in modernist ecclesiastical form dominated by a vault made of tetrahedrons clad in extruded aluminum separated by continuous coloured-glass panels. End walls are glass. Four separate places of worship are combined into one structure: a Catholic chapel, a circular Jewish chapel and an All Faiths Room are located below the main floor devoted to Protestant services.

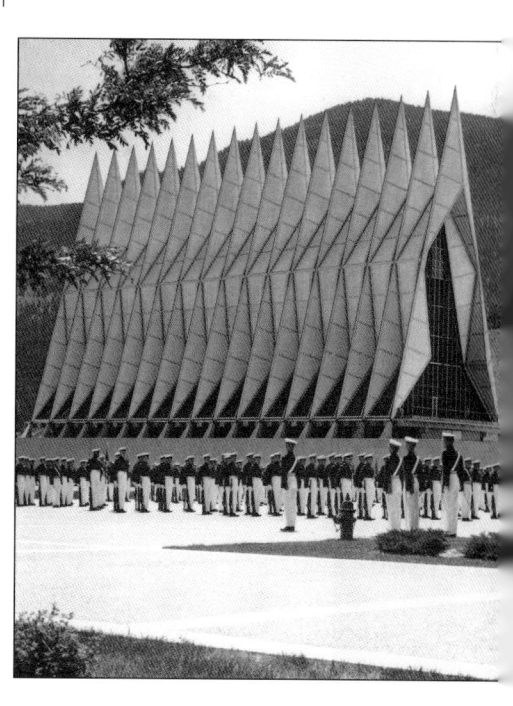

19
Salk Institute for Biological Research
La Jolla, California
1965
Louis Kahn

20
Kimbell Art Museum
Fort Worth, Texas
1972
Louis Kahn

Sited at the head of a ravine along coastal bluffs, the Institute's integrated building complex and natural setting provide a contemplative working environment for a community of scientists. The austere central plaza is flanked by symmetrical, four-storey, semi-detached rows of researcher studies in bays with diagonal walls oriented toward the sea. Behind, linked to the studies by bridges, are free plan laboratory spaces.

The museum is a series of low, cycloid vaults punctuated by courts which together define human-scaled, articulated spaces on the interior and linear porticos to the outside. The building combines exquisite proportions, craftsmanship and integration of natural light to create spaces where quiet modernism brings grace to the experience and enjoyment of art.

Selected Bibliography :
Mock E (ed)
Built in USA 1932-1944
New York 1944

Hitchcock H-R & Drexler A (eds)
Built in USA. Post-War Architecture
New York 1952

McCoy E
Five California Architects
New York 1960

Heyer P
Architects on Architecture: New Directions in America
New York 1966

Jordy WH
American Buildings and their Architects: the Impact of European Modernism in the Mid-Twentieth Century
New York 1976, 1986

McCoy E
Case Study Houses 1945-1962
Los Angeles 1977

McCoy E & Goldstein B
Guide to US Architecture 1940-1980
Santa Monica 1982

Stern R, Gilmartin G & Mellins T
New York 1930: Architecture and Urbanism between the Wars
New York 1987

Wilson RG & Robinson SK (eds)
Modern Architecture in America: Visions and Revisions
Ames 1991

Photographic Credits :
Julius Shulman
2, 8, 11
Library of Congress, Prints and Photographs Division, Historic American Buildings Survey
1, 3, 4, 6
Chicago Historical Society
7
Hedrich-Blessing
12
W. Boychuck Collection
9
Ezra Stoller ESTO
5, 10, 13, 14, 16, 19, 20
Skidmore, Owings & Merrill
18

Acknowledgements :
David Fixler
Jo Goldberger
Gary Koll
Hélène Lipstadt
Anthony Merchell
Henry Moss
Kathleen Randall
Nina Rappaport
Julius Shulman
Erica Stoller ESTO
Katherine Rinne
Amy Weisser
Andrew Wolfram

Literature of the Modern Movement in architecture | An international bibliography of books & periodicals

This bibliography combines key texts of the Modern Movement with a selection of later histories and commentaries. Monographs on individual architects are so numerous that these are only included for a few architects whose work was seminal to the development of the whole international movement. For extensive bibliographies on individual architects readers are refered to: Sharp D, **Sources of Modern Architecture: A critical bibliography** (London 1981) in the list of books below. Likewise works on individual countries are only included where these are under-represented in the general literature.

Catherine Cooke | Dennis Sharp

Books

Arkin D (ed)
Arkhitektura sovremennogo zapada
Moscow 1932

Banham R
Theory and Design in the First Machine Age
London 1960

Banham R
Guide to Modern Architecture
London 1962
New edition as:
Age of the Masters
London & New York 1975

Banham R
The New Brutalism
Stuttgart, London & New York 1966

Banham R
The Architecture of the Well-tempered Environment
London & Chicago 1969

Bargellini P & Freynie E
Nascita e vita dell' architettura moderna
Florence 1947

Bauer C
Modern Housing
New York 1934

Bauziene M (ed)
Lietuvos Moderno Pastatai
Vilnius 1998

Bayer H, Gropius W & Gropius I
Bauhaus 1919-1928
New York 1938, London 1939
German edition Stuttgart 1955

Behrendt C
Modern Building
London 1938

Benevelo L
Storia dell'architettura moderna
2 vols Bari 1960
English translation as:
The History of Modern Architecture
2 vols London & New York 1972
French translation as:
Histoire de l'architecture moderne
4 vols Paris 1978, 1979, 1980, 1988

Benton C
A Different World: Emigré Architects in Britain 1928-1958
London 1995

Benton T, Benton C & Sharp D (eds)
Form and Function: A Source Book for the History of Modern Architecture and Design 1890-1939
London 1975

Blau E
The Architecture of Red Vienna 1919-1934
Cambridge (Mass) 1999

Blau E & Platzer M (eds)
Shaping the Great City: Modern Architecture in Central Europe 1890-1937
Munich & London 2000

Boesiger W (ed)
Le Corbusier. Oeuvre complète
Zürich 1929-1965 in 7 volumes
Paris 1933-
London & New York 1966-

Cacciari M
Architecture and Nihilism: on the Philosophy of Modern Architecture
New Haven & London 1993

Cârneci M (ed)
Bucuresti anii 1920-1940 între Avangarda si Modernism
Bucharest 1994

Cetto ML
Modern Architecture in Mexico
Stuttgart & London 1961

Cheney S
The New World Architecture
London 1930

CIAM (eds)
Die Wohnung für das Existenzminimum: Auf Grund der Ergebnisse des II Internationalen Kongresses für Neues Bauen
Frankfurt am Main 1930, repub Stuttgart 1933

CIAM (eds)
Rationelle Bebauungsweisen. Ergebnisse des 3 Internationalen Kongresses für Neues Bauen
Stuttgart 1931

Cohen J-L & Eleb M
Casablanca: Mythes et figures d'une aventure urbaine
Paris 1998

Collins P
Changing Ideals in Modern Architecture
London 1965

Cunningham A (ed)
Modern Movement Heritage
London 1998

Curtis WJR
Modern Architecture since 1900
London 1982 and later editions

Czerner O & Listowski H
Awangarda Polska. Architektura i Urbanistyka 1918-1939
Warsaw & Paris 1981

Deutscher Werkbund
Bau und Wohnung. Die Bauten der Weissenhofsiedlung in Stuttgart errichtet 1927; 'Die Wohnung'
Stuttgart 1927

Doesburg T van
De Stijl en de Europese architectuur
Nijmegen 1986
German translation as
Uber Europaische Architektur
Basel 1990
English translation as:
On European Architecture: complete essays from 'Het Bouwbedrijf' 1924-1931
Basel 1990

Dorfles G
L'architettura moderna
Milan 1954

Ferris H et al
Machine Age Exposition: catalogue
New York 1927

Frampton K
Modern Architecture. A Critical History
London 1980
French translation as:
Histoire critique de l'architecture moderne
Paris 1985

Fry EM & Drew J
Tropical Architecture in the Dry and Humid Zones
New York 1964

Giedion S
Space, Time and Architecture
Cambridge (Mass) 1941 repub 1982

Giedion S
A Decade of New Architecture
Zürich & New York 1951

Ginzburg M
Zhilishche
Moscow 1934

Gossel P & Leuthauser G
Architecture in the 20th Century
Cologne 1990

Gropius W
Internationale Architektur
Munich 1925 repub 1927

Gropius W
The New Architecture and the Bauhaus
London 1936
German edition 1965

Herbert G
Martiensson and the International Style
Cape Town 1975

Heynen H
Architecture and Modernity: A Critique
Cambridge (Mass) 1998

Hitchcock H-R
In the Nature of Materials: the buildings of Frank Lloyd Wright 1887-1941
New York 1942, repub London 1973

Hitchcock H-R & Johnson P
The International Style. Architecture since 1922
New York 1932 repub 1966

Hitchcock H-R
Latin American Architecture since 1945
New York 1955

Jackson N
The Modern Steel House
London 1996

Jencks C
Modern Movements in Architecture
Harmondsworth 1973

Joedicke J
A History of Modern Architecture
Stuttgart & London 1959

Joedicke J
Architecture since 1946
Stuttgart & London 1972

Joedicke J & Plath C
Die Weissenhofsiedlung Stuttgart
Stuttgart 1977

Johansson G
Funktionalismen I Verkligheten
Stockholm 1931

Johnson P & Hitchcock H-R et al
Modern Architecture International Exhibition: catalogue
New York 1932

Johnson P
Mies van der Rohe
New York 1947

Jong C & Mattie E
Architectural Competitions: vol I 1792-1949, vol II 1950-Today
Cologne & Naarden 1994

Kirsch K
Werkbund ausstellung 'Die Wohnung' Stuttgart 1927. Die Wiessenhofsiedlung.
Stuttgart 1993

Klotz H (ed)
Vision der Moderne. Das Prinzip Konstruktion
Munich 1986

Kopp A
Quand le moderne n'était pas un style mais une cause
Paris 1988

Krischanitz A & Kapfinger O
Die Wiener Werkbundsiedlung: Dokumentation einer Erneuerung
Vienna 1985

Lampugnani VM (ed)
Encyclopaedia of 20th Century Architecture
London 1986

Lange E de
Geen Officiële maar Levende Schoonheid: het internationale nieuwe bouwen tot 1940
's-Gravenhage 1983

Le Corbusier
Vers une architecture
Paris 1923
English translation as:
Towards a New Architecture
London 1929

Le Corbusier
Urbanisme
Paris 1925
English translation as:
The City of Tomorrow and its Planning London 1929
Russian translation with additions as: **Planirovka goroda**
Moscow 1933

Le Corbusier
The Athens Charter
New York 1973

Lesnikowski W (ed)
East European Modernism: Architecture in Czechoslovakia, Hungary & Poland between the Wars
London & New York 1996

Lindner W & Steinmetz G
Die Ingenieurbauten und ihre Entwicklung
Leipzig 1923

Loghem JB van
Bouwen. Bauen. Bâtir. Building.
Amsterdam 1932 repub Nijmegen 1990

Lopez Rangel R
La Modernidad aquitectonica mexicana 1900-1940
Azcapotzalco 1989

Lundahl G (ed)
Nordisk Funktionalisme
Uppland 1980

Machedon L. & Scoffham E
Romanian Modernism: The Architecture of Bucharest 1920-1940
Cambridge (Mass) 1999

Mambriani A
L'Architettura Moderna nei paesi Balcani
Bologna 1970

Meyer P
Moderne Architektur
Zürich 1928

Minorski J
Polska Mysl Innowacyjna w Architekturze 1918-1939
Warsaw 1970

Moholy-Nagy L
Von Material zu Architektur
Munich 1929
English translation as:
The New Vision from Material to Architecture
New York 1930

Monnier G
L'architecture du XXe siècle
Paris 1997

Moravanszky A
Die Erneuerung der Baukunst: Wege zur Moderne in Mitteleuropa 1900-1940
Salzburg 1988

Müller M
Architektur und Avantgarde
Frankfurt am Main 1984

Myers IE
Mexico's Modern Architecture
New York 1952

Newman O
CIAM '59 in Otterlo: themes, buildings, projects
London 1961

Norberg-Schultz C
Principles of Modern Architecture
London 2000

Oud JJP
Nieuwe Bouwkunst in Holland en Europa
Amsterdam 1935 republ 1981

Pica A
Nuova Architettura nel Mondo
Milan 1936

Platz G
Die Baukunst der neuesten Zeit
Berlin 1927, 1930

Rentsch V (ed)
Sigfried Giedion 1888-1968: Der Entwurf einer modernen Tradition
Zürich 1989

Richards JM
An Introduction to Modern Architecture
Harmondsworth 1940 repub 1965
US edition Baltimore 1962

Roth A
La Nouvelle Architecture. Die neue Architektur. The New Architecture 1930-1940
Zürich & Munich 1939 republ 1948 1975

Roth A
A Decade of Contemporary Architecture
Zürich 1951

Sartoris A
Gli elementi dell'architettura funzionale
Milan 1932 replub 1935
Revised edition as:
Taschen B (publ)
Functional Architecture. Funktionale Architektur. Le Style International.

The International Style 1925-1940
Cologne 1990

Sartoris A
Introduzione all'architettura moderna
Milan 1949

Sartoris A
Encyclopédie de l'architecture nouvelle
Milan 3 volumes 1954-1957

Scully V Jr
Modern Architecture: The Architecture of Democracy
London & New York 1961

Sfaellos C
Le fonctionalisme dans l'architecture contemporaine
Paris 1952

Sharp D
Sources of Modern Architecture: A critical bibliography
London 1981

Sharp D
Twentieth Century Architecture: A visual history
London 1991

Steinmann M
CIAM-Dokumente 1928-39
Basel & Stuttgart 1978

Syrkus H
Ku idei osiedla spolecznego 1925-75
Warsaw 1976

Sweeney R
Frank Lloyd Wright. An annotated bibliography
Los Angeles 1978

Tafuri M
Viena Rossa. La Politica residenziale nella Viena socialista 1919-33
Milan 1980

Tafuri M & Dal Co F
Modern Architecture
New York 1976

Taut B
Die Neue Baukunst in Europa und Amerika
Stuttgart 1929
English translation as:
Modern Architecture
London 1929

Teige K
Nejmensí byt Prague 1932

Uhlig G
Kollektivmodell "Einküchenhaus": Wohnreform und Architekturdebatte zwischen Frauenbewegung und Funktionalismus 1900-1930
Berlin 1981

various
Wohnung und Werkraum. Werkbund ausstellung. Ausstellungs - Führer Breslau 1929

Wang Shao-Zhou
A Pictorial Handbook of Chinese Modern Architecture
Shanghai 1989 (in Chinese)

Wedebrunn O (ed)
Modern Movement Scandinavia
Copenhagen/Aalborg 1998

Wingler HM
Das Bauhaus 1919-1937
Bramsche 1962
English translation as:
The Bauhaus
Cambridge (Mass) 1969

Witt D de & Witt ER de
Modern Architecture in Europe: A Guide to Buildings since the Industrial Revolution
London 1987

Woud A van der
Het Nieuwe Bouwen Internationaal – CIAM Volkshuisvesting Stedebouw
Delft 1983

Wright FL
An Autobiography
New York 1932

Wright FL
An Organic Architecture
London 1939

Wright FL
When Democracy Builds
New York 1945

Yerbury FR
Modern European Buildings
London 1928

Yorke FRS
The Modern House
Cheam 1934

Yorke FRS & Penn C
A Key to Modern Architecture
London 1939

Zevi B
Towards an Organic Architecture
London 1950

Zevi B
Storia dell'architettura moderna
Turin 1950, repub 1955

Periodicals

ABC: Beiträge zum Bauen
Series 1 no 1 Zürich 1924
Series 1 nos 2-6 Basel 1924-1925
Series 2 nos 1-4 Basel 1926-1928
Reprinted Eindhoven 1969

Abstraction-Création
Paris 1933

Archigram
London 1961-77

The Architects' Journal
London 1919-

Architects' Year Book
London 1945-1975

Architectura
Amsterdam 1881-1917

Architectural Design and Construction
London 1935-1946
became:
Architectural Design 1947-

**Architectural Forum:
the Magazine of Building**
Orange (Conn) 1892-1974

Architectural Record. The Record and Guide
New York 1891-

The Architectural Review
London 1896-

Architecture
Sydney 1916-1958
became:
Architecture in Australia 1955-75
Architecture Australia 1976-

Architecture, Mouvement et Continuité (AMC).
Paris 1967-73
became:
Moniteur Architecture AMC
1973-

Architecture in Greece
Athens 1967-

L'Architecture Vivante
Paris 1923-1933

L'Architecture d'Aujourd'hui
Boulogne sur Seine 1929-

Der Architekt
Vienna 1895-1922

Architekten
Copenhagen 1899-1929
became:
Arkitekten 1929-1956
Arkitektur 1957-1971
Arkitektur DK 1972-

L'Architettura. Cronache e storia
Rome 1955-

L'Architettura Italiana
Turin 1905-1943

Arhitectura
Bucharest 1935-

Arkhitekt
Sofia 1927-1936

Arkhitektura: Journal of Theory History and Criticism
Sofia 1949-

Arkhitektura MAO
Moscow 1923 two issues only

Arkitektur
Stockholm 1909 -

Arkkitehti-Arkitekten
Helsinki 1903-

Arquitectura espanola
Madrid 1923-1928

Arquitectura México
Mexico City 1940-

Arquitectura e Urbanismo
São Paulo 1936-1942

Art et Technique
Liège 1913-1914

L'Art libre
Brussels 1919-1922

Arts & Architecture
Los Angeles 1944-1967; 1981-

Au Volant
Brussels 1919
became:
7 Arts 1922-1928

Der Aufbau: Monatsschrift fur Planen, Bauen und Wohnen
Vienna 1926-1988
became
Perspektiven 1988-

Der Baumeister
Munich 1902-
Bauwelt: Zeitschrift für das Gesamte Bauwesen
Berlin 1910-45
became:
Neue Bauwelt 1946-52
Bauwelt 1952-

Blok
Warsaw 1924-1926

Bouwkundig Weekblad
Amsterdam 1881-1969
became:
Plan 1970-

Axis
London 1935-6

Bâtir
Brussels 1932-1940

Bauen und Wohnen
Ravensburg 1946-79

**Bauhaus:
zeitschrift für gestaltung**
Dessau 1926-9, 1931

Het Bouwbedrijf
Amsterdam 1924-1938
became:
Bouwbedrijf en openbare werken
1939-1951

Byggekunst
Oslo 1919-

Cahiers d'Art
Paris 1926-

Le Carré Bleu
Paris 1958-

La casa bella
Milan 1928-1932
became:
Casabella 1933-1938
Casabella-Costruzioni 1938-9
Costruzioni-Casabella 1940-3, 1946
Casabella-Continuità 1954-1964
Casabella 1965-

Circle annual
London 1937 one issue only

La Cité
Brussels 1919-1935

Clarté
Brussels 1928-1939

La Construction Moderne
Paris 1885-1914, 1919-

De 8 en Opbouw
Amsterdam 1932-43

Design Review
Wellington 1948-1954

Deutsche Bauzeitung
Munich 1867-

Deutsche Kunst und Dekoration
Darmstadt 1897-1934

277

Devetsil: Revolucni sbornik
Prague 1922 one issue only

Disk
Prague & Brno 1923-1925

DOCOMOMO Newsletter
Eindhoven 1989-1993
became:
DOCOMOMO Journal
Eindhoven 1993-1998, Delft 1999-

Le Document
Brussels 1922-1939

Documentos de Actividad Contemporanea (AC) GATEPAC
Barcelona 1931-1937

Domus
Milan 1928-

De Driehoek
Antwerp 1925-1926

Eesti arkitektide almanak
Tallinn 1934

L'Effort Moderne
Paris 1924-1927

L'Emulation
Brussels 1874-1914; 1921-1939

L'Equerre
Liège 1929-1939

L'Esprit Nouveau
Paris 1920-25

Ezhegodnik MAO annual
Moscow no 5 1928, no 6 1930

Ezhegodnik OAKh annual
Leningrad 1928, 1930, 1935

Focus
London 1938-9 four issues only

Die Form
Berlin 1922, 1925-35

Forum
Amsterdam 1946-

Forum
Berlin 1926-1933

Frühlicht
Berlin 1920-1 Magdeburg 1921-2

G. Zeitschrift für elementare Gestaltung
Berlin 1923-6

L'Habitation à bon marché
Brussels 1921-1940

House & Home
New York 1952-1977

Der Moderne Stil
Stuttgart 1899-1905

Izvestiia ASNOVA
Moscow 1926 one issue only

The Japan Architect
Tokyo 1956-

Journal of the Indian Institute of Architects
Bombay 1934-

Kritisk Revy
Copenhagen 1926-1928

Kunst
Brussels 1930-1935

Das Kunstblatt
Berlin, Weimar, Potsdam 1913-32

Latvijas Arhitektura
Riga 1938-1940; 1995-

MA: aktivista folyóirat
Budapest 1916-19, Vienna 1920-26

Metron
Rome 1945-1954

Moderne Bauformen
Stuttgart 1902-44

Der Moderne Stil
Stuttgart 1899-1905

Das Neue Frankfurt
Frankfurt am Main 1926-1931
became:
Die Neue Stadt 1931-1933

New Zealand Institute of Architects' Journal
Wellington 1922-1977
became:
New Zealand Architect 1977-1987
Architecture New Zealand 1988-

Nuestra Arquitectura
Buenos Aires 1929-

Opbouwen
Antwerp 1928-1937

Het Overzicht
Antwerp 1921-1925

Pencil Points
New York 1920-1945
became:
Progressive Architecture
1945-1995

Plan
Oslo 1933-1936

Plastique
Paris 1937 five issues

Praesens: architektura
Warsaw no 1 1926, no 2 1930

PROA: Urbanismo Arquitectura Industrias
Bogota 1946-

Quadrante
Milan 1932-1936

Rassegna di Architettura
Milan 1929-1940

Royal Architectural Institute of Canada Journal
Toronto 1924-June 1966

South African Architectural Record
Johannesburg 1915-

Sovremennaia Arkhitektura (SA)
Moscow 1926-1930
superceded by:
Sovetskaia arkhitektura 1931-33

Spazio
Rome 1950-1953

Spazio e societa
Milan 1977-1984
Florence 1984-

Stavba
Prague 1922-1931

Stavitel
Prague 1919-1933

De Stijl
Delft 1917 no 1
then Leiden 1917-1931

Stroitel'stvo Moskvy
Moscow 1924-1941

Der Sturm
Berlin 1910-1932

Styl
Prague 1908-1938

Technika Chronika
Greece 1930s

La Technique des Travaux
Liège 1925-1977

Techniques et Architecture
Paris 1941-

Tekhné
Liège 1911-1912

Tér és Forma
Budapest 1928-48

Tvorba
Prague 1926-1937

Urbanistica
Turin 1932-

Veshch' Gegenstand Objet
Berlin 1922 two issues only

Volne smery
Prague 1897-1949

Wasmuths Monatshefte für Baukunst
Berlin 1914-1929
became:
Wasmuths Monatshefte für Baukunst und Stadtbau 1930-1932
Wasmuths Monatshefte 1933-1942

Wendingen
Amsterdam 1918-1931
also English edition 1921-4

Das Werk
Berne 1913-1915, Zürich 1915-1972
became:
Archithèse 1972-1976
Werk-Archithèse 1977-1979
Werk: Bauen und Wohnen 1979
Archithèse 1980-

The West African Builder and Architect
Ibadan 1960-1968

Western Homes and Living
also as **Western Living** et al
Vancouver 1950-

Zivot II: sbornik nové krásy
Prague 1923

Zodiac
Milan 1957-1973 annual
New series 1989-

Conservation

The following books deal with conserving and restoring Modern Movement buildings.
For a full list of DOCOMOMO's own publications, see: Cunningham A (ed) Modern Movement Heritage (London 1998) or the DOCOMOMO International website:
www.docomomo.com

Fiorini L & Conti A
La conservazione del moderno: teoria e practica. Bibliografia di architetture e urbanistica
Florence 1993

Henket H-J & Jonge W de
Het Nieuwe Bouwen en Restaureren
Zeist & The Hague 1990

Macdonald S (ed)
Modern Matters: Principles and Practice in Conserving Recent Architecture
Shaftesbury 1996

280

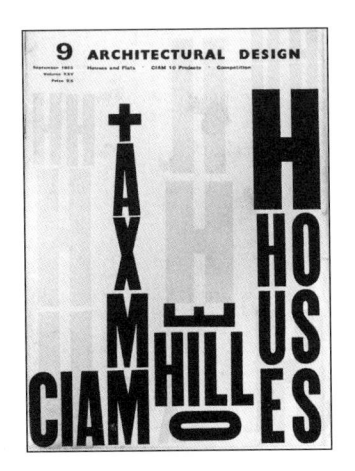

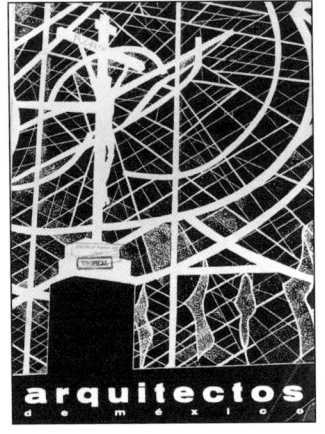

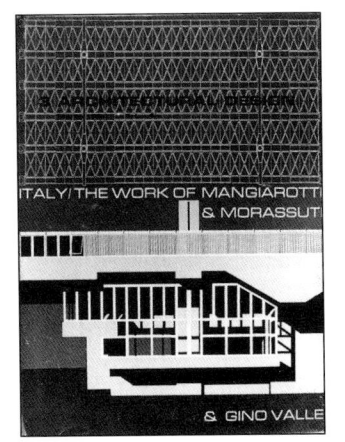